Chemists and Chemistry
in Nature and Society
1770–1878

Professor Trevor H. Levere

Trevor H. Levere

Chemists and Chemistry
in Nature and Society
1770–1878

VARIORUM 1994

ACR 1344

This edition copyright © 1994 Trevor H. Levere.

Published by VARIORUM
   Ashgate Publishing Limited
   Gower House, Croft Road,
   Aldershot, Hampshire GU11 3HR
   Great Britain

   Ashgate Publishing Company
   Old Post Road,
   Brookfield, Vermont 05036
   USA

ISBN 0-86078-412-6

British Library CIP data
   Levere, Trevor H.
   Chemists and Chemistry in Nature and
   Society, 1770-1878. - (Variorum Collected
   Studies Series; CS 439)
   I. Title II. Series
   540.9

The paper used in this publication meets the minimum requirements of the
   American National Standard for Information Sciences – Permanence
   of Paper for Printed Library Materials, ANSI Z39.48-1984. ∞ ™

Printed by Galliard (Printers) Ltd
   Great Yarmouth, Norfolk, Great Britain

COLLECTED STUDIES SERIES CS439

QD
18
E85
L48
1994

CONTENTS

This volume contains xiv + 298 pages

PUBLISHER'S NOTE

The articles in this volume, as in all others in the Collected Studies Series, have not been given a new, continuous pagination. In order to avoid confusion, and to facilitate their use where these same studies have been referred to elsewhere, the original pagination has been maintained wherever possible.

Each article has been given a Roman number in order of appearance, as listed in the Contents. This number is repeated on each page and quoted in the index entries.

It has not been possible to reproduce all the illustrations originally included in these articles; in some cases new illustrations have been substituted.

PREFACE

Chemistry has long been a science of shifting borders and protean identity. Sometimes the centre and at other times the periphery has attracted greater attention, and chemists have alternated between seeking to emphasize the autonomy of their discipline, and uniting their science with other sciences. One brand of chemical philosophy was dominant within Robert Fludd's Renaissance cosmology. Under Robert Boyle, chemical philosophy in Britain became part of the mechanical philosophy, even while laboratory practice was strengthening chemistry's identity. The iatrochemistry of Paracelsus made chemistry part of medicine. This tradition was preserved throughout Europe in schools which taught chemistry within the medical curriculum, as Hermann Boerhaave did at Leiden. Martinus van Marum, largely responsible for the introduction of Antoine Laurent Lavoisier's new or antiphlogistic chemistry into the Netherlands (I), first learned his chemistry as part of an education for medicine. Later in the century, Joseph Black's dissertation on *magnesia alba* was written for a degree in medicine. Meanwhile, Newtonian chemists attempted the methodological reduction of chemistry to physics, an enterprise in which Laplace and Berthollet later participated. Newtonian physics provided not only a conceptual model, but, through the work of instrument makers and demonstrators, provided an extension of the tools and methods of physicists into the chemical laboratory. Those chemists who, like Van Marum, had learned about the experimental Newtonianism epitomized in the work of Willem Jacob 'sGravesande and of the brothers Jan and Petrus van Musschenbroek, manifested that influence in the design of chemical apparatus in their laboratories. Lavoisier's own apparatus, developed partly through his collaboration with the physicist and astronomer Laplace, and more extensively through interaction with his instrument makers and fellow chemists, also marked a shift in the relations between chemistry and physics. This was primarily evinced in Lavoisier's stress on a quantitative as well as a qualitative chemistry. Enlightenment empiricism and the concomitant drive for an autonomous chemistry had stressed chemical qualities as they could be experienced through the senses, of sight, smell, touch, and above all of taste. Lavoisier, like Black and Henry Cavendish before him, added quantitative rigour to qualitative subtlety. He made the balance and the gasometer both keys and regulators for his system of chemistry (IV).

Chemistry is a practical and an applied science, not only in medicine, but also in agriculture, in metallurgy, and in industry. It accordingly impinges on many facets of material and social culture. It was an important science for the early Fellows of the Royal Society of London, with their Baconian program for a history of trades. It was similarly significant for the *Encyclopédistes*, concerned to bridge the gap between the philosopher's science and the artisan's craft. It was to remain important for the participants in the subsequent Scottish enlightenment, for improving landlords throughout the eighteenth century, and for the members of that extraordinary constellation of natural philosophers and industrialists, the Lunar Society of Birmingham. A late eighteenth-century scientific tour of England had to take in the learned Lunatics, as well as Joseph Banks's breakfasts, and the shops of the instrument makers of London, by that date the heart of the European instrument trade. Chemistry was part of an international scientific culture, aspects of which are explored in II and III, concentrating on Anglo-Dutch relations in the eighteenth century.

The second set of essays (V-VIII) uses the career of Thomas Beddoes to examine issues in the relations between chemical science and medicine, politics, and society. Educated in Edinburgh as a physician, a pupil and almost a disciple of Joseph Black, Beddoes was for a while reader in chemistry at Oxford. He largely although not uncritically accepted Lavoisier's chemical revolution, and with his instrument maker developed laboratory apparatus to demonstrate the truths of the new system. His lectures and demonstrations were well received, and he seemed likely to be appointed to the proposed Regius chair in the discipline. But Oxford politics were tory, if not reactionary, while Beddoes's were democratic, and thus, in the years following the French Revolution, radical and verging on seditious. Beddoes's association with francophile members of the Lunar Society, and with their more radical offspring, further hampered his candidacy. Rejected by the university, he left for Bristol. There, he established an institution for investigating the therapeutic effects of breathing different gases, with the assistance of young Humphry Davy as director of the chemical laboratory. Beddoes's scientific work continued to be prejudiced by his involvement in political protest.

The turn of the eighteenth and nineteenth centuries was an eventful time. Georg Wilhelm Friedrich Hegel was not alone in seeing the new century as a time of birth and transition. The French Revolution had been succeeded by the Napoleonic Wars, British democracy had been all but stifled by the government's gagging bills, industrial revolution was in full swing, and so was its philosophical and literary opposition in the romantic movement. In chemistry, Lavoisier's definition of provisional and practically determined elements was complemented by John Dalton's atomic theory, facilitating greater discrimination between chemical species, and anticipating the possibility of novel chemical syntheses and the expansion of chemical industry. Soon added to this complex was the Prussian reform of higher education, leading effectively to the birth of the university research laboratory as a training ground for doctoral students. IX and X lightly explore aspects of these developments, within the history of chemical ideas, and more broadly in the context of the historiography of nineteenth-century science. X touches primarily on Romanticism, historicism, scientific institutions, and Humboldtian science. IX has as its main theme the complexity arising from newly discovered elements, and from ever larger organic molecules, seen against the simplicity of the rules of chemical combination — the rich economy of nature.

In spite of prior inroads from both chemistry and physics, many if not most chemists by the beginning of the nineteenth century considered that their science enjoyed full autonomy. There were, however, those who were unhappy with such a compartmentalization of the sciences. Michael Faraday, for example, although he began work as Humphry Davy's assistant in the chemical laboratory, refused to be limited by the label of chemist, and held firmly to the title of natural philosopher. For post-Kantian German idealist philosophers, chemistry was a centrally significant science, arising from the powers of matter and intimately connected both to geology and to the sciences of life.

XI to XVI look at what Davy and Faraday both regarded as chemical philosophy, a fusion of ideas and empirical knowledge yielding intellectual insight, like Francis Bacon's experiments of light. Davy (XI) moved from Bristol to the Royal Institution in London, and there rapidly established himself as the most visible and brilliant British scientist of the day. He was ambitious, regarding himself as one of the heroic sons of genius whose achievements would deserve immortality. Dalton for Davy was chemistry's Kepler. Davy was determined to be its Newton. But Davy, admiring the ideas informing chemical discovery, was also imbued with an understanding of the importance to society of those applications deriving from chemical science — not least of them his own invention of what miners came to know as the Davy lamp. Davy's ideas were what excited the poet and philosopher Samuel Taylor Coleridge, who saw in chemistry "poetry realized in nature" (XII). In a scheme deriving primarily from German philosophy, notably in the writings of Friedrich Schelling and Heinrich Steffens, Coleridge made chemistry a crucial science (XIII). He saw it as providing the basis for a theory of life, and resting upon the seminal powers of matter and their elaboration in the history and structure of the earth. Hegel had a similar view of the place of chemistry in the hierarchy of the sciences, and saw it as emerging from geology (XIV). Faraday explored the operation and interaction of the chemical and electrical powers of matter, material ripe for exploration in the laboratory, as well as by philosophers of nature. His electrochemistry (XV) built directly upon experiments inspired by ideas about powers, and rested upon a conception of matter derived from Newtonian theories, as well as the partly Leibnizian ideas of Roger Joseph Boscovich. Faraday added one other extra-laboratory ingredient to his theorizing about matter, a brand of the theology of nature that he used to reinforce his particular brand of dynamism (XVI).

The relations of matter to its powers, and of both to chemical qualities, were important not only to natural philosophers, but also to those who, like Gay-Lussac and Berzelius, saw themselves and were recognized as chemists. The final group of essays in this book deals with what were strictly chemical debates. To account for chemical qualities had long been a fundamental problem in chemistry.

In the rise of organic chemistry in the first half of the nineteenth century, that problem took the particular form of a methodological debate: should one advance in organic chemistry using the tried and proven methods and assumptions of inorganic chemistry, or should one use organic chemistry as the new norm? In the former case, the individual atoms, or sometimes their aggregates, would have to carry the main explanatory burden: the nature of the atoms would count for more than their putative arrangement. In the latter case, in contrast, similarities in the properties of two different substances were supposed to be mainly the result of similar although unknown arrangements of atoms. This is the debate explored in XVII. The next essay looks at the debate between Joseph Louis Gay-Lussac and Humphry Davy, asking especially about the causes of acidity and alkalinity, and whether those properties derived from any particular substance or principle, or were the result of the modes of combination of constituent substances. The final essay (XIX) looks at the assumptions and ideas involved in different ideas about chemical arrangement, showing wherein they differed from the truly stereochemical ideas of Jacobus Henricus van't Hoff and Joseph Achille le Bel.

These essays were written over a span of twenty-six years. Sometimes there is an overlap between different essays within a section, for example in those on Beddoes. Each of the papers does, however, make different points, and I have therefore let them stand unrevised. On the other hand, it has been desirable, for technical reasons, to reset VIII, XV, XVIII, and XIX. During the process of resetting, I have taken the opportunity silently to correct typographical errors, and to make minor stylistic changes.

The history of chemistry has undergone something of a revival in the past eighteen months. Until 1992, the last major one-volume history of chemistry had been Aaron Ihde's, written primarily for chemists, and noteworthy for tackling the recent as well as the remote past. 1992 saw the publication of an elegant essay by David M. Knight, *Ideas in Chemistry* (Athlone Press: London), as well as William H. Brock's substantial and admirable *History of Chemistry* (Fontana Press: London), addressed primarily to chemists, but also to historians of chemistry. More recent still is Bernadette Bensaude-Vincent and Isabelle Stengers, *Histoire de la Chimie* (La Découverte: Paris, 1993). Brock sees chemistry as taking a recognizably modern shape at the turn of the eighteenth and nineteenth centuries. Bensaude-Vincent and Stengers explicitly avoid the dichotomy between premodern and modern chemistry, and emphasize the ways in which chemistry has constantly been in a process of redefinition. Both accounts recognize the importance of social, industrial, professional, and institutional factors, and both are very welcome additions to the literature.

Recent historiography of science has made much of rhetoric and language, and some of it has been unconvincing. A welcome exception to that trend, important for its discussion of chemistry's audience and of the need for chemists to convince that audience, is Jan Golinski, *Science as Public Culture: Chemistry and Enlightenment in Britain, 1760-1820* (Cambridge University Press: Cambridge, New York, and Melbourne, 1992). His book elaborates the context for V-VIII and XI in this volume.

There is a large recent literature on the chemical revolution, encouraged by the recent bicentenary of Lavoisier's seminal *Traité élémentaire de chimie*. There are useful essays in *Osiris*, 2nd Series, **4** (1988), edited by Arthur Donovan, and in *Lavoisier et la Révolution Chimique* (SABIX, Ecole Polytechnique: Palaiseau, 1992), edited by Michelle Goupil, with the collaboration of Patrice Bret and Francine Masson. Maurice Crosland has written two studies particularly important for the study of French chemistry at the turn of the eighteenth and nineteenth centuries, in which chemistry and its context are well integrated. These books are *The Society of Arcueil: A View of French Chemistry at the Time of Napoleon I* (Heinemann: London, 1967), and *Gay-Lussac: Scientist and Bourgeois* (Cambridge University Press: Cambridge, London, New York, and Melbourne, 1978.

The best introduction to the interdependence of language and theory is William Randall Albury, *The Logic of Condillac and the Structure of French Chemical and Biological Theory, 1780-1801*, (Ph.D. Dissertation, The Johns Hopkins University, 1972). John H. Brooke has written a useful and subtle analysis of methodological debates in organic chemistry in *Enlightenment Science in the Romantic Era: The Chemistry of Berzelius and Its Cultural Setting*, edited by Evan M. Melhado and Tore Frängsmyr (Cambridge University Press: Cambridge, New York, and Oakleigh, 1992). Valuable introductions to chemical instruments are provided by Gerard L'Estrange Turner in *Nineteenth-Century Scientific Instruments* (Sotheby Publications and University of California Press: London, Berkeley, and Los Angeles, 1983), pp. 203-25, and *Storia delle Scienze: Gli Strumenti* (Giulio Einaudi: Torino, 1990). My favourite introduction to chemistry as a laboratory science remains Michael Faraday's classic *Chemical Manipulation: Being Instructions to Students in Chemistry, on the Methods of Performing Experiments of Demonstration or of Research, with Accuracy and Success* (W. Phillips: London, 1827).

TREVOR H. LEVERE

Toronto
1993

ACKNOWLEDGEMENTS

Most of these essays were written since I came to the Institute for the History and Philosophy of Science at the University of Toronto twenty-five years ago. I am grateful for support and encouragement to my colleagues here, and to others in Oxford, Cambridge, and Haarlem. I should particularly like to thank the late Professor R. J. Forbes and Mme. Michelle Goupil, Professors Gerard Turner, Stillman Drake, and Alistair Crombie, the President and Fellows of Clare Hall, Cambridge University, and the staff of Teyler's Museum, Haarlem. I am grateful for material help to the Social Sciences and Humanities Research Council of Canada, the Humanities and Social Sciences Committee of the Research Board of the University of Toronto, the Killam Program of the Canada Council, Victoria College in the University of Toronto, and the Directors of Teyler's Stichting and of the Hollandsche Maatschappij der Wetenschappen.

Permission to reproduce or reprint articles was granted by the following institutions, journals, and presses: *Janus* (I), The Royal Society of London (II, VII); *History of Science* (III); the Ecole Polytechnique, Palaiseau (IV, XVIII); *Ambix*, with the consent of the copyright holder, the Society for the History of Alchemy and Chemistry (V, XVII); *BJHS* (*The British Journal for the History of Science*) (VI, XVI); *ISR: Interdisciplinary Science Reviews* (VIII); Kluwer Academic Publishers (X); University of California Press (IX) the Royal Society of Canada, Ottawa (XI); Taylor and Francis, Ltd. (XII); *Studies in Romanticism* (XIII); Klett-Cotta (XIV); The Electrochemical Society, Inc. (XV); the American Chemical Society (XIX).

I

MARTINUS VAN MARUM (1750-1837)

The introduction of Lavoisier's chemistry into the Low Countries.

Part of Spaarne 17, a superb eighteenth century mansion in Haarlem, is now occupied by the Dutch Society of Sciences which has happily preserved for itself three fine period rooms. Looking out from these, across the river, one is confronted by the mistakenly magnificent facade of Teyler's museum and library. Teyler's is now a quiet centre of study, but it was not always so peaceful. In 1811, the Foundation was visited by the Emperor NAPOLEON, who came with the ostensive resolve to find fault with and to stifle its independence. In the event, he acted far otherwise, even granting the Director of the museum an annual augmented pension, to enable him more fruitfully to continue his work there. NAPOLEON's generosity, coupled with the tolerance shown by the French commissioners for the reorganisation of Dutch science, protected Teyler's, so that it was one of the institutions to suffer least under imperial domination.

The Dutch Society of Sciences also flourished at this period, so that in 1817 its secretary was forced to explain to a friend who was somewhat impatient of entry to membership that

since our society has become increasingly famous, the title of member is in such demand among men of letters, that for twenty years only professional savants have been admitted.

One man, Martinus VAN MARUM, as Director of Teyler's museum and secretary of the Dutch Society of Sciences, was responsible for the health, survival and increasing celebrity of the two foundations. A worker of tireless industry and remarkable versatility, he typified and epitomised the eighteenth century's ideal of the man of science. He dabbled earnestly in education and theology, shunned politics (except where such action would have invited scientific oblivion), and immersed himself vigorously and to the full in the scientific currents of his time. There was an impatience in his energy which was to limit his posterior fame — devotion to a single science would have meant a narrower, but perhaps a deeper reward, for even then the full range of science was beyond the reach of the most inspired polymath.

It is in the field of chemistry that he best deserves our remembrance, serving as the prime missionary exponent of Lavoisier's system in the Low Countries. In the following pages I propose to outline this contribution, and shall trace VAN MARUM's progress from adherence to PRIESTLEY's phlogistic chemistry, to complete acceptance of the Neologues' theories.

When, in 1764, Petrus VAN MARUM, self-made commercial industrialist, moved with his family from Delft to Groningen, his son Martinus was swift to enrol, as a student of medecine and philosophy, at the civic University. Aided by the benevolent guidance and inspired instruction of Petrus CAMPER, VAN MARUM enthusiastically undertook research in botany and plant physiology. His efforts were intended, when complete, for publication in his Doctoral thesis, but they were still unfinished when they achieved premature celebrity as his Doctoral dissertation, which he submitted to Prince WILLIAM V, Rector of the University. Two weeks after this initial publication, he produced a second thesis, for which he was awarded the degree of Doctor of Medicine. This auspicious beginning — two doctorates in the space of two weeks — led him confidently to expect that he would succeed CAMPER in the chair of Botany. Instead, Wynoldus MUNNIKS, a contemporary of VAN MARUM, received the coveted post. Martinus, wounded by what he considered a palpable injustice, retired from the suddenly unrewarding pursuit of botany. After so painful and so unexpected a discouragement, he tells us, 'I wanted to carry out other researches in the Natural Sciences, in order to distract myself. To this end, I chose Electricity'.

Joseph PRIESTLEY's *History and Present State of Electricity* served as seed and spur to his subsequent efforts, impelling him along a course of study which he had already begun in 1772. His early attempts in the field, which involved the investigation of 'explosive airs', were a perilous and resounding success, and LE ROY, of the Academy of Sciences in Paris, seemed as impressed by the risks run as by the value of the results.

VAN MARUM's reaction to the rebuff at Groningen extended beyond a mere change of subject — he left city and university alike, and moved to Haarlem, seat of the Dutch Society of Sciences, and favoured with a populace where the merchant classes took both a dilettante's and a patron's interest in the progress of science. On his arrival there in 1776, VAN MARUM set up as a physician, and to this he soon added the post of lecturer, and a position on the Council of the Dutch Society of Sciences.

Then, in 1780, VAN MARUM's entry to a competition, set by Teyler's Second Society on 'phlogisticated and dephlogisticated air', was adjudged the winner and crowned with gold. It was published by the Society in the following year as the first volume of the Treatises issued by Teyler's Second Society. The subject was one of immediate and topical interest, for the competition followed closely upon the appearance of volume III of PRIESTLEY's *Experiments and Observations on Different Kinds of Air*, and VAN MARUM's paper was eagerly received.

'You do very well, Sir', wrote LE ROY, 'to follow the new career opened by Mr. Priestley . . . His discoveries are infinitely curious, and offer a new and vast field to physics'.

In this, the first of the three physico-chemical treatises which VAN MARUM wrote as a phlogistonist, he displayed little originality, being in almost complete agreement with the ideas of previous writers. Indeed, he freely admitted that 'one has mainly to thank the untiring zeal of the discerning Dr. Priestley' for the discoveries concerning phlogisticated and dephlogisticated air, and in this paper he merely aimed at collecting the data currently available, wishing to present them in a more consequential manner — an aim which he achieved admirably. He accepted MACQUER's definition of phlogiston as 'elementary fire, combined and become one of the principles of combustible bodies,' and agreed that dephlogisticated air consisted of fine particles of an earth combined with an acid. In combustion, air accepted phlogiston, so that atmospheric air consisted of earth, acid and phlogiston. VAN MARUM was aware of the discoveries of INGENHOUSZ and SENEBIER in the field of photosynthesis, and ecstatically pointed out the balance which obtains in the atmosphere by virtue of the complementary effects of animal and vegetable respiration.

What a beautiful arrangement, by which the Ruler of the Cosmos has cared for the maintenance of animal and plant life! I think that no doubter can be so irrational that he will let not himself be convinced, by such a demonstration, ... of the existence of an eternally wise Creator.

Typically, the paper ended with an enquiry into the useful consequences which could be derived from the discoveries about phlogisticated and dephlogisticated airs, and his final section reads like a set of hospital instructions. He emphasised the further healthful possibilities for the latter air.

For example, it can probably be used in resuscitating drowned men: if the cause of death in such cases is the blood's inability to relieve itself of surplus phlogiston, what better way could there be to save these people than by using an air which has so strong an attraction for phlogiston?

The next paper which VAN MARUM wrote (this time in collaboration with the Amsterdam merchant and chemist Adriaan Paets VAN TROOSTWYK) dealt with harmful gases and vapours. Although it included no investigation of the chemical processes involved in the formation of the harmful exhalations discussed, it did give a general picture of the way in which men tried to apply chemical knowledge. One of the few purely chemical discoveries included in the treatise was the observation that glowing coals gave off, beside fixed air (carbon dioxide), another gas (carbon monoxide) which so contaminated the air that its harmful effects were swiftly apparent.

Throughout, VAN MARUM displayed his concern with the usefulness of the sciences which he studied. His suggestions were never purely academic, and he never became so deeply immersed in the theory of his researches as to ignore their practical possibilities. A steady stream of papers came from him on divers applied topics, generally relating to medecine.

In the same year that his first chemical treatise appeared, VAN MARUM married, thereby becoming a man of property. Two years later, at the request of the Directors, he took upon himself the direction of Teyler's cabinets of physics and of natural history. This offered him the welcome opportunity to devote more time to research, and he proposed, as a first step, 'to perfect several instruments, whose faults experience had shewn me!'

One of the first fruits of this plan was the 'extraordinarily large electric machine', which to this day stands in Teyler's museum. It seemed to him axiomatic that if a machine, larger than any hitherto built, were available, then new discoveries would result. So he set John Cuthbertson the task of realising the practical limits of an electrostatic disc generator. The outcome was a machine capable of producing sparks of the thickness of a fountain pen and two feet in length — surely the most awesome display of artificial discharges thus far demonstrated. The lateral branches of the spark all tended in the same direction, whence VAN MARUM deduced the superiority of FRANKLIN's single fluid theory of electricity over the 'dualist heresy': which 'proof' FRANKLIN himself was only too happy to accept.

VAN MARUM, aided by VAN TROOSTWYK, subjected various gases, metals and their calces, to the torrential discharge of the machine. They analysed ammonia, formed ozone from oxygen (they merely noted its strong smell, which they attributed to the electric 'matter'), and electrified atmospheric air. The last underwent a volume decrease, thereby convincing them that 'the atmospheric air has received phlogiston in all these experiments'. The correct explanation had to await CAVENDISH's results, and VAN MARUM's conversion to Lavoisierian chemistry: but for the present he was convinced that the electric matter 'is either phlogiston itself, or at least that it contains a lot of this principle'. This was supported by observations that electric discharges could reduce metal calces, i.e., give them back their phlogiston. However, an electric discharge, passed through iron in air, produced the reverse effect, which exiged the conclusion that electricity was capable both of donating and abstracting phlogiston — a paradox which VAN MARUM could neither resolve nor evade.

Naturally, VAN MARUM and VAN TROOSTWYK published their results, and distributed copies to the leading scientists and principal Academies of Europe. The reception, from London and Paris, at home and abroad, was here ecstatic, there sober, but every recipient expressed his wholehearted approbation. VAN MARUM had achieved international stature as a scientist.

In June of the same year (1785), he set out, armed with copies of his work, for the Academy of Sciences in Paris, and, though he did not yet know it, for the new chemistry.

VAN MARUM's arrival in Paris coincided with a critical phase in the development of antiphlogistic chemistry. For some years now, LAVOISIER had made strenuous attacks on the phlogistic stronghold, and had decried phlogiston as 'the *Deus ex Machina* of the Metaphysicians, a substance which explains everything, and which explains nothing, to which one attributes in turn opposite qualities'. Even in his own country, however, he found little support for his theories prior to the discovery of the composition of water. The rise of the antiphlogistic movement in France dates effectively from 1785, when BERTHOLLET publicly attached himself to the Neologues. At the height of the swing towards LAVOISIER, VAN MARUM arrived in Paris, and was not a little astonished at the turbulence of the debate.

During his visit, he made the acquaintance of several leading chemists and members of the Academy, including 'the celebrated founders of modern chemistry', as he was later to refer to LAVOISIER, BERTHOLLET and MONGE. The last of these especially took pains to explain to our curious doctor the ideas of the new system of chemistry, and eagerly demonstrated or indicated the critical experiments on which the theory was principally founded. It was the force of these arguments, 'founded entirely on facts', which brought VAN MARUM seriously to doubt the validity of the phlogistic system. As a result, on his return to Haarlem, he spent the entire winter of 1785-1786 absorbed in evaluating the claims of the Lavoisierian system, and concluded that 'all the foundations of the ancient phlogistic system were completely shaken by the new facts, of which I had just been instructed.' The synthesis of water from its elements, and the calcination of metals in air-free water, by means of electric discharges, were two of the main instruments in his conversion.

In 1787, he published an account of his latest experiments with the great electrical machine, giving to the results a consistently antiphlogistic interpretation. The appendix to this volume, written only in Dutch, was intended to explain the principles of the new system of chemistry, since these were still largely unknown in the Netherlands. This was the first appearance of a coherent exposition of the antiphlogistic system in any country, and reached the press two years before LAVOISIER's *Traité Elémentaire de Chemie*. VAN MARUM made his sketch as brief as was compatible with comprehensiveness, and systematically listed the cardinal points of the theory. This was certainly VAN MARUM's most important and influential single work, but since the main thread of LAVOISIER's argument is readily available, it is unnecessary to describe it in detail. However, VAN MARUM's reasons for accepting the new teaching are instructive: —

Martinus van Marum (1750-1837).

Van Marum's Electric Machine at Teyler's Foundation, Haarlem.

I

PLATE IV

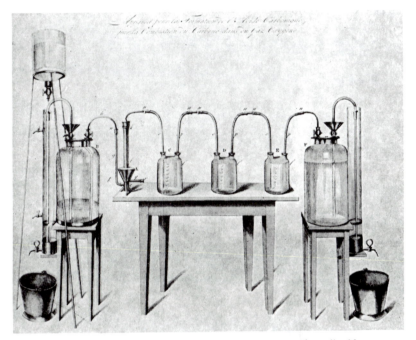

Van Marum's apparatus for the synthesis of carbon dioxide.
(Note his gasometer).

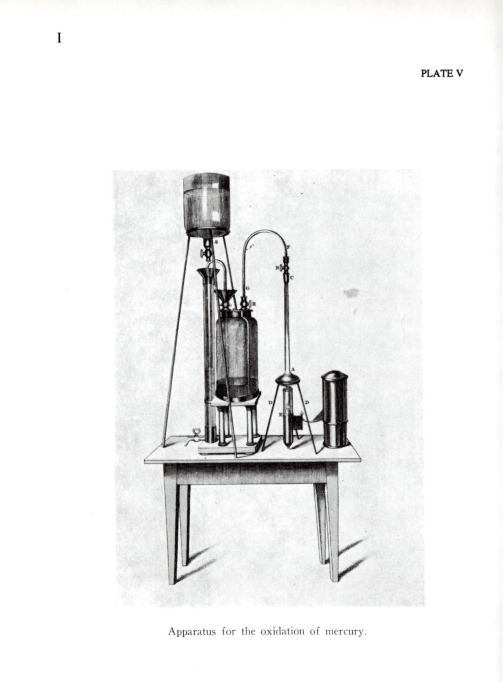

Apparatus for the oxidation of mercury.

1. Every principle of the system has been proven by decisive experiments, with one exception. (This refers to caloric, and VAN MARUM's uncertainty on this point made him defer consideration of the hypothetical entity to the end of his exposition. LAVOISIER, in contrast, being eager to lay the ghost of phlogiston for all time, placed it at the beginning of his treatise.)

2. On the other hand, there has been no direct proof of contending theories, in particular the existence of phlogiston has never been proven, but merely assumed because it explained a number of phenomena.

3. The new teaching gives simple and clear explanations of many phenomena, including a number which could not be explained on the basis of the older system.

The final page of his exposition also deserves full quotation.

... although it is quite clear that this teaching, as far as it goes, is thoroughly founded on experiment, and that it sheds much light on our knowledge of Nature, it is however far from being the case that I consider it adequate in all respects. On the contrary, I freely recognize that there are many matters which, though closely connected to the undertaking, remain completely unknown. Further, the teaching regards some substances, such as sulphur and carbon, as principles: but this is in no way because these principles are regarded as *simple* principles, but because their composition is so far unknown. Since this theory has brought to light the composition of a number of substances which had previously been thought of as simple principles, we should be wary of the delusion of regarding substances whose composition is unknown to us, as principles. So, however much light this theory sheds, it also shews us on the other hand, how much further research remains. This is indeed the fate of a Natural Scientist, that every newly discov ered truth generally brings before him other unknown matters, concerning which he had not previously noticed his ignorance.

This treatise, which opened the attack on phlogiston in the Netherlands, marked the beginning of a new era of chemistry there. In the following year, it was translated into German, and NAHUIJS in the Low Countries published a paper in which he declared that he retained not the slightest doubt in favouring LAVOISIER's theory far above that of STAHL or of any of his supporters. Subsequently, in 1793, two of that illustrious Amsterdam fraternity, the Dutch Chemists, published further summaries of LAVOISIER's system.

I

Initial reactions to VAN MARUM's paper were decidedly mixed, ranging from the near ecstasy of the Neologues, to the combative misery of the phlogistic rearguard. The issue was not yet clear, but the time was ripe and the theory sound, so that within fifteen years there was not a phlogistonist of note throughout the Netherlands.

The end of the eighteenth century was an age of violent flux in European politics, as in science, and Holland shared to the full in the turbulence of the times. In 1787, the year in which VAN MARUM's *Sketch of Mr. Lavoisier's Teaching* appeared, the Patriotic Party forced temporary capitulation on WILLIAM V, and his return to the Hague on the bloodless tide of Prussian muskets was followed by the dissolution and reorganisation of the more severely Patriotic municipal councils, including that of Haarlem. VAN MARUM was invited to join the reformed council, but he declined involvement with any political party. His only concern with politics was where it impinged on his scientific independence and endowments, and the revolution of 1787 affected him only in so far it temporarily inhibited the funds of Teyler's Foundation.

The next major shock was not so easily and gently surmounted. At the height of the Terror in Revolutionary France, 'many scoundrels on whom Justice has wreaked her vengeance, tried to extinguish every light, by slaughtering men of merit : and of such, we have unfortunately suffered great losses'. Happily, when the French armies crossed the frozen rivers to the south, and entered Holland in January 1795, ROBESPIERRE had fallen, and with him the excesses of the Terror : but still, the future for science must have appeared all too uncertain. INGENHOUSZ wrote nervously to his friend VAN MARUM.

'You are pleased to believe that you have nothing to fear for your person and your home, seeing that *qui timet bis miser est*. For a long time our friend Lavoisier flattered himself with the same hope, and did not escape for all that.'

As soon as the French arrived, VAN MARUM entered on what was to become his habitual course of action, and presented Claude ROBERJOT and Faujas DE ST. FOND, commissioners for scientific reorganisation in the Low Countries, with volumes of his researches. He had met both these gentlemen on the most friendly terms, during his visits to Paris in 1785 and 1788. On 2 March 1795, the insurance policy matured, and VAN MARUM received a dispensation relieving him from the obligation of billetting French troops in Haarlem: he was thereby enabled to carry on limited research. Furthermore, presuming on his acquaintance with the Commissioners, and deploying to the full his powers of persuasiveness, he so far prevailed with the invaders that Teyler's Museum was left in its entirety, and was not stripped for the enrichment of the Paris museum.

Even with this good fortune and adroit manoeuvring, he was hindered in the pursuit of his researches by that recurrent curse, 'the general scarcity of money (which) has made necessary all possible economy'. In spite of this, VAN MARUM, firmly resolved not to become enmeshed in the administrative net, was still at liberty to continue his chemical and physical occupations. This was in marked contrast to the fate of many scientists, who had become involved in the affairs of government, to the detriment of scientific research in the Low Countries. He was even fortunate in not receiving a preferred chair at Utrecht, for not only would there have been no immediate financial advantage, but in the succeeding years of French occupation, the University was replaced by a secondary school.

As Director of the collections, and then Secretary, of the Dutch Society of Sciences, VAN MARUM had more than just political feelings with which to reckon, and his scientific ambitions rode rough-shod over many less determined sensibilities. The election of that heterodox and controversial divine, Joseph PRIESTLEY, was met with bitter indignation, and J. F. D'ORVILLE considered that

it would be dishonourable to remain any longer a Director of a Society in which Priestley, who publicly undermines our religion, is admitted as a Member. It has deeply pained me to witness this, especially in a land whose principle support is the maintenance of the Pure Reformed Religion.

VAN MARUM replied that only scientific merit should be considered in matters of election, and D'ORVILLE resigned in protest. But the difficulty encountered in this case was an isolated instance, and the scientists VAN MARUM proposed were generally elected, at least in the early years of his secretaryship. (This was before the increasing demand for membership consequent on the Society's increasing celebrity made entry more difficult.) Avidly, he gathered leading scientists — BERTHOLLET, LAVOISIER, MONGE, KLAPROTH, PRIESTLEY and many others—under the aegis of membership.

He was, moreover, just as eager to achieve his own election to other societies of note, and in all but two cases was immediately successful. In the one, the Academy of Sciences in Paris, the delay was temporary and occasioned by rules of precedence; but the Royal Society in London was much more difficult of access.

He began his campaign conventionally, sending copies of his works to Sir Joseph BANKS, the autocratic President. Then, in 1790, he came to London, in part to shop around for Teyler's among the famous instrument makers, but more especially to follow INGENHOUSZ's advice in making the acquaintance of influential members of the Royal Society, who might forward his enterprise. VAN MARUM's irascibility and impatience of professional etiquette had already incurred the dislike of Henry CAVENDISH, and he hoped that personal encounter might overcome the eccentric genius' unfortunate antipathy. The number of foreign Fellows was limited to one hundred, the certificate of election required the signature of at least six of the leading Fellows, and the initials F.R.S. were then avidly sought by gentlemen as being among the necessary perquisites of social standing. The difficulties were thus considerable, and van MARUM returned to Haarlem without having succeeded in his object.

The seed had been sown, however, and at last, CAVENDISH must have relented, for in 1798 he was one of the signatories to the certificate of van MARUM's election.

All this striving after international recognition was merely a backcloth against which van MARUM carried on his more serious researches. He was above all concerned to demonstrate the truth of the new system of chemistry, by experiment, publication and disputation. He retained in addition his early interest in pneumatic chemistry, and in relation to the new teaching opined that

The theory I have presented sheds much light on the origin and properties of the different storts of air, which for some years, especially since the discoveries of Dr. Priestley, have begun to form a new and very remarkable branch of knowledge. This Natural Science of airs has been brought, by the theory presented above, to such a degree of simplicity and clarity that would particularly recommend itself on this account alone, even if it were not based on direct experimental proof ...

When he sent his first volume of researches to Sir Joseph BANKS, the Royal Society was in recess. However, the President must have shewn the volume to Charles BLAGDEN, former Secretary of the Society, and research assistant to Henry CAVENDISH. It was owing to his familiarity with CAVENDISH's work that BLAGDEN wrote to VAN MARUM, referring to his electrification of atmospheric air.

From Mr. Cavendish's experiments I think we may conclude, that the electric spark does not communicate any phlogiston to the air, but acts simply as making it red- or white-hot, and inducing the elective attractions corresponding to that degree of heat. Therefore, your dephlogisticated air being unmixed, that is having nothing to combine with it, was not diminished or impaired, but the common air, consisting of dephlogisticated and phlogisticated air mixed together, was both diminished and impaired, because none of the former was employed in converting a small portion of the latter into nitrous acid, in consequence of the increase of their elective attractions by the heat ... If Mr. Lavoisier's hypothesis, excluding phlogiston, be adopted, the facts may still be explained with the same ease ...

With this letter, BLAGDEN enclosed a copy of CAVENDISH's Memoir, which VAN MARUM read. He concurred with BLAGDEN in thinking that LAVOISIER's antiphlogistic system would provide a simple explanation of CAVENDISH's results. Further,

As these experiments shed a lot of light on many phenomena, which I had seen while testing the effects of the electric ray on different kinds of airs, I wanted to see from my own experiments the results described by Mr. Cavendish ... I flattered myself that the superior force of our machine would lead to more convincing proofs.

The results obtained were indeed in fundamental agreement with CAVENDISH's: but there was a quantitative discrepancy which puzzled VAN MARUM, and induced him to write to CAVENDISH. The latter replied somewhat tersely, and later opined that 'the others' failed to achieve identical results 'through want of patience'. It was VAN MARUM's published spurt of irritation at this reply which caused the breach between them.

Besides sparking atmospheric air, thereby producing nitric oxide and thence nitric acid, VAN MARUM and VAN TROOSTWYK used the electrical machine to spark nitric oxide. From the results of this experiment, VAN MARUM deduced that nitrous air contained nitrous acid, while LAVOISIER regarded the gas as a constituent of nitric acid. (The terms nitric and nitrous were used interchangeably by VAN MARUM). His error here arose from his tacit assumption that the power of an electric discharge was purely destructive, so that he ignored the possibility of decomposition followed by recombination of the constituents.

In addition to trying the effects of electric discharges on different airs, VAN MARUM investigated the action of these airs on metal wires when strong discharges were passed through them. When he used tin in nitrous air, he was surprised to note that calcination proceeded 'as readily as in atmospheric or in pure air', whence he deduced that the metal was capable of abstracting oxygen from nitrous air, and combining with it to form a calx. This interpretation would clearly have been impossible without a just appreciation of LAVOISIER's system, of which the 'acidifying principle', or oxygen, was the keystone.

If the discovery of oxygen formed the basis of the antiphlogistic theory, then that of the composition of water confirmed and completed it, and it was most important for the acceptance of the theory that this composition should be effectively demonstrated, both analytically and synthetically. We have already come across VAN MARUM's calcination of iron wires in water: and over the years, he investigated, with moderate success, means of decomposing water merely by electric shock. (DEIMANN and VAN TROOSTWYK, in 1789, carried out an experiment which achieved both the synthesis and decomposition of water, without the possibility of any external reagent.) The large-scale synthesis of water, however, seemed to offer the best way of winning converts. It was true that LAVOISIER had designed an apparatus to effect the synthesis quantitatively, but, as Gaspard MONGE complained, 'the trouble is ... that Mr. Lavoisier has carried out his experiments with apparatus which is too costly, and all physicists think that, to ensure success, it is necessary to lay out, as he did, five or six thousand pounds'. It was this situation, coupled with the conviction that the composition of water was the most illuminating discovery made in his lifetime, that induced VAN MARUM to devise an apparatus which would combine the requisite accuracy with relative cheapness. The result was a gasometer where the flow of gas was regulated by hydrostatic pressures, rather than by the system of balances which LAVOISIER had employed. It was as accurate as LAVOISIER's and had the advantage of being over six times cheaper.

VAN MARUM used his gasometers in lecture demonstrations in Teyler's museum from 1791 onwards, and the apparatus is still

exhibited there. It was one of the pieces which he shewed to
Napoleon when the Emperor visited Haarlem, and apart from the
great electrical machine is certainly his most famous instrument. Its
appearance created international interest, and copies were made for
the universities of Leiden, Utrecht, Berlin and Dorpat. Alessandro
Volta, writing from Pavia, expressed his enchantment with the apparatus—'there is no need to say how much I prefer it to the
Gasometer made by Messrs. Lavoisier and Meusnier'.

Van Marum spent a considerable part of his time prior to 1798
in inventing and improving apparatus whereby to demonstrate 'those
experiments upon which the new system was especially founded'. To
so staunch an empiricist, the most effective instrument of persuasion
was clearly direct experimental proof. Stubborn, irreducible facts,
incontrovertibly presented, were the surest means of conversion. Let
the phlogistonists build their fantastic, ingenious structures—it shall
not avail them against a system of facts! The natural pity is that he
regularly betrayed his own faith—if so much of the theory worked,
as it most definitely did, then surely it must all be true. And so,
gradually, we find him relinquishing his critical attitude for one of
unquestioning acceptance. For the present, however, he still stands
on a basis of fact.

Besides the composition of water, the oxidation of metals and the
reduction of their oxides provided another mainstay of the new
system. The reversible thermal oxidation of mercury furnished a
decisive demonstration of the principle, but the reaction was uncons-
cionably slow when carried out in Lavoisier's apparatus. Lavoisier
himself admitted that

this apparatus suffers from the great inconvenience, that the air does
not renew itself sufficiently; but, on the other hand, if one were to
give the outside air too free a circulation, it would carry away mercury,
dissolved in it, and at the end of a few days, there would be none
left in the vessel. Since the experiments on mercury are the most
conclusive of all those which one can perform on the oxidation of
metals, it is to be wished that one could devise a simple apparatus by
means of which one could demonstrate this oxidation, and the results
obtained, in public courses'.

Van Marum tackled the problem. He tried the oxidation using an
Argand lamp to heat mercury in a Boyle's flask, and provided the air

from one of his gasometers. The quantitative results seem to have been eminently satisfactory, and again he used the apparatus in his own lecture courses.

Descriptions of other apparatus of VAN MARUM's invention were published in French, Dutch, German and English, and practical chemists throughout Europe were reaping the benefits that accrued from the simple, comprehensive experiments made possible by his ingenuity. It was as a practical chemist that he was known and respected, as an instrumentalist that he was sought out. His thrusts played no inconsiderable part in the gathering momentum of the antiphlogistic campaign in Germany and the Netherlands, and today one can still admire the elegant design and constant purpose displayed in his equipment in Teyler's Museum.

VAN MARUM's contributions to Lavoisierian chemistry were indeed preeminently practical, but his efforts at assimilating and employing its theoretical implications present a valuable microcosm of the transition from the old to the new system. We have already seen how LAVOISIER adopted William CLEGHORN's material theory of heat, and introduced caloric at the very beginning of his treatise. Since the new theory was intended to supplant the phlogiston theory in the minds of chemists, it was imperative that it should account for the perplexing phenomena of fire and heat which accompanied chemical reaction. The current materialism of all experimental philosophy, coupled with LAVOISIER's insistence on the conservation of mass in chemical reactions, required that the matter of fire should be imponderable, and LAVOISIER's dissatisfaction with what he considered a necessary paradox did not make the acceptance of his ideas any easier. Some chemists, like DE LA METHERIE, were sceptical of caloric, and considered that it bore a suspicious resemblance to the phlogiston it was designed to oust. Others, like VAN MARUM, at first regarded caloric as the least essential part of the antiphlogistic system, and paved the way for the eventual shedding of this fictitious entity. Caloric might have provided one of the most far-reaching subjects in Natural Science, but it lacked a respectable experimental lineage, and VAN MARUM was accordingly uneasy about it. But it was not long before its convenience as an explanatory tool (an argument) which he had scorned as inadequate in his rejection of phlogiston) induced him to shed his doubts, in practice if not in theory.

The first surviving lecture notes we have, where VAN MARUM introduced the subject of caloric, do not use the term, which 'sounded odd in Dutch'. His lecture of 19 January 1793 effectively summarized his ideas at that date:

1. Whenever vapours or fluid bodies change to aeriform substances, a very remarkable quantity of the matter of heat unites with them.

2. Vapours cannot attain the aeriform state when no matter of heat combines with them.

3. Union with the matter of heat gives to steam no greater warmth. (This refers to latent heat).

4. When vapours change to aeriform substances, by being taken up by the atmosphere, the matter of heat is also united with them.

5. Aeriform substances release the matter of heat whenever they return to the liquid state.
6. Warmth is caused by an individual substance.

Where the sixth point was concerned, VAN MARUM admitted that

The adequacy of a proposed substance to explain a number of natural phenomena can never prove the actual existence of such a substance. We need a more complete proof of the existence of caloric.

From the above, it follows that oxygen gas consists of the principle of oxygen, combined with caloric: in combustion, the increased temperature causes a change in the balance of affinities or elective attractions between caloric, oxygen and the combustible, so that the last two combine, and the matter of heat and light is evolved as flame. Lavoisier had at first stated that oxygen was necessary for any combustion, and that metals, sulphur and phosphorus contained very little caloric. Thus a serious objection to his theory of combustion was raised when the Dutch Chemists remarked, in 1794, that metals would burn in heated sulphur in the absence of oxygen. DEIMAN, VAN TROOSTWYK, NIEUWLAND and BONDT put forward their observations without any controversial intent, and merely as a piece of experimental fact—and as something of a puzzle. They admitted that they were unable to give a completely satisfactory explanation of the phenomena, but noted that the sulphur and metals had ceased, following their inflammation, to be merely a mechanical mixture, and had combined to form metallic sulphides. To account for this, they postulated a higher caloric content for sulphur than had been suspected: the exothermal nature of the reaction could then be attributed to a change in heat capacity, the sulphide having a smaller specific heat than the sum of the specific heat of the mixture and the heat of fusion of the sulphur, so that the formation of a sulphide was accompanied by the evolution of free caloric (heat).

VAN MARUM's first acquaintance with these experiments came from a communication in which the explanation I have just given was not included, so that he was left to frame his own account of the causes. Quite independently, he arrived at the same explanation. His attitude towards the experiments was far less disinterested than that of the Dutch Chemists, and he immediately published his intention of shewing 'that these experiments not only do not contradict the Lavoisierian system as a whole, but that in certain respects, they actually serve to confirm it'. After some terminological hair splitting, in which he distinguished between combustion and glowing, he seized upon LAVOISIER's eventual recognition of the existence of caloric in all bodies, and continued:

Now when sulphur combines with metals, caloric is set free: and it is apparent that this amount of caloric is enough to raise the bodies to a temperature high enough for them to glow ...

This glowing certainly gives a striking proof of the amount of caloric that some bodies possess. Moreover, it confirms that part of Lavoisier's theory, according to which the amount of caloric existing in different bodies may vary very greatly ... it is indeed remarkable that no-one until now has thought of using the glowing of a mixture of tin and sulphur as a proof of this.

In 1794, he published his account of a discovery of quite a different sort, but here again he relied for his explanation upon caloric. On 4 December 1793, he was setting up the apparatus for a lecture demonstration of the combustion of phosphorus in oxygen. He proposed to ignite the phosphorus by tying a cotton thread round it, rubbing the thread with resin, and sparking this in pure air (oxygen). This involved evacuating the vessel and introducing oxygen prior to ignition. To his surprise, as he evacuated the vessel, he found that 'when the mercury was one inch lower than in the barometer, the phosphorus took fire'. (Presumably the initial glow was due to chemiluminescence, and the process was a chain reaction—this would explain the upper pressure limit). VAN MARUM's account of this indicated his final and completely unquestioning acceptance of caloric, and rivalled in ingenious fantasy the elaborate façades of late phlogistic argument. He invoked 'the principles of modern chemistry':

Exhalations continually rise from the surface of phosphorus when it is exposed to the atmosphere . . . but as soon as the air is rarified to a certain degree, the exhalations cannot rise; for these particles will not be elevated but during the time that the surrounding air is heavier than themselves. Whenever, therefore, the air is rarified to this degree, the exhalations must remain and surround the phosphorus from which they came. The union of oxygen with these phosphorus exhalations must then be made only in the vicinity of the phosphorus . . . (as shewn by the light of the disengaged caloric . . .) This caloric, which is disengaged from the oxygen, must also, on account of its greater density, give heat to the phosphorus. Hence may be clearly seen the reason for the combustion . . . Woollen and cotton stuffs have the property of preventing the dispersion of caloric (because they impede the circulation of the air, by which the heat would else be conducted off).

On 31 December 1796, he wrote to Guyton DE MORVEAU of these experiments, which threw some light 'on the slow combustion of phosphorus, which some German chemists claim to have observed in azot'. The observation that phosphorus ignited when oxygen pressure was reduced had led some chemists to deduce that nitrogen was better able to support combustion than was oxygen. VAN MARUM, however, backed by the investigations of FOURCROY and VAUQUELIN, was able to argue conclusively that GOTTLING and others had used impure samples of nitrogen, which contained some oxygen—when this was used up, the glow ceased, but was instantly renewed upon the introduction of even the smallest quantity of oxygen. Following this discovery, DEIMAN wrote to CRELL in Germany that he was astounded that the German savants were at such pains to explain so simple a phenomenon—indeed, only confirmed phlogistonists were not convinced of the soundness of VAN MARUM's explanations.

The experiments on phosphorus represented his last theoretical contribution to the progress of the antiphlogistic system of chemistry. His work on the catalytic dehydrogenation of alcohol, following PRIESTLEY's discovery, did indeed win Marsilio LANDRIANI to the cause, but served more to clarify his own ideas on the nature of carbon than to promote the system to which he adhered. His work on electricity, carried out at VOLTA's instigation, lies beyond the scope of this paper. One isolated achievement, however, deserves recognition before we leave his practical researches. His conviction that 'apparatus is improved when it is simplified', coupled with his desire for ever more efficient equipment, led him to modify and perfect SENGUERD's air pump. It was soon apparent that the pneumatic machine could be used in reverse, as a compressor, and so employing it to compress ammonia vapour in March 1787, he found the 'the aeriform state of some fluids ceases, and that they change into liquids, when they are subjected to the requisite pressure'. This cautious generalization, to which VAN MARUM attached no great significance, celebrated his liquefaction of ammonia, the first time ever that man had liquefied a gas by pressure alone.

VAN MARUM had turned to chemistry at a critical point in its history, when the modern system was struggling to be born, and chemical science was growing at an accelerating and wholly unprecedented rate. Happily, the eighteenth century gentleman's certain knowledge that progress was inevitable and that the present age must necessarily be the best, was tempered in him by historical consciousness:

So far as the history of Natural Philosophy is concerned, there has been no period in which that branch of science called Chemistry has contributed so much, as in the last eighteen or twenty years. And when one compares the present state of chemistry with that of ten years ago (this was written for a lecture in the autumn of 1794), one must wonder at the great and unexpected progress which has been made in this science in so short a time . . .
. . . The new chemical system, based on unequivocal experimentation and expounded with extraordinary clarity, could not avoid attracting the attention of many. Divers persons who had hitherto been concerned with other branches of Natural Philosophy, were now attracted by the new light, into which chemistry had been brought, and in this way the science obtained in a short time a far greater number of practitioners than seems ever to have been the case at any earlier time.

VAN MARUM's enthusiasm for science, however, ivolved more than a modern devotion to research for its own intrinsic merit (and for intellectual renown). Religion provided a constant impetus to his work, and he believed that

when one really understands what is meant by Natural Philosophy, then one finds it all the more satisfying, for it gives us a more accurate knowledge of the nature, the composition and the underlying mechanism of those things which the Creator of the world has found good to place on the surface of the earth ... what science is better designed than this (chemistry) to satisfy one's desire for knowledge? ...The greater the knowledge we have of those things which we have investigated, the more apparent becomes the great power, wisdom and goodness of the Creator.

With the certain menace of Imperial French invasion, continued devotion to chemical science was not going to be easy, for in NAPOLEON's educational scheme there was little room for academic research. There was a thorough-going insistence on useful, and especially military, science, at the expense of theoretical understanding, an attitude which was anathema to VAN MARUM, in whom the practical and theoretical scientist were intimately fused. Before the invasion, he had pleaded his cause, stressing the use of chemistry.

It is to be hoped that man will always bear in mind the wide uses of chemistry ... and that although the times in which we live are suited to attract attention to various contemplative and less useful sciences, *right-thinking* scientists will however be allowed to continue with their diligence in furthering this science. It is therefore to be wished that, amidst the great events of our times, people will always remain mindful of encouraging this science ...

Then, following the Batavian Revolution, he shrewdly announced a complete shift in his scientific values:

Fellow citizens! In the great reform of civic life through which we are now living, ... I consider it my especial duty specifically to apply the knowledge which I have obtained by practising physics or chemistry, or neighbouring sciences, so that, as far as lies in my power, something to the good of society may flow from it.

As I have already indicated, the ploy was successful, and amidst the general cessation of scientific work, VAN MARUM was able to work on in relative tranquility. NAPOLEON's visit to Haarlem in 1811, with its emphasis on useful work, only served to confirm VAN MARUM in his position, and to strengthen Teyler's Foundation—no mean achievement.

After 1798, VAN MARUM effectively ceased from chemical research. LAVOISIER's theory had attained general acceptance in the Low Countries, and it seemed that there were no new concepts to investigate, no dramatic advances in sight—there was little point, to VAN MARUM's impatient temperament, in continuing with the subject. He turned briefly to geology, and introduced HAUY's system of mineralogy into the Netherlands. (This has been discussed by HOOYKAAS). Thereafter, he retreated to administration, and, like CANDIDE, to his garden. (He possessed one of the finest botanical collections in Europe, and his correspondence on this subject was vast). His intellectual arteries had hardened, and he remained indifferent to the next dramatic step in chemistry—the rise of chemical atomism.

His administration, however, was far from ineffectual. The minute book of the Dutch Society of Sciences records in 1826 that during VAN MARUM's secretaryship, the Society

has risen to such a state of prosperity and fame, that it shines in the first rank of the learned societies of the civilized world. Membership is thus avidly sought by the most renowned savants of all nations, while the real use that (the Society) serves for the sciences in general, and in particular for those which are of more immediate influence on the prosperity of our fatherland, cannot be denied.

He was not a great genius, and his fame has not endured. Today, only the curious visitor to Teyler's Museum in Haarlem will gain any immediate impression of his achievement, and may perhaps wonder at his industry. Yet he was quick to recognize men of the front rank, and was eager, inventive and energetic in promoting their insights. Most certainly, he should be remembered as one of the last great polymaths. The dictum by his friend and fellow, the Genevan pastor Jean SENEBIER, may well serve as his epitaph, and my conclusion.

Les bon esprits ont bientôt apperçu qu'on n'est pas savant quand on a seulement aprofondi une science, ou plutôt ils voient d'abord que la science est une, qu'elle embrasse toutes les connoissances possibles, & que celui là seulement est le plus savant qui en a embrassé un plus grand nombre.

This article is in effect an abstract of a fuller paper of the same title, which will appear, with full references and acknowledgements, in volume I of a series of Van Marum Studies (in press) under the auspices of the Dutch Society of Sciences. I am indebted to the Society for permission to reproduce material from that paper.

This paper was made possible by the generous hospitality of R. J. FORBES and the Dutch Society of Sciences, and by the leniency of Dr. A. C. CROMBIE and the university authorities at Oxford, who gave me leave to spend some months last year studying the complete Van Marum archives in the possession of the Dutch Society. I should particularly like to thank Professor Forbes for his kindness and helpfulness to me during my stay in Haarlem.

II

FRIENDSHIP AND INFLUENCE
MARTINUS VAN MARUM, F.R.S.

[*Plates 5 and 6*]

IN 1798, after more than ten years of an involved campaign, Martinus van Marum, Secretary of the *Hollandsche Maatschappij der Wetenschappen* (Dutch Society of Sciences), at last achieved his election as a Foreign Member of the Royal Society. This note, after briefly introducing van Marum in time and place, relates the progress of that campaign.

The mid-eighteenth century was an age when scientific societies spawned across Europe. There was a continuing and ever-quickening interest in experimental natural philosophy, and especially in its newest and most dramatic branch, that of electricity; and cabinets of natural curiosities multiplied apace.

The Netherlands, which had long been a stronghold of experimental Newtonianism, harboured a middle class of bankers, merchants and local politicians who wanted instruction and guidance in the new sciences. Civic pride moved Haarlem, before any other Dutch city, to pay for this guidance, and to put it upon a secure and regular footing. In 1752 the *Hollandsche Maatschappij der Wetenschappen* was founded by seven members of the Haarlem town council, to play the same role in Holland as the Royal Society did in England, and the *Académie Royale des Sciences* in France. The Hollanders were determined that their new Society should do more than cater for specialists. The Directors, the men who founded and financed it, were wealthy citizens and amateurs rather than practitioners of science. They invited scientists to become non-paying members, and extended a degree of patronage to them. Contact was thus promoted between the commercial and the scientific world in Haarlem, to mutual advantage (1).

In 1776 Martinus van Marum (1750–1837), attracted to Haarlem as a vigorous and flourishing scientific centre, came there from Groningen and set up as a physician. His old teacher at Groningen, the celebrated physician and naturalist

Petrus Camper (1722–1789), already belonged to the *Hollandsche Maatschappij der Wetenschappen*. He now proposed his pupil for membership, and Van Marum was duly elected. In the following year, 1777, Van Marum was appointed as director of the Society's cabinet of natural curiosities. In 1793 the first secretary, C. C. H. van der Aa (1718–1793) died, and in 1794 Van Marum became secretary.

The other important centre of scientific learning in Haarlem was in *Teyler's Stichting*, a literary, theological, philanthropic and scientific foundation, established from the legacy left by Pieter Teyler van der Hulst (1702–1778), a prosperous merchant. In 1784 Van Marum became director of the museum and library of the scientific part of this foundation (2). He was energetic in carrying out administrative duties in all his posts, and in addition found time for a programme of teaching and of research which was highly competent over a remarkably wide range.

In some fifty years of active work, he explored and helped to develop almost every science of his day. His contributions to electrical science were greatly admired by Volta and Franklin. He was an active supporter of Lavoisier's system of chemistry, and succeeded in ensuring its early acceptance in the Netherlands. He also introduced Haüy's crystallography to Dutch scientists, possessed one of the finest botanical gardens in late eighteenth-century Europe, and was an enthusiastic naturalist, geologist and palæontologist. He designed and improved a great deal of chemical and physical apparatus, realizing that experimental demonstration was worth far more than a barrage of mere words; to this realization he owed most of his success and fame both as a teacher and as an experimentalist (2).

The *Hollandsche Maatschappij der Wetenschappen*, flourishing under his forceful supervision, rose to a place of honour among European academies (3). Van Marum steered it ever more firmly into the paths of the natural sciences, secured the election to it of most of the leading scientists of his day, and at the same time took care to look after his own reputation (4). By means of an impressive sequence of researches, coupled with a skilful series of manoeuvres and alliances, he contrived to be elected to nearly thirty scientific societies in forty hectic years. He, in return, frequently had to reward his worthy collaborators in science and Societies with the reciprocal honour of membership of the *Hollandsche Maatschappij der Wetenschappen*. In the early years of Van Marum's career, such exchanges were easily and often accomplished. At that period in Holland, the situation was one which had not long before obtained in England. Then, as Lord Brougham would later remark, 'whoever wished to add the title of F.R.S. to his name, as author of a book or as a Divine seeking preferment, or as a

Plate 5

MARTINUS VAN MARUM, For. Mem. R.S.
(1750-1837)
Reproduced from the original in the Hollandsche Maatschappij der Wetenschappen

Plate 6

The Teylerian electrical machine

Physician in quest of a practice, had only to become acquainted with [the Secretaries], and obtain their good will' (5).

As a rule, this game of reciprocal honours was played with zest by both parties; L. F. F. von Crell, for example, thanking Van Marum for arranging his election to the Dutch Society of Sciences, asked him to carry on the good work by doing the same for him with other Dutch literary and scientific societies. In return, Crell would do all he could to secure Van Marum's election to the leading German societies, which would be honoured to welcome so eminent a scientist (6).

Few elections, however, were conducted on the basis of personal favour alone. Van Marum's proposals for membership were in general good for the Society, whose Directors rarely rejected them. Even before Van Marum became Secretary in 1794, Berthollet, Le Roy, Lavoisier, Monge, Blagden, Priestley and other leading chemists owed their membership to him (7); in these and many other cases, friendship was coupled with real scientific merit. There is no doubt that Van Marum's influence with the Dutch Society was used to that Society's advantage.

Competition for membership increased as the *Hollandsche Maatschappij* acquired greater renown; the desire for election grew until it simply could not be met. In 1817 Van Marum wrote to a friend whose election was presenting problems that '[f[ormerly they were less difficult when it came to choosing members; but since our Society has become more and more famous, the title of "member" has been in such demand among men of letters, that for twenty years we have only admitted professionals who are Professors, or who have acquired their reputation by works which they have published or presented to the Society' (8).

Van Marum himself, in seeking his own election to foreign and domestic Societies, generally met with little or no trouble. Only twice was he denied immediate entry. Unfortunately for him, the reluctant Societies were the most prestigious in existence—the *Académie Royale des Sciences* in Paris, and the Royal Society of London. To the former, within which he had powerful support, Van Marum had long been seeking the post of scientific correspondent from the Low Countries, and his election merely waited until rules of precedence were satisfied (9).

The Royal Society proved much more difficult of access.

STEPPING STONES TO THE ROYAL SOCIETY

The physical and chemical experiments designed by Van Marum and performed by him with the apparatus in Teyler's Museum were widely broadcast and widely acclaimed. As a matter of common courtesy, he distributed copies of his publications to the secretaries and presidents of the sister societies of the *Hollandsche Maatschappij der Wetenschappen*, and to his friends and fellow scientists. As a matter of common prudence, he made sure that his copies went where they would do him and his Society most good. Sir Joseph Banks (1743–1820), President of the Royal Society of London, accordingly became an early target for the published results of Van Marum's researches (10), which, in a scarcely disguised attempt to recommend their author for election, were always accompanied with a request that Banks present a copy to the Fellows of the Royal Society (11).

Unhappily, before the campaign was well under way, Van Marum quarrelled with the Hon. Henry Cavendish. He wrote to this shy eccentric (12), asking about the products formed when a mixture of azot (nitrogen) and dephlogisticated air (oxygen) was subjected to a powerful electric discharge. Cavendish had performed this experiment first (13), and Van Marum had repeated it on a larger scale. There was a considerable quantitative discrepancy between their results, and the Dutchman wanted to know why. Cavendish's reply (14) was peculiarly unhelpful and Van Marum was angry enough to publish his indignation in his next volume of researches (15). Cavendish no doubt found this reaction embarrassing and annoying in about equal parts—he took many years to get over it. Banks was presumably aware of the circumstances of this affair, and he was Cavendish's friend. When Van Marum sent Banks the account of the first continuation of his experiments with the Teylerian electrical machine (16), and stated that he would like to be considered for Foreign Membership of the Royal Society, he received no encouragement.

Nothing daunted, Van Marum sent a copy of his latest book to the gossipy unofficial London agent for Continental science, J. J. Magellan (1722–1790), explaining his position (though without mentioning Cavendish), and asking Magellan's advice and help (18). The reply came almost by return, listing rules and instructions on 'How to become a foreign F.R.S.' (19). The affair then seems to have stagnated for a while. Though Van Marum continued to ply Banks with the results of his researches and engaged him in a botanical correspondence, nothing came of it. Banks was elected a member of the *Hollandsche Maatschappij*, an honour which he gracefully acknowledged in 1790 (20), but there was still no word of Martinus van Marum, For.Mem.R.S.

The next move in the game came as a result of Van Marum's responsibilities as Director of the library and museum of Teyler's Foundation. One of his main concerns around 1790 was the enrichment of Teyler's collection of physical instruments, for he wanted to make the museum a research and teaching centre of international importance. Local materials and local craftsmen were unable to satisfy his requirements, and he looked eagerly to London as the home of the best instrument makers of the day. Dollond, Adams, Ramsden, Nairne and many others could supply his every want. His friend and would-be confident, the natural philosopher Jan Ingenhousz, court physician to the Viennese Imperial family, temporary resident of London, and Fellow of the Royal Society, urged on him the desirability of a visit to London. There he would be able to describe and buy all the instruments he wanted, and incidentally to meet the top London scientists (21). The proposition was very attractive—a visit to London in the best tradition of eighteenth-century Dutch Newtonians (22), the pick of the finest instrument market in the world, and the chance of meeting influential members of the Royal Society and of overcoming all objections to his election as For.Mem.R.S. Van Marum sought and obtained permission from the Directors of Teyler's Foundation to go to London for the purpose of enriching Teyler's museum and library (23), and on 6 July 1790 he set out (24, 25).

Unfortunately he arrived at a time when the Royal Society was in recess for the summer, but Ingenhousz was there to receive him. Banks was hospitable, Blagden charming, Herschel and De Luc entirely courteous. Only Cavendish's goodwill was wanting. Once, when Ingenhousz was introducing a foreign scientist at Sir Joseph Banks's, Cavendish, tongue-tied with embarrassment, looked for a way through the crowd and bolted from the room (26). Van Marum may well have been the offending foreign scientist.

Van Marum returned to Haarlem later that summer, his For.Mem.R.S. seemingly no nearer. Ingenhousz, however, refused to give up, and throughout the following spring urged his friend to return and to try again. Ingenhousz had meanwhile been elected to the Council of the Royal Society, and felt that his support for Van Marum's candidacy might now carry more weight. Alas that there were so many applicants for the few vacant places. 'Never before', the new councillor wrote in mingled sorrow and pride, 'never before has the honour of becoming a member been the object of such aspiration as it is now'. Being a *gentleman* was no longer enough to guarantee election. 'A mere med. doctor, with no scientific accomplishment outside his profession, may well be rejected. They are getting very strict about foreign Members . . . I don't think they'll elect any this year'. None the less he promised his continued support (27).

Van Marum gratefully dedicated a paper to him (28), and had him elected to the *Hollandsche Maatschappij der Wetenschappen* (29). Ingenhousz kept up the campaign, approaching Blagden, who had assisted Cavendish in his research and was a friend of Banks and a former Secretary of the Royal Society. Blagden seemed favourably inclined towards Van Marum, though he gave the impression that Cavendish was still peeved, and had Banks's sympathy. Obviously Van

Marum had done himself nothing but good by his visit to London, and Ingenhousz repeatedly urged him to return (30).

But this was no time for foreign travel—even before the French army invaded the Netherlands in 1795, that country was suffering from considerable political instability, and from a corresponding shortage of funds. It was difficult merely to maintain a research programme, let alone to contemplate buying new instruments. The Directors of Teyler's Foundation wisely decided not to overreach themselves, and resisted Van Marum's repeated demands for more money for the museum.

From Holland, Van Marum renewed his frontal attack, and once more wrote to Banks that he would feel highly honoured if his zeal for the progress of the physical and chemical sciences could one day procure him the 'distinguished honour of being a foreign member or associate of the illustrious body of *savants* of which you are the President' (31).

Banks did not reply directly. Two years later, in 1797, Ingenhousz stirred the pot again, reporting to Van Marum the news that the Royal Society had changed its rules. Formerly, he wrote (32), it had been necessary for the signatories to an election certificate to know the candidate personally. Henceforth, a man's publications would suffice to recommend him. Things would be easier for Van Marum now—Ingenhousz at once put him down as a candidate for election.

At the first meeting of the Royal Society after Easter 1798, Van Marum was balloted for and elected; no one black-balled him. Ingenhousz made sure that his own signature was first on the certificate (33), and also that it was he who first brought the good news to Van Marum.

There is only one note to add to this tale. Although Van Marum had qualified as an M.D., he was, as his certificate stated, 'a Gentlemen [*sic*] distinguished for his knowledge in Natural Philosophy and particularly in Chemistry'. Yet the signatories to his election certificate were mainly physicians and botanists—and what is more they were, with the exception of Ingenhousz, strangers to him. These surprising supporters were: Maxwell Garthshore (1732–1812), physician; Samuel Foart Simmons (1750–1813), physician; Edward Whitaker Gray (1748–1806), botanist; Joseph Correa da Serra (1750–1823), botanist; and George Pearson (1751–1828), physician and chemist. Why should these men have supported Van Marum? For the answer, it is necessary to go back to Van Marum's old teacher, Petrus Camper, who visited London for the last time in 1785 (34). Garthshore and Pearson had entertained Camper on that occasion, Simmons had travelled to Friesland to see Camper and had later been his host in London. Their respect for Camper would have been, indeed, *was* enough to secure their support for his pupil. Gray and Correa da Serra supported Van Marum as fellow botanists (35), Ingenhousz as a friend and natural philosopher.

Van Marum was a remarkable man, tireless and industrious in many fields of science. Perhaps he should also be remembered as a determined and successful albeit tactless academic politician.

POSTSCRIPT

Glimpses of scientific personalities serve to illuminate the more conventional side of the history of science. Van Marum is a neglected figure whose career illustrates many of the vicissitudes of late eighteenth- and early nineteenth-century science, and as such he well deserves the attention of scholars. He is at last receiving recognition in a series of studies (2) now appearing under the aegis of the *Hollandsche Maatschappij der Wetenschappen*.

ACKNOWLEDGEMENTS

The Canada Council has generously provided a grant for my work on Van Marum.

In preparing this note I have had to lean heavily and gratefully on the unfailing help and courtesy of many authorities. It is a pleasure to express my especial indebtedness to Professor R. J. Forbes and the Directors of the *Hollandsche Maatschappij der Wetenschappen*, to Mr I. Kaye, Librarian of the Royal Society, to Drs J. G. de Bruijn, Librarian of Teyler's Foundation, Haarlem, to Mrs E. Patterson, and to the librarians of the British Museum and the University libraries of Oxford and Toronto.

NOTES

(1) J. A. Bierens de Haan, *De Hollandsche Maatschappij der Wetenschappen 1752–1952*. Haarlem, 1952.

(2) For biographical details of Van Marum, including a survey of his scientific (especially chemical) work, see R. J. Forbes, ed., *Martinus van Marum Life and Work*, Vol. 1. Haarlem: Tjeenk Willink, 1969. Three more volumes are planned.

(3) See for example art. 'MARUM, MARTIN VAN', *Encyclopaedia Britannica*, 11th edn., Cambridge University Press, 1910–1911.

(4) Bierens de Haan, *op. cit.*, chapter 2. Forbes, *op. cit.*, chapters 1 and 2.

(5) Cited in J. R. Partington, *A History of Chemistry*, Vol. 3, London, 1962, p. 241.

(6) Van Marum Archives, *Hollandsche Maatschappij der Wetenschappen*, Haarlem (microfiche published by Micro-Methods Ltd., East Ardsley, Yorkshire), microfiches 50, 51.

(7) Forbes, *op. cit.*, p. 36.

(8) Van Marum Archives, letter to J. Parmentier, 13 June 1817.

(9) *Ibid.*, Part I, microfiche 147, letters of 2 May 1778, 20 August 1778, 23 August 1783 from Nicholas-Christien, Comte de Milly.

(10) M. van Marum, *Verhandelingen uitgegeeven door Teyler's Tweede Genootschap*, **3, 4, 9, 10.**

(11) *E.g.* Van Marum Archives, Part I, microfiche 7, makes it clear that Van Marum was sending his works as propaganda as much as courtesy.

(12) *Ibid.*, microfiche 44.

(13) H. Cavendish, 'Experiments on Air', *Phil. Trans.*, **75**, 372 (1785).

(14) Van Marum Archives, Part I, microfiche 44, letter of 22 January 1786.

(15) Van Marum, *Verh. Teyler's IIde. Gen.*, **4**, 194 (1787).

(16) *Ibid.*, **4.** The machine is described in Van Marum, *ibid.*, **3,** 2–28 (1785), and in B. Dibner, 'The Great Van Marum Electrical Machine', *The Natural Philosopher*, **2**, 87–103 (1963).

(17) British Museum Add. MS. 8096.471: letter of 10 April 1787.

(18) Van Marum Archives, Part I, microfiche 341, letter of [April 1787].

(19) *Ibid.*, microfiche 141, letter of 17 April 1787. This letter refers to the new rules described in Royal Society MS. Council Minutes, 8 March 1787.

(20) Banks to Van der Aa, 10 December 1790, archives of the *Hollandsche Maatschappij der Wetenschappen*.

(21) Van Marum Archives, Part I, microfiche 111.

(22) P. Brunet, *Les Physiciens Hollandais et la Méthode Expérimentale en France au XVIIIe Siècle*. Paris: Librairie Scientifique Albert Blanchard, 1926. See also I. B. Cohen, *Franklin and Newton*. Cambridge, Mass.: Harvard University Press, 1966, pp. 214–261.

(23) Teyler's Foundation, Director's Minutes, MS. Vol. I, pp. 212–213, 18 June 1790.

(24) The diary of Van Marum's visit to London will be published in Forbes, *op. cit.*, Vol. 2, forthcoming.

(25) The main purpose of Van Marum's London visit was the purchase of instruments: see *Martinus van Marum Life and Works*, Vol. 4, forthcoming.

(26) G. Wilson, *The Life of the Hon.*[ble.] *Henry Cavendish*. London: for the Cavendish Society, 1851, p. 166.

(27) Van Marum Archives, microfiche 111, letter of 11 March 1791.

(28) Van Marum, 'Lettre à Jean Ingenhousz, contenant la description d'une machine électrique, construite d'une manière nouvelle et simple, et qui réunit plusieurs avantages sur la construction ordinaire', *Journal de Physique*, **38**, 447–459 (1791).

(29) Bierens de Haan, *op. cit.*, p. 363.

(30) Van Marum Archives, Part I, microfiche 112, letter of 22 June 1791.

(31) Royal Society of London, Misc. MSS.III, 112, letter of 20 December 1795.

(32) Van Marum Archives, Part I, microfiche 113, letter of 25 June 1797. For the rules in effect when Van Marum was elected, see *Record of the Royal Society of London*, 4th edn. London: The Royal Society, 1940, pp. 95–96.

(33) Royal Society of London, MS. Certificate Book. Van Marum was balloted for and elected on 19 April 1798.

(34) P. Camper, 'Itinera in Angliam, 1748–1785', *Opuscula Selecta Neerlandicorum de Arte Medica*, **15** (1939).

(35) See for example M. Van Marum, *Catalogue des Plantes, cultivees au printemps 1810; dans le jardin de M. van Marum a Harlem*. Haarlem: printed privately, 1810.

III

RELATIONS AND RIVALRY:
INTERACTIONS BETWEEN BRITAIN AND THE NETHERLANDS IN EIGHTEENTH-CENTURY SCIENCE AND TECHNOLOGY

THE NETHERLANDS are small and dominated by water, providing, by virtue of their geographical location, a focus for many trade routes. Dutch history has long been influenced by these factors. The densely populated Netherlands straddle major river deltas giving access to the heart of Europe, and are surrounded by larger, militarily more powerful nations. Dutch prosperity, in these circumstances, has long depended upon trade and commerce, and upon a populace educated to take its place in a world of international competition, thriving on acquired skills and transmitting its culture where it lacked more tangible native resources. The history of the Netherlands is a history of relations and of transmission —of men and materials, of books and ideas, of science and technology.

Dutch relations with Britain have played an important part in this history—near neighbours competing for world trade, sometimes by force of arms, mutually supporting in the intellectual realm, frequently related by education and for a while by a common monarchy, the Netherlands were a favoured refuge for Englishmen in turbulent times, and a willing medium for the reception and transmission of British ideas. Nor was the benefit one-sided. In agriculture and engineering, navigation and business practice, printing and scientific education, Britain gained greatly from her Dutch neighbours. The richness of the interaction between the two countries offers an area for study which is fruitful for the historian, whatever his chosen perspective.

In 1964 the Victoria and Albert Museum provided a splendid introduction to this wealth in its exhibition, "The Orange and the Rose". Historians of science could profitably pursue and develop this introduction. So far, they have scarcely tried, perhaps because there is still a temptation to approach the history of science as if it dealt only with great men, and with their triumphs in the face of obstinate foolish reaction. The historiographical area I wish to consider has few such figures. Again, the very richness of the interaction may have provided a strong disincentive to serious study, requiring a broader-based approach than is provided by internalist or intellectualist history of science. Scientific relations between England and Holland in the eighteenth century (I shall allow myself to stray slightly beyond the confines of that century) involve a good deal of the social history of science, entangled with fashions and politics as much

III

as with philosophy and experiment. Compartmentalisation distorts the pattern of relations, while an unstructured view of the field leaves the impression of insignificant chaos. Yet British-Dutch relations can furnish a well-placed strategic entry to the whole of eighteenth-century science. Their breadth makes heavy demands on the historian, who may in turn anticipate corresponding rewards.

The seventeenth century, the years of the Dutch Republic, constituted the golden age of the Netherlands, in science and technology no less than in art. Dutch hydraulic engineers were called in to drain English fens, and directed many large-scale engineering works in Britain. London was first supplied with drinking water by Peter Morice in 1582, Cornelius Vermuyden (?1590–1677) was the greatest drainage engineer in all Britain, the English were largely apprenticed to the Dutch in printing and agriculture—it seems likely that even 'Turnip' Townshend (1674–1738) in the following century was merely introducing established Dutch practices— and Dutch cartography and navigational science were supreme, as the works of Blaeu (1571–1638) and of Waghenaer (fl. 1577–1598) clearly show. It was through the Netherlands too that many of the scientific ideas of southern Europe were transmitted to the North and West. The names of Huygens (1596–1687) and Leeuwenhoek (1632–1723) suffice to indicate the independent value of Dutch contributions to science.

In the eighteenth century, the Netherlands loom less large on the international scene. Their decline may be seen as relative merely. One factor, strongly contributing to it, arose because the very conditions they had helped to create in the seventeenth century—most important among them being unhindered trade based upon Grotius's doctrine of the freedom of the seas—now worked strongly in favour of Britain. The latter's rival prosperity came to eclipse that of the Dutch, who therefore, throughout most of the eighteenth century, could not afford war with England. The years of peace facilitated intellectual contact between the two countries, while the bloodless revolution of 1688 created intimate diplomatic relations with cultural exchanges in their train. A particularly significant instance occurred in the reign of George I, when 'sGravesande (1688–1742) came to England as secretary to the Dutch ambassador at the English court: he met Newton, attended lectures by Desaguliers (1683–1744) on natural philosophy, and conceived a great enthusiasm for their brand of science. When he subsequently returned to Holland, his own lectures at Leiden were extremely valuable to the Newtonian cause. Voltaire (1694–1778), arch-anglophile and popularizer of Newton's physics, made a special point of visiting 'sGravesande, and Desaguliers's translation of 'sGravesande's work into English brought the cycle of propaganda and influence full circle.

The Netherlands, from being the first cradle of Cartesianism outside

France, became the first stronghold of Newtonianism outside England. Experimental Newtonian physics, indeed, was developed more vigorously in the Netherlands than in Britain in the early eighteenth century, and, as Brunet has shown, 'sGravesande, Desaguliers and P. Musschenbroek (1692–1761) were extremely influential in spreading Newtonian ideas to France. Desaguliers visited Holland and lectured there on Newton's natural philosophy, Musschenbroek studied medicine under Boerhaave (1668–1738) and then, like 'sGravesande, worked in London under Newton and Desaguliers. Boerhaave did much to reconcile chemistry with the new natural philosophy, and his teaching was enormously influential. From 'sGravesande's time, the professor of philosophy in the United Provinces was first and foremost a physicist. Even the incorporation of Newtonian physics with natural theology, often regarded as peculiarly English, is epitomized, at great length, in the work of a Dutchman, Bernard Nieuwentijt—cosmology became the praise of God through experimental physics.

The experimental orientation and emphasis of eighteenth-century Dutch physics cannot be overstressed. Dutch Newtonians were concerned to demonstrate the truth of their physics by experiment, and accordingly designed and built whole arsenals of apparatus. Historians of scientific instruments usually concentrate on English work in the second half of the eighteenth century, when Nairne (1726–1806) and Dollond (1706–1761), Ramsden (1735–1800) and Adams (1750–1795) made the London instrument market the greatest in the world. There survive, however, magnificent collections of scientific instruments in Leiden, Utrecht and Haarlem, containing exemplars of the work of leading Dutch craftsmen, and the trading networks established by Dutch merchants opened lines for the purchase of instruments from London to St. Petersburg. There are many fine Dutch instruments in English museums, and eighteenth-century Dutch Newtonians, from Volder (1670–1705) at the opening of the century to Van Marum (1750–1837) at its close, visited England for the express purpose of buying scientific instruments. The Netherlands even imported instrument makers from London, John Cuthbertson (1743–1806) among them. The experimental bent of Dutch science appears not only in physics, but also in chemistry, where the acceptance of Lavoisier's theory was aided by the use of Dutch apparatus, and in biology, where Dutch microscopes, from Leeuwenhoek to Harting, were especially fine. The study of scientific instruments is a hitherto neglected part of the history of science, and, although there are some admirable pioneering efforts, Anglo-Dutch relations in the instrument field are particularly important and have formerly been undeservedly ignored.

Another major factor contributing to the spread of Newtonian physics was the vogue for scientific amusement, at its elegant height in the writings of Fontenelle, Voltaire and Algarotti. Advertisements in the

Spectator encouraged ladies to carry pocket microscopes on their walks, literary society was entranced with science, George III collected scientific instruments, and Louis XIV amused himself by having an electric shock passed through a long line of monks. Science was in the *salons* with a vengeance. It is here that the Anglomania of early eighteenth-century literary Dutch society helped the diffusion of British ideas in natural philosophy. Justus van Effen was a major agent in this process. He visited England as an under-secretary to the Embassy, met Newton, and gained election to the Royal Society. He later edited the *Hollandsche Spectator*, which was closely modelled on its English namesake, and introduced Newton's scientific ideas to a wide public. Steele (1672–1729), in England, offered the resources of his lecture hall, the *Censorium*, to Desaguliers. Anglo-Dutch influence operated in both directions. It was not long before the growing Dutch interest in science led to the foundation of a number of scientific societies, of which the first, the Hollandsche Maatschappij der Wetenschappen, was founded in Haarlem in 1752. The role of fashionable and popular science in creating a climate favourable to serious science has yet to be studied in the Anglo-Dutch context.

At the popular level of scientific education, England seems to have provided the model for the Netherlands. At a more professional level, however, the roles were emphatically reversed in the eighteenth century. With a high density of population and little in the way of natural resources, the Dutch had to base their prosperity on native wit and acquired skills. The educational system set up in response to this need largely accounts for the fact that at the beginning of the eighteenth century the Dutch were among the most literate people in Europe. Their book trade was extremely important in the international diffusion of ideas; thus many English ideas of the early eighteenth century reached France via Holland. The technical quality of Dutch printing was far superior to the English, and English licensing acts and libel laws contributed to keeping the balance in favour of the Netherlands.

Late seventeenth-century Britain was in political and religious turmoil, from which the Netherlands provided safe haven. When political upheavals had died down, Scottish Calvinists and English dissenters were still educationally at a disadvantage, being excluded from the English universities; and besides, scientific training, where it existed at those universities, was generally far from adequate. For all these reasons, many Britons studied at the universities of Leiden, Utrecht and Franeker. It has been estimated that in 1700, about one-third of the students at Leiden were British, and that during the eighteenth century some two thousand British students matriculated there, many of them proceeding to their M.D. in Holland after taking their B.A. at Oxford or Cambridge.

From the stand-point of British-Dutch relations, the most important teacher was undoubtedly Herman Boerhaave, *communis Europae praecep-*

tor. Boerhaave's influence extended in many directions, largely because he taught *all* the subjects on the medical curriculum. In medicine, he ranged himself between the opposing schools of the iatro-chemists and the iatro-physicists, though leaning at first towards the latter. His chemical lectures and writings went into many translations and editions, approved and otherwise. They provided standard text-books throughout much of the eighteenth century, establishing chemistry as a science in its own right, related to physics and to medicine but not dependent on them. Boerhaave was in charge of the University botanical garden at Leiden: collecting and exchanging specimens necessitated an extensive correspondence, useful in making and maintaining contacts with foreign scientists. In this way Boerhaave forged his closest links with the Royal Society of London, even though it was as a physician and a chemist that he was most highly regarded. England learned much from Holland about gardening. Both nations sent ships to the ends of the earth, and, by controlled exchange, built up many splendid botanical collections. Boerhaave's botanical correspondence is far from unique—Sir Joseph Banks, who ruled the Royal Society of London, and van Marum, who effectively ran the Dutch Society of Sciences, owed many of their scientific contacts to their untiring and vast correspondence, which they used even for diplomatic ends.

Boerhaave's chemical teaching had the greatest effect on British science. In England, Peter Shaw (1694–1763) first translated his work, using it as a platform from which to argue for the rational application of chemistry to industry and agriculture. Henry Pemberton, a product of Leiden, gave chemical lectures at Gresham College in 1730-31, in which he reflected an interest in manufactures. Later in the century, Bryan Higgins, M.D. (Leiden, 1765) continued the tradition by founding a school of practical chemistry in Soho. Between 1709 and 1738, 178 students graduated under Boerhaave, of whom about a quarter were English-speaking: 31 came from England, 5 from Scotland, 5 from Ireland, and 2 from the British Colonies. These figures, taken out of context, are misleading: Scotland made far greater and more sustained use of Boerhaave's teaching than did England. The first medical school in Edinburgh, soon to rank foremost in Britain, was founded by four pupils of Boerhaave, while the first Scottish chair of chemistry, established in Edinburgh in 1713, was occupied by James Crawford, another of Boerhaave's pupils. Plummer, one of the first medical professors at Edinburgh and a pupil of Boerhaave, taught John Roebuck, one-time partner of James Watt, and William Cullen, Black's mentor. Scottish medicine, chemistry and chemical industry can all be directly connected to the teaching of Herman Boerhaave.

The Boerhaave old-boy network was prolific, and its ramifications were exceedingly complex. For example, Boerhaave taught van Swieten, who

became Court Physician to Maria Theresa. He also taught John Pringle
(1707–1782), who corresponded with van Swieten. Jan Ingenhousz
(1730–1799) took over from van Swieten at the Austrian court, met
Pringle in Holland, and later in England was introduced by him to such
physicians as William Hunter (1718–1783) and Alexander Munro (1679–
1767), one to the founders of the Edinburgh medical school. From this
point, the network of correspondence expands exponentially, until one is
left with the impression that everyone knew everyone else within the
profession.

    Personal correspondence, of course, is but one channel of communication.
Travel between the Netherlands and Britain was common, and some
detailed accounts of such trips survive. For example, John Smeaton
(1724–92) visited the Netherlands in 1755, and recorded in his diary his
impressions of Dutch science and technology; later in the century, the
anatomist Petrus Camper (1722–1789) and the scientific polymath
Martinus van Marum separately visited England. The travel diaries of
all three have been published, and indicate close and co-operative relations
between the scientists of both countries. Historians of science have
hitherto made little use of these diaries. It would be useful to investigate
the role of scientific tours in the transmission of ideas and techniques.

    These tours were probably most important in facilitating agricultural
and technological exchanges: books would suffice for those sciences where
orthodox ideas were already established. Our present knowledge of the
extent of Britain's debt to Dutch agriculture is fragmentary, consisting
mainly of isolated pieces of information about such men as Lord Townshend, Bakewell (1725–1795) and the Earl of Stair (1673–1737). Fragmentary or not, it is enough to suggest that the debt is strong. The
general problem is wide open. One might begin by investigating the
history of the Society of Improvers in the Knowledge of Agriculture,
which was founded in Edinburgh in 1723, and helped to inaugurate a
major agricultural revolution in the 22 years it lasted. The undoubted
relation of Scottish to Dutch chemistry, and the equally clear relation
between that chemistry and agricultural practice, offer a rich field for
research.

    As far as technological exchanges go, Dutch expertise in hydraulic
engineering was important even into the eighteenth century, in draining
fens and building canals. Many Dutch families moved to England to
forward such enterprises. John Roebuck, who sought to use chemical
knowledge in the Carron ironworks, had acquired his scientific knowledge
at Edinburgh and Leiden. Watt's steam engine aroused considerable
Dutch interest, long frustrated by the patent laws of England. Dutch
mechanics were invited to Manchester in the mid-eighteenth century to
build engines, for example, the swivel loom. The Lunar Society had
many points of contact with the Netherlands. It would be easy to

multiply instances, harder but well worth-while to evaluate the Dutch contribution to the British industrial revolution. I strongly suspect that it will be found very considerable.

The splendours of the Dutch Republic did not last long into the eighteenth century. Britain gradually eclipsed her neighbour in science and philosophy, in trade and technology. It is tempting to view the relations between the countries as increasingly unbalanced. The influence, however, is not as uni-directional as is often implied; the relations were rich and complex, and in the realms of science and technology, Britain, home of Newton and of Locke, may perhaps have gained as much as she gave. The possibility is at least worth considering, particularly since few of the fields for investigation have received any real attention.

It was suggested at the outset of this paper that the very richness of interaction might appear as diffuseness, repulsive to the historian who seeks tidy answers to tidy questions. There is perhaps a more serious, because unavoidable, obstacle in the way of the would-be investigator of any field of Dutch history, and that is the Dutch language. Adam may have spoken High Dutch, but in spite of the optimism of Simon Stevin, that language has not yet been universally recognized as the best for science, nor, for that matter, for the history of science. There is, alas, no easy way out. But at least the Dutch are traditionally better linguists than the English. The practical result is that much of the primary material for the first half of the century is in Latin, while for the second half English and French become more widespread—French partly as a consequence of invasion,which strained communications between England and the Low Countries and opened a whole new field connecting education, politics and science. This field is sure to yield a rich harvest for historians of science, when they begin to study it.

Because of the elaborate and close-woven texture of British-Dutch relations in the eighteenth century, sources present a real problem of selection—almost any major collection is bound to have some relevant material, and the best starting-points may not be immediately apparent. There are, however, a number of collections of primary sources with a high concentration of pertinent material. Haarlem has some of the finest collections of books, instruments and manuscripts, principally located in Teyler's Stichting and the Hollandsche Maatschappij der Wetenschappen. The library of Teyler's Stichting, too little known and frequented, is one of the richest in existence for science in the second half of the eighteenth century. It is complemented by an equally fine museum of philosophical instruments, mineral and palaeontological specimens. The Hollandsche Maatschappij der Wetenschappen possesses the lectures, diaries and correspondence of Martinus van Marum, who was involved in almost every science of his day and exchanged letters with most leading contemporary scientists. These invaluable papers are now available on

III

micro-fiche. The Dutch national centre for the history of science is the Rijksmuseum voor de Geschiedenis der Naturwetenschappen in Leiden, with extensive library and archive facilities and an impressive museum of instruments. University collections also contain much useful material. The University Museum of Utrecht, for instance, has a splendid collection of microscopes, much of Musschenbroek's apparatus—and plenty besides. Since navigation has played a major rôle in both Dutch and British history, maritime museums (there is a fine one in Amsterdam) are rich sources for some areas of the history of science and technology. In Britain, the Royal Society of London, the British Museum, the Science Museum, and the Maritime Museum at Greenwich all contain a wealth of material. The relations between Scotland and the Netherlands were at times so close that there must surely be great deal of relevant material in the older Scottish universities.

The bibliography here appended reflects the state of the literature—uneven, with no general surveys and few monographs, yet far richer than is generally recognized. Works from which specific information has been taken or to which reference has been made in this paper are indicated by an asterisk, in place of footnotes in the text.

Acknowledgements

I am grateful to the Canada Council for generous support. Mr J. McHale Jr. provided much assistance in assembling material. It is a pleasure to acknowledge the hospitality and assistance of the directors and officers of those institutions listed above as major sources. Dr R. P. W. Visser suggested valuable additions to the bibliography.

SELECT BIBLIOGRAPHY

E. N. Andrade & D. C. Martin, "The Royal Society and its foreign relations", *Endeavour*, xix (1960) 72–80.
E. Baasch, *Holländische Wirtschaftsgeschichte* (Jena, 1927).
A. J. Barnouw & B. Landheer, *The contribution of Holland to the sciences* (New York, 1943).
J. F. Bense, *Anglo-Dutch relations from the earliest times to the death of William III* (London & The Hague, 1925).
D. Bierens de Haan, *Bibliographie Néerlandaise historique scientifique des ouvrages importants dont les auteurs sont nés aux 16e, 17e, et 18e siècles sur les sciences mathématiques et physiques, avec leurs applications* (Rome, 1883).
J. Bierens de Haan, *Van oeconomische tak tot Nederlandsche Maatschappij voor Nijverheid en Handel 1777–1952*, (Haarlem, 1952).
*J. Bierens de Haan, *De Hollandsche Maatschappij der Wetenschappen 1752–1952* (Haarlem, 1952).
D. A. K. Black, "Johnson on Boerhaave", *Medical history*, iii (1959) 325–329.
P. Bockstaele, "Bibliographie van de geschiedenis der Wetenschappen in de Nederlanden", *Scientiarum historia*, iii (1961) 50–56, 102–113, 209–226; iv (1962) 91–112.
H. Boerhaave, *De comparando certo in physica* (Leyden 1715).
H. Boerhaave, *A new method of chemistry; including the theory and practice of that art*, translated by P. Shaw and E. Chambers, with notes, 2 vols (London, 1727).
H. Boerhaave, *Elementa chemiae, quae anniversario labore docuit, in publicis, privatisque, scholis*, 2 vols (Lugduni Batavorum, 1732).
H. Boerhaave, *Elements of chemistry: being the annual lectures of Herman Boerhaave*, translated from the Latin by Timothy Dallowe, 2 vols (London, 1725).

H. Boerhaave, *A new method of chemistry; including the history, theory, and practice of the art*, translated, from the original Latin of Dr Boerhaave's *Elementa chemiae* as published by himself, by Peter Shaw, second edition, 2 vols (London, 1741).

H. Boerhaave, *Elemens de chymie*, traduit du Latin par J. N. S. Allamand, 2 vols (La Haye, 1748).

H. Boerhaave, *Memorialia Herman Boerhaave, optimi medici* (Haarlem, 1939).

H. C. Bolton, *A catalogue of scientific & technologic periodicals (1605–1800) & chronological tables and library check list* (Washington, 1885).

H. J. M. Bos, *Descriptive catalogue. Mechanical instruments in the Utrecht University Museum* (Utrecht, 1968).

J. B. Botsford, *English society in the eighteenth century, as influenced from overseas* (New York, 1924).

J. S. Bromley & E. H. Kossmann, ed., with introduction by P. Geyl, *Anglo-Dutch conference. Britain and the Netherlands* (London, 1960–64).

I. Brugmans, *Paardenkracht en Mensenmacht: sociaal-economische geschiedenis van Nederland 1795–1940* (The Hague, 1961).

*P. Brunet, *Les physiciens Hollandais et la méthode expérimentale en France au XVIII* siècle* (Paris, 1926).

P. Brunet, *L'introduction des théories de Newton en France au XVIII* siècle; avant 1748* (Paris, 1931).

W. Burton, *An account of the life and writings of Herman Boerhaave* (London, 1743).

D. S. L. Cardwell, "Science and technology in the eighteenth century", *History of science*, i (1962) 30–43.

R. S. Clay & T. H. Court, "English instrument making in the eighteenth century", *Transactions of the Newcomen Society*, xvi (1935–36) 45–54.

A. & N. Clow, *The chemical revolution, a contribution to social technology* (London, 1952).

J. A. Chaldecott, *Handbook of the King George III Collection of scientific instruments* (London, 1951).

J. G. van Cittert-Eymers & W. J. Lavèn, *Descriptive catalogue. Electrostatical instruments in the Utrecht University Museum* (Utrecht, 1967).

E. Cohen, "Een physisch-chemische caricatuur", *Chemisch Weekblad*, ii (1905) 4–19.

E. Cohen, "Teruggevonden manuscripten en briefwisselingen van Herman Boerhaave", *Bijdragen tot de geschiedenis der geneeskunde*, xviii (1938) 147–50.

E. & W. Cohen, "Katalog der Wiedergefunden Manuskripte und Briefwechsel von Herman Boerhaave", *Verh. Nederlandsche Academie van Wetenschappen (tweede sectie)*, xl (1941).

I. B. Cohen, *Franklin and Newton: an inquiry into speculative Newtonian experimental science and Franklin's work in electricity as an example thereof* (Cambridge, Mass. 1966).

F. J. Cole, "The University of Leyden—contributions to biology and medicine", *Nature*, (1941) 161–163.

J. D. Comrie, "Boerhaave and the early medical school in Edinburgh"; see Boerhaave, *Memorialia* (1939).

C. A. Crommelin, *Physics and the art of instrument making at Leyden in the 17th and 18th centuries* (Leiden, 1929).

C. A. Crommelin, "Het NederlandschHistorisch Natuurwetenschapelijk Museum", *Oudheidkundig Jaarboek*, x (1930) 10–25.

C. A. Crommelin, "De Hollandse natuurkunde in de XVIIIᵉ eeuw en de oorsprong der natuurkundige instrumentmakerskunst", *Sudhoff Archiv für Geschichte der Medizin*, xxviii (1935) 119.

C. A. Crommelin, "Die Holländische Physik in 18 Jahrhundert mit besonderer Berüksichtigung der Entiwicklung der Feinmechanik", *Sudhoffs Archiv für Geschichte ˙er Medizin*, xxviii (1935) 129–142.

C. A. Crommelin, "Die Elektrisiermaschine des Dr Deiman und deren Verfertiger John Cuthbertson. (Mit einer Nachschrift über Jonathan Cuthbertson)", *Zeitschrift für technische Physik*, xvii (1936) 105–108.

C. A. Crommelin, *Descriptive catalogue of the physical instruments of the eighteenth century (including the collection 'sGravesande - Musschenbroek) in the Rijksmuseum voor de Geschiedenis der Natuurwetenschappen (National Museum of the History of Science) at Leyden* (Leiden, 1951).

D. A. Cronick, *A history of scientific and technical periodicals: the origins and development of the scientific and technologic press, 1665–1790* (New York, 1962).

M. Crosland, "The development of chemistry in the eighteenth century", *Studies on Voltaire*, xxiv (1963) 369–441.

W. Cunningham, *Alien immigrants to England* (London, 1897).

J. Cuthbertson, *Algemeene eigenschappen van de electriciteit, onderrigting van de werktuigen en het nemen van proeven in dezelve*, 2nd ed., 3 vols (Rotterdam, 1782–1794).

III

J. Cuthbertson, "An account of improvements in electrical batteries; a method of augmenting their power, with experiments, showing the proportional lengths of wire fused by different quantities of electricity, and a description of a new universal electrometer", *Journal of natural philosophy*, ii (1799) 525–535.

J. Cuthbertson, "A series of experiments upon metals with an electrical battery, shewing their property of absorbing the oxygen from the atmosphere when exploded by electric discharges", *Journal of natural philosophy*, v (1802) 136–147.

T. L. Davis, "The Vicissitudes of Boerhaave's textbook of chemistry", *Isis*, x (1928) 33–46.

*M. Daumas, *Les Cabinets de physique au XVIII⁰ siècle* (Paris, 1952).

M. Daumas, *Les instruments scientifiques aux XVII⁰ et XVIII⁰ siècles* (Paris, 1953).

T. Dekker, "De popularisering der natuurwetenschap in Nederland in de achttiende eeuw", *Geloof en wetenschap*, liii (1955) 173–188.

J. T. Desaguliers, *A course of experimental philosophy*, 2 vols (London, 1734–1744).

J. T. Desaguliers, "Some thoughts and experiments concerning electricity", *Philosophical transactions*, xli (1739–40) 186–210.

B. Dibner, *Early electrical machines. The experiments and apparatus of two enquiring centuries (1600–1800) that led to the triumphs of the electrical age* (Norwalk, Conn., 1957).

G. Doorman, *Patents for inventions in the Netherlands during 16th, 17th and 18th centuries, with notes on the historical development of techniques*, abridged English version translated by J. Meijer (The Hague, 1942).

R. Dossie, *Memoirs of Agriculture and other economic aids*, 2 vols (London, 1768).

Encyclopaedia Britannica, 4th ed. (Edinburgh, 1805–1810), vol vii, Art. "Electricity", pp. 645–808.

H. Engel, "Alphabetical list of Dutch zoological cabinets and menageries", *Bijdragen tot de Dierkunde*, xxvii (1939) 247–346.

B. Fay, "Learned societies in Europe and America in the eighteenth century", *American historical review*, xxxvii (1932) 255–266.

*R. J. Forbes, ed., *Martinus Van Marum*, i & ii (Haarlem, 1969). [Vols. iii, iv forthcoming.]

R. J. Forbes, "Een reis naar Londen in 1790", *Olie*, xix (1966) 242–246.

R. J. Forbes, "The Royal Society and the progress of science abroad", *Nature*, clxxxvii (1960) 100–102.

P. Gauthier, "L'enseignement de la chimie au milieu du XVIIIᵉ siècle", *L'enseignement scientifique*, ii (1929) 163–8.

*F. W. Gibbs, "Peter Shaw and the revival of chemistry", *Annals of science*, vii (1951) 211–237.

F. W. Gibbs, "Boerhaave and the botanists", *Annals of science*, xiii (1957) 47–61.

F. W. Gibbs, "Boerhaave's chemical writings", *Ambix*, vi (1958) 117–135.

'sGravesande, *Mathematical elements of natural philosophy, confirmed by experiments; or an introduction to Sir Issaac Newton's philosophy*, written in Latin, translated into English by J. T. Desaguliers, 2nd ed., corrected, 2 vols (London, 1726; 5th ed., 1737; 6th ed., 1747).

P. George, "The scientific movement, the development of chemistry in England, as seen in the papers published in the *philosophical transactions* from 1664/5 until 1750", *Annals of science*, iii (1952) 302–322.

A. A. M. De Haan, *Het wijsgerig onderwijs aan het Gymnasium Illustreen de Hogeschool te Harderwijk 1599–1811* (Ph.D. thesis, Leyden University, 1960).

S. B. Hamilton, "Continental influence on British civil engineering to 1800", *Archives internationales d'histoire des sciences*, xi (1958) 347–355.

J. E. Handley, *Scottish farming in the eighteenth century* (London, 1953).

*N. Hans, *New trends in education in the eighteenth century* (London, 1951).

S. Hart, *Recueil de plusieurs pièces de physique ou l'on fait voir principalement l'invalidité du système de Newton* (Utrecht, 1722).

R. Hatton, *Diplomatic relations between Great Britain and the Dutch Republic, 1714–1721* (London, 1950).

G. van den Haute, *Les relations anglo-hollandaises au début du XVIII⁰ siècle, d'aprés la correspondance d'Alexandre Stanhope, 1700–1706* (Louvain, 1932).

M. ten Hoor, "Philosophy": see A. J. Barnouw & B. Landheer (1943).

R. Hooykaas, *Rede en ervaring in de natuurwetenschap der 18⁰ eeuw* (Loosduinen, 1946).

H. L. M. v. d. Horn v. d. Bos, E. Cohen & C. Hoitsema, "Liste des ouvrages chimiques écrits avant 1865 par des hollandais ou par des étrangers habitant la Hollande, ou publiés en Hollande", *Chemisch Weekblad*, iii (1906).

J. H. van't Hoff, *Das Teyler-Museum in Haarlem und die Bedeutung historischer Sammlungen für Naturwissenschaft und Technik* (Munchen, 1905).

A. H. Israels & C. E. Daniels, *De verdiensten der hollandsche geleerden ten opzichte van Harvey's leer van de bloedsomloop* (Utrecht, 1878).

J. Kendall, "Some eighteenth century chemical societies", *Endeavour*, i (1942) 106–109.

III

52

A. Kent, ed., *An eighteenth century lectureship in chemistry* (Glasgow, 1950).
M. Kerker, "Herman Boerhaave and the development of pneumatic chemistry", *Isis*, xlvi (1955) 36–49.
W. J. King, "Christian Huygens and the mechanical philosophy of the eighteenth century", *Isis*, xlvii (1956) 61.
H. S. van Klooster, "Hermann Boerhaave", *Journal of chemical education*, xxx (1956) 546–547.
L. Knappert, "Les relations entre Voltaire et 'sGravesande", *Janus*, (1908) 249–257.
D. A. Kronick, "The Fielding H. Garrison list of medical and scientific periodicals of the seventeenth and eighteenth centuries", *Bulletin of the history of medicine*, xxxii (1958) 456–474.
D. A. Kronick, *History of scientific and technical periodicals, 1665–1790* (New York, 1962).
*J. P. N. Land, "Philosophy in the Dutch universities", *Mind*, iii (1878) 87–104.
J. P. N. Land, "Schotse wijsgeren aan Nederlandsche Hoogescholen", *Verslagen en Mededelingen d. Kon. Akad. v. Wetensch. afd. Letterkunde*, 2nd series, part 7, 168–182.
B. Landheer, *The Netherlands* (Berkeley, 1944).
Alle de brieven van Antoni van Leeuwenhoek (*The Collected Letters of Antoni van Leeuwenhoek*) (Amsterdam, 1939–   ).
W. R. Lefanu, "4 letters from Boerhaave", *Janus*, xxxviii, (1934) 70–76.
[Leiden University Student list], *Album studiosorum Academiae lugduno batavae 1575–1875* (The Hague, 1875).
T. H. Levere, "Martinus van Marum (1750–1837). The introduction of Lavoisier's chemistry into the Low Countries", *Janus*, liii (1966) 115–134.
T. H. Levere, "Friendship and influence—Martinus van Marum, F.R.S.", *Notes and records of the Royal Society of London*, xxv (1970) 113–120.
G. A. Lindeboom, *Boerhaave's correspondence*, 2 vols (Leiden, 1962).
G. A. Lindeboom, ed., *Iconographia Boerhaavii* (Leiden, 1963).
*G. A. Lindeboom, *Herman Boerhaave, the man and his work* (London, 1968).
E. Malins, *English landscaping and literature, 1660–1840* (London, New York, & Toronto, 1966).
J. B. Manger, *Recherches sur les relations économiques entre la France et la Hollande pendant la Révolution française, 1785–1795* (Amsterdam, 1923).
P. Mathias, *The first industrial nation: an economic history of Britain 1700–1914* (London, 1969).
H. Metzger, *Newton, Stahl, Boerhaave et la doctrine chimique* (Paris, 1930).
H. Metzger, "La Litérature chimique Françaisè au 17e et 18esiècle", *Thales*, ii (1935 [1936]) 162–166.
H. Michel, *Scientific instruments in art and history*, translated by R. E. W. Maddison and F. R. Maddison (London, 1967).
P. F. Mottelay, *Bibliographical history of electricity and magnetism* (London, 1922).
R. Mousnier, *Progrés scientifique et technique au XVIIIe siècle* (Paris, 1958).
R. Murris, *La Hollande et les Hollandais au XVIIIe siècle vus par les Français* (Paris, 1925).
*A. E. Musson and E. Robinson, *Science and technology in the industrial revolution* (Manchester and Toronto, 1969).
P. Neill, *Journal of a horticultural tour through some parts of Flanders, Holland and the north of France in the autumn of 1817 by a deputation of the Caledonian Horticultural Society* (Edinburgh, 1823).
W. A. Nicholson, "A comparison between electrical machines with a cylinder, and those which produce their effect by means of a circular plate of glass. With a description of a machine of great simplicity and power, invented by Dr Martinus Van Marum", *Journal of natural philosophy*, i (1797) 83–88.
B. Nieuwentijdt, *The religious philosopher*, 3 vols (London, 1718–1719).
B. Nieuwentijdt, *Fundamentals of certitude, or the right method of mathematics in the ideal as well as the real* (London, 1720).
G. Oldham, "Peter Shaw", *Journal of chemical education*, xxxvii (1960) 414–419.
W. J. Pienaar, *English influences in Dutch literature, and Justus van Effen as intermediary* (Cambridge, 1929).
L. M. Price, "Holland as a mediator of English-German literary influences in the seventeenth and eighteenth centuries", *Modern language quarterly*, ii (1941) 115–122.
O. Pringsheim, *Beiträge zur wirtschaftlichen Entwicklungsgeschichte der vereinigten Niederlande im 17. und 18. jahrhundert* (Leipzig, 1890).
L. A. J. Quetelet, "Memoir of G. Moll, LL.D., Professor of Physics and Sciences in the University of Utrecht, and member of the Academy of Brussels", *The London and Edinburgh philosophical magazine and journal of science*, [N.S.] xiv (1839) 288–298.
H. S. Reed, "Jan Ingenhousz plant physiologist; with a history of the discovery of photosynthesis", *Chronica botanica*, xi (1947/8) 285–393.

III

E. Robinson, "The Lunar Society: its membership and organisation", *Transactions of the Newcomen Society*, xxxv (1962–1963) 153–177.

*E. Robinson & A. E. Musson, *Science and technology in the industrial revolution* (Manchester & Toronto, 1969).

M. Rooseboom, *Bijdrage tot de geschiedenis der instrumentmakerskunst in de Noordelijke Nederlanden tot omstreeks 1840* (Leiden, 1950).

M. Rooseboom, "The history of science and the Dutch collections", *The museum journal*, lviii (1958) 199–208.

A. Scnuit, "Astronomy": see A. J. Barnouw & B. Landheer (1943).

R. E. Schofield, ed., *A scientific autobiography of Joseph Priestley, 1733–1804* (Cambridge, Mass., 1966).

C. Singer, E. J. Holmyard, A. R. Hall, & T. I. Williams, *A history of technology*, 5 vols (New York & London, 1954–58).

D. W. Singer, "Sir John Pringle and his circle—Part I. Life", *Annals of science*, vi (1946–1950) 127–180.

John Smeaton's diary of his journey to the low countries, 1755, The Newcomen Society for the Study of the History of Engineering and Technology, Extra publication no. iv (London, 1938).

R. W. Innes Smith, *English-speaking students of medicine in the University of Leyden* (Edinburgh & London, 1932).

E. G. R. Taylor, *The mathematical practitioners of Hanoverian England, 1714–1840* (London, 1966).

P. Van der Star, *Catalogus uit de kinderjaren van de elektriciteit, de geschiedenis van de electriciteit van 1606 tot ca. 1831* (Leiden, 1961).

C. J. Uphoff, "Botany": see A. J. Barnouw & B. Landheer (1943).

J. Versluis, *Geschiedenis van het onderwijs in Nederland* (Utrecht, 1916).

The Orange and the Rose, Holland and Britain in the age of observation, 1600–1750 [Victoria & Albert Museum Exhibition Catalogue] (London, 1964).

R. P. W. Visser, "De Nederlandsche geleerde genootschappen in de 18e eeuw", *Werkgroep 18e eeuw, Documentieblad* no. vii (1970) 7–18.

R. Wailes, *The English windmill* (London, 1954).

*C. H. Wilson, *The Dutch Republic* (New York & Toronto, 1968).

IV

BALANCE AND GASOMETER

IN LAVOISIER'S CHEMICAL REVOLUTION

In the historical introduction to his essay on chemistry in the *Encyclopédie Méthodique,* Antoine François de Fourcroy, at once participant and historian of the chemical revolution, entered on a discussion of the physical handling of gases before Lavoisier. He wanted particularly to draw attention to the technical, instrumental, and manual aspects of chemistry. His reason for this was clearly stated. Differences, novelties, and improvements in chemical apparatus had accompanied successive discoveries. New facts might have been necessary for the conception and construction of new and improved apparatus, but once that apparatus was used in experiments, it in turn gave rise to new facts (1). Instruments were of course not enough for discovery : the ingenious apparatus devised by Mayow and Hales did not, as Fourcroy observed, become laboratory instruments or research tools (2). Fourcroy argued that Joseph Priestley's apparatus had been the true origin of all subsequent instruments for the handling of gases, and hence of the discoveries made with them (3) ; even Lavoisier admitted that Priestley had a share in pneumatic discoveries :

"Ces découvertes importantes dues principalement à MM. Priestley et Lavoisier ont conduit à des appareils très ingénieux à l'aide desquels on peut déterminer jusqu'à un certain point le degré de salubrité de l'air, la quantité de fluide respirable qu'il contient, la nature des miasmes dangereux avec lesquels il est mêlé... " (4).

But Priestley, for all his discoveries, and for all his apparatus, had not revolutionized chemistry. The chemical revolution was not just Lavoisier's, but it was in large part his achievement.

From time to time after Fourcroy, historians of chemistry have paid attention to the role of instruments and apparatus (5). But historians and philosophers of science generally have not been overly concerned with the importance of instruments and apparatus in the development of science, although the recently burgeoning interest in the nature of experiments suggests a corrective (6).

Instruments can serve many purposes ; two of the main ones are the revelation of minute and otherwise imperceptible phenomena, and quantification. The result of using new or improved instruments for these purposes sometimes results in the transformation of a science (7).

Increasing exactitude may be revealed by what Hackmann (8) has called passive instruments, to distinguish them from active instruments like the air pump that reveal novel phenomena ; but the distinction breaks down when increased precision transforms a science, by revealing hitherto indemonstrable regularities or constancies. That was one of the things that happened in the chemical revolution, when balances of increased sensitivity were used to confirm and give credence to the crucial concept of conservation, based on the non-creation and non-destruction of ponderable matter.

The balance, although necessary, was not sufficient to bring about the chemical revolution. Gas chemistry, and the apparatus that made it possible, were also crucial, as Fourcroy and latterly Bensaude have pointed out (9). Lavoisier's laboratory had more than six thousand pieces of glassware, many of them used for pneumatic chemistry, and some of them quantitative. I shall discuss the gasometer, and its immediate precursors, below. But the balance was the prime instrument in the chemical revolution, and so I shall begin with it here.

The balance was greatly modified between 1760 and 1785. As Daumas tells us : "La chape disparaît et le couteau repose sur un plan d'acier porté par une colonnette métallique ; le fléau n'est plus suspendu, il est posé sur un pied stable. Le couteau n'est plus pris dans la masse du fléau, mais il est rapporté ; il est en acier plus dur et bien qu'il conserve une section arrondie, son arête est plus finement taillée ; pour ménager cette arête et lui éviter une usure trop rapide qui entraînerait un travail de réfection difficile et coûteux, on essaie divers systèmes pour soulever le fléau au repos" (10). These improvements, taken together, produced an instrument so superior as to be virtually new.

Before they were implemented, Joseph Black, an admirable and meticulous experimentalist, gave results for his work on magnesia alba to the nearest grain (one grain = 64.8 milligrams) (11). The first great precision balance was made for Henry Cavendish by John Harrison, inventor of the marine chronometer and a highly skilled clockmaker. Cavendish was soon carrying out observations accurate to 1/10 grain, a ten-fold increase in accuracy over Black's (12). Jesse Ramsden, arguably the finest instrument maker of the eighteenth century, made a balance that was used in the Royal Society of London in the 1780s, and was sensitive to a hundredth of a grain, a further ten-fold increase in accuracy (13). Similar instruments were made for Lavoisier in Paris in the 1780s, by Pierre-Bernard Mégnié and Nicolas Fortin. What lay behind this rapid emergence of the precision balance ?

It is worth looking for an interplay between conceptual and instrumental development in science (14). Historians of scientific instruments have tended to argue that the precision balance was constructed in response to the needs of scientists (15) ; and Lavoisier has generally been given the credit for articulating those needs, from the vantage point of his belief in the conservation of mass in chemical processes (16).

This is certainly part of the story, but it is not the whole of it. Experimental tactics are sometimes dictated by instrumental capacity (17). The seventeenth century witnessed an increasing desire for a general observation-based quantification of nature. This desire, reinforced by the eighteenth-century didactic vogue for experimental demonstration, encouraged the development of various kinds of precision apparatus. The whole process also gained from the competitive search for accurate chronometers to determine longitude at sea. Encouraged by the consequent pressures and opportunities, a new generation of instrument-makers arose, developing and using new tools to produce instruments of unprecedented precision and sophistication (18). Ramsden's combination of high craftsmanship and the finest dividing engines exemplified the best of the new work, which was found first in London and then in Paris.

In the 1790s, such skills and tools made possible the long considered introduction of the metric system, facilitated by new, extraordinarily precisely graduated instruments for the standardization and calibration of weights and measures. The work took place primarily through the Académie des Sciences, and some of it took place in Lavoisier's own laboratory (19). In his **Traité** of 1789, Lavoisier wrote of his long-standing

"projet de faire diviser la livre poids de marc en fractions décimales, et ce n'est que depuis peu que j'y suis parvenu. M. Fourché, balancier, successeur de M. Chemin, rue de la Ferronnerie, a rempli cet objet avec beaucoup d'intelligence et

316

d'exactitude, et j'invite tous ceux qui s'occupent d'expériences à se procurer de semblables divisions de la livre : pour peu qu'ils aient d'usage de calcul des décimales , ils seront étonnés de la simplicité que cette division apportera dans toutes leurs opérations" (20).

Thus there was a dynamic process in which the needs of science sometimes virtually required the development of new apparatus (Lavoisier's use of the balance provides a prime example), but in which the development of new standards and tools of craftsmanship also indicated and sometimes virtually dictated the development of science. A precise gravimetric chemistry depended upon the availability of precision balances.

Lavoisier's approach to chemistry was conditioned in part by the skills of his instrument makers, especially Fortin and Mégnié (21), in part by his collaboration with colleagues in the Académie and his methodological approximation of chemistry to physics (22), in part by Stahlian and Encyclopaedic notions of chemistry (23), and by his reading of Condillac's *Logique* (24).

Let us first consider the *Encyclopédie*. Written by several authors, it spoke with several voices, often in only approximate accord. But there were some comments in d'Alembert's introduction that are worth keeping in mind as one reads Lavoisier. First was the division of the science of nature into general physics, concerning the general properties of matter, and particular physics, which studied the bodies in themselves, including their qualities. Chemistry, in this scheme, was part of particular physics, a categorization that Lavoisier would welcome. Secondly, for d'Alembert, chemistry was confined to the composition and experimental decomposition of bodies. These operations were central to the program of eighteenth-century French chemistry, and indeed to chemistry throughout Europe : the German and Dutch words for chemical science meant "the art of separation". Such an approach was unsurprisingly at the core of Lavoisier's chemical revolution (25). When he wrote a *"Note pour l'article chimie"*, he began by pointing out the most dramatic recent changes in the science ; progress in analysis and in the processes of composition and decomposition headed the list (26). Finally, d'Alembert pointed out that in the *Encyclopédie,* the presentation of the arts, embodying craft skills and science, would combine theory with the description and illustration of the pertinent operations and tools ; theory and practice were to be reconciled (27). Lavoisier's *Traité Elémentaire de Chimie* was to devote one of its three parts to a description of the operations and instruments of chemistry.

The methodological incorporation of chemistry with particular physics and the importance of apparatus for that enterprise have been well documented for the collaboration of Lavoisier with Laplace in their memoir on heat (28). The clarity with which Lavoisier perceived his goals is revealed in an anonymous review of Lavoisier's first book, of which the very title, *Opuscules physiques et chymiques* (29), suggests at least the kinship of two sciences. The review, we are told by Grimaux*, was written by Lavoisier himself ; he explained that

> *"M. Lavoisier... applique à la chimie, non-seulement les appareils et la méthode de la physique expérimentale, mais cet esprit d'exactitude et de calcul qui caractérise cette science. L'union qui paraît prête à se faire entre ces deux branches de nos connaissances sera une époque brillante pour les progrès de toutes deux, et M. Lavoisier est un de ceux qui, jusqu'ici, ont le plus contribué à cette réunion vainement désirée depuis longtemps"* (30).

The importance of Condillac for Lavoisier is well known as far as chemical language and the organization of chemical knowledge are concerned (31). I want to go further and argue that Lavoisier's use of instruments in the laboratory, and his presentation of those instruments in his *Traité,* parallel his use of a new chemical nomenclature, and have something of the same pedagogical (32) and even epistemological force as his chemical language.

Condillac's ideas were common currency for Lavoisier's generation. Condillac's *Logique,* published within weeks of his death in 1780, was the most important of his works for Lavoisier, who read

---

* NDE : Grimaux, éditeur des tomes V et VI des *Oeuvres de Lavoisier* affirme en effet, t. V, p. 320, sans plus de précision, qu'il existe un rapport de Lavoisier sur son ouvrage. Ce rapport autographe est effectivement conservé aux Archives de l'Académie des Sciences, fonds Lavoisier, dossier 93 mais n'est pas totalement identique au rapport présenté à l'Académie et imprimé en 1777, *Histoire et Mémoires de l'Académie Royale des Sciences,* pour 1774, pp. 71-78 et repris in *Oeuvres,* t. II, pp. 89-96. Sur cette question voir : W. C. Ahlers.- "P. J. Macquer et le rapport sur les *Opuscules physiques et chimiques* de Lavoisier", *Actes du XIIe Congrès International d'Histoire des Sciences,* Paris, 1968, Paris, A. Blanchard, 1977, pp. 5-9 et C. E. Perrin.- "Did Lavoisier report to the Academy of sciences on his own book ?", *Isis,* t. 75, 1984, p. 343-348.

it soon after it was published (33). He did not adopt Condillac wholesale (34), but none the less drew heavily on him in the formulation of his own methodology and pedagogy.

What was there for him to learn from Condillac (35)? The answer, in one word, is "analysis", coupled with his perception that language was not merely the passive instrument of thought, but through words and their relations controlled the form of present thought and the possible range of later perception and thought (p. 208-9) (36).

Algebra presented the epitome of a language based upon analysis, and hence could be a model for demonstrative reasoning in every science (p. 279, 285). Algebra's superiority arose because the reasoning process advanced by the recognition of identity from one stage to the next, and that identity was most apparent when algebraic signs were used (p. 299), most clearly in algebraic equations.

Lavoisier's concern with the logic of his arguments is clear from an early date. He read the **Logique** soon after its publication (37), and soon began to stress analysis, and to tie it to quantification and algebra. In the early 1780s, he reflected more generally on chemical method :

"Ainsi la première chose en physique et en chimie est de ne rien supposer et de partir toujours d'expériences sûres. Ces dernières doivent être [ensuite] considérées commes les données d'un problème d'après lesquelles on doit procéder à la recherche de l'inconnu. C'est alors que le physicien commence à mettre du sien mais il n'y doit apporter que [la procédure sage analyse], il ne doit rien ajouter aux données... C'est la méthode analytique qu'il faut emprunter [des géomètres] et cette méthode qui est la vraie logique est applicable à toutes les sciences" (38).

Just what Lavoisier meant by the analytic method in chemistry emerged in his writings over the next few years. First of all, analyses would be based upon the careful determination of the quantitative proportions of constituents, an enterprise at the very foundation of chemistry and one promising an unprecedented degree of rigour in the science (39). This meant weighing constituents, composed of elements that persevered unchanged through any number of chemical changes. Lavoisier was already convinced of what he was soon to state explicitly in his **Traité** :

"... rien ne se crée, ni dans les opérations de l'art, ni dans celles de la nature, et l'on peut poser en principe que, dans toute

opération, il y a une égale quantité de matière avant et après l'opération : que la qualité et la quantité de principes est la même, et qu'il n'y a que des changements, des modifications."

"C'est sur ce principe qu'est fondé tout l'art de faire des expériences en chimie : on est obligé de supposer dans toutes une véritable égalité ou équation entre les principes du corps qu'on examine et ceux qu'on en retire par l'analyse" (40).

The terms in a chemical statement would have the same invariance as those in an algebraic one ; and the balance was to be the instrument demonstrating that invariance. There would be an equation relating constituents and their weights, before and after reaction : chemical equations would be congruent with algebraic equations. In 1782, discussing the dissolution of iron in nitric acid, Lavoisier set up the two sides of an equation in terms of the reactants and products, with coefficients representing their weights : and he solved the equation (41). Three years later, discussing the analysis of a salt, Lavoisier explained his reasoning :

"Il est clair d'abord que, si j'ai voulu faire le calcul exact des quantités, j'ai été obligé de supposer que le poids des matières employées était le même avant et après l'opération, et qu'il ne s'était opéré qu'un changement de modification. J'ai donc fait mentalement une équation dans lesquelles les matières existantes avant l'opération formaient le premier membre, et celles obtenues après l'opération formaient le second, et c'est réellement par la résolution de cette équation que je suis parvenu au résultat" (42).

Lavoisier's experiments, sometimes using apparatus of his own invention, were presented so that they had a rhetorical force, carrying conviction and urging a unique reading of the results. Lavoisier insisted, basing himself on Condillac, that theory, language, and scientific observations were indissolubly implicated in one another (43) ; in his **Traité,** at once a primer of the new chemistry and its manifesto, he gave care and prominence to explaining the rules for his language, and to describing the instruments and techniques on which his observations rested.

The description of instruments and their use was, he insisted, an important and novel aspect of the book :

"Enfin j'ai donné dans la troisième partie une description détaillée de toutes les opérations relatives à la chimie moderne.

Un ouvrage de ce genre paraissait désiré depuis longtemps, et je crois qu'il sera de quelque utilité. En général, la pratique des expériences, et surtout des expériences modernes, n'est point assez répandue ; et peut-être, si, dans les différents mémoires que j'ai donnés à l'Académie, je me fusse étendu davantage sur le détail des manipulations, me serais-je fait plus facilement entendre, et la science aurait-elle fait des progrès plus rapides... On s'apercevra aisément que cette troisième partie n'a pu être extraite d'aucun ouvrage, et que, dans les articles principaux, je n'ai pu être aidé que de ma propre expérience" (44).

Lavoisier was not going to give unnecessary credit to his predecessors.

When he wrote about the originality of his experiments, he was talking sometimes about the form and method of those experiments, and sometimes also about the novelty of the apparatus used in them. Now although much of the apparatus described in the *Traité* was not new, Lavoisier was faced with a tradition in which chemical texts and lectures gave little space to the description of apparatus. There were of course exceptions, and Fourcroy, in the article which I mentioned at the outset, gives much and due credit for their apparatus to earlier as well as contemporary investigators of the physics and chemistry of airs, most notably Priestley. Most of the apparatus necessary for experiments in pneumatic chemistry was available through their labours, and had been described in their works. Larry Holmes has recently pointed out that most of Lavoisier's *early researches* in gas chemistry used such apparatus (45) ; Lavoisier in fact modified it, to greater or lesser degree. I stress *researches* to distinguish them from the *demonstrations* in the *Traité*, which often depended on demonstrations using new apparatus and a theory implicit in new language. And I stress *early*, because as Lavoisier's researches developed, he increasingly used purpose-built apparatus, especially when quantification was involved. For example, in 1785 his experiments on the composition and decompostion of water used cylindrical vessels for holding the gases, with an approximation to constant pressure to ensure uniformity of gas flow, and a manometer to indicate the level of the air in the cylinders ; volumes of air were noted, and converted to weights of air (46). The apparatus described is well on the way to constituting a gasometer. Gasometers were among those key instruments in the arsenal of the new chemistry that were themselves new, invented by Lavoisier, his collaborators, and his instrument makers (47) ; the ice calorimeter (dating from Lavoisier's collaboration with Laplace), and Monge's combustion globe are also such instruments. Lavoisier had not begun his career by stressing the importance of instruments, and he came to regret this. A careful discussion of instruments would indeed have helped in ensuring the replicability and acceptability of results, and would have reinforced the didactic role of demonstration experiments.

When he came to the third part of the *Traité*, on the instruments and operations of chemistry, he repeated his view of the inadequacy of existing texts for his purposes.

> *"Indépendamment de ce qu'il n'en existe aucun où les expériences modernes se trouvent décrites avec assez d'étendue, il leur aurait été impossible de recourir à des traités où les idées n'auraient point été présentées dans le même ordre, où l'on n'aurait pas parlé le même langage ; en sorte que le but d'utilité que je me suis proposé n'aurait pas été rempli "* (48).

The first instrument that he described was, appropriately, the balance (49). Standardization of weights had not proceeded very far in Europe in 1789 ; Lavoisier urged his readers to use their local system of weights, so as to determine relative weights :

> *"ces rapports seraient les mêmes pour les savants du monde entier, et l'on aurait véritablement pour cet objet un langage universel"* (50).

Accuracy in determining these relative weights was crucial. Lavoisier, when he wrote the *Traité* referred to three precision balances made by Fortin, who had earlier contributed to the preparation of apparatus for various experiments on the composition of water. In 1787, he was appointed certificated engineer to the king, and in the following year he made for Lavoisier a balance with a beam about a metre long, which Lavoisier claimed to be superior to all others except Ramsden's (51). A twentieth-century estimate puts the accuracy of Fortin's great balance at 1/400,000. This instrument survives in the Conservatoire des Arts et Métiers ; so too do Lavoisier's other two precision balances from this period, made by Mégnié the younger, which have an estimated accuracy of 1/125,000 and 1/50,000 respectively (52). The list of Lavoisier's chemical and physical instruments, drawn up after his execution, includes not only these three precision balances, but nineteen other balances, including twelve wretched badly made small ones (53) ; there was an enormous difference between balances for everyday rough work, and exact instruments for research.

Lavoisier was a skilled experimentalist. And, as he intended, he used his instruments in imposing logic on his results. If the total weight of the products in an experiment was either more or less than the weight of the reactants,

> "il y a erreur, et il faut recommencer l'expérience jusqu'à ce qu'on ait un résultat dont on soit satisfait, et qui diffère à peine de 6 ou 8 grains par livre de matière mise en expérience" (54).

Thus he had clearly defined the acceptable limits of experimental error.

There were two other instruments, central to Lavoisier's chemistry, and wholly absent from the work of earlier chemists : the ice calorimeter, and the gasometer, which was built for Lavoisier by Mégnié in 1783.

The calorimeter was needed because reactions involving heat are found everywhere in chemistry, and if that science was to be quantified as Lavoisier wished and Laplace dreamed, then heat (or, for Lavoisier, its material substrate) had to be measured. The calorimeter was a conceptually elegant device even if it did look like a bucket ; it consisted of a central compartment surrounded by two jackets, one within the other, and both containing ice. Ice melted gradually in the outer jacket, and until it had all melted, it constituted an isothermal barrier insulating the inner jacket and central compartment from the warmth of the atmosphere. Any water in the inner jacket was run off from a tap at the start of the experiment, an exothermal reaction was arranged in the central compartment, and water thereby melted in the inner jacket was run off and weighed at the end of the reaction. Knowing the latent heat of fusion of ice, one could then readily calculate the heat of the reaction under investigation (55).

The gasometers in their final form were the most elaborate of all the new pieces of apparatus. Constant pressure was kept upon a gas in the main reservoir, by means of weights on a mechanical balance using rolling bearings to minimize friction. Pressure of the gas in the reservoir could be measured by a manometer. The whole instrument looked like and indeed was the fruit of a marriage between engineering and physics, but in Lavoisier's hands, aided by his collaborator Meusnier, it became what Lavoisier called

"un instrument précieux par le grand nombre des applications
qu'on en peut faire, et parce qu'il est des expériences à peu près
impossibles sans lui" (56).

Holmes's findings suggest that Lavoisier used mostly the
pneumatic apparatus of Hales and Priestley in his initial researches
(57). The notebooks certainly show him using such apparatus, and
continuing to use it (58). But they also show that Lavoisier modified,
added, and used increasingly sophisticated apparatus (59).

Daumas has made it clear (60) that Lavoisier first improved the
pneumatic trough, went on to invent, with suggestions from Meusnier,
a pneumatic device that was essentially a pneumatic trough with taps
for the entry and egress of gases ; and by 1783, had two of them built,
for handling two gases. This was a prerequisite for the demonstration
of the formation of water by the combustion of hydrogen. These
pieces of apparatus were not true gasometers, since they could not
measure the gases that they dispensed. Meusnier made suggestions for
transforming them into true gasometers. Between 1783 and 1785,
Mégnié tackled their construction, and that assignment was completed
by the end of 1785. Further improvements, conceived by Meusnier,
were incorporated in new gasometers built by Mégnié and presented
to the Académie in March 1788. Meusnier's collaboration was
important, and is admirably indicated in the most recent volume of
Lavoisier's correspondence (61).

These special pieces of apparatus were expensive ; chemistry, in
approximating itself to physics, had like physics become big science.
Fortin's great balance cost 600 livres ; two ice calorimeters cost
another 600 livres the pair ; and Lavoisier's gasometers cost 636
livres. Lavoisier paid the bulk of cost, but the Académie also
contributed (62). Apart from the time spent on the construction of the
gasometers by his workers, Mégnié had spent 92 days on the job
himself (63). Lavoisier acknowledged that using the gasometers
became expensive :

"Ce qui le renchérit, c'est qu'un seul ne suffit pas : il le faut
double dans un grand nombre de cas, comme dans la formation de
l'eau, dans celle de l'acide nitreux, etc. C'est un effet inévitable de
l'état de perfection dont la chimie commence à s'approcher, que
d'exiger des instruments et des appareils dispendieux et
compliqués : il faut s'attacher sans doute à les simplifier, mais il
ne faut pas que ce soit aux dépens de leur commodité et surtout de
leur exactitude" (64).

Here was a problem. In order to be persuaded of the validity of the new chemistry, one needed to adopt the new nomenclature and perform the new experiments ; chemistry was an empirical science, and nobody should be persuaded merely by reading about it. But replicating Lavoisier's experiments meant having a set of his instruments, and that was generally a forbiddingly expensive proposition.

Only great private wealth, a royal exchequer, or a major university could contemplate equipping a laboratory like Lavoisier's . Lavoisier financed his laboratory mostly with his inherited wealth. The king of Spain, on Lavoisier's recommendation, brought Joseph-Louis Proust to Segovia, where :

"I succeeded, through the force of hard work, courage and perseverance, in erecting the most wonderful laboratory known anywhere in Europe today... I succeeded in developing the most complete chemical establishment for instruction in chemistry, the richest school in experiments that it to be seen" (65).

Thomas Beddoes in Oxford wrote to Joseph Banks in 1791 that the

"laboratory at Oxford has been for a considerable time past undergoing a thorough repair, which I hope will make it one of the best in Europe..."

The apparatus was mostly made by J. Sadler, better known for his work on steam engines and balloons ; later that year, Beddoes told Black that Sadler had constructed :

"a very valuable assortment of chemical apparatus - a gasometer very much improved upon Mr. Lavoisier's &c - so that I am able to shew any & every experiment in his book" (66).

Unfortunately the improved gasometer and the rest are lost.

One set of simplified apparatus that does survive is in Teyler's Stichting, Haarlem. It was built according to Martinus van Marum's design, because he recognized that :

"one of the principal reasons why [Lavoisier's] theory formerly enjoyed such slight attention among Physicists and Chemists in this country seemed to me the fact that they had no opportunity to see or to repeat the experiments, the results of which formed the

basic principles of the new chemical theory. Indeed, the necessary apparatus as made by the generous Lavoisier at his own expense could hardly be obtained, owing to its costliness and to the difficulty of constructing it with the precision required" (67).

Van Marum's solutions, in brass, glass, and stoneware, succeeded in making fair approximations to Lavoisier's logical and experimental demonstrations available to a wider public ; they brought the chemical revolution to the Netherlands. And they did so by drawing, even more closely than Lavoisier had done, upon the existing apparatus designed by experimental physicists (68). Van Marum's simplified apparatus supplied laboratories as far away as Tartu and St. Petersburg (69).

Simplified apparatus carried conviction in demonstrations at public lectures and elsewhere. And certainly, it was possible to discover and to demonstrate the composition of water without Lavoisier's apparatus. It could not be otherwise, since Lavoisier was not the first to discover it. And for many chemists, that experiment argued decisively against the phlogistic hypothesis. The chemical revolution did not need the refinements in apparatus that Lavoisier deemed essential. But he committed himself to costly precision apparatus. He did so for two main reasons. First was his wish to make chemical proof a matter of demonstration, with the rigour of mathematical demonstration. The other and related reason was that only with such apparatus could the conservation of weight be rigorously used as the regulative principal bringing quantitative order to chemistry.

IV

ACKNOWLEDGEMENT :

The bulk of this paper is new ; but it derives from an essay in T.H. Levere and W.R. Shea, eds., *Nature*, Experiment, and the Sciences... (Kluwer Academic Publishers, Boston and Dordrecht, 1990), p. 207-223. Passages here reproduced from that work remain in the copyright of Kluwer Academic Publishers, by whose permission they appear here.

NOTES AND REFERENCES

Oeuvres de Lavoisier, 6 vol., Paris, Imprimerie Nationale, 1864-1893, are here after designated *"Oeuvres".*

1 - Fourcroy, art. "Chimie" in Guyton de Morveau, Fourcroy, and Vauquelin, *Encyclopédie Méthodique, chimie, pharmacie et métallurgie* 6 vols + 2 vols plates (Paris, 1786-1815) vol. 3 p. 389. I am grateful to my colleague Prof. Janis Langins for drawing my attention to the importance of this article.

2 - Ibid. p. 407.

3 - Ibid. p. 413.

4 - *Oeuvres,* vol. 5, p. 299.

5 - A notable example is the oeuvre of Maurice Daumas ; see below, and also his essay, "Les appareils d'expérimentation de Lavoisier", *Chymia,* 3 (1950) 45-62. See also Truchot, "Les Instruments de Lavoisier. Relation d'une visite à la Canière...", *Annales de chimie et de physique* 5e série 18 (1879) 249-319.

6 - Some very promising directions are explored in D. Gooding, T. Pinch, and S. Schaffer, eds... *The uses of experiment. Studies in the natural sciences.* Cambridge University Press, 1989.

7 - Cf. W.S. Jevons, *The Principles of Science* ... 3rd edn. London : Macmillan 1879. p. 270.

8 - **Op. cit.** Gooding p. 39.

9 - Bernadette Bensaude-Vincent, "Lavoisier : une révolution scientifique", in Michel Serres, ed. , *Eléments d'histoire des sciences.*Paris : Bordas, 1989. p. 362-385 at p. 366.

10 - Maurice Daumas.- *Les instruments scientifiques aux XVIIe et XVIIIe siècles.* Paris : 1953. p. 292, where an even more compressed development is proposed, between 1760 and 1770. See also John T. Stock.- *Development of the Chemical Balance.* London : Her Majesty's Stationery Office, 1969.

11 - J. Black.- "Experiments upon magnesia alba, quicklime and some other alcaline substances", *Essays and observations, Physical and Literary, read before a Society in Edinburgh and Published by them, 2 : 157 (1756).*

12 - Stock, *op. cit.* , p. 11.

13 - Ibid. , p. 11-14.

14 - See e. g. W. Hackmann.- "The relationship between concept and instrument design in 18th-century experimental science", *Annals of Science,* 36, 1979. p. 205-224.

15 - Daumas, *op. cit.* , p. 290.

16 - Stock, *op. cit.*, p. 2 ; Gerard L.E. Turner.- *Nineteenth-Century Scientific Instruments.* Berkeley : University of California Press, 1983. p. 64.

17 - Gooding **op. cit.** p. 1.

18 - Daumas, *op. cit.* E.G.R. Taylor.- *The Mathematical Practitioners of Hanoverian England 1714-1780.* Cambridge : Cambridge : University Press, 1966.

19 - Daumas, *op. cit.* , p. 161-179 ; 249-270.

20 - *Oeuvres* vol. 1, p. 249. Ed. de 1789, t. 2, p. 7-8.

21 - M. Daumas.- *Lavoisier théoricien et expérimentateur.* Paris : Presses Universitaires de France, 1955.

22 - H. Guerlac.- "Chemistry as a branch of physics : Laplace's collaboration with Lavoisier", *Historical Studies in the Physical Sciences 7,* 1976, p. 193-276 gives the most extended illustration of this aspect of Lavoisier's work.

23 - H. Metzger.- *Les doctrines chimiques en France de début du XVIIe siècle à la fin du XVIIIe siècle.* Paris, 1969. M. Fichman.- "French Stahlism and chemical studies of air, 1750-1770", *Ambix 18,* 1971, p. 94-122. See also Gough, note 25 below.

24 - Etienne Bonnot de Condillac.- *La Logique. Logic,* translated and introduced by W.R. Albury. New York : Abaris, 1980.

25 - R. Siegfried and B.J. Dobbs.- "Composition : a Neglected Aspect of the Chemical Revolution", *Annals of Science,* 24 1968, p. 275-93. J.B. Gough.- "Lavoisier and the Fulfillment of the Stahlian Revolution", *Osiris,* 2nd Series, *4,* 1988, p. 15-33 at 16.

26 - *Oeuvres,* vol. 5, p. 298.

27 - Jean Le Rond d'Alembert.- *Preliminary Discourse to the Encyclopedia of Diderot,* translated by R.N. Schwab and W.E. Rex. Indianapolis : The Bobbs-Merril Company, 1963, p. 54, 95, 124.

28 - Guerlac, op. cit. *Memoir on Heat read to the Royal Academy of Sciences, 28 june 1783, by Messrs. Lavoisier and Laplace, of the same Academy,* translated with an introduction and notes by Henry Guerlac. New York : Neale Watson Academic Publications, Inc. 1982.

29 - Lavoisier, *Opuscules...* Paris : Durand et Didant le Jeune, 1774.

30 - *Oeuvres,* vol. 2, p. 96.

31 - The fullest statement is Albury, *op. cit.* See also Maurice P. Crosland, *Historical Studies in the Language of Chemistry.* London : Heinemann, 1962. p. 170-171.

32 - Lavoisier's pedagogy is clear in his *Traité,* and also in the report that he drew up, and that was presented posthumously, in 1798 : "Réflexions sur l'instruction publique, présentées à la Convention Nationale par le Bureau de Consultation des Arts et Métiers", *Oeuvres,* vol. 6, p. 516-31.

33 - Daumas.- *Lavoisier,* p. 101.

34 - Wilda C. Anderson.- *Between the library and the laboratory. The Language of chemistry in eighteenth-century France.* Baltimore : The Johns Hopkins University Press, 1984.

35 - For a wide-ranging account, see Isabel F. Knight.- *The Geometric Spirit : The Abbé de Condillac and the French Enlightenmen.* New Haven : Yale University Press, 1968.

36 - Cf. Anderson, *op. cit.,* p. 39.

37 - Daumas.- *Lavoisier*, p. 101.

38 - Lavoisier.- "Discours préliminaire, logique de l'abbé de Condillac", p. 117, Académie des Sciences, Lavoisier MSS cote 1260 : text reproduced in Albury, *op. cit.* , p. 275-6.*

39 - *Oeuvres,* vol. 4, p. 544.

40 - *Oeuvres,* vol. 1, p. 101.

41 - This is pointed out by R. Albury (1972), p. 145, and by Michelle Goupil, in *Du flou au clair. Histoire de l'affinité chimique,* de **Cardan à Prigogine**. Paris, éd. du CTHS, 1991, p. 174-177. Thèse de doctorat d'état ès sciences (Université de Bordeaux I, 1986), p. 211 et seq., concerning Lavoisier, "Considérations générales sur la dissolution des métaux dans les acides", *Histoire de l'Académie des Sciences* pour 1782 (1785) p. 492-511.

42 - *Oeuvres,* vol. 3, p. 778.

43 - *Oeuvres* , vol. 4, p. 359.

44 - *Oeuvres,* vol. 1, p. 14.

45 - Paper at the IUHPS Conference, Munich, August 1989.

46 - Lavoisier, Archives de l'Académie des Sciences, MS registre de laboratoire tome 10, 1785, f21r-28v, describing the "Expérience de la décomposition de l'eau, faite le 27 février 1785" ; the description of the apparatus is on f26v-28v.

47 - See below.

48 - *Oeuvres,* vol. 1, p. 245-6.

49 - *Ibid,* vol. 1, p. 248 et seq.

---

* NDE : En réalité ce passage se trouve bien dans le dossier 1260, sur une feuille séparée intitulée seulement "Discours préliminaire" et non pas "Discours préliminaire, Logique de Condillac", mention qui figure sur deux feuilles du dossier 1259 mais qui ne comportent pas le passage cité, dont la transcription correcte est "il n'y doit apporter que la part d'une sage analyse".

50 - *Ibid,* vol. 1, p. 249.

51 - *Oeuvres*, vol. 1, p. 252. Daumas, *Les Instruments Scientifiques....,* p. 366. Daumas, *Lavoisier*, p. 134. Fortin adapted well to revolutionary institutions in France, and made a balance and a set of weights for the Commission des Poids et Mesures.

52 - Daumas.- *Lavoisier.-*, p. 138, citing Marcel Guichard.- *Essai historique sur les mesures en chimie.*1937. Vol. 2, p. 18. Fortin's balance in Conservatoire des Arts et Métiers (CNAM) n° 19887 ; Mégnié's are CNAM n° 19886 and 19885. Mégnié's career ran a successful course similar to Fortin's : Daumas.- *Les Instruments Scientifiques...* p. 275-8.

53 - A. Deluzarche.- "Le sort des instruments et de la collection minéralogique de Lavoisier", *L'actualité chimique,* Jan.-Feb. 1989, p.7-11 at 7. "Inventaire après décès de Lavoisier", "Physique n° 8 Inventaire des Instrumens de Physique et de Chymie du Cabinet de Lavoisier, cy-devant Fermier Général, et de l'académie de sciences, Boul[e]vard de la Madelaine", Archives nationales, Minutier central des notaires.

54 - *Oeuvres,* vol. 1, p. 323.

55 - *Oeuvres,* vol. 1, p. 284-93, and plate VI.

56 - *Oeuvres,* vol. 1, p. 267.

57 - See Holmes, *op. cit.*

58 - E. g. Lavoisier MS Archives de l'Académie des Sciences, laboratory notebooks (Registre de laboratoire) for March 1774-February 1776, f° 6 ; for Nov. 1786 to end 1787, f° 167r and loose leaf insert.

59 - See e. g. note 45 above, and the discussion below.

60 - Daumas.- *Lavoisier* p. 47-54.

61 - Lavoisier.- *Correspondance...* , fascicule IV 1784-1786. Paris : 1986. Annexe III p. 299-304.

62 - Daumas.- 1950, p. 54.

63 - Daumas.- *Lavoisier.* p. 135, 141, 146.

64 - *Oeuvres*, vol. 1, p. 267.

65 - Ramon Gago.- "The New Chemistry in Spain", *Osiris,* 2nd series, *4, p.* 169-92 at 175, translated from Guerra Moderna, leg. 5696, leg. 5735 (quotation) ; Archivo General de Simancas.

66 - Thomas Beddoes to Joseph Banks, 3 Jan. 1791, British Museum (Natural History) Dawson-Turner Collection vol. 7 f°. 189-90. Beddoes to Joseph Black, 15 april 1791, MS Edinburgh University Library. J.E. Hodgson.- "James Sadler 1753-1828 of Oxford, aeronaut, chemist, engineer, and inventor", *Transactions of the Newcomen Society 8,* 1927-8, p. 66-82. T. H. Levere.- "Dr. Thomas Beddoes at Oxford : Radical Politics in 1788-1793 and the Fate of the Regius Chair in Chemistry", *Ambix, 28,* 1981, p. 61-9.

67 - Martinus Van Marum.- "Beschryving van eenige nieuwe en verbeterde chemische werktuigen, behoorende aan Teyler's Stichting, en van proefneemingen met dezelve in 't werk gesteld", *Verhandelingen uitgegeeven door Teyler's Tweede Genootschap, 10,* 1798, i-viii, p. 1-123; translated in *Martinus Van Marum Life and Work [MvM],* ed. E. Lefebvre and J. G. de Bruijn, vol. 5. Leyden : Noordhoff International Publishing, 1974, p. 239-298. See also T. H. Levere.- "Martinus Van Marum and the Introduction of Lavoisier's Chemistry into the Netherlands", *MvM* ed. R. J. Forbes, vol. 1. Haarlem : Tjeenk Willink & Zoon, 1969, p.158-286. H.A.M. Snelders.- "The New Chemistry in the Netherlands", *Osiris,* 2nd series, 4, 1988, p. 121-145 at 131.

68 - G. L'E. Turner and T.H. Levere, *MvM* ed. Lefebvre and de Bruijn, vol. 4, *Van Marum's Scientific Instruments in Teyler's Museum.* Leyden : Noordhoff International Publishing, 1973, especially p. 103-116 & 247-252.

69 - *MvM* vol. 6, 1976, p. 271-5.

V

DR. THOMAS BEDDOES AT OXFORD: RADICAL POLITICS IN 1788–1793 AND THE FATE OF THE REGIUS CHAIR IN CHEMISTRY

INTRODUCTION

THOMAS Beddoes (1760–1808) studied chemistry under Joseph Black at Edinburgh, and, possibly with Black's support, was licensed at Oxford where he gave chemical lectures. While at Oxford, he styled himself Reader in Chemistry; after his removal to Bristol, he began to refer to the time when he had been Professor of Chemistry.[1] The University's official record has no mention of Beddoes as Professor. He was always sanguine, retrospectively as well as prospectively; but he was no liar. What was the substance of his supposititious chair in chemistry?

Part of the answer is suggested by a satirical epistle, addressed to Beddoes purportedly by Erasmus Darwin:

> BOAST of proud Shropshire, Oxford's lasting shame,
> Whom none but Coxcombs scorn, but Fools defame,
> Eternal war with dulness born to wage,
> Thou Paracelsus of this wondrous age;
> BEDDOES, the philosophic Chymist's Guide,
> The Bigot's Scourge, of Democrats the Pride;
> Accept this lay; and to thy Brother, Friend,
> Or name more dear, a Sans Culotte attend.[2]

Beddoes was embarrassing to Oxford precisely because he was a democrat. The fate of the Oxford chair in chemistry was decided by Beddoes' politics.

He studied medicine first at London and then, from 1780 to 1786, at the University of Edinburgh. He then went to Oxford, where he graduated as M.D.[3] He repeated an experiment on the production of artificial cold in Oxford on 21 March 1787.[4] In November of that year he announced to Black that he was embarking on a new manual of chemistry.[5] Beddoes' address was now Fleet Street, London, but he appears to have been already firmly ensconced in Oxford, for in the same year he had printed *A Memorial concerning the state of the Bodleian Library, and the conduct of the principal Librarian, Addressed to the Curators of that Library, by the Chemical Reader.* Whatever the significance of Beddoes' "readership" at this point, the *Memorial* shows that he had held it at least from February 1787.[6]

THE CHEMICAL READER

He began optimistically, finding at Oxford "increasing ardour" for the pursuit of chemistry.[7] In February 1788 he wrote to Black:

> I have begun my lectures & although my numbers cannot be put in competition with one at Edin[r]. yet the desire of knowing something of Chemistry seems to be spreading, since people have perceived that it is neither a petty branch of medicine nor one of the black arts, as they are termed, but simply an inviting & important

part of Nat. Phil. I think my numbers will be greater this than the last course, though I had then the largest class that has ever been seen at Oxford, at least within the memory of man, in any department of knowledge.[8]

Black visited Oxford in 1788, greatly impressing the Dean of Christ Church and other dignitaries,[9] and presumably visiting Beddoes, who continued to lecture with a special dispensation from John Cooke, Vice-Chancellor of the university.[10]

In 1789, Wedgwood was supplying Beddoes with porcelain tubes for the laboratory,[11] and two years later Beddoes wrote to Joseph Banks that the "elaboratory at Oxford has been for a considerable time past undergoing a thorough repair, which I hope will render it one of the best in Europe; in the mean time, I have been prevented from making any experiments".[12] The apparatus for the laboratory was mostly made by J. Sadler, better known for his work on steam engines, and as a balloonist. Sadler constructed "a very valuable assortment of chemical apparatus—a gazometer very much improved upon Mr. Lavoisier's &c—so that I am able to shew any & every experiment in his book".[13]

The lack of experiment was, however, a reflection of Beddoes' newly dejected state. "The spirit of Chemistry", he wrote to William Withering, probably in 1789, "has almost evaporated at Oxford, as indeed I always expected it would. The young men are generally speaking regardless of every thing . . . Accordingly my class was chiefly composed of the senior members of the University . . . the stock of curiosity seems nearly exhausted."[14] By the Spring of 1791, Beddoes was complaining that science, and chemistry in particular, would never flourish at Oxford "under the shadow of ecclesiastical & scholastic institutions".[15]

OXFORD, POLITICS, AND THE FRENCH REVOLUTION

What had happened to Beddoes' enthusiasm, and to his audiences? What had made him only now despondently aware of the authority of tradition in a Tory university? The French Revolution had happened, with all the alarms it conjured in its wake in the minds of the British establishment. Even before 1789, the hundredth anniversary of the English revolution of 1688 had raised hopes of constitutional reform, proposed by radicals who went back to lost glories.[16] Beddoes was indignant, writing to Davies Giddy that "to talk of restoring our constitution to its antient state is to me very offensive nonsense. And I am grieved to hear so many people found our right to reformation on what they suppose our forefathers to have possessed."[17] He was, however, no great admirer of the constitution, and he supported the Revolution in France without equivocation or concealment, although he was later horrified at the excesses of the Paris mob, which could only undermine the National Assembly.[18] He was increasingly critical of Pitt, whom he came to see as the source of repressive legislation at home, and of war-mongering abroad.[19] He was an old acquaintance of Sir James Mackintosh, M.P., whose *Vindiciae Gallicae* of 1791 he saw as an able and popular answer to Burke's *Reflections on the Revolution in France*, London, 1790.[20] What could one do in Oxford with an avowed Democrat? One could shun his lectures, and this the young men of Oxford did.

The Priestley riots flared in Birmingham in July 1791.[21] Beddoes was so widely connected with the members of the Lunar Society including Priestley, that he could almost be considered as their associate.[22] He certainly shared Priestley's political views, complaining that the English newspapers misrepresented the essentially justifiable chain of events in France, while regretting the "intolerable" excesses of the people in the tribunes.[23]

Riots in England and revolution abroad polarized British political life, and Henry Dundas, since 1791 Secretary of State for Home Affairs in Pitt's cabinet, was increasingly engaged in confrontations with the English democratic movement.[24]

In these confrontations Oxford, whose Chancellor was then Lord North, sided solidly with the party of King and country. When Beddoes expressed himself, as he frequently did, in terms critical of the medical profession, and with particular reference to hospitals, the response from the medical members of the University seems to have been predictable. "As to the unfavourable opinion entertained at Oxford with regard to [my] sentiments on hospitals", Beddoes wrote in January 1792 to Davies Giddy:

> you will readily believe that anticipated disapprobation falls light. You know as well as I do, the orbit in which Oxford minds move. I suppose one might trace a chain of ideas from the French Revolution to doubts concerning the extensive use-fulness of hospitals; & one might venture to foretell that neither the one nor the other would be well received in the house adjacent to the Divinity-school or the tower of St. Angels. Establishments would be equally respected in both.[25]

Over the next few months of 1792, the second part of Thomas Paine's *Rights of Man* was published; James Watt junior visited the French jacobins; a Royal Proclamation was issued (21 May) against seditious writings; it was decided to prosecute Paine for seditious libel; and Beddoes was doing what he could to ensure the free diffusion of information and the frustration through publicity of the measures taken by government "to continue the people in their prejudices".[26] He proposed a petition, never sent, in which the dangers to be apprehended from popular unrest were seen as far less alarming than "the bigotry turned against the protesting populace".[27] In the same year, Beddoes had printed *Alexander's Expedition . . . to the Indian Ocean*, which was a sustained and well-supported invective against the excesses of British imperial policy in India. "These possessions", he wrote, "undoubtedly enable ministers to enlist more recruits under the banners of Corruption."[28] At about the same time, he issued his *Letter to a Lady*, in which oppression of the poor is portrayed as likely to lead to violence; injustice invited rebellion.[29]

HOPES FOR A REGIUS CHAIR IN CHEMISTRY

Beddoes, by the summer of 1792, was an unsettling man to have in Oxford; nor was Oxford any longer congenial to him. He decided to resign, and in June went to the Vice-Chancellor. In an undated letter of 1793, Beddoes looked back on his career in Oxford and described the interview to Giddy:

> I said that I had no desire to read any more lectures; but that as I had given no chemical lectures that year, & as I thought it unjustifiable to keep possession of the Elab^y. with^t. reading lectures & as I cd. not immediately with convenience remove my specimens &c, I wd. not formally resign till *this* summer [1793]. I added that I wd. offer to read *this* spring & if I had a tolerable class, wd. proceed—that course however shd. certainly be the last—& if they wd. fix upon a successor, I wd. certainly resign to him this year: & I thought the person, whoever he might be, wd. be obliged to me for giving him notice so long beforehand.—The V. Chanc^r. said, this was extremely liberal—'but Sir as it is as much to be desired that some salary shd. be annexed to the Chem^l. Chair[30] & we cannot ask it in the name of any person so *eminent* as yourself, I wish you wd. draw up a memorial to be sent to the Sec^y. of State & keep the lectureship, till an answer be given to that memorial'.—I drew up the memorial. L^d. Guildford [Lord North] gave it to Dundas, who, as appeared

from a letter of L^d. Guildford's received it very favourably—I went into the country, became *eminently* & much beyond my importance, odious to Pitt & his gang, as I know from an hundred curious facts—the memorial from this & other causes was forgotten or destroyed.[31]

Beddoes' account of events is substantially accurate. There was, briefly in 1792, a possibility of acquiring a Regius Chair in Chemistry for the University, and Beddoes, at that time Oxford's most distinguished chemist, suddenly became valuable to the University. The first move was an approach by John Sibthorp, professor of botany since 1784, to Dundas through Lord North, requesting an improvement in status and emoluments. In the days of Charles II, the professor of botany had received £200 a year from the royal exchequer, more than twice the stipend in 1792.[32] Sibthorp hoped that Dundas would persuade George III to restore the chair to its former glory and double his income. He seems to have succeeded, for in early July 1792, Lord North wrote to Dundas requesting him "to lay the University of Oxford Dr. Sibthorpe & me at his Majesty's feet, & in all our names to return our most heartfelt acknowledgements for the very gracious & benevolent condescension with which he has received our petition"[33].

A few days later, however, Charles Willoughby returned from attending the Quarter Sessions, where he had discussed Sibthorpe's hopes with "some of the Heads of the University". Cambridge had a chair in botany and a chair in chemistry, each enjoying a stipend of £100 a year. Neither chair was held by warrant from the Crown, but funds came from the exchequer. "Now", reported Willoughby to Guilford, "I can from authority state to you that it appears to be of more public utility to reduce the salary [requested by Sibthorpe] & transfer a moiety of it Viz. £100 per ann. to a Professorship in Chemistry which is at this time *totally* unprovided for in this University [Oxford] which wo^d. put these two new Professorships (as far as the Royal bounty is concerned) on the same footing as those at Cambridge—The Botany Professor of Oxford has already near £100 pr. ann.—"[34] Guilford was clearly irritated by the University's tiresome stand. It was most gracious of his Majesty to endow a chair of botany, for which the University should be properly grateful. He had known nothing of the University's wish for an endowed Professorship of Chemistry.[35]

He was soon to be fully informed. The very next day the Vice-Chancellor wrote to him about the proposed Chair of Chemistry, and about the prime claimant for it, Thomas Beddoes, reiterating the substance of Willoughby's report, stressing the need for parity with Cambridge, and enclosing a memorandum from Beddoes, with this recommendation: "[He] (tho' as he says for a short time) has so unequivocal a claim in his Line to our utmost assistance and has given such ample satisfaction by Courses of Chemical Lectures to a larger class of Pupils than ever was before collected in that branch of useful Science, that I trust your Lordship's known candour and goodness will pardon this last attempt in your Vice-Chancellor to render some material & lasting Service to your University."[36] Cooke thus confirms Beddoes' account, including his determination to resign.

Chemistry at Oxford had long been unevenly and uncertainly supported. Plot was appointed Professor of Chemistry in 1683.[37] A list of 1710 mentions "Mr. Rd. Frewin, Prof. Chimistry, whenever he gaines a Class."[38] Other eighteenth-century professors were John Freind (1675–1728), and Martin Wall (1747–1824) who, describing himself as Public Reader in Chemistry, gave chemical lectures in the early 1780s.[39] Now, on 17 July 1792, Lord North acceded to Cooke's request, sent his letter and Beddoes' brief and hastily-composed memorandum to Dundas' office, and felt he had done his duty. Since North died less than three weeks later, on 5 August 1792, he could scarcely have done more. Beddoes' argument stressed the cost of apparatus and the expense of running the laboratory, and otherwise rehearsed familiar ground—the need for parity with Cambridge. There seemed every reason to assume that Oxford would shortly have its Regius Chair in Chemistry.[40]

THE HOME OFFICE AND THE PERILS OF DEMOCRACY

Beddoes and the Home Office between them made certain that no such pedestrian course was followed. The tenor of Beddoes' political conversation may be gathered not only from *Alexander's Expedition* and his *Letter to a Lady*, but also from his correspondence that summer, for his private and public utterances were alike uncompromising. "... defamation", he wrote from Oxford on 18 July, "is always very busy in disseminating reports concerning religious & political heresy . . . . And I wish the republican spirit may now become universal, as it is evidently the prevailing."[41]

Only now, after the University and Beddoes had approached Dundas, did anyone take public notice of Beddoes' political character. Willoughby wrote from Baldon House on 21 July to warn Dundas against Beddoes as one undeserving of his Majesty's bounty. He admitted his "thorough knowledge of chymistry", and that he "reads most able lectures which are well attended". But "in his political character I am informed, he is a most violent *Democrate* and that he takes great pains to seduce Young Men to the same political principles with himself". The Vice-Chancellor, Willoughby added, "feels much hurt at the information I am now giving you and hopes that it may not prevent his Majesty's bounty being bestowed on the University at some future time". Of course the Vice-Chancellor recognized the impossibility of any longer advancing Beddoes' claims. "I am likewise informed", Willoughby concluded, "that Dr. Beddows has expressed his intention to quit the University of Oxford after he has read his next course of lectures, which it is hoped he may do and then his Majesty *may appoint* a chymical Proffessor in case he sho^d. think proper at that time to comply with the wishes of the University."[42] The whole affair was meanwhile to be suspended, and kept strictly confidential.

One week later, Beddoes appeared on a Home Office list of "Disaffected & seditious persons". He was there in the excellent company of his friend Joseph Priestley.[43] This list may serve as a reminder of the undoubted connection between reformers and the Friends of Liberty with natural scientists in the 1790s.[44] Beddoes' case was in this respect not unique, and, once the Home Office was alerted to it, he had clearly lost his chair, and equally clearly could not be told why.

A broadsheet that he issued in October 1792 would in any case have ensured his departure from Oxford. In the summer of 1792 the King had instructed the bishops to organize an appeal to support the French clergy who had fled to England. Beddoes opposed the subscription, describing the priests as pests who had oppressed society, and whose support would "inflame the people of England to the thirst of blood against the French". The September Massacre in Paris had outraged English opinion. Beddoes, privately horrified, was still the friend of France and liberty, and accordingly entitled his broadsheet: "REASONS For believing the friends of liberty in France not to be the authors or abettors of the crimes committed in that country; humbly addressed to those who from time to time constitute themselves Judge and Jury upon affairs public and private, and without admitting any testimony but the gross lies of Beldame Rumour, damn their neighbours individually, and the rest of the world by the lump." With such diplomacy did Beddoes address the issue. "The enormities of September 2d.", he argued, " . . . were not, in a sense more extensive, the crime of the French Nation than the Birmingham and London riots, the *horrid barbarities* exercised by Englishmen in America, Asia and Africa, are or were the crimes of the English nation; nor indeed, I fear in one so extensive. Considering the occasions, the design to roast Dr. Priestly alive (although but one man, and that man an Unitarian and a Philosopher) betrays as sanguinary a spirit as that of the Paris Mob. And would it be justifiable to criminate the whole English Nation on this account?"[45] Beddoes deplored the failure of the metropolitan and country press to report events in France accurately, and tried for some months to set on foot "a country newspaper, such as should teach the people their rights & a respect for those of others. . . . To me it appears extremely urgent to humanize the people, for I think our government cannot stand long."[46]

Beddoes' position mirrored that of the reform societies in their support of the French, arousing the same conservative reaction and contributing to the public identification, however inaccurate, of reformers as English Jacobins.[47] The Home Office received an account of Beddoes' activities of "sowing sedition" in the neighbourhood of Shifnall, "particularly by the distribution of Pamphlets of a very mischievous and inflammatory tendency, and such as ought to be publicly noticed". Ewan Nepean, permanent under secretary at the Home Office, tried unsuccessfully to collect information that would justify arraigning Beddoes on a charge of sedition.[48]

Over the next few months, Beddoes continued to fear popular violence in England, arguing that constitutional reform and the free diffusion of information were the best ways to avoid a crisis. By mid-November he felt that democracy was gaining: "The Nth. of England & Scotland all democratic—London rapidly democratizing—Vive l'egalité, vice G- S- the K- . . . No cause of apprehension, but in the wretched State, moral and physical, which our happy C[onstitutio]n in Ch[urch] & State has left the poor."[49]

On 1 December a Royal Proclamation was issued, calling up the militia to control riots and insurrection. On the same day, another Proclamation sought to encourage naval recruitment; there followed the Proclamation of 26 December, offering increased bounties to enlisting sailors. Louis XVI was beheaded in Paris on 21 January 1793, eleven days before France declared war on England; and on 1 March a general fast was proclaimed in England, before God and in preparation for the French wars.[50]

RESIGNATION AND DEPARTURE FROM OXFORD

Beddoes had, about Christmas 1792, been urged to resign. He had already become reluctant to deliver further lectures: "My political sentiments and the manner in which I expressed them saved me from all embarassment."[51] He was told that he would have no audience, and that he would probably be succeeded by one Stacey. "I much wished Stacey to succeed me, as he has a large family & wd., on acc^t. of his being able to make apparatus with his own hands, be likely to give as good a course as any body I knew at Oxford. I chearfully resigned—& Dr. Bourne is appointed."[52] On 7 April 1793 Beddoes wrote to Giddy that he was about to leave Oxford, being then engaged in packing up his laboratory. Even then, Beddoes remained an optimist: "I own to you that I expected to find strong marks of aversion in the looks and conduct of the clergy here—I was conscious that I had no title to their kindness." But with only one exception, "I have remarked an unusual forwardness of civility in the rest of my acquaintence. It can be no wonder that men's exterior should become more smooth as their alarms subside; yet it feels to me as a mark of the increased liberality of the age."[53]

Beddoes left Oxford for Bristol shortly thereafter. On 26 July 1793 the Duke of Portland was installed as chancellor of Oxford, and in the following year succeeded Dundas in the Home Office, while Dundas became Secretary of State for War. By the end of the decade, the English democratic movement was effectively stifled, and with it all illusions of "the increased liberality of the age".[54]

ACKNOWLEDGEMENT

The research for this paper was supported by a grant from the Social Sciences & Humanities Research Council of Canada. Dr. W. A. Smeaton read a draft of this paper and made valuable suggestions. I am grateful for permission to reproduce correspondence in the Davies–Giddy papers, Cornwall Record Office.

REFERENCES

1. Beddoes' self-bestowed titles appear in his *A Memorial concerning the state of the Bodleian Library and the conduct of the principal librarian, Addressed to the Curators of that Library, by the Chemical Reader*, Oxford, 1787, and in his *A letter to Erasmus Darwin, M.D. on a new method of treating pulmonary consumption, and some other Diseases hitherto found Incurable*, Bristol, 1793, p. 29. F. W. Gibbs & W. A. Smeaton, "Thomas Beddoes at Oxford", *Ambix*, **9** (1961), 47–9.

2. *The Golden Age, a Poetical Epistle from Erasmus D--n, M.D. to Thomas Beddoes, M.D.*, London, printed for F. Rivington & Co., & J. Cooke, Oxford, 1794, p. 3.

3. J. E. Stock, *Memoirs of the life of Thomas Beddoes, M.D.*, London, 1811.

4. Gibbs & Smeaton (1), 48–9, based on R. T. Gunther, *Early Science in Oxford*, Vol. 1, 1923, 204.

5. Beddoes to J. Black, 6 Nov. 1787. Black correspondence, Edinburgh University Library (EUL).

6. The *Memorial* is dated Pembroke College, 31 May 1787, but (p. 13) refers to his activities in Oxford over the past three months. Gibbs & Smeaton (1), p. 49.

7. Beddoes to Black, 6 Nov. 1787 (EUL).

8. Beddoes to Black, 23 Feb. 1788 (EUL).

9. Maxwell Garthshore to Black, 7 Oct. 1788 (EUL). Davies Giddy states that Beddoes was made an honorary member of the Common Room at Christ Church: Cornwall Record Office (CRO) MS DD DG, Giddy's Diary, entry dated 1826 facing entry for 18 July 1791.

10. C. Willoughby, Baldon House, 21 July 1792, to [?Henry Dundas], Public Record Office (PRO), Home Office MSS HO.42.208. Beddoes to Black, 21 April 1789 (EUL).

11. Wedgwood MS 563–1 in Keele University Library.

12. Beddoes to Banks, 3 Jan. 1791. British Museum (Natural History) Dawson-Turner Collection **7** ff 189–190.

13. Beddoes to Black 15 April 1791 (EUL). J. E. Hodgson, "James Sadler (1753–1828) of Oxford, aeronaut, chemist, engineer, and inventor", *Transactions of the Newcomen Society*, **8** (1927–8), 66–82. Beddoes also used Milner's syllabus at Oxford: Beddoes to J. Watt jr. 25 Feb. 1798, Birmingham Public Libraries M IV B.

14. Typescript of letter at McGill University, Bibl. Osler no. 1988.

15. Beddoes to Black 15 April 1791 (EUL).

16. Albert Goodwyn, *The Friends of Liberty. The English Democratic Movement in the Age of the French Revolution*, Harvard University Press, Cambridge, Mass., 1979.

17. CRO MS DG 41.58, n.d. Giddy subsequently changed his name to Gilbert, and as Davies Gilbert became President of the Royal Society of London. See A. C. Todd, *Beyond the Blaze: A Biography of Davies Gilbert*, D. Bradford Barton Ltd., Truro 1967.

18. Correspondence with Giddy, 1789–1793, CRO MSS DG 41; MS DG 41.6, 5 May 1791.

19. Beddoes, *A Word in Defence of the Bill of Rights against Gagging-bills*, 1795; *An Essay on the Public Merits of Mr. Pitt*, 1796.

20. Beddoes to Giddy, CRO MS DG 41.15, [26] May 1791. Goodwyn, *The Friends of Liberty* (16), 19, 69, and chap. 4.

21. R. B. Rose, "The Priestley Riots of 1791", *Past and Present*, **18** (1960), 68–88.

22. R. E. Schofield, *The Lunar Society of Birmingham*, Clarendon Press, Oxford, 1963, 373–377, makes a weaker claim for Beddoes.

23. Beddoes to Giddy, 2 Feb. 1792, CRO MS DG 41.13.

24. Goodwyn, *The Friends of Liberty* (16), chap. 6. R. R. Nelson, *The Home Office, 1782–1801*, Duke University Press, Durham, N.C., 1969.

25. Beddoes to Giddy 9 Jan. [1792], CRO MS DG 41.40.

26. Goodwyn, *The Friends of Liberty* (16), chaps. 6 & 7. E. Robinson, "An English Jacobin: James Watt, Junior, 1769–1848", *Cambridge Historical Journal*, 1955, 349–55. PRO, Treasury Solicitor's Papers, MS TS 11 962/3508, 19 April 1792. Beddoes to Giddy 3 April [1792], with enclosures from James Keir to Beddoes, CRO MS DG 41.50.

27. Beddoes to Giddy 4 July 1792. CRO MS DG 41.16. Giddy signed and sent an address, dated 10 July 1792, of a much more conservative tenor than Beddoes': CRO DG 41.35.

28. *Alexander's Expedition Down the Hydaspes & the Indus to the Indian Ocean*, London, 1792, 82; printed but not published.

29. *A Letter to a Lady on the subject of early Instruction, particularly that of the poor* [1792], printed but not published.

30. Beddoes had already made that point in March 1789: Stock, *Beddoes* (3), p. 21.

31. Beddoes to Giddy, CRO MS DG 41.22 [1793].

32. C. Willoughby to [Guilford] 11 July 1792, PRO MS HO 42.208.

33. Guilford to [Dundas] [7] July 1792, PRO MS HO 42.21.

34. Willoughby 11 July 1792, PRO MS HO 42.208. Tho. Martyn 14 July 1792, PRO MS HO 42.21 gives information about the chairs at Cambridge.

35. Guilford to [Dundas] 15 July 1792, PRO MS HO 42.208.

36. John Cooke to Guilford 16 July 1792, PRO MS HO 42.208.

37. Oxford University Register. Fletcher, *Collectanea*, 1st. series, pp. 298–299.

38. Bodleian Library MS TOP Oxon e. 365, 1710, p. 24.

39. *Letters of Radcliffe and James*, ed. M. Evans, Oxford Historical Society, 1888, p. 148. I am grateful to Mrs. V. Jobling for the information in this note and nn. 37–38. Wall published *A syllabus of a course of lectures in chemistry, read at the Museum*, Oxford, 1782.

40. PRO MS HO 42.208, 17 July 1792.

41. Beddoes to Giddy, 18 July 1792, CRO MS DG 41.14.

42. Willoughby to Dundas, 21 July 1792, PRO MS HO 42.208. No Regius Professor of Chemistry was subsequently appointed at Oxford. North's death, and the subsequent vacancy in the chancellorship until July 1793, may have been partly responsible for the matter of the regius chair being shelved. Sibthorp did however become Regius Professor of Botany: Sibthorp to [Dundas] 17 Sept. 1792, PRO MS HO 42.21. A chair in chemistry (not a regius chair) was founded in 1798, but not occupied until 1803: Gibbs and Smeaton (1), p. 47 n.

43. "Disaffected & seditious persons. Goodmans fields 28 July 1792", PRO MS HO 42.21.

44. A similar argument is made by J. Money, *Experience and Identity. Birmingham and the West Midlands 1760–1800*, Manchester University Press, 1977, 225, & in Rose, "The Priestley Riots" (21), 76.

45. The broadsheet (CRO DG 41.25) is also described in Beddoes to Giddy 21 Oct. 1792, CRO MS DG 41.20.

46. Beddoes to Giddy 21 Oct. & 8 Nov. 1792, CRO MS DG 41.20 & 41.5. Goodwyn, *The Friends of Liberty* (16), 231, mentions an independent newspaper established by "a radically disposed bookseller" in Leicester at about this time. Beddoes was concerned about the moral as well as the material condition of the poor. For background, see R. Quinalt & J. Stevenson, eds., *Popular Protest and Public Order*, London, 1974, including J. Stevenson, "Food riots in England, 1792–1818", pp. 33–74.

47. Goodwyn, *The Friends of Liberty* (16), pp. 266–7.
48. Nepean to Isaac Hawkins Browne, 1 Nov. 1792, PRO MS HO 42.22. The Home Office network of "spies" was decidedly limited: see C. Emsley, "The home office and its sources of information and investigation 1791–1801", *English Historical Review*, **94** (1979), 532–61.
49. CRO MS DG 41.5. Beddoes to Giddy 19 Nov. 1792, CRO MS DG 41.38.
50. The Proclamations are widely available: I consulted them in the Bristol Record Office, 1792 Box (26)—containing documents for 1792 to 1793.
51. Beddoes to Giddy [1793], CRO MS DG 41.2.
52. Beddoes to Giddy, 7 April [1793], CRO MS DG 41.22. [R. Bourne], *A syllabus of a course of chemical lectures read at the Museum . . . in 1794*, Oxford, 1794.
53. CRO MS DG 41.2.
54. Goodwyn, *The Friends of Liberty* (16), chap. 12.

VI

Dr. Thomas Beddoes (1750–1808): Science and medicine in politics and society

Introduction

THE career of Thomas Beddoes was moulded by British responses to the French Revolution. Beddoes, until appalled by the events of the Terror, saw France as the model for mankind.[1] The government of England took the very different view that democracy was closely allied with jacobinism and sedition. The Home Office was the agency most immediately engaged in opposing sedition, and any criticism of the King, or of the constitution in church and state, was scrutinized as being potentially seditious. In 1793, England and France went to war, and the following years saw treason trials and gagging bills, profoundly disturbing even to the more conservative among the friends of peace and liberty in England, Beddoes among them.[2]

Beddoes was a friend of most of the members of the Lunar Society of Birmingham. When the mob rose in that city against Joseph Priestley, Beddoes made public his detestation of the 'Church and King' riots,[3] his sympathies with France, his admiration for French scientists and social scientists, and his opposition to the war. It is not surprising that the Home Office investigated him.

Beddoes saw his responsibility as a physician as primarily one of preventing disease, which meant understanding and tackling its social, material, and physiological causes. He was an advocate of public health measures and reforms a full generation before Chadwick, at a time when England lagged behind France in organized medicine.[4]

---

[1] For the ideological role of science in the French Revolution, see J. Fayet, *La revolution française et la science, 1789–1795*, Paris, 1960; E. Maindron, *L'Académie des Sciences*, Paris, 1888; L. P. Williams, 'Science, education and Napoleon I', *Isis*, 1956, *47*, 368–82; H. Guerlac, 'Lavoisier', *D.S.B.*, viii, 69–91.

[2] C. Emsley, 'The home office and its sources of information and investigation 1791–1801'. *English Historical Review*, 1979, *94*, 532–61. R. R. Nelson, *The Home Office, 1782–1801*, Durham, North Carolina, 1969. A. Goodwin, *The Friends of Liberty. The English democratic movement in the age of the French Revolution*, Cambridge, Mass., 1979. J. E. Cookson, *The Friends of Peace. Anti-war Liberalism in England, 1793–1815*, Cambridge, 1982.

[3] R. E. Schofield, *The Lunar Society of Birmingham*, Oxford, 1963. R. B. Rose, 'The Priestley Riots of 1791', *Past and Present*, 1960, *18*, 68–88.

[4] E. P. Hennock, 'Urban sanitary reform a generation before Chadwick', *Econ. Hist. Rev.*, 1957, II, *10*, 113–120. B. Hamilton, 'The medical profession in the XVIIIth century', *Econ. Hist. Rev.*, 1951, II, *4*, 148. C. C. Hannaway, 'The Société Royal de Médicine and epidemics in the Ancien Régime', *Bull. Hist. Med.*, 1972, *46*, 257–73. David M. Vess, *Medical Revolution in France 1789–1796*, Gainsville, Fla., 1975. Toby Gelfand, *Professionalizing Modern Medicine: Paris Surgeons and Medical Science and Institutions in*

Beddoes's friends and supporters in his Pneumatic Institution[5] included Coleridge, who had also been investigated by the Home Office, James Watt junior, an English jacobin, and other known radicals. Beddoes kept his reputation as a jacobin long after he had given up political agitation and turned his attention almost entirely to social medicine.[6]

Revolution and Riot: the Lunar Society, Beddoes, and Politics

The English establishment's response to the Revolution was predictable. Edmund Burke's *Reflections on the Revolution in France*, London, 1790, was the conservative manifesto of that response; it provoked Tom Paine's counter-manifesto *The Rights of Man*, Part I, London, 1791; Part II, London, 1792.[7] Paine's message was direct and strong, and more than likely to exacerbate divisions within society. Beddoes, although a friend of the Revolution, dreaded the Paris mob, and had no wish to see its counterpart in England. He was therefore relieved when his old acquaintance Sir James Mackintosh published *Vindiciae Gallicae*, 1791, a work that 'has almost satisfied my [Beddoes's] desideratum of an able and popular answer to Burke.'[8] Such works, far from generating sympathy with the democratic movement in England, may instead have provoked a counter-reaction, thus indirectly fuelling the outrages of the Priestley riots of July 1791, when the Birmingham mob rose against the local dissenters, destroyed Priestley's papers and scientific apparatus, burned his house and the houses of more than twenty-five others, and made the members of the Lunar Society an especial object of their fury.[9]

In November, Beddoes visited James Keir at his house near Birmingham; Keir was a member of the Lunar Society, a democrat, and a phlogistonist in chemistry who tried unsuccessfully to persuade Beddoes to join him in composing a new work on chemical theory. 'As our opinions in chemistry were different and in politics the same,' Beddoes recorded, 'and he is the intimate friend of Darwin and Day,[10] we should have been unlucky indeed if we had wanted conversation.' Their conversation ranged over chemistry and politics, especially the aftermath of the Birmingham riots. 'I am told our country newspapers are full of abuse in which dissenters are united with the well-wishers of the French rev[n]. Priestley's friends believe

the Eighteenth Century, Contributions to Medical History, Westport, Conn., and London, 1980. For the fashionable French view of hygiene, see M. Foucault, *Power/Knowledge*, ed. C. Gordon, New York, 1980, 166–82. J.-P. Goubert, 'L'art de guérir: Médecine savante et médecine populaire dans la France de 1790', *Ann. Écon. Soc. Civilisations*, 1977, *32*, 908–26. The standard article on French hygiene, for a slightly later period, is E. Ackerknecht, 'Hygiene in France, 1815–1848', *Bull. Hist. Med.*, 1948, *22*, 117–155.
    [5] T. H. Levere, 'Dr. Thomas Beddoes and the establishment of his Pneumatic Institution', *Notes and Records of the Royal Society of London*, 1977, *32*, 41–49.
    [6] Coleridge, *The Watchman*, 17 March 1796. E. Robinson, 'An English Jacobin: James Watt, Junior, 1769–1848', *Cambridge Historical Journal*, 1955, 349–55.
    [7] Goodwin, op. cit. (2), 100.
    [8] Beddoes to Giddy, 5 May and [?26] May 1791: Davies–Giddy (DG) papers, Cornwall Record Office (CRO), MSS DG 41/6 & 41/15.
    [9] Goodwin, 180–183. Rose, op. cit. (3), 76.
    [10] Thomas Day, 1748–1789, another of the Lunar circle. Schofield, op. cit. (3), 52.

he would certainly be destroyed were he to appear at Birm[ingham] ... At the time of the riots Keir certainly saved his house by taking measures for a vigorous defence.'[11]

Beddoes was convinced that the English newspapers were doing everything they could to misrepresent and bring discredit upon events in France, and upon the friends of France in England. He also supposed that magistrates in Birmingham had encouraged the mob in its excesses; and he became increasingly alarmed.[12]

In January 1792 he wrote his *Letter on Early Instruction, Particularly that of the Poor.* His message was simple; injustice and oppression, partly exercised through the poor laws, provoked fanaticism and mob violence. It was therefore urgently necessary to humanize 'the minds of the poorer class of Citizens.'[13] Humanization for Beddoes involved education, the amelioration of material conditions, the removal of abuses, and the renunciation of violence; it was a decidedly paternalistic variant of democratization. The mob, whether for the established order or for revolution, was a fearful thing.

The second part of Paine's *Rights of Man* appeared in February 1792, with plans for a Democratic welfare state; as Keir wrote to Beddoes, the volume 'has alarmed Government much.'[14] In May, the London Revolution Society published its correspondence with the National Assembly and jacobin clubs in France. James Watt junior, Beddoes's friend, had recently been in Paris as an English jacobin. On 21 May the government's alarms found expression in a Royal Proclamation directed against Paine and other authors of seditious writings. The anti-jacobinism of the gentry led them to assume a connection between democracy, seditious writings, and what E. P. Thompson has called 'popular self activity'[15]; protest was accordingly repressed. Beddoes indignantly asserted that food riots and similar disturbances were much less alarming than the counter-measures instituted against the protesters.[16]

Beddoes, although no rioter, had become one of the protesters. His *Letter on Early Instruction* was followed by an epic poem entitled *Alexander's Expedition to the Indian Ocean*, London, 1792, prompted by the abuses revealed in the Warren Hastings affair. But just as the former *Letter* had moved rapidly from a consideration of the moral education of the young[17] to an examination of the ills of society, so, in *Alexander's Expedition*,

[11] Beddoes to [Giddy], 21 Nov. 1791. MS DG 41/48, CRO.

[12] Beddoes to Giddy 4 Nov. 1791. MS DG/41, CRO.

[13] Beddoes, *Letter on Early Instruction*, 1792, 1, 20.

[14] MS DG 41/50, CRO, 3 April 1792. Public Record Office (PRO) MS TS 11 962/3508, 19 April 1792.

[15] E. P. Thompson, 'The moral economy of the English crowd in the eighteenth century', *Past and Present*, 1971, *50*, 76–136 at 129.

[16] Goodwin, op. cit. (2), 200. Robinson, op. cit. (6). Beddoes to Giddy 4 July 1792, MS DG 41/16, CRO.

[17] Dorothy Stansfield, 'Thomas Beddoes and education', *History of Education Society Bulletin*, 1979, *23*, 7–14.

Beddoes's historical subject served merely to introduce essentially Whiggish reflections on British imperial policy in India, on the evil effects of missionary activity, and on the corruption of government ministers. The work was not published,[18] Beddoes thereby avoiding the possibility of prosecution for sedition.

Beddoes, supporter of Priestley and critic of the establishment, was not a comfortable presence in the Tory university of Oxford. But he was Oxford's most distinguished chemist, and the vice-chancellor, John Cooke, President of Corpus, wanted to use Beddoes's scientific reputation to secure a Regius Chair in chemistry for the university.[19]

The proposal went from Cooke to the chancellor of the university, and from him to the Home Office, where it was at first approved. Then, however, in July 1792, information reached Henry Dundas, the Home Secretary and thus the official responsible for suppressing sedition and riot, that Beddoes was a 'most violent *Democrate* and that he takes great pains to seduce Young Men to the same political principles with himself.'[20] Clearly such a person could not be the recipient of royal favour; at a word from the Home Office, Beddoes and the University of Oxford were deprived of a Regius Chair in chemistry.[21]

Beddoes offended the Home Office not only by his activities in Oxford, but also in Shropshire, where he had been 'sowing sedition', 'particularly by the distribution of Pamphlets.'[22] His name also appeared, with Joseph Priestley's, on a list of disaffected and seditious persons who had gathered near Derby. It is worth remarking that Beddoes's politically suspicious presence, near Shrewsbury and near Derby, may have been connected with Erasmus Darwin's Derby Philosophical Society and with his son Robert's group at Shrewsbury, especially since the Home Office noticed the latter among the 'Associations for the Relief of Pretended Grievances' in October 1792. The Lunar Society was not the only philosophical society that came under political suspicion and scrutiny.[23]

There is, alas, no proof that Beddoes was active in either of the Darwins' societies. But he undoubtedly saw himself as an aspiring

[18] MS note by Wm. Anstice, 9 Oct. 1819, in Yale University's copy of *Alexander's Expedition*.

[19] Guilford to [Dundas] [7] July 1792, C. Willoughby to Guilford 11 July 1792, J. Cooke to Guilford 16 July, 1792, in PRO MSS HO 42.21, 42.208. Beddoes to Giddy, MS DG 41/22, CRO 1793.

[20] Willoughby to Dundas, 21 July 1792, PRO MS HO 42.208.

[21] T. H. Levere, 'Dr. Thomas Beddoes at Oxford: Radical Politics in 1788–1793 and the Fate of the Regius Chair in Chemistry', *Ambix*, 1981, *28*, 61–9.

[22] E. Nepean to I. H. Browne, 1 Nov. 1792, PRO MS HO 42.22.

[23] J. Money, *Experience and Identity. Birmingham and the West Midlands 1760–1800*, Manchester, 1977, 225. E. Robinson, 'The Derby Philosophical Society', *Annals of Science*, 1953, *9*, 368–76. 'Disaffected & seditious persons'. Goodmans fields 28 July 1792', PRO MS HO 42.21. For other scientific societies and sedition (mostly at a later date) see Ian Inkster, 'London Science and the Seditious Meetings Act of 1817', *BJHS*, 1979, *12*, 192–6; Paul Weindling, 'Science and Sedition: How Effective Were the Acts Licensing Lectures and Meetings, 1795–1819?', *BJHS*, 1980, *13*, 139–53; Ian Inkster, 'Seditious Science: A Reply to Paul Weindling', *BJHS*, 1981, *14*, 181–7. For the relations between Beddoes and Erasmus Darwin, see J. E. Stock, *Memoirs of the Life of Thomas Beddoes, M.D.*, London & Bristol, 1811; D. King-Hele, *Doctor of Revolution: The Life and Genius of Erasmus Darwin*, London, 1977; D. King-Hele (ed.), *The Letters of Erasmus Darwin*, Cambridge, 1981.

democrat. On 19 November 1792 he wrote to his former student and close confidant Davies Giddy. 'Venit summa dies et ineluctabile tempus,' he exclaimed, 'as I have preached for the last three months to our rich democrates and Aristocrates—but not in vain—they begin now to tremble and sing low, the latter I mean . . . The inclosed papers, from Shrewsbury to Birming[ham] and from Whitchurch to Ludlow, have produced a stronger sensation than I could have conceived possible . . . The Nth of England and Scotland all Democratic—London rapidly democratizing—Vive l'egalité, vice G[od] S[ave] the K[ing] . . . No cause of apprehension but in the wretched state, moral and physical, which our happy C[onstitution]n in Ch[urch] and State has left the poor.' The reference to the moral state of the poor again suggests Whiggish paternalism more than democracy; Beddoes's ambivalence was perhaps reflected in his attempts to establish a country newspaper that would not be subject to government control, and that would contribute to the goal of humanizing the people, by teaching them their rights and the rights of others, including the French. He had also, in October, composed and distributed a broadsheet opposing a subscription for the relief of exiled French priests, on the grounds that such a subscription would fan British hatred of the French, who were justified in deposing Louis because tyrants invite rebellion. He compared the September massacres with the Priestley riots, neither being typical of the nation in which they occurred.[24]

Beddoes feared popular insurrection, even while sympathizing with democratic protest; the government, in contrast, wanted to suppress such protest. On 1 December 1792 a Royal Proclamation was issued calling up the militia to control riots and insurrection, together with another proclamation for encouraging naval recruitment. Louis XVI was beheaded on 21 January 1793, and eleven days later England and France were at war.

The Home Office was at this stage responsible for security in England, and for the conduct of the war. The friends of liberty were associated with the jacobin enemy abroad. Beddoes could not remain in Oxford in such a climate of opinion. Chemistry in the 1790's could provide a career only in a university or, less genteelly, in a manufactory. Beddoes had tried the former and, unlike his friends in the Lunar Society, was not tempted by the latter. Thomas Beddoes, M.D., would return to medicine.

He had already at Edinburgh carried out experiments upon animal respiration.[25] As early as 1791, while visiting Davies Giddy in Cornwall, he had dreamed of a research institution to investigate the therapeutic effects

---

[24] Beddoes to Giddy, 19 Nov. 1792, MS DG 41/38, CRO. Giddy had studied under Beddoes at Oxford and, as Davies Gilbert, was to succeed Davy as P.R.S. See A. C. Todd, *Beyond the Blaze. A Biography of Davies Gilbert*, Truro, 1967. Beddoes, *Reasons for believing the friends of liberty in France not to be the authors or abettors of the crimes committed in that country* [1792]. Beddoes to Giddy, 21 Oct. & 8 Nov. 1792, MSS DG 41/20, 41/5, CRO.

[25] Beddoes, *A Letter to Erasmus Darwin, M.D., on a new method of treating pulmonary consumption, and some other diseases hitherto found incurable*, Bristol, 1793, 28–29.

192

of different gases.[26] Leaving Oxford in 1793, he determined to embark upon research and practice in pneumatic medicine.

Consumption would be his main target. It was the most devastating of all respiratory diseases, accounting for approximately one quarter of recorded deaths in a predominantly urban sample of 20,000 burials a year in the 1790's.[27] Even if one recognizes that consumption was a catch-all category in the 1790's, it is clear that respiratory infections were a leading cause of death; malnutrition among the poor would have been a significant contributing factor. Beddoes sought a spa town, a resort of invalids, as a source of patients, both visitors and the resident poor. Clifton and the adjoining city of Bristol answered his needs; it had its Hotwell, supposedly effective in the cure of consumption; it had an infirmary, an additional source of patients; and, as a lively intellectual centre, it was likely to be receptive to his innovative proposals.[28] Beddoes was reassured by his reception: 'The medical people here wish, pretend at least to wish, me success and are upon a friendly footing with me.'[29]

He had high hopes for pneumatic medicine, believing it to be of very wide application. 'I have it in contemplation', he wrote in June 1793, 'to undertake several incurable diseases besides consumption.'[30] Beddoes announced his plans for the creation of a pneumatic institution in a public letter to Erasmus Darwin, whose name he thereby enlisted in the enterprise.[31] Beddoes had the greatest admiration for Darwin, whose views would, he believed, 'make a vast change in the practice of medicine', and whose writings would place him 'among the greatest of mankind—the founders of sciences.'[32]

Beddoes's *Letter to Erasmus Darwin, M.D., on a new method of treating pulmonary consumption* (1793) was followed in 1794 by a quarto pamphlet bearing the title, *The Golden Age. A poetical epistle from Erasmus D—n, M.D. to Thomas Beddoes, M.D.* The pamphlet was evidently not by Darwin; since it was printed for an Oxford publisher,[33] it may well have been written by one of Beddoes's former colleagues.

The mottoes on the title page were taken from Beddoes's writings, and were chosen so as to expose his politics and his science alike to ridicule.

---

[26] Todd, op. cit. (24), 25.

[27] Beddoes, *Hygëia; or Essays, Moral and Medical on the causes affecting the personal state of the middling and affluent classes*, 3 vols., Bristol, 1802–3, ii, 5. Ibid., p. 6: 'Of 1654 buried in one parish in Bristol—683 stand under the title of consumption or decline: and from a register at Shrewsbury it will be presently seen that for ten years, above one death in four is appropriated to consumption.' Beddoes also gives figures for Chester, from J. Haygarth, 'Observations on the Bill of Mortality in Chester, for the Year 1772', *Phil. Trans.*, 1774, *64*, 67–78, & 'Bill of Mortality for Chester for the Year 1773', *Phil. Trans.*, 1775, *65*, 85–90.

[28] J. Nott, *Of the Hotwell Waters, near Bristol*, Bristol, 1793. C. A. Weber, *Bristols Bedeutung für die englische Romantik . . .*, Halle, 1935.

[29] Beddoes to Giddy, MS DG 41/7, CRO, 31 July 1793.

[30] Beddoes to Giddy, MS DG 41/28, CRO, 15 June 1793.

[31] Beddoes, op. cit. (25).

[32] Beddoes to Giddy, 29 Oct. 1793 & June 1796; MSS DG 41/4, 42/20, CRO.

[33] Rivington & Cooke.

Dr. Thomas Beddoes (1750–1808) 193

Footnotes like Darwin's in *The Botanic Garden* quoted Beddoes on the glories achieved by French science since the Revolution; on the similarities between vegetable and animal oils, which suggested that chemistry and physiology might, 'by regulating the vegetable functions, teach our woods and hedges to supply us with Butter and Tallow'; and on the advantages owed by France to the overthrow of the monarchy, the nobility, and the clergy. These advantages were listed in Beddoes's *Reasons for believing the Friends of Liberty in France not to be the Authors or Abettors of the crimes committed in that Country*, 'the celebrated Hand bill circulated in Shropshire, which eventually occasioned his resignation of the Chemical Chair in the University of Oxford.'[34]

The pseudonymous author apostrophized Beddoes:

> Boast of proud Shropshire, Oxford's lasting shame,
> Whom none but Coxcombs scorn, but Fools defame,
> Eternal war with dulness born to wage,
> Thou Paracelsus of this wondrous age;
> BEDDOES, the philosophic Chymist's Guide,
> The Bigot's Scourge, of Democrats the Pride;
> Accept this lay; and to thy Brother, Friend,
> Or name more dear, a Sans Culotte attend.[35]

Bristol: a Turbulent City

Bristol was scarcely a revolutionary city; but it did experience disturbances and threats of riots during the latter half of the eighteenth century.[36] At least one of these threats was in reaction against dissenters. In July 1791, the very month of the Priestley riots, the mayor of Bristol was told: 'We are coming Near two 2,000 Good harty hail strong Rufins which will Pull Down your fine Manchin house and your fine Baptis Meating and not your Meating only but Prespterines. Likewise the Romands and all your Decenters houses shall share the same fate as them at Birmingham.'[37] Nothing came of that threat, but there were disturbances and threats of disturbances in Bristol throughout the decade. These were not radical or seditious in any significant sense, although this was not always clear to the authorities; the issues were tolls, tithes and what were seen by the protesters as abuses of the market economy, leading to unjustifiable prices for bread and meat. Disturbances, in short, were frequently assertions of traditional social values. The mayor, however, was nervous, and on 17 August 1792 Dundas promised him that the cavalry quartered nearby would come to his aid when needed. On 30 September 1793, there was a riot at the toll bridge, in which the militia fired on the rioters, killing fifteen and wounding around fifty others. Dundas was not even informed, and was

[34] *The Golden Age*, 6, 14.   [35] Ibid., 3.
[36] Rose, op. cit. (3), 71; 'Eighteenth-century price riots and public policy in England', *International Review of Social History*, 1961, 6, 277–92. Thompson, op. cit. (15).
[37] PRO MS HO 42.19, quoted in Money, op. cit. (23), 227.

indignant. It was later suggested that the riots had been encouraged by an agitator from London; official thoughts must immediately and erroneously have turned to the friends of liberty. In November, the mayor wrote to Home Office to ask that a troop of horse be stationed in the city during the winter. A French dancing master and a miniature painter came under suspicion as disaffected and seditious persons.[38]

Amid these suspicions and discontents, the Bristol Society for Constitutional Information, an essentially conservative middle class reform organization, entered in January 1794 into correspondence with the leading national democratic body, the London Corresponding Society, reporting, somewhat pathetically, that 'our Number is *now* considerably increased . . . it is our firm Opinion, could we but arouse them, that Patriots would become nearly the Majority of our City.' They received no reply, but their letters were seized with the books of the London Corresponding Society, and scrutinized for possible use in the treason trials of 1794.[39]

Beddoes's sympathies were both patriotic and reforming, if only cautiously democratic. He was delighted at the acquittal of Thelwall, Horne Tooke, and the others in the treason trials, who, he wrote, 'had fallen upon times when the violence of a sanguinary faction in a foreign country [France] had rendered the very name of reformation odious here.'[40]

Efforts to promote reforms were certainly looked on with little favour; when in February 1795 Beddoes and others wanted to make a petition, the mayor of Bristol refused to take the chair or to lend the Guildhall for the meeting.[41] Poor harvests and rising prices made the state of the poor so alarming that Beddoes delayed advertising in the London papers for the subscription for the Pneumatic Institution, 'partly from the necessity of contributions to keep the poor alive' this hard winter.' He feared, not without cause, that there was a danger 'from a general fermentation among the working class', and hoped that the English aristocracy in their blindness would not suffer the same fate as the French.[42]

The Kingswood colliers near Bristol threatened to rise over the issue of tithes, and the militia stood by. Meanwhile, fears of invasion were mounting. In July 1795, the Home Office drew up a plan, 'In Case of Invasion', insisting that 'every attempt at Sedition or Disturbance shall be repressed with a High Hand.'[43]

[38] PRO MS HO 43.4, pp. 81–82. Emsley, op. cit. (2). Bristol Record Office (BRO), 1793 Box, MS 1 Oct. 1793. PRO MSS HO 42.26, 42.27, 43.4.

[39] PRO MS TS 11, entries for 28 Jan. & 24 April 1794. Much useful light is shed on radical politics in London in the 1790's in *The Autobiography of Francis Place (1771–1854)*, ed. M. Thale, Cambridge, 1972.

[40] Beddoes to Giddy [? Jan./Feb. 1795], MS DG 42/4, CRO.

[41] Beddoes to Giddy, n.d., MS DG 42/36.

[42] Beddoes to T. Wedgwood, March ? 1795, MS W/K. Beddoes to Giddy, 14 March 1795, MS DG 42/30. W. M. Stern, 'The bread crisis in Britain, 1795–6', *Economica*, 1964, *N.S.*, 31, 168–187, 169 gives the monthly rise in the price of wheat in England and Wales.

[43] Mayor of Bristol to Home Office, 13, 17, 18 March 1795; PRO MSS HO 42.29, 42.34, 'Invasion', PRO MS 42.40.

On 29 October, the King in his coach was attacked on the way to the opening of parliament. Seditious propaganda was blamed for the outrage, and a royal proclamation was issued on 4 November to suppress the distribution of seditious writings and the holding of seditious assemblies, which meant any assemblies not first approved by a magistrate. A protest meeting was held in Bristol, where Beddoes 'spoke to the purpose', and a petition was drawn up against the proclamation, that Beddoes saw as an assault on the rights of Englishmen. His pamphlet, *A Word in Defence of the Bill of Rights, against Gagging Bills*, 1795, was a trenchant statement addressed to the citizens of Bristol.

Beddoes's public position was by now prominent; it was at about this time that he, although Bristol's leading natural philosopher, was debarred from membership in the Bristol Philosophical Society because of his 'opinions in regard to religion'[44]—opinions attributed to him but about which he was extremely reticent.

In 1796, Beddoes published *An Essay on the Public Merits of Mr. Pitt*, a slashing attack on his domestic and foreign policies. Maintenance of ignorance about the conditions of the poor was among the failings of Pitt's ministry; so too was its negligence of the usefulness of scientific knowledge.[45] The latter was in contrast to revolutionary France, where science was officially an instrument of national reconstruction.[46] Beddoes followed this work with another, whose title, *Alternatives Compared: or, What shall the Rich do to be Safe?*, London, 1797, was answered by the injunction to get rid of Pitt. While Beddoes published his polemics, the Home Secretary and the mayor of Bristol corresponded about seditious persons in Bristol; fears of invasion following an abortive French landing across the Bristol Channel in Wales; the distribution of seditious papers and posters; rumours of a meeting of democrats in Bristol; gun boats in the Bristol Channel; and treasonable societies of United Irishmen.[47]

Pneumatic Medicine and Pneumatic Chemistry

Amid such fears, Beddoes simultaneously campaigned for freedom of speech, and for funds for his proposed Pneumatic Institution. Inevitably, even the latter campaign was perceived as having its political dimension, arousing support and opposition through political association, as well as scientific debate. Beddoes enjoyed some success in Bristol and Edinburgh, but his main support came from the Wedgwoods in Birmingham, and from the ironmaster William Reynolds in Shropshire. The Lunar Society was

[44] *Star* report of Bristol Guildhall Meetings of 17 & 20 Nov. 1795, reproduced with annotations in *The Collected Works of Samuel Taylor Coleridge*, general ed. K. Coburn: *Lectures 1795 on Politics and Religion*, ed. L. Patton & P. Mann, London & Princeton, 1971, Appendix B1; Appendix B2 reproduces the Petition of the Inhabitants of Bristol Against the Two Bills, & Appendix B3 reproduces Beddoes, *A Word in Defence of the Bill of Rights, Against Gagging Bills*.
[45] Beddoes, *An Essay* . . ., 1796, 13, 155. Coleridge reviewed the work in *The Watchman* of 5 May 1796.
[46] Fayet, op. cit. (1).
[47] PRO MSS 43.8, 43.9, 42.20, 43.10, 43.11, Jan. 1797–Aug. 1799.

most supportive; Matthew Boulton, Erasmus Darwin, Richard Lovell Edgeworth, James Keir, James Watt, and no less than seven of the Wedgwoods subscribed. Professors Joseph Black, Andrew Duncan, and Alexander Munro, the geologists James Hutton and Sir James Hall, and the Royal Medical Society of Edinburgh were listed among the subscribers from Edinburgh in 1795.[48] The Duchess of Devonshire not only subscribed, but sought to persuade Sir Joseph Banks to do so: she failed. Banks had his doubts about the pneumatic practice, and had besides, as James Watt junior guessed, 'seen Beddoes's cloven *Jacobin* foot and it is the order of the day to suppress all *Jacobin innovations* such as his is already called.' James Watt junior was perhaps the most vigorous agent for the institution, and his reputation was more jacobin than Beddoes's.[49]

It is little wonder that the London establishment in science was scarcely represented among Beddoes's supporters. Sufficient funds did, however, accrue, thanks largely to the generosity of Reynolds and the Wedgwoods, and on 21 March 1797, Beddoes announced the opening of a new medical institution, where free treatment was offered to patients suffering from consumption, or from other diseases 'which ordinary means have failed to remove.'[50]

Beddoes was now able to test his theories, and to find just how true his hopes would prove:

> Pneumatic art unfixes Cancer's claw,
> And shields the victim doomed to Phthisis' maw.
> See Palsy dance! his hollow Macies fill,
> And Asthma pace without a puff uphill.'[51]

Neither Beddoes's success in obtaining funds for his institution, nor his optimism about pneumatic chemotherapy, were sufficient to purify him politically. He had been engaged, not altogether competently, in promoting public scientific and medical lectures in Bristol; shortly thereafter plans were afoot for building the 'Bristol Philosophic Theatre'. One plan was for a theatre by College Green, in sight of the cathedral. The Dean and

[48] Beddoes's career was in England, but part of his education had been at Edinburgh under Black. This may suffice to account for the Scottish support for Beddoes's Pneumatic Institution (Levere, op. cit. (5)). One should also note the extent of democratic protest in Edinburgh in the years immediately preceding the treason trials of the 1790's (Goodwin, op. cit. (2)). There were significant parallels between English and Scottish interactions between science and politics. See, e.g., J. B. Morrell, 'The Leslie affair: Careers, Kirk, and politics in Edinburgh in 1805', *Scottish Historical Review*, 1975, *54*, 62–82, and 'Professors Robison and Playfair, and the *Theophobia Gallica*: Natural Philosophy, religion and politics in Edinburgh, 1789–1815', *Notes and Records of the Royal Society of London*, 1971, *26*, 43–63. Beddoes & J. Watt, *Considerations on the Medicinal Use and Production of Factitious Airs*, Bristol, 1795, Part 3, 111–12.

[49] Sir J. Banks to Giorgiana, Duchess of Devonshire, 30 Nov. 1794, British Museum (Natural History) Dawson-Turner Collection, MS vol. 9 ff. 124–5. The correspondence is summarized in W. R. Dawson, *The Banks Letters*, London, 1958, pp. 207–8. J. Watt, Jr. to Ferriar, 19 Dec. 1794, Gibson-Watt MS 20.

[50] *Bristol Gazette*, 21 March 1799.

[51] Quoted in Beddoes & Watt, op. cit. (48), Part 3, ix.

VI

Chapter demurred, however, because of Beddoes's reputation as a jacobin.[52]

Once Beddoes had succeeded in establishing his pneumatic institution, he had his own base for lectures, which were again successful. He planned to offer further public lectures accessible to all by reason of a very low admission charge. Such proposals scarcely assuaged fears of democracy. When a barrel of frogs, intended to serve as experimental animals in Beddoes's Institution, was dropped and burst on Bristol Quay, bystanders were dismayed as hundreds of frogs made their escape; the people of Bristol thought the animals were 'meant as food for the French revolutionaries concealed in the city.'[53]

Beddoes's work in pneumatic medicine derived in part from researches in pneumatic chemistry, that indicated a connection between air, respiration, and life. John Brown, whose work Beddoes had publicized in 1795, had argued that illness arose from an excess or deficiency of excitability in a patient's system; effective therapy would act so as to restore excitability to the level in the system that corresponded to health. In treating respiratory diseases, it seemed possible that one of the newly discovered gases might act appropriately. Beddoes's institution would explore the therapeutic action of different factitious airs in the treatment of consumption and other illnesses.[54]

Oxygen, Priestley's eminently respirable air, promised well. The other principal component in the atmosphere, nitrogen, was reputed to be thoroughly unhealthy; Samuel Latham Mitchill in New York identified one of its derivatives, nitrous oxide, as the principle of contagion. Meanwhile, Priestley, observing that nitric oxide supported combustion but not life, had suggested that a comparative study of oxygen and nitric oxide would contribute to the understanding of respiration.[55]

Here, in brief, was the background to the researches begun at the Pneumatic Institution in 1799. These researches were executed by Humphry Davy, the Institution's newly appointed chemical superintendent, recommended to Beddoes by Davies Giddy.

Davy soon discovered that Mitchill's theory was wrong: he and Priestley independently proved that nitrous oxide could be breathed

[52] Beddoes to Giddy, 1 June 1798, MS DG 42/37, CRO, *Bristol Infirmary Biographical Memoirs*, MS iv, 536–38, BRO. Other information about public lectures involving Beddoes is in ibid., 528–34; Beddoes to Giddy, Oct. 1797, MS DG 42/29, CRO; Beddoes to J. Watt, Jr., 10 April 1798, Birmingham Public Libraries, M IV B. See also Inkster & Weindling, op. cit. (23).

[53] C. C. Abbott, 'The parents of T. L. Beddoes', *Durham University Journal*, 1941–2, N.S., *3*, 159–175, 168.

[54] T. H. Levere, 'Dr. Thomas Beddoes. The Interaction of Pneumatic and Preventive Medicine with Chemistry', *Interdisciplinary Science Reviews*, 1982, *7*, 137–147, elaborates and documents these and the following medical and chemical themes. Beddoes's most extensive Brunonian statement is in J. Brown, *The Elements of Medicine*, new ed., with biographical prefaces, introduction by T. Beddoes, 2 vols., London, 1795.

[55] J. Priestley, *Experiments and Observations relating to various branches of natural philosophy; with a continuation of the observations on air*, Birmingham, 1785, iii, 321. For further details, see Levere, op. cit. (54).

without producing ill effects. Indeed, Davy found that nitrous oxide was exhilarating, and appeared to function as a stimulant. Beddoes accordingly pinned his hoped on nitrous oxide as a cure for consumption.[56]

Davy carried out exhaustive researches on nitrous oxide, but he became highly critical of Brown's theory of excitability, arguing that it was 'probably founded on a false generalization. The modification of diseased action may be . . . specific in different organs.'[57] In that case, diseases in different parts of the body would need different treatments, so that nitrous oxide would fail as a cure for all diseases of deficient sensibility. That did not mean that nitrous oxide could not cure consumption; Beddoes, far more sanguine than Davy, was confident that the gas would overcome consumption and paralysis, and was simply the most beneficial discovery ever made.

Beddoes's advocacy, Davy's skill, and the beneficient effects of nitrous oxide, made breathing the gas a popular pastime in Beddoes's circle. Members of the Lunar Society and West country radicals gathered at the Pneumatic Institution, inhaled the exciting air from Watt's apparatus or from a silk bag, and described their sensations. Southey and Coleridge, Edgeworth and Thomas Wedgwood, and Beddoes himself, were among those who tried the gas.[58]

The Pneumatic Institution was the resort of reformers, democrats, and dissenters. It drew the attention of Canning's satirical and polemical journal, the *Anti-Jacobin Review and Magazine*, which in 1800 published 'the pneumatic revellers. An eclogue',[59] over the motto,

—Trifles, light as air,
Are to the *Theorist* confirmation strong.

There are in the eclogue parodies of the verses of Southey and of the moralising Mrs. Barbauld, and personal attacks on Beddoes and his fellow revellers. But the motivation for the satire emerges as political when 'Dr. B—s' is made to announce:

If the food I create for the palate and paunch
Debar the fond wish for a slice of the haunch,
The gluttons on rich calipashes that revel,
And the soup-meagre cottagers bring to a level . . .
[ALL *Drink* again; and *dance* and *sing*.]
Then hail, happy days; when the high and the low,
All nourish'd alike, from this air—hospitality,

[56] Beddoes did, however, criticize Brown's theory. See e.g. Davy to H. Penneck, 26 Jan. 1799, American Philosophical Society BD 315.1/1969 1821 MS.

[57] *The Collected Works of Sir Humphry Davy, Bart.*, ed. J. Davy, 9 vols., London, 1839, iii, 330. For Davy's attitude towards medicine and a medical career, see M. Neve, 'The Young Humphry Davy: or John Tonkin's Lament', in *Science and the Sons of Genius. Studies on Humphry Davy*, ed. S. Forgan, London, 1980, 1–32.

[58] Beddoes to Boulton, 17 Jan. & 27 June 1799, Birmingham Public Libraries Box B2, 18, 21. F. F. Cartwright, *The English pioneers of anaesthesia (Beddoes, Davy, and Hickman)*, Bristol, 1952. Beddoes, *Notice of some observations made at the Pneumatic Medical Institution*, Bristol, 1799.

[59] *Anti-Jacobin Review and Magazine*, 1800, 6, 111–18.

Shall together with Gas-born benevolence glow,
And prove, that true bliss must arise from equality.
When Britons and Gauls, ye shall revel and sing,
Light, lighter than Gossamers twinkle and glance;
Here, thridding a maze, and there link'd in a ring,
And scarcely touch earth, as ye kindle the dance.

Beddoes, 'enthroned on his airy monster', was ridiculed for hubris in science, for making claims that went well beyond experience or reason. But the eclogue and review were intended to undermine a man who preached equality, friendship for France, and care for 'soup-meagre cottagers'—a phrase that attacks Count Rumford with his plans for feeding the poor with nutritious and inexpensive soup. Rumford, another philanthropist, was also a danger to the established order of society.[60]

Food Riots, the Condition of the Poor, and the Potential of Science
The price of bread rose sharply in 1795 and 1796, enhancing both rural and urban distress. Poor harvests and wartime blockade lay behind the high prices. Shortage of grain was matched by a shortage of beef. On 6 June 1795 there were attacks on butchers' shops in the High Street Market in Bristol.[61]

Beddoes saw the condition of the poor as arising largely from malnutrition and the diseases that followed in its wake; he estimated conservatively but with reasonable accuracy that in London, at least half the children of the poor perished before the age of three.[62] His studies in vegetable and animal chemistry persuaded him as early as 1792 that chemical research, properly supported, would enable mankind to convert the vegetable matter of the hedgerows into wholesome food[63]—hence the satire in the *Golden Age* of 1794:

No more the lazy Ox shall gormandize
And swell with fattening grass his monstrous size;
No more trot round and round the groaning field,
But tons of Beef our loaded thickets yield!

[60] Ibid., 1800, *6*, 424–28. For Rumford's philanthropy, see M. Berman, *Social Change and Scientific Organization. The Royal Institution, 1799–1844*, Ithaca, N.Y., 1978, chap. 1. Rumford's philanthropic concerns are evident in his writings, see e.g. his 'Of Fundamental Principles on which General Establishments for the Relief of the Poor May Be Formed in All Countries', & 'Of Food: and Particularly of Feeding the Poor', *Collected Works of Count Rumford*, ed. Sanford C. Brown, 5 vols., Cambridge, Mass., 1968–70, v, 99–166 & 167–262.
[61] Beddoes to Giddy, MS DG 41/16, CRO. Stern, op. cit. (42). See also the MS Assize of Bread, BRO. J. Latimer, *Annals of Bristol in the 18th Century*, Bristol, 1893, 516. See Thompson, op. cit. (15) for a caution against the simplistic assumption that such attacks were simply reflex responses to shortages and high prices.
[62] BRO, MS (n.d.) 1794, Box 10. Beddoes, *A guide for self preservation, and parental affection; or plain Directions for enabling people to keep themselves and their children Free from several Common Disorders*, Bristol, 1794. Beddoes slightly underestimated infant mortality; for the best modern demographic estimates, see E. A. Wrigley & R. Schofield, *The Population History of England 1541–1871: A Reconstruction*, Cambridge, Mass., 1982. There are useful essays in D. V. Glass & D. E. Eversley, eds, *Population in History. Essays in Historical Demography*, London, 1965; a brief impressionistic account is given by Roy Porter, *English Society in the Eighteenth Century*, Penguin Books, 1982.
[63] Beddoes, *Observations on the nature and cure of calculus, sea scurvy, &c.*, 1792, 109.

> The patient Dairy-Maid no more shall learn
> With tedious toil to whirl the frothy Churn,
> But from the Hedges shall her Dairy fill,
> As pounds of Butter in big drops distill![64]

But the shortage of food was real, and, in so far as it arose from war, man-made. Pitt's policies were blamed—Pitt, the members of whose party and the officers in whose army powdered their wigs with flour that could ill be spared from baking. 'LICENSED TO WEAR HAIR POWDER. PITT FOR EVER!' proclaimed a bandeau that Beddoes distributed.[65]

The port of Bristol received less flour and wheat than formerly. In July 1795 the mayor petitioned the Privy Council to avoid a shortage by sending 'some of the ships laden with Grain expected from the Baltic.' The reply was that 500 quarters[66] of wheat had lately been consigned to the city; to which the mayor replied that it had not come, and in any case represented less than four days supply for a city of 100,000 inhabitants. By the end of the month, the Home Secretary had to write that he could send no more wheat to relieve Bristol.[67]

Instead of direct relief, the Lords of the Privy Council had undertaken to reduce the consumption of wheat in their own families, by using other grain. This was merely symbolic. The master bakers of Bristol complained in September that some flour, instead of being distributed to the bakers for the benefit of the people, was being bought 'by Factors who sold dear to the bakers.' This near monopoly was forcing prices up, and might soon force the bakers to 'stop their Ovens and shut their Shops.'[68]

By October, mobs had become so demanding that dealers would not risk sending wheat and flour to Bristol; and, whereas in July there had been a month's reserve, the Master Wardens and Company of Bakers now estimated that the reserve would only last five days—and then there would be no more baking, 'to the great inconvenience of their Customers (particularly the Poor).'[69] There were protests, for the most part peaceful, in early October; by the end of the month an anonymous letter, signed 'Ego Amor Pax' (sic), warned the mayor that if prices did not fall within a fortnight, the people would sack the corn warehouses and bakers' and butchers' shops. The colliers were prepared to take up arms, '& we have also three regiments of soldiers on our side.' All the government could do that winter was to urge a reduction in the consumption of wheat by the use of coarser bread, and of other grain than wheat.[70]

Early in 1796, Beddoes addressed a printed *Letter to the Right Hon.*

[64] *The Golden Age*, 5–7.
[65] A specimen ribbon is enclosed in Beddoes to Giddy, 16 June 1795, MS DG 42/26.
[66] A quarter of wheat was 8 bushels or 64 gallons; the fifth(!) part of a load (O.E.D.).
[67] BRO 1794 Box 17, 4 July 1795. PRO MSS HO 43/6, 43/7.
[68] PRO MS HO 42.35. BRO 1795 Box 42, 28 Sept. 1795. Again, see Thompson, op. cit. (15) for a gloss on the relations between marketing practices and popular protest.
[69] BRO 1795 Box 42, 16 Oct. 1795.
[70] PRO MS HO 42/36. BRO 1794 Box 18, 11 Dec. 1795, 22 Dec. 1795, 28 Dec. 1795.

William Pitt, on the means of Relieving the present scarcity, and preventing the diseases that arise from meagre food. Britain was consuming more than she produced, and Pitt's economies concerning grain would not pass muster in the school of Adam Smith[71]. Beddoes's solution was to turn to science for help. 'If a moderate contribution could be collected from the rich, and if a few persons acquainted with chemistry and medicine would unite with a few others of leisure and activity to conduct a train of simple experiments', then there was every hope of finding new ways of feeding people nutritiously. Reverting to his old idea, Beddoes suggested that science should seek ways of converting grass to food, with Pitt's vital support. If Pitt would become the patron of scientists, and 'if the recent glories of your administration should become the subject of an epic poem, one book should be devoted to those heroes of chemic and mechanic science that thronged to your standard . . . I hardly doubt of your success in procuring the conversion of fodder into meat for man.'

Beddoes had other suggestions. Could not cattle be reared on potatoes? Rumford's soup kitchens should be multiplied, barley should be saved from the distillers and from the brewers of strong beer, pilchards should be more widely eaten, and opium should be investigated to see how far it could replace food.[72]

Pitt clearly was unconvinced by Beddoes's proposals, to which he did not respond. Beddoes retaliated with his *Essay on the Public Merits of Mr. Pitt* later that spring, and with an essay in *The Watchman* on the 'sufferings and death of a worthy, overworked, and poor labourer.'[73]

Beddoes's imaginative remedies were not tried. Shortages continued throughout the 1790's, and were accompanied by fears of popular risings. The government did manage to bring in foreign shipments of grain in the latter half of the decade, thereby averting real famine; the riots were mostly in reaction to prices when they rose too rapidly, and to marketing practices seen as unjust. But government policies were imperfect; a royal proclamation was issued in 1800 to suppress food riots, and to encourage 'the free Supply of the Markets'—free, that is, from popular regulation.[74]

There was, however, distress among the poor, whose condition Beddoes judged in 1800 to have been worsening 'for many years.' Despairing of the breakthroughs that might come from significant state patronage of science, he turned increasingly to preventive medicine. He saw large numbers of patients at his institution. 'I go on well with the poor,' he announced in 1801, 'especially with their young families—for whom

---

[71] In fact, Pitt was closer to Adam Smith than to the traditional market economy—see Thompson, op. cit. (15).

[72] Beddoes, *Letter . . .*, London, 1796, 4, 11, 13, 16, 18, 21, 27–8.

[73] Beddoes in *The Watchman*, 27 April 1796.

[74] PRO MS HO 42.28. Copies of the royal proclamations issued in the 1790's were sent to Bristol, and may be consulted in many libraries, including PRO and BRO. R. B. Rose, op. cit. (3). J. Stevenson, 'Food riots in England, 1792–1818', in *Popular Protest and Public Order*, ed. R. Quinalt & J. Stevenson, London, 1974, 33–74.

they wd not have thought of applying for advice had I not called for the children to examine—They get more regular every week.' Their regularity was encouraged by Beddoes's policy of charging them a fee at the beginning of a course of treatment, and refunding it only when the course was completed.[75]

He wrote to the Wedgwoods about a public health scheme that would take in all the poor of Bristol. As he moved away from pneumatic experiments to preventive medicine, he changed the name of his foundation to the Institution for the Sick and Drooping Poor. When Beddoes retired from practice in 1807, he estimated that his institution had treated more than ten thousand patients. What he had done in Bristol was but a small sample of what was needed on a national scale. In his last major publication, he made proposals for a national organization for preventive medicine.[76] That he did so in a work addressed to 'the middling and affluent classes' merely recognized the sources of power and patronage in society. Beddoes, distressed by the bloody excesses of the Terror in Paris, was no jacobin revolutionary, but rather a liberal reformer and philanthropist.

Epilogue

Philanthropy in the decade following the French Revolution attracted support and criticism from two opposite directions. On the one hand, philanthropy implied sympathy with the poor, and was accordingly suspect, as tainted with democracy, a disease of French politics. On the other hand, philanthropy, by removing the worst grievances of the poor, could preserve the social order and work against democracy.

Beddoes was open to the same contrary criticisms. He made no secret of his sympathy with the principles that underlay the French Revolution, of his dissatisfaction with the British government's policies, or of his concern for the condition of the poor. He insisted, however, that riots had to be suppressed, and his insistence that the poor had to be humanized was motivated as much by a desire to avoid revolution as it was by philanthropy. He was thus exhibiting attitudes close to those of the members of the Society for Bettering the Condition of the Poor, and of the Board of Agriculture, who provided the support for the Royal Institution of Great Britain in its early days.[77]

Beddoes, like the founders of the Royal Institution, saw science as at once a stabilizing and an enriching force in society, that could, by improving the lot of all classes, avert social catastrophe. But his sympathy for France was disturbing, especially for his contemporaries outside the fold of social and religious dissent,[78] so that his scientific career foundered in

---

[75] Beddoes to [J.] Wedgwood [Nov. 1801], MS W/K.
[76] Ibid., 21 July 1803 & 19 June 1807, MSS W/K. Beddoes, op. cit. (27), iii, 86.
[77] Berman, op.cit. (60), chap. 1.   [78] Cookson, op. cit. (2).

Oxford and was hampered in Bristol, for example by his exclusion from the philosophical society, and by the obstacles he encountered in trying to build a lecture theatre.

His medical career, too, was at best a partial success. Erasmus Darwin and other members of the Lunar Society had confidence in him as a physician, and so, presumably, did the large numbers of 'sick and drooping poor' who attended his Institution. The research programme of the Pneumatic Institution was not, however, successful; nitrous oxide, later widely used as an anaesthetic, did not cure consumption, and Beddoes did not develop Davy's discovery of the analgesic properties of the gas.[79] Beddoes long clung to his belief that pneumatic medicine would work, writing in 1804: 'I have no confidence in my old speculations nor tenderness for them, but I hold it as a fact that the gasses [*sic*] have salutary powers—and that in a high degree.'[80] And yet, at the end of his life, his confidence failed. In his last letter to Davy, written days before his death, he lamented that, 'like one who has scattered abroad the *avena fatua* of knowledge from which neither branch, nor blossom nor fruit has resulted, I require the consolation of a friend.'[81]

His radical friends did not consider him a failure, but admired and supported his endeavours. Coleridge in 1796 had begun his review of Beddoes's *Letter to . . . Pitt* with a precise identification of his mixture of science, politics, and philanthropy:

> To announce a work from the pen of Dr. Beddoes is to inform the benevolent in every city and parish, that they are appointed agents to some new and practicable scheme for increasing the comforts or alleviating the miseries of their fellow-creatures. The present letter is introduced by an attack on our Minister for his criminal improvidence in not having guarded against the contingency of unproductive years; and contrasts his supineness with the successful activity of the enemy. In a strain of keenest irony the Doctor notices the singular fact that, while the French have pressed into their service all the inventive powers of the chemist and mechanic, the sons of science in Britain (almost without an exception) are known to regard the system and measures of the Minister with contempt or abhorence: nor does he omit to glance on the recent practice of electing Members of the Royal Society from the colour of their political opinions.[82]

When Beddoes died in 1808, the enemies of liberalism sighed with undisguised relief.

Acknowledgements
Professors J. Beattie, P. Mazumdar, and L. Stewart, and Mr. Paul Wood

[79] Cartwright, op. cit. (58). R. H. Ellis, ed., *Essays on the first Hundred Years of Anaesthesia*, 3 vols., Edinburgh, 1982. W. D. A. Smith, *Under the Influence. A History of Nitrous Oxide and Oxygen Anaesthesia*, Basingstoke, 1982; E. B. Smith, 'A Note on Humphry Davy's Experiments on the Respiration of Nitrous Oxide', in S. Forgan, op. cit. (57), 231–8.

[80] Beddoes to ?, 27 Nov. 1804, Birmingham Public Libraries, Boulton & Watt papers, M IV B.

[81] Quoted in A. Treneer, *The Mercurial Chemist. A Life of Sir Humphry Davy*, London, 1963, 113.

[82] Coleridge, *Watchman*, 17 March 1796.

VI

204

have made valuable suggestions and criticisms. I am grateful to the staff of the Public Record Office; the Birmingham Reference Library and Mr. J. Warner-Davies (Boulton & Watt papers); the Bristol Record Office and Miss J. Close; the British Museum, Natural History (Dawson-Turner collection); the Cornwall Record Office and Mr. J. C. Edwards (Davies-Giddy papers); Major D. Gibson-Watt (Watt papers); Messrs. Josiah Wedgwood & Sons Ltd., of Barlaston, Stoke-on-Trent, the owners of the Wedgwood papers; Keele University Library, where the Wedgwood papers are deposited, and Dr. I. Fraser; the Osler Library, McGill University, and Dr. P. Teigen; and the Sterling and Beineke Libraries of Yale University, and Miss E. Patterson. Manuscripts are quoted by permission. The research for this paper was supported by a grant from the Social Sciences and Humanities Research Council of Canada.

VII

DR THOMAS BEDDOES AND THE ESTABLISHMENT
OF HIS PNEUMATIC INSTITUTION:
A TALE OF THREE PRESIDENTS

INTRODUCTION

IN 1793 Dr Thomas Beddoes (1760–1808) moved from Oxford to Bristol where he worked to found his Pneumatic Institution. Davies Giddy (Gilbert) (1767–1839), once his protégé and subsequently President of the Royal Society, supported Beddoes in this enterprise. He recommended young Humphry Davy (1778–1829), another future P.R.S., as superintendent of the Institution's Laboratory. Joseph Banks (1743–1820), P.R.S., firmly withheld his name and his purse from the Institution, which became a focus for political and medical controversy. The Watts and Wedgwoods campaigned for Beddoes. This note follows him to Bristol and traces the vicissitudes that he encountered there.

BEDDOES AT OXFORD

Beddoes studied medicine at London and at Edinburgh, where he attended Joseph Black's (1728–1799) lectures, the source of 'any just views I may entertain of chemistry', and 'the most perfect system of practical logic, that is to be found any where' (1). After graduating as M.D. at Oxford, he assumed an uncertain and independent post there, variously styling himself 'chemical reader' and 'professor' (2). He began with his customary optimism, finding at Oxford 'increasing ardour' for the pursuit of chemistry (3). On 23 February 1788 he wrote to Black that he had begun his lectures on chemistry, a subject now perceived as interesting in its own right, and one which in his last course had attracted the largest attendance ever seen at Oxford, 'at least within the memory of man, in any department of knowledge' (4). This enthusiasm was short lived. Beddoes, writing in the spring of 1791 to congratulate Black on his rejection of the phlogiston theory, complained that science, and chemistry in particular, would never flourish much at Oxford 'under the shadow of ecclesiastical & scholastic institutions' (5). Decreasing interest in chemistry and decreasing attendance at his lectures meant a lower income for Beddoes, who was paid by the students in his classes and not by the university (6). Then came the philosophical and political epic poem on *Alexander's Expedition*, in which Beddoes denounced British imperial ambitions in India. His open sympathy for the French Revolution was a further source of friction (7). Politically, intellectually, and financially Oxford had become uncongenial. He left it in 1793, and went to Bristol.

Bristol: the idea of a Pneumatic Institution

Beddoes had a longstanding interest in the chemistry of airs. He was familiar with the works of Scheele and Priestley, and in 1790 had edited and published extracts from John Mayow's writings (8), with reflexions on the chemistry of respiration. At the same time Beddoes's work as a doctor regularly confronted him with consumptive patients. Since airs interacted with the blood in the lungs, and since consumption was a disease of the lungs, Beddoes thought of using pneumatic chemistry to treat consumption. In a public letter to Erasmus Darwin, M.D. (1731–1802), Beddoes explained that he had fixed on Bristol Hotwells to pursue this problem, 'because this resort of invalids seemed more likely than any other situation to furnish patients in all the various gradations of Consumption' (9).

Beddoes, corresponding with Darwin about his practice and proposals, had meanwhile become engaged to Anna , daughter of Richard Lovell Edgeworth (1744–1817). Edgeworth observed of his future son-in-law that he was

> . . . a little fat Democrat of considerable abilities, of great name in the Scientific world as a naturalist and Chemist—good humored good natured— a man of honor & Virtue, enthusiastic & sanguine . . . His manners are not polite—but he is sincere & candid—. . . The Doctor will settle at Clifton and if he will put off his political projects till he has accomplish'd his medical establishment he will succeed and make a fortune—But if he bloweth the trumpet of Sedition the Aristocracy will rather go to hell with Satan than with any democratic Devil (10).

Edgeworth's assessment was shrewd. Beddoes's plans attracted many medical supporters and good financial backing, even while they aroused suspicion and downright hostility because of his unconcealed radicalism. Throughout the 1790s and early 1800s Beddoes was politically prominent, protesting against the Pitt-Grenville 'Gagging Bills' (11), offering unsolicited advice on such questions as *What shall the Rich do to be Safe* (12), and attacking Pitt on social and political grounds. This was enough to ensure widespread opposition to his most apolitical

43

proposals. His attack on the Royal Society for its 'recent practice of electing Members . . . from the colour of their political opinions' (13) scarcely endeared him to Banks, and prejudiced his case. But he remained sanguine.

He was convinced that the application of elastic fluids to the cure of diseases was 'both practicable and promising', that an Institution in Bristol was the best vehicle for such application, and that a medical pneumatic institution capable of receiving twelve patients would fully 'answer the purpose. . . . In two or three years, such an establishment ought to render itself useless, by so far simplifying methods and ascertaining facts, that every practitioner of medicine, at least, may both know how to procure and how to apply the different elastic fluids, supposing they should be found serviceable in any species of disease' (14).

THE CAMPAIGN FOR THE INSTITUTION:
BANKS AND THE LUNAR SOCIETY

On 29 July 1794 he proposed to open and advertise the subscription, hoping that three or four thousand pounds would suffice. The Institution would need apparatus to generate and administer the airs, and a superintendent 'to direct the chemical processes, and to administer airs and medicines under the direction of the Physician' (14).

Darwin and probably Edgeworth had given advice. Now other members of the Lunar Society and Fellows of the Royal Society were to become involved. James Watt's (1736–1819) daughter had died of consumption at an early age. Watt, sharing Beddoes's hopes for pneumatic medicine, corresponded with Beddoes, designing and manufacturing an apparatus for the preparation and administration of different airs (15). Watt selectively solicited subscriptions, from, among others, Black, who agreed to have his name set down for a few guineas. Black was guardedly optimistic, believing that the sum wanted could not fail 'to be very quickly made up in England, if his proposals are at all listened' (16).

So too thought the younger James Watt (1769–1848), who had been in Paris during the Terror, and for whom family, science, and politics combined to favour Beddoes. By 8 November 1794 Watt had obtained subscriptions from William Withering (1741–1799), Matthew Boulton (1728–1809), James Watt, and [Samuel] Galton [b. 1753], while expecting to succeed with James Keir (1735–1820) on the morrow. These were local notables. 'I have no co[g]-noscentical acquaintance in London', he wrote, 'but will try what I can do there by means of the Ignoranti' (17). Nine days later he was claiming the support of all the Birmingham physicians (18).

The Lunar Society and Birmingham physicians were valuable, but if the appeal was to succeed with the Royal Society's Fellows in London and the south, Joseph Banks's name was needed. It was not forthcoming. Georgiana, Duchess of Devonshire, was the first to solicit his support as 'a protector of any effort towards improvement', and was courteously but firmly refused:

> Sir Jo⁵ had once his doubts concerning the propriety of his giving public countenance of any kind [to] a man who has openly avowd opinions utterly inimical in the extreme to the present arrangement of the order of Society in this Country, but the Dutchesses better opinion of the Dʳ has wholly satisfied him on that head; his doubts are now confined to the ... Doctor's project of trying the effect of Gas's upon patients [labouring] under the consequences of pulmonary diseases. On that hand Sir Jo⁵ is of opinion that there is a greater probability of a waste of human health, if not of life, being the consequence of the experiment, than an improvement in the art of Medicine being derived from the results: he cannot therefore with a safe conscience give encouragement, either public or private, to an undertaking in his opinion more likely to be attended with mischievous than [with] beneficial consequences (19).

A second appeal from the Duchess met with an equally firm refusal, buttressed by Banks's unwillingness to apply the results of experiments on animals to human patients (20). No sooner had Sir Joseph concluded this correspondence than he found himself again approached on Dr Beddoes's behalf, this time by James Watt. Banks reiterated his argument, and concluded with the request 'that I may not be pressed any more by the Doctor's friends to do what I have already full & ... formally declined to do' (21). The younger James Watt was incensed at Banks's refusal:

> ... So much for this sapient [luminary] opinion, but *latet anguis in herba*. The fact is I suppose he has seen Beddoe's cloven *Jacobin* foot and it is the order of the day to suppress or oppose all *Jacobin innovations* such as this is already called. It is said to be the same spirit operating in a different way. Even the purity of my father's principles cannot absolve him from the contagion of the connection. I apprehend the scout committee of the Royal Society regard him too as a lost sheep.—If there is opposition which I most sincerely hope for, we shall be sure to do good. All the men of real Chemical knowledge (Cavendish excepted) have given their name (22).

Watt was every bit as sanguine as Beddoes, looking forward to the establishment of the Institution upon a brilliant footing, and inspired by the support of the Duchess of Devonshire and the Marquis of Lansdowne to dream of enlisting the Duke of Bedford—a very likely man—and the rest of the aristocracy after Spring 1795, just as soon as the hurry of Parliament business was over (23).

Beddoes himself was buoyant, writing to Giddy with revolutionary zeal, 'I begin to think of ye pneumatic Inst^n scheme ça ira'. Subscriptions had been advertised in 'a Birmingham newspaper ... Thos Wedgwood writes that he & his father & brothers intend subscribing 50 pounds each; & that they will spare neither pains nor expence in promoting the design' (24). By February 1795 subscriptions were in excess of £500 without any advertisement in the London papers, and in spite of some politically motivated obstruction, Beddoes and his friends had enlisted an impressive roll of subscribers. Later in the year, when an additional three hundred pounds had come in, Beddoes published a list of some 180 subscribers (25). Edinburgh was strongly represented by Joseph Black, Professor Andrew Duncan, Sir James Hall (1761–1832), James Hutton (1726–1797), Professor Alexander Monro (1733–1817), the Royal Medical Society, and numerous surgeons and physicians. Then came the Midlands, with the Lunar Society's members comprehensively present. There were many Bristol subscribers, but few from London, Astley Cooper, F.R.S. (1768–1844) being the only eminent London surgeon. Banks and the bulk of the London establishment of the Royal Society were unsurprisingly but notably absent, and the sum subscribed was still far short of what was needed.

1796 saw Beddoes frustrated for lack of funds, though by no means despairing. Davies Giddy had been the recipient of his hopes since they had shared an enthusiasm for chemistry and geology at Oxford. Now Beddoes wrote to him once more with customary optimism:

> You will perhaps wonder to hear that the company at Clifton has been at least thrice as numerous as the last 2 years—But I imagine this has been the most unhealthy season which this country has experienced for years—

This surely must have encouraged Beddoes. Moreover,

> I begin to see a little distinctly the powers of elastic fluids in medicine ... Nothing but the peculiar circumstances of the country wḍ now prevent the establishment of research so often mentioned—We have got a tolerable sum—I suppose £1300 or 1400—& are (or rather wḍ be) likely to get much more. The distress however now felt by ministry for money must soon extend to private life: It is I believe very pressing ... —We shall be obliged to buy peace, shall we not? ... (26).

Two years later, loss of trade appeared to be driving the citizens of Bristol to take up philosophy, and Beddoes intended to set the Pneumatic Institution on foot 'in winter, if the times permit' (27). He planned to use the profits from the first two volumes of his forthcoming *Contributions to physical and medical knowledge* ... to supplement the still barely adequate subscription to the Institution (28). Giddy recommended Humphry Davy, then obscure, as chemical superintendent, and Davy joined Beddoes's establishment in October 1798. The funds were by then almost adequate to Beddoes's purpose, and negotiations were set on foot for a house in Dowry Square (29).

The house was bought, and on the first day of the following spring, when the laboratory was ready, the *Bristol Gazette* bore this announcement:

NEW MEDICAL INSTITUTION

This Institution is fixed at the upper end of *Dowry Square, Hotwells,* corner house. It is intended among other purposes for treating diseases, hitherto found incurable, upon a new plan. Among the Subscribers are almost all the Medical Professors at *Edinburgh,* and a large portion of the Physicians in England, who have done anything to improve the practice of their art.

At present it is only ready for out patients, and the attendance of persons in Consumption, Asthma, Palsy, Dropsy, obstinate Venereal Complaints, Scrophula or King's Evil, and other Diseases, which ordinary means have failed to remove, is desired.

Patients will be treated gratis.

The application of persons in confirmed Consumption is principally wished at present; and though the disease has heretofore been deemed hopeless, *it is confidently expected that a considerable portion of such cases will be permanently cured.*

It has been perfectly ascertained by experience, that none of the methods to be pursued are hazardous or painful.

Attendance will be given from Eleven till One o'clock, by THOMAS BEDDOES, or HUMPHRY DAVY.

Subscriptions for the support of this Institution, received by JOHN SAVERY, Esq.; Narrow Wine-Street, Bristol.

CONCLUSION

The new Institution was active and, within its social sphere, fashionable. Robert Southey, S. T. Coleridge, the younger Wedgwoods, and members of the Edgeworth family were among those who sampled the delights of inspiring nitrous oxide under Davy's superintendence (31). The presence of so many known radicals (Coleridge had even been investigated by a government agent) ensured hostile publicity for the Institution. *The Anti-Jacobin Review and Magazine* dissected Beddoes's *Notice* ... (31) and published 'The Pneumatic Revellers. An Eclogue' under the motto:

Trifles, light as air,
Are to the *Theorist* confirmation strong (32).

The 'Eclogue' clearly and disapprovingly connected Beddoes's medical and pneumatic theories with his politics—legitimately so, since Beddoes associated social and material conditions with the causes of sickness (33). The poor attended the Institution—three hundred patients came in one month in the summer of 1802, and John King (1766–1846), physiological superintendent, treated 678 cases from 1 January to 18 April of that year (34).

The Institution's éclat and retrospective fame diminished after Davy's removal to the Royal Institution, although it is perhaps an overstatement to claim, as the *Dictionary of National Biography* does, that Beddoes's Institution was 'virtually given up' thereafter (35). As late as 1804, he was still sanguine:

I am about to commence a vigorous prosecution of the effect of airs in medicine, being more favourably circumstanced than ever (36).

Dr Thomas Beddoes did not give up.

ACKNOWLEDGMENTS

The work for this paper was supported by a Killam Senior research Scholarship. Correspondence is reproduced by kind permission of Major D. Gibson-Watt and the Trustees of the British Museum (Natural History).

NOTES

(1) T. Beddoes to J. Black, Oxford, 23 Feb. 1788. Black MSS, Edinburgh University Library.
(2) F. W. Gibbs & W. A. Smeaton, 'Thomas Beddoes at Oxford', *Ambix*, **9**, 47–49 (1961). Beddoes's self-bestowed titles appear in his *A Memorial concerning the state of the Bodleian Library and the conduct of the principal librarian. Addressed to the Curators of that Library, by the Chemical Reader*. Oxford, 1787, and in his *A letter to Erasmus Darwin, M.D. on a new method of treating pulmonary consumption, and some other Diseases hitherto found Incurable*. Bristol, 1793, p. 29. Davies Giddy was one of Beddoes's first pupils at Oxford—see F. F. Cartwright, *The English pioneers of anaesthesia (Beddoes, Davy, and Hickman)*. Bristol, Wright, 1952, p. 53.
(3) Beddoes to Black, London, 6 Nov. 1797. Black MSS, loc. cit.

(4) See note (1).

(5) Beddoes to Black, Oxford, 15 April 1791. Black MSS, loc. cit.

(6) See Gibbs & Smeaton, note (2).

(7) C. A. Weber, *Bristols Bedeutung für die englische Romantik und die deutsch-englischen Beziehungen*. Halle (Saale), 1935, p. 92.

(8) T. Beddoes, *Chemical Experiments and Opinions extracted from a Work Published in the Last Century*. Oxford, 1790.

(9) *A Letter to Erasmus Darwin* . . . (note (2) above), p. 40.

(10) Postscript by R. L. Edgeworth to letter from Maria Edgeworth to Mrs. R. Clifton, 21 July 1793. Edgeworth MSS. on loan to Bodleian Library, Oxford; published in Marilyn Butler, *Maria Edgeworth. A literary biography*. Oxford, 1972, p. 110.

(11) John Colmer, *Coleridge, Critic of Society*. Oxford, 1959; reprinted 1967, p. 47n.

(12) T. Beddoes, *Alternatives Compared: or, What shall the Rich do to be Safe*. London, 1797. (Dr W. Farrar told me of a copy in Manchester Central Reference Library.)

(13) S. T. Coleridge, *The Watchman*, 1796, ed. L. Patton. Princeton, 1970, p. 100. Beddoes was regularly reviewed by and contributed to *The Watchman*.

(14) T. Beddoes, *A proposal towards the improvement of Medicine*. Bristol, 1794.

(15) James Patrick Muirhead, *The Life of James Watt, with selections from his correspondence*. London, 1859, pp. 416–417.

(16) Cited by James Watt to T. Beddoes, Birmingham, 31 Oct. 1794. Gibson Watt (GW) MSS 184.

(17) James Watt jr. to Beddoes, Soho, 8 Nov. 1794. GW MSS 10^r.

(18) *Ibid.*, 17 Nov. 1794. GW MSS 11. For the Birmingham background, see R. E. Schofield, *The Lunar Society of Birmingham*. Oxford, 1693.

(19) Banks to G. Devonshire, 30 Nov. 1794. British Museum (Natural History) Dawson-Turner Collection (DTC) f. 125.

(20) DTC ff. 126–129.

(21) DTC ff. 133–134.

(22) J. Watt jr. to Ferriar, 19 Dec. 1794. GW MSS 20.

(23) J. Watt jr. to Beddoes, 2 Jan. 1795. GW MSS 22^v.

(24) Beddoes to Giddy, [Jan. or Feb. 1795]. Cornwall Record Office, MS DG. 42. According to J. E. Stock, *Memoirs of the Life of Thomas Beddoes, M.D.* . . . ., London & Bristol, 1811 p. 154, Thomas Wedgwood subscribed £1000.

(25) Beddoes to Giddy, 12 Feb. 1795, Cornwall R. O., MS DG. 42. The list of subscribers is in T. Beddoes and J. Watt, *Considerations on the Medicinal Use and Production of Factitiou Airs*, Part 3. Bristol, 1795, pp. 111–112.

(26) Beddoes to Giddy, 31 July 1796. Cornwall R. O., MS DG. 42. A. C. Todd, *Beyond the Blaze* Truro, 1967, Part I, gives valuable background here.

(27) *Ibid.*, Beddoes to Giddy, 21 March 1798.

(28) Advertisement dated 29 Aug. 1798 (copy in Bristol Public Library). *Contributions* . . appeared in 1799.

(29) J. A. Paris, *The Life of Sir Humphry Davy, Bart. Ll.D.* . . . ., 2 vols. London, 1831. Vol. ↓ pp. 52–66.

(30) Bristol Gazette, 21 March 1799. An over-enthusiastic account of the significance of th Institution is A. H. Miller, 'The Pneumatic Institution of Thomas Beddoes at Clifton 1798', *Ann. Med. Hist.*, **3**, 253–260 (1931).

(31) T. Beddoes, *Notice of some observations made at the Medical Pneumatic Institution*. Bristol, 1799, pp. 1–16, 40; reviewed in *The Anti-Jacobin Review and Magazine*, **6**, 424–428, (1800).

(32) *Anti-Jacobin . . .*, **6**, 111–118, (1800).

(33) See, e.g., T. Beddoes, *Hygeia: or Essays moral and medical on the causes affecting the personal state of our middling and affluent classes*, 3 vols. Bristol, 1802–1803.

(34) Anna Maria Beddoes to D. Giddy, Aug. 1802. Cornwall R.O., MS. DG. 89. *Hygeia* (note (33)), Vol. 2, preceding 'Essay seventh'.

(35) Davy's appointment to the R.I. is described in H. Hartley, *Humphry Davy*. London, 1966. The *D.N.B.'s* article on Beddoes is by Richard Garnett.

(36) Letter from Beddoes, 19 April 1804. British Library Add. MS. 18–204, f. 55.

VIII

Dr. Thomas Beddoes: The Interaction of Pneumatic and Preventive Medicine with Chemistry

Summary

Chemistry has often been pressed into the service of medicine. In the years following Lavoisier's chemical revolution, the attention of chemists focused upon gases. Thomas Beddoes (1760-1808) developed a research program that explored the therapeutic effects of different gases in the treatment of tuberculosis and other diseases. Beddoes was inspired by the discoveries of Joseph Priestley, employed young Humphry Davy as an assistant in his researches, received advice and encouragement from Erasmus Darwin, and used pneumatic apparatus designed by James Watt. He also engaged in efforts directed at social reform and at reforms in public health, being especially concerned with the condition of the poor. His Pneumatic Institution in Bristol was at one and the same time a research centre and a health clinic. This paper explores the interaction between chemistry and medicine in Beddoes' career, within a context of scientific and social ferment.

Chemistry in the eighteenth century was often taught as part of the medical curriculum in universities, from Herman Boerhaave at Leiden at the beginning of the century to Joseph Black at Edinburgh at its close. At the same time, chemistry was emerging as an autonomous discipline, so that relations between medicine and chemistry changed greatly in the course of the century.

Changes in science were matched by changes in society. The Enlightenment had a vision of the improvement of society by science, which was to be organized and used for the benefit of mankind. This vision had medical and chemical aspects, with application to public health and to industry. Ventilation of prisons, hospitals, factories and ships, the connection between dirt, malnutrition and illness, and the need for the collection and dissemination of medical data, were topics of wide concern in the latter half of the century. In Britain, reforms in hygiene and health in these years were most prominent in the army and navy, although there were calls for action in society as a whole, with limited effect in the generations before Chadwick.[1]

Thomas Beddoes, the subject of this review, was trained in medicine, skilled in chemistry, and a strong proponent of medical and social reform. He conceived and founded the Pneumatic Institution of Bristol, home of the first systematic practice of pneumatic medicine — that is, medicine based upon the chemistry of gases — a new and exciting prospect in the years around Lavoisier's chemical revolution. There was a significant interaction of medicine and pneumatic chemistry in the work of Beddoes and of his protégé, Humphry Davy, whose first major researches were carried out in Beddoes' Institution. The lack of necessary provisions for public health was a spur to chemical researches that involved not only Beddoes and Davy, but also members of the Lunar Society of Birmingham, including Erasmus Darwin and James Watt.

PNEUMATIC CHEMISTRY AT OXFORD

Beddoes studied medicine at London and then at Edinburgh, where the University's matriculation records show him as registered from 1780 to 1782, and from 1784 to 1786. While there, he attended Joseph Black's lectures, later styling them the source of "any just views I may entertain of chemistry".[2] Black was to be Beddoes' model. When Beddoes planned to write a new manual of chemistry, he requested and received permission to dedicate it to Black. He then graduated as M.D. at Oxford, travelled in France, returned to Oxford, and was licensed to give chemical lectures there.[3]

Beddoes' lectures were initially well attended. In 1792 came the prospect of a regius chair in chemistry, which the vice-chancellor privately offered to Beddoes.[4] Medicine had provided a sure path to a professional career in chemistry. The timing could not have been better, for Lavoisier's new theory was hotly debated, and chemistry seemed at once the most exciting and most useful of the sciences, at least to its practitioners. Whatever position one took in the debate between the phlogistonists and the neologues, there was no denying the significance of achievements in pneumatic chemistry. Of all those achievements, Black's were uniquely well regarded on both sides of the Channel.

Black had moved from medicine, via pneumatic chemistry and his classic work on fixed air and magnesia alba,[5] to a chair in chemistry. Now Beddoes, his protégé, seemed likely to follow the same path. He had travelled in France, visiting leading French chemists.[6] He was active in the debates about the chemical revolution, a contributor to pneumatic chemistry, and one alert to its connections with medicine. In 1790 he brought out a volume of *Chemical Experiments and Opinions extracted from a Work Published in the Last Century*, celebrating the writings of John Mayow, notably his *Tractatus Quinque* (Oxford, 1754). Mayow had given a chemical history of nitre and nitro-aerial spirit, and had investigated the role of the latter in respiration and combustion. Here, clearly, was a contender for recognition in the pneumatic chemistry stakes, and one who had perceived the physiological importance of chemistry.

Beddoes' own chemical opinions moved rapidly during his years at Oxford. These years saw the publication of Lavoisier's manifesto of the chemical revolution, his *Traité élémentaire de chimie* (2 vols., Paris, 1789). By the mid-1790s, most chemists had come to accept Lavoisier's theory that combustion was combination with oxygen, and had rejected the phlogiston theory, according to which combustion was a process in which a burning substance lost phlogiston, the principle of combustibility.

Joseph Priestley was the staunchest defender of the old theory. He wrote many essays and books supporting the phlogiston theory, from the 1770s, when it was generally received, until the 1800s, when scarcely anyone else still held to the theory; he published *The Doctrine of Phlogiston established and that of the Composition of Water refuted* in Northumberland, Pennsylvania, in 1800, and brought out a second edition in 1803. Priestley's main contributions to chemistry had been in the field of gas chemistry, to which Black also had contributed. Ironically, Priestley's own discoveries contributed to the overthrow of the theory that he defended.

When Beddoes arrived in Oxford, he was convinced that discoveries in pneumatic chemistry, Black's among them, had destroyed the old arrangement, and might lead one to "despair altogether of the theory of Chemistry. But the light which has been afforded by the recent discoveries of Mr. Cavendish, Mr. Lavoisier, Berthollet and some others, seems to me to suggest better hopes, except to those who have had the folly or the misfortune to fix their [opinions] inalterably." That was never Beddoes' misfortune, and he proposed the rejection of phlogiston or any other principle supposed to be common to all inflammable bodies; he also agreed that there should be no separate class of elastic fluids, for the gaseous state depended upon combination with fire.[7]

Two years later, in 1789, Beddoes was inclined to return to the old theory, informing Black that "Dr. Priestly (*sic*) seems totally to have overthrown the antiphlogist[ic] theory – I am anxious to hear what the French chemists have to say on the other side – I have seen some of their private objections to [Dr.] Priestly's inferences, but they are totally insignificant – Still however we owe much to Mr. Lavoisier for having taught us the combination of pure air."[8] By 1789, following the publication of Lavoisier's *Traité* in the same year, Beddoes had again swung away from "the old chemical theory", and wrote to congratulate Black for having renounced it too.[9]

Whatever his theoretical enthusiasms, Beddoes' remained very interested in the practice of pneumatic chemistry. The "very valuable assortment of chemical apparatus" that he had assembled at Oxford included "a gazometer very much improved upon Mr. Lavoisier's"; and he proudly claimed that he could show "any and every experiment" in Lavoisier's *Elements of Chemistry*. Much of his prize equipment had been built by James Sadler, the first Englishman to make a balloon ascent, whom Beddoes described as a pastry cook and "a perfect prodigy in mechanics". Sadler had made, among other items, "an airpump which exhausts perfectly – and of course is constructed on principles totally new – [and] a balance which I have seen turn with 1/100 of a grain when loaded with a pound at each arm – I have all these instruments in the Elaboratory...."[10]

But in spite of these good things — a well-equipped laboratory, the lively debates about contemporary chemistry, especially pneumatic chemistry, and its promising potential for medicine — Oxford became increasingly uncomfortable for Beddoes, who had supported the French Revolution and advocated democratic policies in England. Pressure was brought to bear by the Home Office, and the regius chair in chemistry was lost to Beddoes and to the university. [11]

PNEUMATIC MEDICINE AT BRISTOL

Once Beddoes had been frustrated in his chemical career at Oxford he was virtually forced back into medicine by his professional training and by the dearth of direct openings in chemistry. Pneumatic medicine was his choice. In his book on Mayow, he had looked forward to the time when chemistry would confer upon medicine "the same power ... over living, as is at present exercised over some inanimate bodies; and ... not only the care and prevention of diseases, but the art of protracting the fairest season of life and rendering health more vigorous, will one day ... realize half the dream of Alchemy".[12] Beddoes had shared the widespread interest in the eminently respirable air, oxygen, discovered in 1774 by Priestley and earlier by Scheele. He even edited a translation of Scheele's chemical essays. [13] He had become acquainted with Dr. Edmund Goodwyn, whose work on the function of respiration he considered to be "most masterly". Goodwyn had explored the connection of life with respiration, examining the effects on animals of asphyxiation, strangulation and drowning.[14]

At Edinburgh, Beddoes "made or witnessed many experiments upon animals", to elucidate the action of air on the blood on its passage through the lungs. He also reflected upon Lavoisier's view that atmospheric air should be understood not only as "an elastic fluid capable of decomposition", but also "as a chemical agent capable of taking up, in the way of solution, miasmata of various kinds".[15] Malaria and gaol fever were just two of the diseases that were believed to be spread by "miasmata". The emphasis upon ventilation in public health reforms of the 18th century arose directly from such views of the role of the air in transmitting disease. Sir John Pringle's *Observations on the Diseases of the Army* (London, 1752), John Heysham's *An Account of Jail Fever or Typhus Carcerum as it Appeared at Carlisle in the Year 1781* (1782), James Currie's *Medical Reports* (Liverpool, 1797) and John Haygarth's *A Letter to Dr. Percival on the Prevention of Infectious Fever* (1801), all discussed ventilation as a factor in reducing the incidence of disease.

There was, in short, a connection between air, respiration and life, both in health and sickness. Consumption was unquestionably the most devastating respiratory disease in Britain in the 1790s. Beddoes examined bills of mortality and found, for the sample of some 20,000 burials that he scrutinized, that approximately 5,000 a year were accounted for by consumption, as against approximately 2,000 by fevers and, on average, somewhat less than 2,000 a year by smallpox. Deaths from consumption were consistently high, while those from fevers and smallpox fluctuated considerably.[16] Consumption was clearly an urgent problem for physicians. Since airs interacted with the blood in the lungs, and since consumption was a disease of the lungs, Beddoes thought of using pneumatic medicine to treat it. Whereas the connection between respiration and health was widely recognized, Beddoes seems to have been a pioneer, and initially a lone one, in giving this connection a chemical interpretation, and in seeing in pneumatic chemistry a key to health. He tells us that "from the moment I first became acquainted with the effects of pregnancy in suspending the progress of Consumption, I conceived hopes that by combining this fact with the discoveries daily made in pneumatic chemistry, a successful method of treating this disease, in some of its stages at least, might be devised".[17]

He fixed on Bristol Hotwell to pursue his investigations, because, as he explained in a public letter to Erasmus Darwin "this resort of invalids seemed more likely than any other situation to furnish patients in all the various gradations of Consumption".[18] He might also have mentioned that political opposition made a career within the establishment impossible, so that London was closed to him; that Bristol was a thriving medical centre with a lively intellectual and political culture;[19] and that the Bristol Infirmary was, as a source of patients and data, the next best thing to London hospitals.[20]

The Hotwell had provided a fashionable supplement to Bath Spa during the 18th century. Analyses and accounts of the virtues of the Bristol waters had appeared throughout the century.[21] In 1779, Joseph Priestley published a letter "on the Air extracted from the Water of the Hot-well".[22] In 1793, when Beddoes removed to Bristol, Dr. John Nott published yet another account of the Hotwell, claiming that its waters were indubitably efficacious in the treatment of phthisis. Beddoes' timing seemed good.[23]

He began confidently, writing in June 1793 that he had prosecuted his ideas on consumption: "I have found them to answer so well that I (with three other friends) have taken an house and set up an air apparatus here - I have scarce been here a fortnight at a time but have had a few [patients]. ... I have it in contemplation to undertake several incurable diseases besides consumption."[24]

He hoped that pneumatic medicine would overcome a range of desperate complaints. Beddoes believed, for example, that scurvy offered "an application of the pneumatic chemistry, nearly as direct and beautiful as the phaenomena of respiration". He had long supposed that scurvy arose from "a gradual abstraction of oxygene from the whole system". It should therefore be curable by the administration of oxygen-enriched air; and so, by a similar argument, should herpes.[25]

Beddoes in 1793 believed that scurvy and many other diseases arose from a deficiency of vital energy. His views were here broadly in accordance with Brunonian physiology, named after its inventor, John Brown, a pupil of Cullen. Brown postulated that every living being was endowed with its portion of excitability, the principle on which life depended. Excitability, located in the medullary portion of the nerves, had to be maintained in proportion to the stimuli acting on the system, or illness, even death, would ensue. Thus the treatment of disease that he advocated was directed towards adjusting stimuli so as to restore its proper balance with excitability in the patient, whether by augmenting or diminishing it. [26]

In the early 1790s, Beddoes saw oxygen as directly affecting excitability, and asked Black and his fellow physicians: "Supposing the proportion of ingredients in the atmosphere be that best adapted to the average state of health, is it not likely that there may be certain deviations from this state, where that fluid body contains too little vital air, and other deviations, where it contains too much?"[27] Beddoes, although often critical of Brunonian physic for being too general to be helpful in treating different specific diseases,[28] was here using it as a model for pneumatic therapy.

THE NEED FOR AN INSTITUTION

Beddoes was convinced that the use of oxygen and other elastic fluids for the cure of diseases was "both practicable and promising", that an Institution in Bristol offered the best prospects for exploring pneumatic medicine, and that a medical pneumatic institution capable of receiving twelve patients would fully "answer the purpose". He advertised his plans on 29 July 1794, proposing to open a subscription for three or four thousand pound sterling. The Institution would need apparatus to generate and administer the airs, and a superintendent "to direct the chemical processes, and to administer airs and medicines under the direction of the physician".[29]

The campaign for the Institution[30] quickly became embroiled in politics, for Beddoes did not leave his democratic and radical concerns behind when he left Oxford. The medical community was effectively polarized, with the London establishment opposing Beddoes, while extensive support came from Edinburgh and the Midlands. Particularly generous support came from the Wedgwoods; Thomas Wedgwood was in these years the constant recipient of Beddoes' enthusiasms: "This [pneumatic] practice however continues universally successful in cancers and foul ulcers -- That the experience of others confirms by obs[ns]. with regard to phthisis pulm." was shown by reports from the Birmingham Dispensary.[31]

By December 1794, Beddoes was able to refer to "various trials of *factitious airs* in the Bath and Manchester hospitals as well as in private practice", all promising cures. "Experiments upon animals in a state of health corroborate these facts and suggest the application of the same practice to the distemper in dogs and the murrain in cattle."[32] Joseph Banks, firmly declining to have anything to do with Beddoes' proposals, wondered how experiments upon healthy animals could bear upon the treatment of consumptive humans. All in all, he thought Beddoes' experiments more likely to lead to "a waste of human health" than to any improvement in the art of medicine.[33]

Physicians outside London were, however, more inclined to give factitious airs a trial. On 17 March 1795, Beddoes reported to Tom Wedgwood that a patient nearing the last stages of consumption had been cured at the Birmingham dispensary. This success had provided so persuasive an argument for the practice that "a ward in the Birm: hospital is to be appropriated this spring to pneumatic medicine".[34]

Beddoes and other physicians were by now exploring the use of different gases for different diseases. In the spring of 1795 Beddoes discussed oxygen for chlorosis, hydrogen for phthisis, hydrocarbonate for the same disease, and a mixture of hydrogen and atmospheric air for tightness of the chest.[35] In June he expressed his satisfaction that Erasmus Darwin had prescribed oxygen for Mrs. Josiah Wedgwood: "It is certainly a specific stimulus to the arterial system and Mrs. J. W.'s arterial system was palpably too languid."[36]

If only pneumatic medicine could be rendered fashionable, it would prosper. The Duke and Duchess of Devonshire and the Earl of Dartmouth had already subscribed.[37] Now Beddoes proposed printing a pamphlet "on elegant paper", with a vignette of a patient inhaling from a bag.[38] The pamphlet was never printed, nor did the world of fashion succumb to Beddoes' blandishments. But if the practice did not conquer fashion, it at least became practicable, thanks to James Watt's breathing apparatus.[39] This was essentially a simplified version of Lavoisier's gasometer for containing gases and regulating their flow, connected by a tube to a mouthpiece or mask. In 1796 Watt produced "an account of a simplified [apparatus], which will soon be manufactured and will suit a kitchen or parlour common fire". The simplified apparatus (see Fig. 1) consisted of one chamber containing a furnace for the synthesis of gases, connected by a tube or pipe to a second chamber in which gases could be stored, and from which they could be dispensed to patients.[40]

Techniques for administering the airs were now available, funds for the Institution continued to come in, and Beddoes enlarged his aims: "My plan is to assemble everything mechanics, chemistry and art in general can supply for the relief of the sick." [41] 1796 was a splendid year: "The resort hither is beyond all example; and the harvest for Death and the Doctors has been plentiful accordingly."[42] 1797 saw Beddoes hopefully "arrived at a method of *preventing*

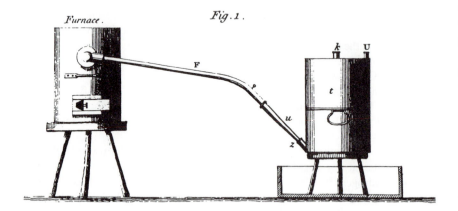

Figure 1. James Watt's simplified apparatus for the preparation and storage of gases, published in 1796. On the left is the furnace containing the vessel in which the required gas is prepared. On the right the gasometer, t, which is initially full of water, with the outlets z closed with a cork. When the gas is produced in a steady stream, outlets k and U are closed, z is opened, and the pipe u inserted into z; the water displaced by the inflowing gas overflows from z into the container below the gasometer. When the gasometer is full, as shown in the illustration, gas will emerge at z which is then closed again. To obtain the gas, outlet k is connected to a tube for the patient, and water is poured into the opening U.

consumption in the majority of cases".[43] And two years later, Beddoes announced the opening of his medical institution: "It is intended among other purposes for treating diseases, hitherto found incurable, upon a new plan. ... At present it is only ready for out patients, and the attendance of persons in Consumption, Asthma, Palsy, Dropsy, obstinate Venereal Complaints, Scrophula or King's Evil, and other Diseases, which ordinary means have failed to remove, is desired. ... The application of persons in confirmed Consumption is principally wished at present; and ... *it is confidently expected that a considerable portion of such cases will be permanently cured.*"[44]

HUMPHRY DAVY, NITROUS OXIDE AND BRUNONIAN PHYSIC

Davy's appointment as chemical superintendent of the Institution is well known; he may be said to have been Beddoes' greatest discovery, as Faraday was Davy's. Beddoes required that his chemical assistant be experienced and "conversant with whatever illustrates the philosophy of chemistry as we find it in Lavoisier". Davy, then young and untried, was far from an obvious choice. Another contender for the post was Thomas Thomson, recommended through Robison to Watt as "one of the most accomplished Chemists" in Scotland'.[45]

Thomson, indeed, went on to become regius professor of chemistry in Glasgow. Besides Davy, the Institution soon acquired the services of John King, a surgeon recommended to Beddoes by John Abernethy of St. Bartholomew's Hospital, London. King had been born in Switzerland as Nicholas Johann Koenig, had studied anatomy and physiology in London, and had then moved to Bristol where, like Beddoes, he married one of the Edgeworth sisters. He remained in Bristol until his death in 1846, and the Pneumatic Institution, transformed into a straightforward medical institution, passed largely into his hands after Beddoes' withdrawal in the early 1800s.[46]

Meanwhile, however, the newly founded Institution was a centre for research in pneumatic medicine and chemistry. Shortly after his arrival in Bristol, Davy wrote to Henry Penneck, a friend in Penzance. First came a list of chemical apparatus for the laboratory, including a double-necked receiver, cylinders, tubes, receivers, a retort and a blow-pipe — a more limited collection than Beddoes had enjoyed in Oxford. Much of the apparatus was supplied by Matthew Boulton, while other pieces came from the Wedgwoods. For Davy, the laboratory of the Pneumatic Institution was "superb", and he looked forward to commencing "experiments on pneumatic medicine".

The mixture of chemistry and medicine, and the interaction of the Pneumatic Institution with the hospitals and the general public, emerge vividly in Davy's letter:

VIII

Figure 2. This caricature by James Gillray of a lecture at the Royal Institution, London, was published on 23 May 1802. It depicts Dr. Thomas Garnett (1766-1802) lecturing to a fashionable audience, with Humphry Davy acting as lecture assistant. Garnett is administering the exhilarating air – with unfortunate results – to Sir John Hippesley, whose nostrils he pinches between finger and thumb. Davy stands by with a pair of bellows, belching forth gas. On the lecture bench, among other things, are bottles of oxygen and hydrogen and a collapsed bladder. Benjamin Thompson, Count Rumford (1753-1814) stands at one side. An open book belonging to one of the audience is inscribed, "Hints on the nature of Air requir'd for the new French Diving Boat". The drawing is entitled "Scientific Researches! - New Discoveries in PNEUMATICKS! – or – an Experimental Lecture on the Powers of Air". (John Read, *Humour and Humanism in Chemistry*, G. Bell, London, 1947; the caricature is reproduced here by kind permission of a private collector to whom the author extends his thanks.)

Bowles and Smith [local surgeons] are lecturing on Anatomy in Bristol, we have had two or three dissections – From my intimacy with Bowles, I am enabled to attend the Hospital whenever I please and to examine the patients. I likewise see the greater number of Dr. Beddoes private patients so that I have greater opportunities for studying Anatomy and Medicine here, than I could [possibly] have had either at London or Edinburgh. .

We had intended to lecture on Chemistry in March but ... the Theatre is not yet erected.... Whenever we lecture we are certain of a numerous class.... Dr. Beddoes will offer [a] chemical course, probably lecture on medicine and Physiology. Both Browns and Darwins Theories seem to be daily losing ground. I have had a number of conversations with Dr. Beddoes on the subject. Dr. Beddoes himself seems to have given up altogether Brown's theory - I consider Dr. Beddoes is the most liberal candid and philosophic [physician] of the age, as He has sufficient [...] to give up his own theories, as well as those He has adopted whenever they appear contradictory to facts.[47]

Beddoes deserved this tribute to his open-mindedness; but he seems to have been curiously stubborn about Brown's theory, preserving it in his practice of medicine while subjecting it to theoretical criticism. He continued to seek ways of combining pneumatic chemistry with Brunonian physiology. His ambivalence is reflected in the introduction and notes he provided in 1795 to a new edition of Brown's *Elements of Medicine*, as a service to Brown's widow .[48]

We have seen that Beddoes early entertained hopes for treatment using oxygen or vital air. Nitrogen, the other principal constituent of the atmosphere, was termed azote in the new French nomenclature, indicating that it would not support life. This idea had been taken up by Samuel Latham Mitchill, Professor of Chemistry, Natural History and Agriculture at New York, the first American advocate of Lavoisier's chemistry, and a former pupil of Black. He identified nitrous oxide as the principle of contagion.[49] Different

contagions and poisons may consist of the same materials, varying but in their proportions, or in some unimportant circumstance, and ... the virus of syphilis, small-pox, and measles, and of the spider, rattlesnake, and other venomous creatures, as being all of animal production, may consist in the main of azote and oxygene, combined perhaps with some other ingredient; and there is high probability that marsh miasmata will be found little else than a similar compound. The ichor of cancer and other corroding ulcers is very probably pretty much the same thing. The disease of rabid animals, and the dread of water, and other miserable symptoms consequent upon their bites, may very probably receive some light from this source; and so perhaps may sibbens, yaws, and leprosy.

Mitchill believed, in short, that there was a single cause of contagion, rather than the many causes formerly believed in, and he viewed this dubious hypothesis as an advance of medical science comparable with the progress from polytheism to monotheism.[50]

Mitchill's views were well known to Beddoes, who had published them in 1795 and in 1796 had reviewed Winthrop Saltonstall's *An inaugural Dissertation on the Chemical and Medical History of Septon. Azote, or Nitrogene* (New York, 1796). An appendix to this work contained "several letters by Dr. Mitchell (*sic*) on the noxious power of the dephlogisticated nitrous air of Priestley; alias, the gaseous oxyd of azote". Beddoes clearly accepted the main thrust of Mitchill's arguments, and expressed his satisfaction at seeing "the philosophers of America at last attempting to make some return for the abundant chemical knowledge which they have received from Europe".[51]

Meanwhile, Priestley had been pursuing the chain of researches stemming from his initial *Experiments and Observations on Different Kinds of Air* (London, 1774-75). In that work, Priestley described his attempts to restore "noxious air" by treating it with the air extracted from saltpetre, an air in which candles burned. His attempts failed. He did, however, discover that nitrous air had remarkable antiseptic properties, and flattered himself that "in time, very great medicinal use will be made of the application of these different kinds of air to the animal kingdom."[52] Because dephlogisticated nitrous air (nitric oxide) supported combustion but not life, Priestley suggested that a comparative study of dephlogisticated air (oxygen) and dephlogisticated nitrous air might enhance our understanding of respiration.[53]

Soon after Davy began his chemical studies in March 1798, his attention was directed to nitrous oxide by Mitchill's theory. "The fallacy of this theory was soon demonstrated by a few coarse experiments made on small quantities of the gas procured from zinc and diluted nitrous acid.... I breathed it mingled in small quantities with common air, without remarkable effects." On Mitchill's hypothesis, Davy should have succumbed to a veritable plague of contagions, but he remained healthy. He resumed the investigation at the Pneumatic Institution in 1799. In March he breathed a mixture of impure nitrous oxide with a slight excess of common air, experiencing mildly depressive but not dangerous results.[54] In the following month, Priestley discovered the respirability of nitrous oxide. Beddoes gave a short account of it in his Notice of Some Observations made at the Pneumatic Institution (1799).

Mitchill's theory was now overturned. Davy, after experimenting upon animals, respired pure nitrous oxide on 11 April 1799. The gas proved in most cases to be exhilarating, and without unpleasantly debilitating after-effects.[55] Most stimulants were not so kind in their action. Davy suggested that stimulants in general acted by increasing the circulation of the blood; this accelerated respiration — the coordination of oxygen "and perhaps nitrogen" — and also accelerated the supply of nutritive matter to the blood. This nutritive matter contained nitrogen, which was supplied directly to the blood by nitrous oxide; it followed that less nutritive matter was required "from the absorbents during the excitement from nitrous oxide, than during the operation" of other stimulants, so that exhaustion seldom ensued.[56]

Nitrous oxide was accordingly likely to prove beneficial in the treatment of diseases "of deficient sensibility", such as paralysis. Carbon monoxide, on the other hand, was by no means a stimulant. Rather, Davy observed, it "diminishes living action as rapidly as nitrous oxide increases it". Brunonian theory indicated that one could adjust the level of "excitability" in a patient by administering one or other of these gases. Davy, having offered the universal prescription, retreated: "The common theory of excitability is probably founded on a false generalization. The modification of diseased action may be . . . specific in different organs; and hence out of the power of agents operating on the whole of the system." In that case, nitrous oxide, demonstrably no longer the principle of contagion, would also fail as a universal cure for diseases of deficient sensibility. Beddoes, however, viewed it with enthusiasm. He believed that it overcame paralysis, and "I see every day consumptive patients and patients on the verge of consumption recovering — Mr. Watt tells me they have not such success at Birm^m. - This is inconceivable." Indeed, for Beddoes, nitrous oxide was "the most beneficial discovery ever made".[57]

CONCLUSION: PUBLIC HEALTH AND PREVENTIVE MEDICINE

Pneumatic medicine might still do good; but it fell far short of Beddoes' early hopes. By 1801, when Davy had removed to the Royal Institution of Great Britain (see Fig. 2), Beddoes was clearly concentrating on providing a health service for the poor and their families, who were becoming regular patients at the Institution. "What I want," he wrote to [Josiah] Wedgwood, "is to have 4 or 5 young medical men —3 perhaps wd. do —I wd. parcel out all Bristol between them and make them call occasionally to see the situation of the family and to ensure general regularity of attendance --The young men can be had cheap — I think £550 a year wd. cover the full benefit of preventive and to a great extent of curative medicine to all Bristol and the counties within attending distance." [58]

Preventive medicine, especially for the poor, was no new concern for Beddoes. In 1793 he had published *The History of Isaac Jenkins, and Sarah his Wife, and their Three Children,* as a moral tale instructing the poor in management for health, and instructing the gentry in philanthropy directed to the same end. 1794 saw the appearance of Beddoes' *A Guide for Self-Preservation, and Parental Affection; or Plain Directions for Enabling People to Keep Themselves and their Children Free from Several Common Disorders.* Then came *Hygeia: or Essays*

Moral and Medical on the Causes Affecting the Personal State of our Middling and Affluent Classes (3 vols., Bristol, 1802-03).

In *Hygeia*, Vol. II, p. 98, discussing consumption, Beddoes expressed his central thesis: "One might engage at once to reduce the tribute of lives we render.... It must first, however, be generally believed with SYDENHAM, that our *chronic maladies are of our own creating.*" Prevention was the key, and it depended on knowledge. What was needed was a national organization for preventive medicine, in which information about public health would be collected by local and regional boards, and disseminated by the metropolitan board. "But *the expence! the danger of a job!* -- the expence! what expence? the expence of a few thousand pounds a year for the greatest benefit that can be conferred on a people, from whom so many millions are drawn." [59].

Beddoes' plans for reforms in public health were well conceived, and in line with the way in which the Hippocratic medicine of "airs, waters, and places" was applied by French bureaucracies before 1789.[60] The reforms that he sought in English urban public health had, however, to wait another generation for Chadwick's work. Ventilation and hygiene were important aspects of that work, unlike pneumatic medicine, of which Beddoes none the less never wholly despaired. But cures were slippery things. "The contrariety of testimony in medicine makes one doubt one's own senses." The greatest need, offering the greatest hope, was for prevention: "I believe there is hardly any possibility of doing uncompensated good but by preventing sickness."

The Pneumatic Institution, now known as the Medical Pneumatic Institution, had from the outset offered free treatment to the poor.[61] It registered 678 patients between 1 January and 18 April 1802.[62] By 1803 it had changed its name to the Institution for the Sick and Drooping Poor.[63] In September 1803, Beddoes had remodelled his Institution at Dowry Square, by ceasing to emphasize pneumatic medicine, and by removing the institution to Broad Quay. In 1804, Stock, Beddoes' biographer, joined the staff, and King became its surgeon. By now, Beddoes had fully determined "to prosecute trials with elastic fluids, when I have fully gained the confidence of the people here and established the preventive scheme — I have no confidence in my old speculations nor tenderness for them - but I hold it as a fact that the gasses [*sic*] have salutary powers - and that in a high degree."[64] In 1807, the year before his death, Beddoes retired. Looking back, he reported that "before I became unable to attend the Institution, above 10,000 patients had been registered, almost all with chronic complaints and among them an unusual number of children".[65]

The 1790s and early 1800s saw food shortages, poor harvests being exacerbated by the distress consequent on the war with France.[66] Beddoes had a social conscience as well as a political one. His Institution was humane and bold in purpose, seeking to relieve distress. Pneumatic medicine turned out to be largely a failure, in spite of its early promise in theory and practice. But his treatment of the poor, and the practical education he offered them in the rudiments of health – nutrition, hygiene, temperance – were more than pious aspirations; they went a little way towards meeting a need that would not be addressed by society for another generation.

LITERATURE CITED

1. E. F. Hennock, "Urban sanitary reform a generation before Chadwick". *Econ. Hist. Rev.* **10**,113-20 (1957); B. Hamilton, "The medical profession in the XVlllth century". *Econ Hist Rev.* 2nd ser. **4**, 148 ff. (1951).

2. T. Beddoes to J. Black, Oxford (23 February 1788), Black MSS, Edinburgh University Library (EUL).

3. Beddoes to Black (6 November 1787), Black to Beddoes (24 November 1787), EUL.

4. T. H. Levere, "Dr. Thomas Beddoes at Oxford: radical politics in 1788-1793, and the fate of the Regius Chair in Chemistry". *Ambix* **28**, 61-9(1981).

5. J. Black, *Dissertatio Medica Inauguralis, de Humore acido a cibis orto, et Magnesia alba*, Edinburgh (1754). Black was Professor of Chemistry at Edinburgh 1766-99.

6. J E. Stock. *Memoirs of the Life of Thomas Beddoes, MD ...*, London and Bristol (1811).

7. Beddoes to Black (6 November 1787), EUL.

8. Beddoes to Black (21 April 1789), EUL. Beddoes was probably referring to J. Priestley, "Objections to the Experiments and Observations relating to the Principle of Acidity, The Composition of Water, and Phlogiston, considered...". *Phil. Trans.* **79**, 7-20 (1789).

9. Beddoes to Black (15 April 1791), EUL

10. *Ibid.*

11 Public Record Office MSS HO 42.21, 42.208. See Note 4 above.

12. *Chemical Experiments and Opinions extracted from a Work Published in the Last Century*, p. 61, Oxford (1790). Beddoes reprinted this passage in his *A Letter to Erasmus Darwin, M.D. on a New Method of Treating Pulmonary Consumption, and Some Other Diseases hitherto found Incurable*, p. 29 n. Bristol [1793].

13, *The Chemical Essays of Charles-William Scheele. Translated from the Transactions of the Academy of Sciences at Stockholm. With additions* [by T. Beddoes], London (1786).

14. *A Letter to Erasmus Darwin ...*, pp 28-29 [1793]; E. Goodwyn, *The Connexion of Life with Respiration; Or, an Experimental Inquiry into the Effects of Submersion., Strangulation, and the Several Kinds of Noxious Airs on Living Animals ...* , London (1788).

15, Beddoes, *Letters from Dr. Withering, Doctor Ewart, Dr. Thornton*, p. 9. Bristol (1794).

16. Beddoes. *Hygeia: or Essays Moral and Medical on the Causes Affecting the Personal State of our Middling and Affluent Classes*, Vol. II, p. 5. 3 vols., Bristol (1802-03). "Consumption" was clearly something of a catch-all.

17, *A Letter to Erasmus Darwin ...*, p. 30 [1793].

18. *Ibid.*, p. 40.

19. C. A. Weber, *Bristols Bedeutung für die englische Romantik und die deutsch-englischen Beziehungen*, Halle (Saale) (1935).

20. Bristol Infirmary Biographical Records, MS BRO; G. M. Smith, *A History of the Bristol Royal Infirmary, Arrowsmith*, Bristol (1917).

21. V. Waite, *The Bristol Hotwell*, pp. 11- 12, 17. Bristol (1970; reprinted 1977).

22. J. Priestley, *Experiments and Observations relating to various branches of natural philosophy, with a continuation of the observations on air*, Appendix IV. London (1779).

23. J. Nott, *Of the Hotwell Waters, near Bristol*, Bristol (1793). The Hotwell declined in popularity during the 1790s: Waite, pp. 12-13.

24. Beddoes to Davies Giddy (15 June 1793), Cornwall Record Office, Davies-Giddy papers, MS DG 41/28. Giddy later changed his name to Gilbert, and as Davies Gilbert succeeded his former protégé, Humphry Davy, as President of the Royal Society of London. See A. C. Todd, *Beyond the Blaze: A Biography of Davies Gilbert,*, D. Bradford Barton, Truro (1967).

25. Beddoes, *Observations on the nature and cure of calculus, sea scurvy, consumption, catarrh, and fever: together with conjectures upon several other subjects of physiology and pathology*, pp. 44-5, 87. London (1793).

26. John Brown, *Elementa medicinae*, Edinburgh (1789); *The Elements of Medicine, trans. by the author, new ed.. with biographical preface and introduction by T. Beddoes*, 2 vols., London (1795); J. Neubauer, "Dr. John Brown (1735-88) and early German Romanticism". *J. Hist Ideas* **28**, 367-82 (1967).

27. Beddoes, *Letters from Dr. Withering* .... [1794] (Note 15 above), p. 5.

28. Beddoes, Introduction to Brown, *Elements* (Note 26 above); H. Davy to H. Penneck (26 January 1795), American Philosophical Society BD 315.1/1969 1821 MS.

29. *Ibid.* pp. 1-3; Beddoes, *A proposal towards the improvement of Medicine*, Bristol (29 July 1794).

30. T. H. Levere, "Dr. Thomas Beddoes and the establishment of his Pneumatic Institution: a tale of three presidents". *Notes Rec. R. Soc.* London **32**, 41-9 (1977).

31. Beddoes to Thomas Wedgwood, with MS advertisement [1794, Wedgwood MSS in Keele University Library (W/M).

32. *Ibid.*

33. Banks to Georgiana Duchess of Devonshire (2 December and 30 November 1794), British Museum (Natural History), Dawson-Turner Collection MSS 9, ff. 128-9, 125.

34. Beddoes to T. Wedgwood (17 March 1795) (W/M).

35. Beddoes to T. Wedgwood (21 May 1795, 9 June 1795) (W/M).

36. Beddoes to T. Wedgwood (17 June 1795) (W/M).

37. MS advertisement [1794] (W/M); see Note 31 above.

38. Beddoes to T. Wedgwood (27 March 1795) (W/M).

39. T. Beddoes and J. Watt, *Considerations on the medicinal use, and on the production of factitious airs*, 5 parts. Bristol (1794, 1794, 1795, 1795, 1796).

40. Beddoes to Giddy (29 June 1796), MS DG 42/20. The simplified apparatus is described by Watt in *Considerations*, part 5 (1796).

41. Beddoes to Giddy (31 July 1796), MS DG 42/33.

42. Beddoes to Giddy (23 August 1796), MS DG 42/7.

43. Beddoes to Giddy (30 September 1797), MS DG 42/27.

44. Advertisement in *Bristol Gazette* (21 March 1799). An over-enthusiastic account of the significance of the Institution is A. H. Miller. "The Pneumatic Institution of Thomas Beddoes at Clifton" 1798. *Ann. Med. Hist.* **3**, 253-260 (1931).

45. Robison to Watt (14 January 1798), in E. Robinson and D. McKie (eds.), *Partners in Science: Letters of James Watt and Joseph Black*, pp. 285-6. Cambridge, Massachusetts (1970); Beddoes to Boyd (2 January 1798), Birmingham Public Libraries, M IV B. Beddoes was delighted with Davy, writing to J. Watt Jr. in September 1798 (Birmingham Public Libraries. M IV B): "I do not recollect to have conversed with a person of so great talents for experimental investigation."

46. Bristol Archives Office, MSS 32688/1-54.

47. Davy to Penneck (26 January 1799). American Philosophical Society BD 315.1/1969 1821 MS; Beddoes to Boulton (17 January 1799), Birmingham Public Libraries Box B2 18. Boulton also acted as Beddoes' agent for German medical and chemical books.

48. See Note 26 above.

49. S. L. Mitchill, *Remarks on the Gaseous Oxyd of Azote and on the Effects it Produces*, New York (1795).

50. Beddoes published Mitchill's views in Appendix I to *Considerations* (1795): Note 39 above.

51. *Ibid.* and *Monthly Review* **20**(2), 490-3 (1796).

52. J. Priestley, *Experiments ... on ... Air*, Vol. I, pp. 75, 227-8.

53. *Experiments and Observations relating to various branches of natural philosophy; with a continuation of the observations on air*, Vol. III, p. 321. Birmingham (1786).

54. H. Davy, "Researches, chemical and philosophical, chiefly concerning nitrous oxide, or dephlogisticated nitrous air, and its respiration". In J. Davy (ed.), *The Collected Works of Sir Humphry Davy, Bart....*, Vol. III, pp. 269-70: 9 vols. London (1839); Nicholson's *Journal of Natural Philosophy, Chemistry, and the Arts* **3**, 93 (1799).

55. *Works*, Vol. III, pp. 186 ff., 270. For the additional import of these experiments see F. F. Cartwright. *The English Pioneers of Anaesthesia (Beddoes, Davy, and Hickman)*, Bristol (1952).

56. *Works*, Vol. III, pp. 325-6.

57. *Works*, Vol. III, pp. 327, 329-30; Beddoes to J. Watt Jr. (27 June 1799), Beddoes to Boulton (18 June 1799, ? summer 1799), Birmingham Public Libraries, Boulton and Watt papers, M IV B, and Box B2, 19 and 24.

58. Beddoes to [T.] Wedgwood [November 1801] (W/M).

59. *Hygeia*, Vol. III, p. 86.

60. C. C. Hannaway, "The Société Royale de Médecine and epidemics in the Ancien Régime". *Bull. Hist Med.* **46**, 257-273 (1972); J. P. Frank, "The civil administrator, most successful physician". Trans. J. C. Sabine, *Bull. Hist. Med.* **16**, 289-318 (1944).

61. Advertisement in Bristol Gazette (21 March 1799).

62. *Hygeia*, Vol. II, p. 96.

63. Beddoes, *Rules of the Institution for the sick and drooping poor* (1803).

64. Bristol Record Office, Bristol Infirmary Biographical Records 9, 72; Beddoes to ? (27 November 1804), Birmingham Public Libraries, Boulton and Watt papers, M IV B.

65. Beddoes to J. Wedgwood (19 June 1807) (W/M).

66. For background see R. Quinault and R. J. Stevenson (eds.), *Popular Protest and Public Order*, London (1974), including Stevenson "Food riots in England, 1792-1818", pp. 33-74.

IX

The Rich Economy of Nature: Chemistry in the Nineteenth Century

Chemical science and with it chemical philosophy took wings in the nineteenth century, reaching from the depths of the earth[1] to the most distant stars,[2] contributing to a unified view of Nature, and increasing steadily in its rich economy. The insistent empiricism of early nineteenth-century chemistry, based upon Lavoisier's proscription of metaphysics,[3] furnished an arena in which the chemist with his tactile imagination could grapple intimately with Nature's products and educts and could even attempt to replicate her creative processes. Through chemistry, as through other powerful branches of natural philosophy, man came to know, to control, and even to supplement Nature.

The chief scientific bases of these aspirations were Lavoisier's identification of elements as "the last point which analysis is capable of reaching,"[4] and John Dalton's view that in chemical combination elements combined in simple proportions by weight.[5] Dalton's laws of combining proportions, which Sir Henry Holland in 1848 viewed typically as "the keystone of Chemistry, and the true index to all the actions involved in it,"[6] were founded on an atomic theory. This theory, while controversial, was also heuristically valuable, and often emerged as

*Research for this essay was assisted by a grant from the Canada Council.

1. For a discussion of early nineteenth-century chemical investigations in geology, see D. M. Knight, "The Chemistry of Palaeontology: The Work of James Parkinson (1755–1824)," *Ambix* XXI (1974): 78–85.

2. W. H. Brock, "Lockyer and the Chemists: The First Dissociation Hypothesis," *Ambix* XVI (1969): 81–99.

3. A.-L. Lavoisier, *Elements of Chemistry*, trans. R. Kerr (Edinburgh, 1790), p. xxiv.

4. *Ibid.*, p. xxiv.

5. J. R. Partington, *A History of Chemistry* (London, 1962), III:784–85.

6. Sir Henry Holland, "Modern Chemistry," *Quarterly Review* LXXXIII (1848): 67.

the very life of chemistry.[7] It was convenient to have a foundation as immutable as the stars,[8] for this facilitated a systematic organization of ever-increasing chemical information. The number of recognized chemical elements grew steadily throughout the century. Lavoisier had listed thirty-three in his seminal treatise of 1789. Ninety years later, Mendeleev listed sixty-three, and another four whose identification he predicted.[9] Complexity arose not merely from proliferating elements, but also from the undreamed-of intricacy of organic constitution. Dalton had gone as far as inorganic compounds with seven elementary atoms. By 1910, chemists like Emil Fischer were at home with organic molecules with two hundred or more atoms. The rise of organic chemistry and the development of organic synthesis brought into focus the relations between mineral and living realms, and vitalists and reductionists found equal satisfaction in the new science.[10] Organic chemistry was a bewildering subject, but at least its constituent elements were few in number. The total maze of elements, however, when reduced to order by systematists in the second half of the century, revealed unexpected harmonies, suggestive even of genetic relations and evolutionary mechanisms.[11] The temptation to cosmic generalization proved sometimes irresistible, and chemistry seemed to provide an unparalleled avenue into the mysteries of Nature.

Humphry Davy, perhaps more than any other chemist of the nineteenth century, saw himself exploring this avenue:

> Oh, most magnificent and noble Nature!
> Have I not worshipped thee with such a love
> As never mortal man before displayed?
> Adored thee in thy majesty of visible creation,
> And searched into thy hidden and mysterious ways
> As Poet, as Philosopher, as Sage?[12]

7. W. H. Brock, ed., *The Atomic Debates* (Leicester, 1967), especially chap. 1; D. M. Knight, *Atoms and Elements: A Study of Theories of Matter in England in the Nineteenth Century* (London, 1967), especially chaps. 2, 5.

8. "The Atomic Controversy," *Nature* I (1869): 44–45.

9. Lavoisier, *Elements of Chemistry*, pp. 175–76; Partington, *A History of Chemistry*, IV:894–95.

10. J. H. Brooke, "Organic Synthesis and the Unification of Chemistry—A Reappraisal," *British Journal for the History of Science* V (1971): 363–92; "Wöhler's Urea and Its Vital Force?—A Verdict from the Chemists," *Ambix* XV (1968): 84–114. See also T. H. Levere, *Affinity and Matter: Elements of Chemical Philosophy 1800–1865* (Oxford, 1971), pp. 156–95. The most detailed monograph is F. L. Holmes, *Claude Bernard & Animal Chemistry* (Cambridge, Mass., 1974).

11. The principal spokesman here was Crookes. See R. K. deKosky, "Spectroscopy and the Elements in the Late Nineteenth Century: The Work of Sir William Crookes," *British Journal for the History of Science* VI (1973): 400–23.

12. J. Davy, ed., *Fragmentary Remains, Literary and Scientific, of Sir Humphry Davy, Bart.* (London, 1858), p. 14. For an account of H. Davy's chemistry, see H. Hartley, *Humphry Davy* (London, 1966), and Levere, *Affinity and Matter*, pp. 23–67.

Davy saw chemistry as giving a bond of union to the appreciation of Nature. Complementary to the aesthetic enjoyment of natural scenery, for example, was the intellectual pleasure that arose from the perception of the connection between landscape and the inner relations of its rudest chemical constitutents, "the destruction of a former order of things, and a system arranged with harmony, filled with beauty and life, formed from its elements, and established on its ruins."[13] Awareness of such natural harmony came only through perceiving the operation of chemical laws revealed by careful attention to the minutiae of laboratory experiments. The chemist, in short, discovered literally the detailed relations of parts to the whole:

> It is surely a pure delight to know, how and by what processes this earth is clothed with verdure and with life, how the clouds, mists and rain are formed, what causes all the changes of this terrestrial system of things, and by what divine laws order is preserved amidst apparent confusion. It is a sublime occupation to investigate the cause of the tempest and the volcano, and to point out their use in the economy of things,—to bring the lightning from the clouds and make it subservient to our experiments,—to produce as it were a microcosm in the laboratory of art, and to measure and weigh those invisible atoms, which . . . constitute the universe of things. The true chemical philosopher sees good in all the diversified forms of the external world . . . . Whilst chemical pursuits exalt the understanding, they do not depress the imagination or weaken genuine feelings; whilst they give the mind habits of accuracy, by obliging it to attend to facts, they likewise extend its analogies; and, though conversant with the minute forms of things, they have for their ultimate end the great and magnificent objects of nature. They regard the formation of a crystal, the structure of a pebble, the nature of a clay or earth; and they apply to the causes of the diversity of our mountain chains, the appearances of the winds, thunder-storms, meteors, the earthquake, the volcano, and all those phenomena which offer the most striking images to the poet and the painter.[14]

The passage from detail to grand object was guided by analogy while restrained by experiment. There was an analogy of Nature, but this could not be discovered by mere speculation, the bane of chemical science, since "Nature has no archetype in the human imagination."[15] Her empire was given only to action, and governed by experience, yet these did not suffice—the selection and even the creation of analogies was possible only for the man of genius, among whom Davy rightly

13. H. Davy, *The Collected Works of Sir Humphry Davy, Bart.*, ed. J. Davy (London, 1840), VIII:200 (from a lecture of 1811).
14. *Ibid.*, IX:361–62; first published in H. Davy, *Consolations in Travel* . . . (London, 1830).
15. Davy, *Works*, VIII:347.

counted himself.[16] His view of himself was matched only by his achievements, but his prescription for discovery in science was widely recognized as valid.[17]

The exercise of genius, the creation of intellectual relations founded on natural harmonies and analogies, a cosmic purview and yet continued emphasis on the significance and primacy of the individual facts of experience—all these were involved in the chemist's view of Nature, but they were scarcely his unique preserve. In 1800 Coleridge had stated clearly that chemistry, uniting "the opposite advantages of immaterializing [the] mind without destroying the definiteness of [the] Ideas," was poetical.[18] Davy and Coleridge could agree about the inspiration of chemistry, but differed radically in their views of poetry. Davy's position here was almost identical with that of Robert Hunt, who, half a century later, affirmed uncompromisingly that the creations of poetry were pleasing, but never affected the mind "in the way in which the poetric realities of nature do."[19] Davy's chemical communion with Nature convinced him that the natural philosopher and the poet viewed the world quite differently.[20] Coleridge knew otherwise, and said so frequently, most explicitly in *The Friend*:

> Thus, as "the lunatic, the lover, and the poet," suggest each other to Shakespeare's Theseus, as soon as his thoughts present him the ONE FORM, of which they are but varieties; so water and flame, the diamond, the charcoal, and the mantling champagne . . . are convoked and fraternized by the theory of the chemist. This is, in truth, the first charm of chemistry, and the secret of the almost universal interest excited by its discoveries. . . . It is the sense of a principle of connection given by the mind, and sanctioned by the correspondency of nature. Hence the strong hold which in all ages chemistry has had on the imagination. If in SHAKSPEARE we find nature idealized into poetry, through the creative power of a profound yet observant meditation, so through the meditative observation of a DAVY, a WOOLLASTON, or a HATCHETT . . . we find poetry, as it were, substantiated and realized in nature: yea, nature itself disclosed to us, . . . as at once the poet and the poem![21]

Thus chemistry, for both Davy and Coleridge, developed the faculty of perceiving intellectual affinities where none had been suspected before.[22] The same point was

16. *Ibid.*, I:27. Cf. S. T. Coleridge, *The Friend*, I, ed. B. E. Rooke, *The Collected Works of Samuel Taylor Coleridge*, ed. Kathleen Coburn (London and Princeton, 1969), IV:530-31.

17. Holland, "Modern Chemistry," p. 42, and M. Faraday to C. F. Schoenbein, 13 November 1845, in G. W. A. Kahlbaum and F. V. Derbyshire, eds., *The Letters of Faraday and Schoenbein* . . . (Basle and London, 1899), p. 149.

18. E. L. Griggs, ed., *Collected Letters of Samuel Taylor Coleridge* (Oxford, 1966), I:557.

19. R. Hunt, *The Poetry of Science*, 3d ed. (London, 1854), p. 293.

20. Davy, *Works*, I:66-67, 147.

21. Coleridge, *Collected Works*, IV:471.

22. S. T. Coleridge, notebook 23, folios 31^r & 31^v, to be published in *The Notebooks of Samuel Taylor Coleridge*, IV, ed. K. Coburn (Princeton, forthcoming).

made in the *Preliminary Treatise* of the *Library of Useful Knowledge*: "That the diamond should be made of the same material with coal; that water should be chiefly composed of an inflammable substance . . . : these, surely, are things to excite the wonder of any reflecting mind."[23]

❀

Chemistry was seized on to illustrate the intellectual unity of the cosmos because its subject matter was immediately accessible, its contrasts sensible, and its demonstrations dramatic. The success of chemical lectures at the Royal Institution[24] in carrying chemistry into literary society was largely due to the practical and imaginative convenience of chemistry. Here was a science whose generalizations were profoundly simple, yet whose web of natural affinities was universal in its reach and almost infinitely complex. The very substance of the earth, acted on by air and moisture, underwent perpetual change and provided nourishment for an astonishing diversity of plant life, which in turn, through chemical metamorphosis, supported the full range of animal life. This would then decay, to be resolved into inorganic aggregates; "and the same elementary substances, differently arranged, are contained in the inert soil, or bloom and emit fragrance in the flower, or become in animals the active organs of intelligence."[25] Chemistry afforded perpetual change, underlying constancy, and symbiotic unity to Nature. In its universal application,[26] chemistry could also subdue Nature to the purposes of life and of society. Nature was still mysterious, wonderful, and beautiful, but she was also beneficent and useful, thanks to the labors of the chemist. The universal harmony of Nature yielded supreme power and riches to Britain, a nation favored alike by a chemical providence and its own chemical genius and industry: "The immeasurable beds of iron-ore, coal, and limestone, which are to be found in the neighbourhood of Birmingham, lying beside or above one another, and to which man has only to help himself in order to procure for his use the most useful of all metals in a liberal measure, may not . . . be considered as mere accident. On the contrary, it in fact expresses the most clear design of Providence to make the inhabitants of the British Isles, by means of this gift, the most powerful and the richest nation on earth."[27]

23. Quoted from H. Brougham, *Preliminary Treatise* of the *Library of Useful Knowledge* (1827), in "Society for the Diffusion of Useful Knowledge," *Edinburgh Review* XLVI (1827): 224–44.

24. G. A. Foote, "Humphry Davy and His Audience at the Royal Institution," *Isis* XLIII (1952): 6–12; H. Bence Jones, *The Royal Institution: Its Founder and Its First Professors* (London, 1871).

25. H. Davy, *Elements of Chemical Philosophy*, pt. I, vol. I (London, 1812); reprinted in *Works*, IV:43.

26. "A Popular Course of Chemistry. I. Introduction," *The Magazine of Popular Science and Journal of the Useful Arts* I (1836): 185.

27. Schoenbein's report of Buckland's address to the British Association for the Advancement of Science, Birmingham, 1839, quoted in C. C. Gillispie, *Genesis and Geology* . . . (1951; reprint ed., New York, 1959), pp. 200–201.

The law-abiding unity revealed by chemical science was more than providential utilitarianism in action. It was a partial revelation of the unity of created Nature and especially of the unity of natural forces. Michael Faraday's lifetime endeavour may be seen as a constant pursuit of this unity.[28] The Danish natural philosopher Hans Christian Oersted explained that "the natural laws of chemistry, as well as those of mechanics, are laws of Reason, and both are so intimately connected, that they must be viewed as a unity of Reason."[29] It is striking that in the supreme statement of the natural philosophy of cosmic harmony, the Kosmos of Alexander von Humbolt, the metaphor chosen to present this harmony was most prevalent in chemistry, with its doctrine of elective affinities. "The aspect of external nature . . . is that of unity in diversity . . . ;—one fair harmonious whole . . . the philosopher arrives at an intimate persuasion of an indissoluble chain of affinity binding together all nature."[30] In 1848, Sir Henry Holland's lengthy review article on modern chemistry underlined the seminal and central importance of that science in attaining the union and simplification of the great laws of Nature.[31]

Such ambitious views of the powers of chemical science had implications even for the definition of culture and education, and the extension of chemical method to analyses of more than materials. First, if Nature was intellectually, materially, and in its powers an harmonious whole, and if it was also rational, then the man of education should himself be in harmony with Nature, and education should be directed towards achieving this mental and physical harmony. Culture, attuned to Nature, should be more than mental and more than an end in itself. The pure studies of German universities and the liberal education of Cardinal Newman were equally inadequate and irrelevant to Nature's demands. Education should involve the intimate experience of Nature, and might well be professional—hence the arguments of Playfair, of the Devonshire Commission, and, most eloquently of all, of Thomas Henry Huxley.[32] Rightly or wrongly, British industrial supremacy was associated with the marriage of chemical and physical science to industrial technology, and the maintenance of that threatened supremacy was seen to depend on a matching popular education. In Huxley's words of 1868:

28. L. P. Williams, *Michael Faraday* (London, 1965), pp. 364–407; Michael Faraday, *Faraday's Diary: Being the Various Philosophical Notes of Experimental Investigation made by Michael Faraday during the Years 1820–1862 . . .*, ed. T. Martin (London, 1933), IV:308 (entry 7872, 20 October 1845). T. H. Levere, "Faraday, Matter, and Natural Theology—Reflections on an Unpublished Manuscript," *British Journal for the History of Science* IV (1968): 95–107.

29. H. C. Oersted, *The Soul in Nature* (1852; reprint ed., London, 1966), p. 104.

30. A. von Humboldt, *Cosmos: Sketch of a Physical Description of the Universe*, trans. E. Sabine, 8th ed. (London, 1850), I:5–9.

31. Holland, "Modern Chemistry," pp. 37–70, and especially 42.

32. Some of these arguments are sketched in David Layton, *Science for the People* (London, 1973).

That man, I think, has had a liberal education who has been so trained in youth that his body is the ready servant of his will, and does with ease and pleasure all the work that, as a mechanism, it is capable of; whose intellect is a clear, cold, logic engine with all its parts of equal strength, and in smooth working order; ready, like a steam engine, to be turned to any kind of work, and spin the gossamers as well as forge the anchors of the mind; whose mind is stored with a knowledge of the great and fundamental truths of Nature and the laws of her operations . . . .

Such a one and no other, I conceive, has had a liberal education; for he is, as completely as a man can be, in harmony with Nature. He will make the best of her, and she of him.[33]

With the mind conceived of as itself but a part of Nature, and chemistry universally applicable, what followed but to advocate, in the spirit of Herbert Spencer, that, since scientific method applied to the whole of Nature, there should be an analysis of minds comparable to that of chemical substances?[34]

The correlation through Nature of science with mind was fundamental to major strands of nineteenth-century natural philosophy, and is merely illustrated rather than limited by chemistry. Humboldt expressed it succinctly: "science is mind applied to nature."[35] Huxley, introducing the opening number of *Nature*, defined the progress of science as "the progress of that fashioning by Nature of a picture of herself, in the mind of man."[36] There was more agitating here than a philosophy tinged with idealism, for Victorian progress was largely material, and followed a revived Francis Bacon molded in its own image. Knowledge was also power, power over Nature, industrial power.[37] Chemistry especially was powerful, yielding explosives, medicines, dyes, fertilizers, metals, subduing the old Nature and giving rise to a new Nature "begotten by science upon fact." This "new Nature created by science" was manifest, said Huxley, "in every chemically pure substance employed in manufacture . . . ."[38] With the message of Liebig's writings clearly although partially apprehended in Britain, where, their author complained, "only those works which have a practical tendency awake attention and command respect,"[39] with the alarming example of Germany's successful industrial

33. T. H. Huxley, "A Liberal Education," address of 1868 in *Science and Education* (New York, n.d.), p. 80.

34. "Purpose and Plan of Our Enterprise," *The Popular Science Monthly* I (1872): 113–15.

35. Humboldt, *Cosmos*, I:64.

36. T. H. Huxley, "Nature: Aphorisms by Goethe," *Nature* I (1860): 9–11.

37. For a dissident comment on "Baconianism," see W. F. Cannon, "History in Depth: The Early Victorian Period," *History of Science* III (1964): 20–38.

38. Huxley, *Collected Essays* (New York: Appleton & Co., 1894), I:51; quoted in F. M. Turner, *Between Science and Religion* (New Haven and London, 1974), p. 8.

39. J. von Liebig to Faraday, 19 December 1844, in Michael Faraday, *The Selected Correspondence of Michael Faraday*, ed. L. P. Williams (Cambridge, 1971), I:429–30.

chemistry,[40] and with the belief that England's continuing greatness rested on the realization of her scientific potential,[41] Huxley's new Nature was ardently pursued. For one thing, the old Nature was not infinite in her resources, but the new Nature might compensate for the limits of the old.[42]

✻

Chemical science, revealing and exploiting the consequences of laws of Nature, worked always for the good of mankind. Materialism and utilitarianism might rest content here, but such a halting place was premature, since material welfare and the power that flowed from it were in Christian lands divinely ordained. Humphry Davy, in an historical lecture around 1810, had indicated the happy consequences of the confluence of science and religion: "It happened that whilst one part of the world were enlightened by Religion, another part were left to Nature; and from this part proceeded the sciences; and from the union of the sciences with true Religion in these latter times, everything grand, everything dignified has arisen."[43] Davy went on to argue that chemistry had been the supremely effective science in this union, and dwelt on the cumulative benefits that this science had given mankind. By contrast, Faraday, Davy's pupil and successor, stressed divine power and benevolence.[44]

Once the connection was established between divine wisdom and natural law, the task for the chemist was ultimately one of tracing design in Nature. Chemistry was ripe for natural theology, and also for more modest and sometimes more sophisticated theologies of Nature.[45] Economy and simplicity were obvious qualities of design, yet Nature as the chemist apprehended her was disconcertingly rich. Even before Lavoisier published his table of elements—a considerable expansion over earlier systems—Bergman had shown, in his classic work on chemical affinities, that more than thirty thousand different experiments remained to be performed before the relations between the elements could be reduced to order. Lavoisier's new table of elements was soon to increase this estimate. The chemist could not but be struck by the "infinite variety of forms under which matter is presented to our senses," nor, as the nineteenth century progressed, could he fail to be aware of the repeated discovery of new elements. One way out of this conflict between the demands of design and the achievements of research was to pursue the

40. L. F. Haber, *The Chemical Industry during the Nineteenth Century* (Oxford, 1969), pp. 121–36, 169–80.

41. Lyon Playfair was an important spokesman here. See W. H. G. Armytage, "Lyon Playfair and Technical Education in Britain," *Nature* CLXI (1948): 752–53; R. G. W. Norrish, "Lyon Playfair and His Work for the Great Exhibition of 1851," *Journal of the Royal Society for the Arts* XCIX (1951): 537–49.

42. Charles Giles Bridle Daubeny, "Address," *Report of the Twenty-Sixth Meeting, B.A.A.S.* (Cheltenham, 1856), p. liv.

43. Davy, *Fragmentary Remains*, p. 164.

44. H. Bence Jones, *The Life and Letters of Faraday*, 2d ed. (London, 1870), II:225.

45. Levere, *Affinity and Matter*, pp. 75–79.

Newtonian doctrine that ultimately all matter was the same, or composed of a very few fundamental principles.[46] Davy, for example, having investigated the chemical effects of voltaic electricity, suggested that prime matter in different electrical states might appear as different chemical species: "Should Chemistry hereafter confirm this idea, it would become the most *important*, and *noblest* of the Sciences;—for it would refer the diversified and multifarious phaenomena of ye terrestrial universe, to powers as simple and uniform, as those which govern the movements of the heavenly bodies;—And thus the *History* of Nature, would form *one System*, as Nature itself forms one intelligent design; and all the changes of matter might be referred to one *law* . . . ."[47] By 1807 Davy had discovered the alkali metals—he was in fact to add substantially to the number of known elements.[48] No whit dismayed, he announced that the researches of "modern chemistry . . . have demonstrated that all natural bodies consist of different arrangements . . . of a few simple parts."[49] Having discovered a couple more elements, and before discovering still more, Davy affirmed the probability

> that the number of elements will be diminished: and that arrangements of a very simple nature will explain those phenomena which are now referred to complicated and diversified agents . . . .
>
> Nature infinitely complicated in the minute details of her operations when well investigated is always found wonderfully simple in the grand mechanism of her works. . . .
>
> The uniformity of the succession of events in our globe, the constant decay, and constant renovation of the forms of things—The infinite mutations of the parts of matter—the conservation of the order of the whole demonstrate at once unity of design and unity of power.[50]

Davy's conviction that chemical substances had few truly basic constitutents led him constantly to probe the inner constitution of bodies—and generally his search for simplicity resulted in the addition of further elements to the corpus of chemistry. Others, notably the great Swedish chemist J. J. Berzelius, were differently motivated but equally successful in discovering new elements, and the fecundity of *Nature* with its rich chemical economy was matter for comment throughout the century.[51]

46. *Ibid.*, pp. 4–8, 18–19, 45.
47. H. Davy, Royal Institution of Great Britain, MS 4: December 1809.
48. Hartley, *Humphry Davy*, pp. 50–63, and *passim*.
49. Davy, *Works*, VIII:168–69.
50. Davy, Royal Institution, MX 4: 1.
51. Berzelius's discoveries are recounted in J. E. Jorpes, *Jac. Berzelius. His Life and Work*, Bidrag till Kungl. Svenska Vetenskapsakademiens Historia VII (Stockholm, 1966). For a comment on chemistry's rich economy, see Thomas Dick, *The Christian Philosopher*, 8th ed. (1842), *The Works of Thomas Dick* (New York, 1884), II:275–76.

The rich diversity of Nature rested on a simple basis that was virtually a necessary assumption for nineteenth-century chemists, for without it they would have been utterly lost. The general interpretation of this assumption came through the application of Dalton's laws of combining proportions to some fifty elements, to explain the formation of thousands of compounds. Organic chemistry, which seemed at first to violate these laws, was swifty brought to heel.[52] Davy's view, that greater simplicity obtained, and that analysis would dramatically simplify the table of elements, was at first neglected. Prout's 1815 hypothesis that regularities among atomic weights showed that heavy elements were composed of integral multiples of the unity of the lightest element, was discredited by sober analysis.[53] Then came a series of discoveries: of isomerism, in which the same atoms, differently combined, yielded compounds with different properties; of allotropy, in which the same element could exist in different physical forms with differing chemical activities—witness the difference between graphite and diamond, both forms of carbon; and of analogies between groups of elements, such as the halogens, that could be correlated with progressions in their atomic weights.[54] Perhaps the dreams of the alchemists were not entirely unfounded, and transmutation might be a reasonable goal for the chemical philosopher. So, in different ways, thought Davy and Dumas, Faraday and Crookes. In 1851 the British Association for the Advancement of Science learned of the discovery of yet another metal, whereupon "Mr. Faraday said he was almost sorry to welcome any more metals; they fell on us like asteroids and confused our reckonings; his hopes were in the direction of proving that bodies called simple were really compound, and might be formed artificially as soon as we were masters of the laws influencing their combination."[55] When Crookes discovered thallium in the early 1860s Faraday told him that what he had achieved was all very well, but "if you could decompose an element and tell us what it is made of—that would be a discovery indeed worth making."[56] Crookes took Faraday at his word, and sought to explain the genesis of the elements in terms of their evolutionary development from a prime matter like that formerly proposed by Prout. Spectroscopy, and particularly the new discipline of stellar spectroscopy, seemed to him to support the evolutionary hypothesis in chemistry, and even to

52. Partington, *A History of Chemistry*, IV:233–64.
53. W. H. Brock, "Studies in the History of Prout's Hypotheses," *Annals of Science* XXV (1969): 49–80, 127–37.
54. References for these developments may be found in Partington, *A History of Chemistry*, IV:*passim*.
55. For background here, see Knight, *Atoms and Elements, passim*. The report of Faraday's statement to the B.A.A.S. was published in the *Chemical Record*, 12 July 1851, and reprinted in Faraday, *Lectures on the Non-Metallic Elements*, ed. J. Scoffern (London, 1853), pp. 160–61.
56. Sir William Crookes, *Report of the Fifty-Sixth Meeting, B.A.A.S.* (1886), p. 559.

suggest that evolution was a cosmic law, "manifest in heavenly bodies, in organic individuals, and in organic species," as well as in chemical elements, the ultimate constituents of stars and organisms alike.[57]

Evolution is a dynamic process, constantly active, whereas chemistry—at least Daltonian atomic chemistry—appears to deal with a disconnected passive world of little things. As C. F. Schoenbein wrote to Faraday in 1852, "Atoms, weight, ratio of quantities, endless production, and formula of compounds, i.e. the 'caput mortuum' of nature, are the principal if not only subjects with which the majority of our Chymists know to deal."[58] But it was possible to be a chemist concerned with more than the *caput mortuum*. Faraday himself saw Nature as a unity of active forces extending through all space: "Do not all bodies act where they are not . . . ?"[59] He even envisioned a chain of activity rising from molecules to living beings, although he would not have gone as far as the universal hylozoism of Thomas Sterry Hunt in his presidential address to the Mathematical, Physical and Chemical Section of the Royal Society of Canada, at its inaugural meeting in 1822:

> The student of inorganic nature, however, soon learns to recognize the fact that all matter is instinct with activities. . . . To all . . . physical . . . activities of matter, supervene those processes which we name chemical, and which give rise to new and specifically distinct inorganic forms. The attaining of individuality by matter . . . has always seemed to me the greatest step in the progress of nature . . . . All the energies seen in nature, are in this view, but manifestations of the essential life or quickness of matter . . . .
>
> When we have attained to this conception of hylozoism, of a living material universe, the mystery of nature is solved . . . . This, it will be said, is the poet's view of the external world, but it is at the same time the one which seems to me to be forced upon us as the highest generalization of modern science.[60]

What, finally, of organic chemistry? It would be strange to have reached the life of Nature without a discussion of life *in* Nature, were it not that organic chemistry was not properly concerned with life. Even for those chemists who were vitalists, life was not in the province of chemistry, although design might well require that the laws of chemistry be subservient to the purposes of life. One widely held view was that living matter and inorganic matter were distinct, and that life was

57. *Ibid.*, p. 561.
58. Kahlbaum and Derbyshire, *Letters of Faraday and Schoenbein*, p. 207.
59. Faraday's Common Place Book, unpublished MS at the Institution of Electrical Engineers, p. 324.
60. T. S. Hunt, "The Relations of the Natural Sciences," *Canadian Naturalist* X (1883): 4–5.

distinguished by organization that chemistry could not explain.[61] At the other extreme, possible after syntheses of organic compounds from their elements, was Marcellin Berthelot's view that organic and inorganic chemical phenomena were identical, and were both mechanical. In the production of organic as opposed to organized bodies, there was thus no room for vitalism.[62] More significant for Victorian chemical philosophers was the gradual demonstration that the organic and inorganic realms of matter were subject to the same chemical laws, and that, through the pursuit of ever-widening analogies between these realms, the great Victorian scientific enterprise of unifying Nature was successfully extended.[63] Then again, and perhaps imaginatively more striking, was the complex proliferation of organic substances from an extraordinarily restricted base.[64] The organic realm was composed almost entirely of four elements: carbon, hydrogen, nitrogen, and oxygen. Simple foundations, an infinitude of creation—here indeed was the rich economy of Nature.

61. For introductory comments on vitalism and reductionism, see E. Mendelsohn. "The Biological Sciences in the Nineteenth Century: Some Problems and Sources," *History of Science* III (1964): 39–59. Important distinctions, including "organized-organic," are made by Brooke, *Ambix* XV (June 1968): 84–114; Davy, *Works*, IX:333–34, gives a clear statement of a major vitalist viewpoint.

62. M. Berthelot, *Science et Philosophie* (Paris, 1886), pp. iv–v.

63. For a survey, see H. l. Sharlin, *The Convergent Century: The Unification of Science in the Nineteenth Century* (New York, 1966). A striking instance of the extent to which this unification could be carried is given by Alexander Bain, "On the Correlation of Force in Its Bearing on Mind," *Macmillan's Magazine* XVI (1867): 372–83.

64. Daubeny, "Address," *Report of the Twenty-Sixth Meeting, B.A.A.S.*, pp. l–li.

X

ELEMENTS IN THE STRUCTURE OF
VICTORIAN SCIENCE
OR CANNON REVISITED

INTRODUCTION

Twenty years ago, the late Walter Cannon addressed the History of Science Society on the historiography of nineteenth-century science. His paper, subsequently revised and published under the title "History in Depth", [1] has served as both gad-fly and encouragement. First, there was the implicit assertion of the dignity of the subject, and the challenge posed by what Cannon portrayed as the failure of other historians. "To be sure", he remarked, "the history of science is no more the true center of British history in the nineteenth century than is the history of Parliament. But it is no less so. And historians of Parliament, or of politics, have amply had their chance, from Halévy on, to produce full and convincing history. And they have failed. So have 'social' historians. And attempts to construct 'cultural' history on the basis of literary culture alone are not very promising".

It is perhaps worth remarking that most historians, of Parliament or of politics, have not been concerned to produce "full and convincing history"; they have often produced admirable answers to deliberately defined and limited questions. Halévy, moreover, in his *History of the English People in the Nineteenth Century*, [2] was sensitive to a breadth of cultural and scientific issues that weakens Cannon's swashbuckling attack. Never the less, it remains true, and typical, that Halévy's consideration of science still treats it as an appendage to culture, itself an appendage to political and economic life. Cannon was right to remind us that the sort of broad-based history that he advocated was not – and indeed is not – much in vogue, and that the history of science was as likely to lead to it as any other sub-discipline, and more likely than most. For the most part, however, we still lack the detailed narratives that must precede the construction of an adequate outline of science in the period. There have been encouraging and significant achievements over the last few years, most notably

1. "History in Depth", *History of Science*, 1964, 3, pp. 20–38, revised in S.F. Cannon, *Science in Culture. The Early Victorian Period*, New York, 1978, pp. 225–252.
2. Halévy's survey in vol. 1 of his *History, England in 1815*, 2nd (revised) ed., London, 1949, displays that breadth well.

J.D. North and J.J. Roche (eds.), The Light of Nature. ISBN 90-247-3165-8.
© *1985, Martinus Nijhoff Publishers, Dordrecht. Printed in the Netherlands.*
Reprinted by permission of Kluwer Academic Publishers.

Morrell and Thackray's account of the early years of the British Association for the Advancement of Science.[3] Gerard Turner has examined the importance of patronage in science, Kargon has constructed a useful portrait of science in Victorian Manchester, Frank Turner has analyzed the professional dimension of the science-religion debate, and social historians of science have sought to provide not only a social framework, but also a social explanation of scientific developments, as in Inkster and Morrell's *Metropolis and Province*.[4] The strong program in social history seems to promise social determinism for science. That promise is, however, limited, for, as Mandelbaum remarked in *History, Man, and Reason*, "when one is not specifically dealing with the history of normative political theory, it is perhaps true that sociological factors exert greater influence on the dissemination of philosophic and scientific views than upon their original formulation and development".[5] Historians in the last two decades have helped in fundamental ways to deepen our understanding, but we remain a long way from a clear apprehension of the structure of Regency and Victorian science.

There was a major shift that effectively transformed the nature of science between 1800 and 1875; I shall draw on the achievements of recent scholarship to suggest a scheme for describing that transformation, in part echoing Cannon, and, while not without a hefty conjectural component, of some heuristic historiographic value. The Romantic movement was prelude to the change, and conditioned the sensibilities that made it possible. I shall argue that, in the wake of that movement, scientific and military entrepreneurial initiatives, and changes in the institutional and social structure of science cooperated to move science firmly beyond the Enlightenment and into the last quarter of the Victorian age. Let me begin by offering a sketch of science in Britain around 1800, and then move rapidly across the decades to 1875. The sketches are partial, and the contrasts are accordingly strengthened, but not falsified. They raise important questions.

3. J. Morrell and A. Thackray, *Gentlemen of Science. Early Years of the British Association for the Advancement of Science*, Oxford, 1981.

4. *The Patronage of Science in the Nineteenth Century*, ed. G.L'E. Turner, Science in History no. 1, Leyden, 1976. R.H. Kargon, *Science in Victorian Manchester. Enterprise and Expertise*, Manchester, 1977. F.M. Turner, "The Victorian Conflict between Science and Religion: A Professional Dimension", *Isis*, 1978, 69, pp. 357–76. *Metropolis and Province. Science in British Culture*, ed. I. Inkster and J. Morrell, Philadelphia, 1983.

5. M. Mandelbaum, *History, Man, & Reason. A Study in Nineteenth-Century Thought*, Baltimore and London, 1971, p. x.

SCIENCE AROUND 1800

The supreme achievements of eighteenth-century science had been in mathematical physics, especially dynamics, and in astronomy, both of them very much Newtonian sciences. Newton's laws and rules of reasoning in philosophy, combined with his *Quaeries* to the *Opticks*, furnished the foundations for the main stream of turn-of-the-century science, from astronomy to chemistry – even John Dalton, whose atomic theory represented in some ways a departure from Newtonian orthodoxy, considered himself to be a disciple of Newton. Nature was very simple, and conformable to herself. [6] The majority of natural philosophers accepted the simplicity of nature, and explored it by the successive application of the methods of analysis and synthesis. Here was a world in which Newtonian law, design, cause and effect operated so securely that David Hume might never have written. William Paley, who well knew that Hume had written, and who was determined to refute him, began his statement of the proof of God's benevolence, power, and wisdom in the creation, the "argument from design", by considering the contrivance of mechanism – specifically, of a watch – and then extending the argument analogically to design in God's creation. [7] Paley went on to take most of his remaining examples from the life sciences, where form was related to function, teleological explanation being unquestioned. Almost every eighteenth-century naturalist explored the reciprocal utility of natural history and natural theology.

Since Paley was determined to rebut Hume, it is necessary to consider whether the argument from design presents a sequence of cause and effect in relation to an object, in which case it fails to meet Hume's objections, or whether it does not rather offer an explanation of cause and effect, in which case it seeks directly to counter Hume. [8] Such subtlety is often lacking in those who followed Paley, and who were dismissed by John Henry Cardinal Newman, as mere physical theologians. [9] Analogical argument, however, remained central to natural theology; the most popular eighteenth-century British treatise on the subject, indeed, was Butler's *The Analogy of Religion, Natural and Revealed, to the Constitution and Course of Nature*, a title that enjoyed continued popularity into the next century, and reinforced the continuity of late eighteenth- and early nineteenth-century natural theology. Nieuwentijt's enthusiastic recognition of divine wisdom and benevolence in protecting the Netherlands from At-

---

6. A. Thackray, *Atoms and Powers*, Cambridge, Mass., 1970. *John Dalton and the Progress of Science*, ed. D.S.L. Cardwell, Manchester, 1968.

7. W. Paley, *Natural Theology*, London, 1802. P. Fayter, seminar paper, "Paley's *Evidences* and David Hume", Toronto, 1980.

8. I owe this point to Prof. Sydney Eisen.

9. J.H. Newman, *On the Scope and Nature of University Education*, London, 1965.

lantic furies by the interposition of the British Isles has its nineteenth-century English counterpart. The British Association for the Advancement of Science was told that British industrial supremacy was divinely ordained, ensured by the judicious proximity of coal and steel in the industrial midlands.

If astronomy and dynamics were essentially Newtonian, chemistry in Lavoisier's hands was heir to Locke and Condillac, [10] at once an empirical and a taxonomic exercise, with leanings towards experimental physics and yet another Newtonian tradition. The taxonomy, moreover, like that of Linnaeus in zoology, expressed static relations among discrete entities with generally externally observable characteristics, rather than genetic and developmental relations and characters based upon some inner nature. The same form of taxonomy characterized mineralogy, at this time the major component of the earth sciences. [11]

Thus, across the sciences in 1800, Enlightenment taxonomy, various forms of Newtonianism, and teleology embedded in design were widespread and dominant.

The choice of 1800 as a starting point is arbitrary, a matter of convenience; but the turn of the century serves pretty well to demarcate the Enlightenment from what came after. 1800 saw the publication of Volta's paper on the electric pile, inaugurating the new sciences of current electricity and electrochemistry, and sounding, as Humphry Davy wrote, as an alarm bell to the whole of Europe. [12] In 1799, Schelling published his *Einleitung zu seinem Entwurf eines Systems der Naturphilosophie*, perhaps the major text for German Romantic scientists; in 1800 there appeared the first number of his short-lived *Zeitschrift für spekulative Physik*. Hutton's *Theory of the Earth* had been published in 1795; Playfair's *Illustrations of the Huttonian Theory* followed in 1802. At the very least, a lot of new things were emerging in science and in the philosophy of science. In this respect, science partook of the excitement that pervaded much of the intellectual realm. As Hegel observed in 1807 in the introduction to his *Phenomenology of Mind*:

> It is surely not difficult to see that our time is a time of birth and transition to a new period. The spirit has broken with what was hitherto the world of its existence and imagination, and is about to submerge all this in the past; it is at work giving itself a new form. [13]

10. A.L. Lavoisier, *Traité Elémentaire de Chimie*, 2 vols., Paris, 1789. R.E. Schofield, *Mechanism and Materialism. British Natural Philosophy in an Age of Reason*, Princeton, 1969. Levere in G.L'E. Turner and T.H. Levere, *Van Marum's Scientific Instruments in Teyler's Museum*, Leyden, 1973, pp. 103–22.

11. Louis Agassiz, *Essay on Classification*, ed. E. Lurie, Cambridge, Mass., 1962, pp. 197–259, offers a succinct history of classification in zoology covering the period under consideration here. Buffon's *Histoire Naturelle* – a work of the Enlightenment (see Goodman, p. 57), offers a variant theme.

12. A. Volta, *Philosophical Transactions of the Royal Society of London*, 1800, 90, pp. 403 ff.

13. Quoted in Mandelbaum, *op. cit.*, p. 4.

FROM 1800 TO 1875

Over the next decades, the genetic or developmental classifications earlier explored by the *Naturphilosophen* increasingly made their way into respectable
biology. William Swainson's system, discussed by Knight in chapter 6, was
open to genetic interpretation. Charles Darwin's theory of the origin of species
confirmed the validity of historical models in biology, and in 1871 his *Descent
of Man*, by applying those models to the human species, underlined their uni-
versality. In the earth sciences, Charles Lyell had made the model of history
part of the definition of geology:

> Geology is the science which investigates the successive changes that have taken place in
> the organic and inorganic kingdoms of nature: it enquires into the causes of these changes,
> and the influence which they have exerted in modifying the surface and external structure of
> our planet.
>
> By these researches into the state of the earth and its inhabitants at former periods, we ac-
> quire a more perfect knowledge of its *present* condition, and more comprehensive views con-
> cerning the laws *now* governing its animate and inanimate productions . . .
>
> Geology is as intimately related to almost all the physical sciences, as is history to the moral.
> . . . The analogy, however, of the monuments consulted in geology, and those available in
> history, extends no farther than as regards one class of historical monuments, – those which
> may be said to be *undesignedly* commemorative of former events. [14]

The emphasis upon historical process and development came to characterize
not only the life and earth sciences, but also the physical sciences. In chemistry,
the development of periodic classifications by Mendeleev, Lothar Meyer, and
others in the late 1860s and early 1870s was accompanied by a revival of interest
in Prout's hypothesis about the fundamental unity of matter. William Crookes,
studying rare earths, new elements, and phosphorescence induced by cathode
rays, applied evolutionary models to chemistry, and proposed a dynamic explanation of periodicity. [15] The historical element of eighteenth-century cosmologies was revived in astronomy, leading for example to Lord Kelvin's denial that
Darwin was entitled to the time he needed for his theory to work. By the last
quarter of the nineteenth century, historical models were firmly established
across a range of sciences.

There were other distinct but related ways in which process became the subject of intensive study, and indeed the central concept of the physical sciences,

14. C. Lyell, *Principles of Geology*, 3 vols., London, 1830–3, vol. 1, pp. 1, 3, 4. Geology is the
supreme "Historic Science" (Coleridge's phrase – see below); there are valuable accounts in D.R.
Oldroyd, "Historicism and the Rise of Historical Geology", *History of Science*, 1979, 17, pp.
191–213 and 227–57, and in M.J.S. Rudwick, "Historical Analogies in the Geological Work of
Charles Lyell", *Janus*, 1977, 64, pp. 89–107.

15. D.M. Knight, *Atoms and Elements. A Study of Theories of Matter in England in the Nineteenth Century*, London, 1967, pp. 132 ff.

as it was of the life sciences. Field theory, with its equations describing variations in a continuum, had taken over from the previous theories of force – a development in which James Clerk Maxwell was pre-eminent, and which culminated in the publication in 1873 of his *Treatise on Electricity and Magnetism*. Wave theory had taken over light and electricity, and physical theory in general had become more unified than earlier studies of heat, light, and electricity and the rest had suggested, thanks to the new sciences of electrodynamics and thermodynamics. In 1824, Sadi Carnot enunciated the principle that one cannot transfer heat from a colder to a warmer body without producing an external effect. The significance of this principle was explored in the 1850s, first by Clausius, then by William Thomson. The subsequent development of thermodynamics, joined to that of kinetic theory and statistical mechanics, culminated in the 1870s in the work of Boltzmann, who gave precise expression to the relationship between disorder or entropy, and probability.

The probabilistic explanations of statistical mechanics, developed in Britain and Germany by the 1870s, represented a real shift from the directly causal explanations dominant in 1800. The use of statistics had been developed for social purposes by French and German bureaucracies, Scottish insurance companies, and others, and was eagerly adopted by Utilitarians and other would-be social engineers. The theory was refined by mathematicians, notably Gauss and Laplace, and came to be adopted increasingly in the sciences, in the study of errors, for example in astronomy, and in the calculation of probabilities. The application of statistics to kinetic theory, to plant hybridization (Mendel's *Versuche über Pflanzenhybriden* was published and generally ignored in 1865), to studies of chemical equilibrium, and to Galton's anthropometry in the 1880s, were all manifestations of the acceptability of the new mode of explanation.[16]

Finally, if statistical explanations were acceptable, then there was no need for teleological ones. This did not mean the death of teleology, which, like natural theology, proved hardy, and inclined to reemerge after every assault, modified and adapted to survival in the new environment – for example, that created by the publication of the *Origin of Species*. But the direct and explicit teleology of the physical theologians had yielded by the 1870s.

Clearly, the choice of 1875 as terminal date for this essay is even more arbitrary than that of 1800 as starting point. Never the less, the undermining of traditional, immediate teleology, the burgeoning of statistical explanations, the emphasis upon historical process, and the increased unification at least of the physical sciences, all indicate a major shift in the style and content of science greater than any that had occurred in the eighteenth century. Faced with two carefully selected synchronic slices, from 1800 and 1875 respectively, it would

16. Sources for this and the previous paragraph may be found in *Science in the Nineteenth Century*, ed. R. Taton, London, 1965.

be tempting for us to accept Foucault's metaphor in his *Archaeology of Knowledge*, and to posit an epistemic discontinuity lying somewhere between 1800 and 1875, with essential continuity in the strata on either side – a continuity also postulated by Levi-Strauss, and explored in Hesse's chapter on the generalization of scientific style.

The metaphor is tempting, and it does have the merit of encouraging us to recognize major changes in the form of scientific knowledge, and common forms in scientific and wider culture in a given period – as, for example, when Laclos in his *Liaisons dangereuses* constructs an account of shifting personal relationships on the basis of contemporary tables of chemical affinity and chemical exchange. The trouble with the metaphor is that it evades any account of historical process, let alone adequate recognition of the duration and complexity of that process.

I propose to take from the metaphor the recognition of real change, and of intracultural similarities, while extracting from the complexity of historical process four among many factors that were ingredients in effecting the shift between 1800 and 1875. My indebtedness to Cannon will be evident; and, as she said about her intellectual debts at the end of the preface to *Science in Culture*, "I would like to hear from the rest of you. A simple postcard will do".

ROMANTICISM

Before introducing and explaining my choice of four factors, I shall briefly discuss the Romantic movement as prelude to change and conditioner of sensibilities. Romanticism serves both a unifying role, and embodies and encompasses diversity. It may be helpful to bear in mind Lionel Gossman's simile concerning the Enlightenment:

> The Enlightenment as we can now envisage it is more like a language than a single idea, imposing by its very nature certain modes of thought on those who use it, while remaining always at the same time an expression, in any actual usage, of particular desires and meanings and a response to particular conditions.[17]

One should also remember that Romanticism has been the subject of more than six hundred books, and remains as resistant to definition as it is susceptible of identification. I shall follow the example of Isaiah Berlin in his radio lectures "On Some Sources of Romanticism", by refusing to be so foolish as to say what Romanticism is. There are, however, clear indications of what kind of science was favored by Romantic thinkers. The Encyclopedists had favored the mechanization of the world picture, seeing in that process the greatest achieve-

17. Quoted in Mandelbaum, *op. cit.*, p. 10.

ment of modern science; "mechanical" was to become the great polemical and perjorative adjective of the Romantic movement in its contemplation of nature. Jean-Paul, typically, spoke of the "all-powerful, blind, lonesome machine of the universe".[18]

In place of mechanism, organic life operated as the central metaphor of romantic science. The metaphor applied to the whole of science: there was, indeed, only one natural science, which was the recognition of unity. Organism and life implied growth and productivity, so that science was concerned to explore dynamic processes rather than simply to classify discrete phenomena; accordingly, classifications were developed to illustrate developmental connections and processes, in contrast to the most successful lines of Enlightenment classification. Process was seen as essentially historical, so that the life of nature and natural history, the history of nature, were interdependent. This history arose from inner development, rather than from externally imposed necessity, so that the meaning of teleology and the status of scientific laws both changed.

At the same time, nature itself achieved a more elevated status, as a subject of awe and almost religious feeling – hence both the nature-poetry of the Lake poets, and much of their subsequent impact upon the development of religious thought in England. The spiritual significance of nature for Romantic poets and philosophers, in England as in Germany, was also the source of a good deal of religious unease, since there was no simple way of avoiding the pantheism of nature worship. This is what Coleridge meant when he condemned Schelling's philosophy of nature as the "Spinozismus" of physics.[19]

The spiritual and mental view of nature as the product of ideas, seductively similar to much Neo-Platonic thought embedded in Christianity, emphasized the essential unity of nature, and hence of natural science. Heinrich Steffens, a Norwegian natural philosopher admired by Coleridge and in occasional correspondence with George Greenough, first president of the Geological Society, moved characteristically from minute questions of crystal morphology to an account of the dynamic origins of the cosmos, and from chemistry to geogony, a kind of vital dynamic geology.

Such an approach, while hubristic, dignified the scientific enterprise by stressing the constitutive role of ideas in nature. Laws of nature were expressions of ideas of the mind, and human ideas were echoes of divine ideas. Positivism following Auguste Comte also saw laws as expressions of ideas, but scarcely countenanced their constitutive origin in the mind of God. The perception of

18. W.D. Wetzels, "Aspects of natural science in German romanticism", *Studies in Romanticism*, 1971, 10, pp. 44–59, at 46–7.

19. T.H. Levere, *Poetry Realized in Nature. Samuel Taylor Coleridge and early nineteenth-century science*, New York, 1981, which is also the source for the following two paragraphs.

countenanced their constitutive origin in the mind of God. The perception of an essential congruence and underlying identity of ideas and of laws relating to natural phenomena led Coleridge to his unusual view of Bacon and Plato as respectively the British Plato and the Athenian Verulam, the former working from nature to mind, the latter from mind to nature. In schemes like these, science and nature both achieved a new and heightened significance. Philosophically and culturally, nature was transformed into a unity of historical process corresponding to the development of human consciousness and divine creativity.

I do not wish to claim that the perceptions of science by poets and philosophers led directly to an emphasis upon historical process and to the unification of the sciences, nor to a different forging of the links between science and religion, and thus to the transformation of traditional teleology. Consider Romanticism for the moment merely as prelude to the four factors for discussion, namely, historicism; institutional changes affecting science, from the reorganization of the Prussian universities under Wilhelm von Humboldt, and later more or less related institutional changes in Britain; the growth of scientific surveys after the Napoleonic wars, and the related growth of what Cannon calls Humboldtian science, after the explorer-scientist Alexander, Wilhelm's brother; and the spread of statistical thinking, with the organizational infrastructure that accompanied that spread. With these dominant themes, I shall want to touch on sub-themes affecting Victorian perceptions of nature; but indeed, this essay offers suggestions rather than conclusions, and even the main themes are merely touched on.

Other factors, such as positivism and accelerating industrial change, could be considered. I would argue, however, that they are less immediately significant here because they had relatively little demonstrable impact on the style and content of science. Few scientists practised what Comte advocated. Positivism did endorse historicism, as did Romanticism; we shall accordingly consider positivism in that context. Industrial change undoubtedly had an enormous impact on Victorian society, but economic historians have failed to trace any convincing connection between industrial and scientific change, and social historians, while arguing irrefutably that there was a social cause both for industrialism and for scientific activity, have done no better in demonstrating the connection; the problem remains, without any promising prospects for its solution.

HISTORICISM

The best definition of historicism that I know is, once again, Mandelbaum's, in *History, Man, and Reason*:

Historicism is the belief that an adequate understanding of the nature of any phenomenon and an adequate assessment of its values are to be gained through considering it in terms of the place which it occupied and the role which it played within a process of development.[20]

One form of historicism had been developed in the Enlightenment, to be revived in the writings of St.-Simon and Comte, with their positive historical laws governing society and science alike. The laws were not the laws expressing the inner nature of beings, but rather the external conformity of those beings to the deterministic processes of history. Whatever teleology exists in this scheme is embodied in external determinism.

Inner necessity or internal determinism characterized organism, the central concept for the form of historicism implicit in the Romantic movement, stressing interconnectedness in the process of growth. Herder is the writer whose historicism was most important for the German Romantics, Hegel the philosopher who developed that historicism into a philosophical system. A succinct statement of it, tightly packed and susceptible of much teasing out, is given by Coleridge in a notebook entry of 1819:

The proper objects of knowledge . . . which may be regarded as the Poles of true Learning, are Nature and History − or Necessity and Freedom. And these attain their highest perfection, when each reveals the essential character of the other in itself and without loss of its own distinctive form. Thus Nature attains its highest significancy when she appears to us as an inner power . . . that coerces and subordinates to itself the outward − the conquest of Essence over Form − when by Life + superinduced Finality she reveals herself as a plastic Will, acting in time and of course finitely. Here there is Process and Succession, in each Plant and Animal as an Individual, and in the whole Planet as at once a System and a Unit − and the Knowledge of Nature becomes Natural History. History e contra ha[s] her consummation, when she reveals herself to us in the form of a necessity of Nature − when she appears as a power ab extra that coerces and takes up into itself the inner power − the conquest of Form over Essence . . . But here is *Law*, and the *Ever-present* in the moving Past, the Eternal as the Power of the Temporal − and the Historic Science becomes a higher Physiology, a transcendent Nature.[21]

Romanticism endorsed the historicism that became embedded in geology, comparative anatomy and physiology, and the developmental taxonomies elaborated above all in Germany. We have already remarked, albeit briefly, on the extent of historicism in nineteenth-century science. Darwin's work established it unassailably, the *Origin of Species* implying the applicability of historicism to the understanding of human social and mental life, the *Descent of Man* making explicit that applicability.

Romantic historicism did not survive; the emergence of the critical historical

20. Mandelbaum, *op. cit.*, p. 42.
21. Quoted in Levere, *op. cit.*, p. 103.

school in Germany, and the waning of Hegelianism, would have weakened historicism generally, had it not been revived by Comte, and adopted by Marx and Engels. "In fact, in his 'Speech at the Graveside of Karl Marx', Engels said: 'Just as Darwin discovered the law of development of organic nature, so Marx discovered the law of development of human history'."[22]

INSTITUTIONS

Romanticism and Enlightenment ideology both favored historicism, even if of different forms; both likewise favored the concept of the unification of the sciences, embodied respectively in the *Encyclopédie* itself, and in the ideal of *Wissenschaft* enshrined in the German universities in the first thirty years of the nineteenth century. Science there was in the faculty of philosophy; it was still there in 1880. When the chemist A.W. Hofmann returned from England, where he had been busy establishing a Germanic research-based school of chemistry, he took up his chair in Berlin with an inaugural address[23] insisting that philosophy and natural science should have one professor; in other German universities the faculty of philosophy had undergone division, with the subsequent birth of faculties of natural science. Such division was deplorable; the natural sciences had "in fact suffered no manner of harm from their union with the philosophical branches". How could it be otherwise when the philosophical faculty was the faculty of pure science, "science free and untrammelled, science for its own sake". He prefaced his address with a quotation from E. du Bois-Reymond:

> To the Philosophical Faculty by its nature is entrusted the Palladium of our strivings after the Ideal, the culture of pure Science, the representation of these before the outside world, and when occasion requires before the government.

This ideal of science was active in the German universities from the beginning of the century, through the Prussian reorganization of the whole system under Wilhelm von Humboldt, who in 1809 was placed at the head of the educational section under the Ministry of the Interior, and, among his other achievements, founded the University of Berlin. The ideal persevered, albeit with growing dissent and specialization, as Hofmann's address indicates, until after 1875 – and indeed into this century.

William Whewell was among the most influential British academics of his day, and one of the most receptive to German ideas, although he recognized

---

22. Mandelbaum, *op. cit.*, p. 76.
23. A.W. Hofmann, *Inaugural Address, Berlin 1880*, Boston, 1883, preface and pp. 8, 19.

the need to dress them in a language more acceptable to English sensibilities. In the 1830s and 1840s he wrote and practised extensively on various aspects of a liberal education, echoing the Germans in his stress upon knowledge for its own sake, and in the comprehensiveness of his views reinforcing the idea of the unity of knowledge. Education at Cambridge, and in the sciences even more at Oxford, failed to live up to Whewell's prescriptions, except in the negative respect that research was no part of education – therein differing greatly from German models.[24]

The German ideal of science, systematic disciplined disinterested knowledge, has parallels not only with Whewell's work at Cambridge, but with John Henry Cardinal Newman's ideal of a curriculum embracing all the sciences, including and especially theology. It is ironic that Newman, in his *Idea of a University* of 1853,[25] justified the teaching of theology because it was a science; back in the 1820s, the founders of London University had propounded their secular curriculum to give prominence to the sciences, without any illusion that theology belonged in their company. Both Whewell and Newman contributed to the perception of the unity of the sciences; for them, that unity was intellectual. The unity of the sciences that was to emerge from London University was primarily social and professional. It was this line, rather than the one facilitated by Romanticism, that was to enlist the labors of Huxley, Tyndall, and other new men in transforming scientific education and the professional status of scientists from mid-century on. Their real effectiveness was shown in the 1860s and 1870s in such governmental enquiries as the Devonshire Commission, as well as in the vitality of London University and its associated metropolitan schools of science.[26]

The establishment against which Huxley and company had to assert themselves displayed attitudes and sensibilities at least consonant with some of those of the Romantic movement, favoring the ideas of the unity of knowledge, the intrinsic value of scientific ideas, and the coherence between science and religion. Let me again stress that I do not wish to argue that such ideas, as applied to science by mid- and late-nineteenth-century Englishmen, were the direct consequence of Romanticism. I do wish to claim an indirect effect, exemplified by Whewell's increasing taste for Coleridge's philosophy, and more generally, by the influence upon the "Cambridge network" of Coleridge's concept of the

24. W. Whewell, *Of a Liberal Education in General, with Particular Reference to the Leading Studies of the University of Cambridge*, London, 1845. *On the Principles of English University Education*, London, 1837. D. McNally, *Whewell's Theistic Cosmology*, Ph.D. dissertation, University of Toronto, 1982. M.M. Garland, *Cambridge Before Darwin. The Ideal of a Liberal Education 1800–1860*, Cambridge, 1980.

25. Newman, *op. cit.*

26. F. Turner, *op. cit.* D.S.L. Cardwell, *The Organization of Science in England in the Nineteenth Century*, 2nd ed., London, 1972.

clerisy. Coleridge, in his *On the Constitution of the Church and State*, wrote of the clerisy as a national church of intellect. Within that church, and under the immediate guidance of clergymen, "the science of theology was the root and trunk of the knowledge that civilized man, because it gave unity and the circulating sap of life to all other sciences, by virtue of which alone they could be contemplated as forming, collectively, the living tree of knowledge". Morrell and Thackray, in *Gentlemen of Science*, describe the scientific intelligentsia as a clerisy, and argue for the effectiveness of that clerisy in the early years of the British Association. [27]

The British Association was the most important scientific organization in early Victorian Britain. It encompassed the complete range of the sciences, with the exception of such dubious and controversial subjects as phrenology. The range corresponded well with the ideology of the unity of the sciences, while the strength of the Cambridge network within the Association testified to the continuing vitality in the first half of the century of the links between science and religion. It also tended to blur the distinction between clerisy and clergy, since the bulk of the scientific clerisy were educated at Cambridge or, to a lesser extent, at Oxford, where many of them retained fellowships. The main function of both universities had long been regarded as the education and preparation of members of the clergy of the Church of England. Fellowships were not open until after the passage of the University Test Act of 1871. It followed that scientists within the ancient universities were established churchmen – a circumstance adding point to the campaign for professionalization free from religious constraint discussed by Turner. Meanwhile, and unsurprisingly, of the inner core of British Association members in the first decade, the 1830s, almost half were clergymen. William Buckland and Baden Powell had both been ordained and had enjoyed Oxford fellowships, while the Reverend William Venables Vernon Harcourt was an Oxford graduate. Charles Daubeny, Fellow of Magdalen College, Oxford, was the son of a clergyman. Humphrey Lloyd and Thomas Romney Robinson were clerical Fellows of Trinity College, Dublin, where William Rowan Hamilton was a professor. John Henslow, George Peacock, Adam Sedgwick, Edward Stanley, and William Whewell were all ordained Cambridge men, while Charles Babbage, George Biddel Airy, Lord Milton, and the Marquis of Northampton were Cambridge graduates. [28] The clerisy was in control, and within the clerisy, the clergy were still dominant.

27. *Gentlemen of Science*, p. 19; quotation from Coleridge, *Church and State*, 1830, p. 47. Patterson's chapter on Mary Somerville's 1817 visit to France gives a glimpse of the French clerisy – who were not clerical fellows of colleges (p. 321).

28. *Gentlemen of Science*, pp. 533–9.

HUMBOLDTIAN SCIENCE[29]

John Herschel, reviewing Whewell on the inductive sciences for the *Quarterly Review*, welcomed his rejection of the metaphysical ravings of Hegel and Schelling, while noting that Whewell dealt out justice with a "leaning to the side of mercy".[30] In similar fashion, Henry Holland, reviewing Humboldt's *Cosmos* for the same journal,[31] welcomed his condemnation of *Naturphilosophie*, while accusing him of being a little infected by it. Von Humboldt was trying to achieve a difficult balance — difficult, that is, in Germany in the 1840s when the scientific revolt against Romantic idealistic philosophy was at its height. He was clear enough about the excesses of that philosophy, "the short saturnalia of a purely ideal science of nature", but was determined to resist the degeneration of science into "a mere assemblage of empirical specialities". "Science", he explained, is "mind applied to nature. The external world only exists for us so far as we receive it into ourselves, and as it shapes itself within us into the form of a contemplation of nature".[32] It was essential for the natural philosopher to continue to seek

> to discern physical phenomena in their widest mutual connection, and to comprehend Nature as a whole, animated and moved by inward forces . . . The separate branches of natural knowledge have a real and intimate connection, which renders these special studies capable of mutual assistance and fructification . . . The aspect of external nature . . . is that of unity in diversity . . . ; — one fair harmonious whole . . . the philosopher arrives at an intimate persuasion of one indissoluble chain of affinity binding together all nature.[33]

Von Humboldt was the supreme explorer-scientist of the nineteenth century. His basic assumption was that world-wide observations would lead to general theories. Here was an invitation to international cooperation in science, as well as to large-scale national ventures requiring elaborate organization and correspondingly extensive funds — which could generally only come from state support. Governmental support of scientific research and of scientific organizations was not prominent in early nineteenth-century Britain, except through the armed forces. In the previous century the Royal Navy had, most notably in Captain Cook's voyages, sponsored far-flung scientific researches. The Napoleonic Wars ruled out a continuation of that style of investigation, too new to be called a program. In the aftermath of the second Treaty of Paris in 1815,

29. The concept and label, "Humoldtian science", is Cannon's; see *Science and Culture*, ch. 3.

30. J.F.W. Herschel, *Quarterly Review*, 1841, 68, pp. 177–238.

31. H. Holland, *Quarterly Review*, 1853, 94, pp. 49–79.

32. A. von Humboldt, *Cosmos: Sketch of a Physical Description of the Universe*, trans. E. Sabine, London, 1850, vol. 1, pp. 63–4.

33. *Ibid.*, preface, and pp. 5, 9.

however, the navy was underemployed; so were the ordnance, the Royal Artillery and the Royal Engineers, whose officers incorporated a corps of scientifically trained manpower. The North-West Passage expeditions that followed may in part be seen as a response to the problem of justifying the maintenance of such a corps. Each expedition collected natural history specimens, and made geodetic, geological, meteorological, and, under Edward Sabine, geomagnetic observations contributing to the world-wide study of terrestrial magnetism from the 1820s. The British Association for the Advancement of Science made that study a special concern in the 1830s, and the Royal Society took a vigorous role, particularly in the 1840s; this activity both built on and was in a direct response to the program promoted by von Humboldt.[34] Naval officers, captains included, became interested in the scientific aspects of their voyages. William Edward Parry, for example, spent most of the time preparing for his arctic voyages by consulting with Fellows of the Royal Society; John Franklin corresponded most helpfully with Robert Were Fox about magnetic apparatus; George Strong Nares, transferred from command of H.M.S. *Challenger* to command the British Arctic Expedition of 1875–76, made significant improvements to techniques of deep-sea dredging. The navy's hydrographic program had as one consequence Charles Darwin's voyage on H.M.S. *Beagle*. On land, John Henry Lefroy, an artillery officer, carried out a heroic magnetic survey over much of Canada in the 1840s, reporting back to Sabine in London.[35] International scientific cooperation was a prominent feature of the magnetic surveys; it reached its nineteenth-century peak in the International Polar Year of 1882–83, precursor of the International Geophysical Year in this century.

Observations of the geographical distribution of species, and of meteorological, magnetic, oceanographic and other geophysical phenomena, correlated across large reaches of the earth, certainly fitted Von Humboldt's program; they were scarcely motivated by Romanticism, but their scope was predicated upon the underlying interconnectedness of phenomena on a global scale, so that proliferating scientific surveys succeeded and reinforced Romantic emphases upon the unity of nature.

34. J. Cawood, "The Magnetic Crusade: Science and politics in early Victorian Britain", *Isis*, 1979, 70, pp. 493–518.

35. Parry MSS., Scott Polar Research Institute, Cambridge. Franklin MSS., Public Archives of Canada. J.H. Lefroy and J. Richardson, *Magnetical and meteorological observations at Lake Athabasca and Fort Simpson, by Captain J.H. Lefroy . . . , and at Fort Confidence, in Great Bear Lake, by Sir John Richardson*, London, 1855.

THE SPREAD OF STATISTICAL THINKING

Cannon argued that the way scientific data were presented helps one to identify the form of science: "If you find a 19th-century scientist mapping or graphing his data, chances are good you have found a Humboldtian". [36]

It is significant that von Humboldt's training had been in the administration of state economic policy; governments rely on census data and the like, bureaucrats are trained to handle data displayed in tables and graphs. This had not been significantly true until the eighteenth century, but it became true in the Enlightenment, and has remained so. Social statistics were needed for public health reforms, penal reforms, and, in the early and mid-nineteenth century, for the kind of reforms favored by a Utilitarian ethos. As Morris Berman observes, "there was in the 1820s a general rise in professional consciousness that affected medicine, education, and government administration, had a Benthamite view of science as part of its ideology, and found its outlet in organizations such as the Statistical Society, the London University, and the S.D.U.K. (Society for the Diffusion of Useful Knowledge)". [37]

Statistical thinking, developed in the calculations of life insurance premiums, validated and sanctioned by the success of mathematical astronomy, came to prominence in Britain in 1833, when the Statistical Section of the British Association was founded, with the aid of Quetelet, Malthus, Babbage, Sedgwick, and the economist Richard Jones – a striking group. [38]

An interest in economic and social questions generated and sustained statistical investigations and proliferating statistical societies – a development that needs a major study of its own. At the same time, the sciences drew increasingly on statistical and probabilistic arguments and on descriptions of processes involving large numbers. In the second half of the century, thermodynamics, kinetic theory, evolution, and eugenics were among the sciences that incorporated modes of explanation formerly characteristic of social sciences, and of astronomy. The burgeoning of statistical explanations in the physical sciences arose because of the increasingly confident adoption of atomic theory and of mechanical models based on that theory. Such models presented physical systems as assemblages of vast numbers of moving atoms, which could only be considered in the aggregate by the application of statistics. "In 1850, Maxwell wrote that the theory of probability was the true logic of the universe". [39] But

36. Cannon, *op. cit.*, p. 96.

37. M. Berman, *Social Change and Scientific Organization. The Royal Institution 1799–1844*, Ithaca, N.Y., 1978, p. 113.

38. Cannon, *op. cit.*, p. 242. M.J. Cullen, *The Statistical Movement in Early Victorian Britain*, Hassocks, Sussex, 1975.

39. *History of Mankind. Cultural and Scientific Development*, vol. 5, ed. C. Morazé, *The Nineteenth Century*, London, 1976, p. 105.

one consequence was that mechanical models, which would seem to invite deterministic mechanical explanations, in fact required statistical explanations, whose determinism was unclear. Maxwell thought that only mechanical explanations were truly deterministic; Boltzmann in 1872 took the opposite tack: "One must not confuse a proposition not fully demonstrated, and whose precision is consequently problematic, with a proposition of the calculus of probability, which is rigorously proven".[40] Scientific explanation had indeed been transformed.

ENVOI

I have not discussed the content of the sciences, and recognize the inconclusiveness of any argument that ignores content. Nor have I demonstrated the significance of the factors discussed above. But I am suggesting that, in the pervasive afterglow of the Romantic rebellion, there was an effective interaction between historicism, the birth of new institutions and models for the organization and patronage of science, scientific and military opportunism, and statistical and probabilistic patterns of explanation. This interaction reinforced the epistemic shift identified at the beginning of this essay. The rapidity and extent of the shift scarcely amounted to a dislocation, or at least, amounted to no more of a dislocation than Victorian society as a whole experienced in its material and mental culture.

ACKNOWLEDGEMENT

Prof. Sydney Eisen read an earlier draft of this chapter, and suggested numerous improvements.

40. Quoted in E. Bellone, *A World on Paper. Studies on the Second Scientific Revolution*, Cambridge, Mass., 1980, p. 92.

Humphry Davy and the Idea of Glory[†]

Sir Isaac Newton could be a modest man, when unopposed. The image that he offered of himself as a small boy preoccupied with the pebble that he had discovered on the beach, while before him lay unperceived the great ocean of truth, is part of the iconography of science. We might hold it in balance with Cotes's view, presumably endorsed by Newton since it appeared in the preface to the second edition of the *Principia*, that there was only one true system of the world, discoverable but once, and in fact discovered by Newton, who thus revealed God's ways to man. Edmond Halley's Ode to Newton echoed this theme, and Pope's 'God said, "Let Newton be!" and all was light' gave it epigrammatic force.

After Newton, the scientist could serve as the embodiment of genius. Here was an absorbing theme throughout the eighteenth century. The idea of genius acquired especial fascination for the leaders and followers of the Romantic movement towards the end of the century. Genius was creative and heroic. There is an aspect of Romanticism that seems to reflect Blake's condemnation of Newton for busying himself with abstractions while closing heart and mind to the true beauties of nature; science could be identified with the deadening effects of mechanization. An alternative style of science did, however, exist in the decades around 1800. The natural philosopher Johann Wilhelm Ritter, for example, used

---

[†] An early version of this paper was presented at the Davy Bicentenary Symposium at the Royal Institution of Great Britain in December 1978. The proceedings of the symposium are to be published by Science Reviews Ltd.

galvanism as the key to a living unity in nature, and was lionized by German Romantics, who came to regard him as the supreme authority in science. Clemens Brentano urged his sister: 'Write to Ritter as you would write to the universe. He is about to spell out the creation.'[1] Henrik Steffens, a philosophical Danish scientist much impressed by Ritter, thought nothing of solving the problem of the origin and history of the cosmos as a prelude to discussing the morphology of minerals.[2] Samuel Taylor Coleridge, enthusiastic for Romantic science and a thorough student of Steffens's writings, used the chemist Humphry Davy as a prime exemplar of genius in *The Friend* of 1818. Davy's discoveries, Coleridge wrote, 'have shed a dawn of *science* on the *art* of chemistry, and give no obscure promise of some one great constitutive law, in the light of which dwell dominion and the art of prophecy.'[3]

Davy's discoveries would surely illuminate the relations between science and Romanticism – so at least I thought when I first conceived this paper. The subject, however, as often happens, revealed a will of its own. Davy had his own understanding of genius and his own idea of glory, using both to shape his career and to make himself the most prominent and colourful English scientist of his day.

In his youth and prime Davy numbered among his regular correspondents the great Swedish chemist Berzelius, who after Davy's death called him the greatest chemist of his time, although he had been critical of Davy for his lack of discipline and system. Berzelius, thorough, precise, and clear, demanded these same virtues in others. Davy viewed hypotheses as heuristically useful; once used, they could be discarded, to be replaced by others that might prove equally short-lived. His audience at the Royal Institution of Great Britain was repeatedly treated to the spectacle of last week's hypothesis demolished by this week's experiments. That, for Davy, was how science worked; consistency in opinion was the slow poison of intellectual life.[4] Such ready and casual use of hypotheses was antipathetic to Berzelius, who found the style of Davy's *Elements of Chemical Philosophy* intensely frustrating. 'Great minds often attach too little importance to details ... Your philosophy is too far above my criticism,' he complained to Davy.

---

1 W. Wetzels, 'Aspects of Natural Science in German Romanticism,' *Studies in Romanticism* 10 (1971), 53.
2 H. Steffens, *Beyträge zur innern Naturgeschichte der Erde* (Freyberg, 1801); *Geognostisch-geologische Aufsätze* (Hamburg, 1810).
3 *The Collected Works of Samuel Taylor Coleridge*, Bollingen Series, LXXV: *The Friend*, ed. B. Rooke, 2 vols. (London: Routledge & Kegan Paul; Princeton University Press, 1969), 1, 530.
4 *The Collected Works of Sir Humphry Davy, Bart.*, ed. J. Davy, 9 vols. (London, 1839), 1, 68.

The result, in Berzelius's view, was that Davy 'left only brilliant fragments.'[5]

Davy left more than brilliant fragments, but even his fragmentary remains were informed by unifying ideas of the order and simplicity of nature. His approach may be exemplified by his remarks on landscape, which yielded not only aesthetic pleasure but also the intellectual satisfaction that came from seeing it as the product of 'the destruction of a former order of things, and a system arranged with harmony, filled with beauty and life, formed from its elements, and established on its ruins.'[6] 'Whilst chemical pursuits exalt the understanding,' Davy wrote, 'they do not depress the imagination or weaken genuine feelings; whilst they give the mind habits of accuracy, by obliging it to attend to fact, they likewise extend its analogies; and, though conversant with the minute forms of things, they have for their ultimate end the great and magnificent objects of nature.'[7] Such statements were sympathetic to Coleridge, who, lacking all scientific training but eager to explore the dynamic unity of nature and the role of ideas in science, apostrophized Davy as 'the Father and Founder of philosophic Alchemy, the Man who *born* a Poet first converted Poetry into Science and *realized* what few men possessed Genius enough to *fancy*.' Davy's chemistry, thus perceived, was simply poetry realized in nature, and Davy, after Wordsworth, was for Coleridge the greatest man of the age.[8]

That two such different men as Coleridge and Berzelius recognized Davy's greatness says something about the range of his achievement and the sympathies it excited. Davy's aspirations were certainly boundless. After a local education, valuable principally for leaving his mind untrammelled, he formulated a plan of study as revealing as it was impossible of realization. He would master theology, geography, botany, pharmacology, nosology, anatomy, surgery, chemistry, logic, half a dozen dead and living languages, physics, mechanics, rhetoric and oratory, history, chronology, and mathematics.[9]

His ambitions were at least on the way to being satisfied when in 1799 he moved from Penzance, where he was an apothecary's apprentice, to Bristol. The former Oxford chemist and lifelong radical Dr Thomas Beddoes employed him as superintendent of the chemistry laboratory in

5 T.H. Levere, 'Coleridge, Chemistry, and the Philosophy of Nature,' *Studies in Romanticism*, 16 (1977), 349–79. *Jac. Berzelius Bref.*, ed. H.G. Söderbaum, 6 vols. with 3 suppl. (Uppsala, 1912–32), 2, 35–59. Harold Hartley, *Humphry Davy* (London: Nelson, 1966), 148.

6 Davy, *Works*, 8, 200.

7 *Ibid.*, 9, 361–2.

8 *Collected Letters of Samuel Taylor Coleridge*, ed. E.L. Griggs, 6 vols. (Oxford, 1956–71), 5, 309. S.T. Coleridge, *The Friend*, ed. B. Rooke, 1, 471; *Philosophical Lectures*, ed. K. Coburn (London, 1949), 25.

9 Davy, *Works*, 1, 13; Hartley, *Davy*, 12.

the newly founded Medical Pneumatic Institution. Once ensconced, Davy expanded his program to give more emphasis to poetry and to metaphysics, and made a '*Resolution* ... To work two hours with pen before breakfast on the "Lover of Nature"; and "The Feelings of Eldon," from six till eight; from nine till two, in experiments; from four to six, reading; seven till ten, metaphysical reading (i.e. system of the universe).'[10] Davy's new-found devotion to the writing of epic poetry was encouraged by Robert Southey. Davy responded vigorously, sending him plans and drafts of poems for criticism, and submitting poems for publication in Southey's *Annual Anthology*.[11] The first volume of this would-be annual contained Davy's 'Sons of Genius,' boldly expressing his personal and scientific aspirations:

> While Superstition rules the vulgar soul,
> Fobids the energies of man to ride,
> Raised far above her low, her mean controul,
> Aspiring Genius seeks her native skies. ...

> To scan the laws of Nature, to explore
> The tranquil reign of mild Philosophy;
> Or on Newtonian wings sublime to soar
> Through the bright regions of the starry sky. ...

> From these pursuits the Sons of Genius scan
> The end of their creation; hence they know
> The fair, sublime, immortal hopes of man,
> From whence alone undying pleasures glow. ...

> Like the tumultuous billows of the sea
> Succeed the generations of mankind;
> Some in oblivious silence pass away,
> And leave no vestige of their lives behind. ...

> Like you proud rocks amidst the sea of time,
> Superior, scorning all the billows' rage,
> The living Sons of Genius stand sublime,
> Th' immortal children of another age.[12]

10 Davy, *Works*, 1, 59–60. The Pneumatic Institution is described in T.H. Levere, 'Dr. Thomas Beddoes and the Establishment of His Pneumatic Institution,' *Notes and Records of the Royal Society of London*, 32 (1977), 41–9.
11 *Fragmentary Remains, Literary and Scientific of Sir Humphry Davy, Bart.*, ed. J. Davy (London, 1858), 34. J.Z. Fullmer, 'The Poetry of Humphry Davy,' *Chymia*, VI (1960), 102. *The Annual Anthology*, ed. R. Southey, 2 vols. (Bristol, 1799–1800), 1, 93–9, 120–5, 172–6, 179–80, 281–6; 2, 293–6.
12 Reprinted in J.A. Paris, *The Life of Sir Humphry Davy, Bart.*, 2 vols. (London, 1831), 1, 25–9.

This was practically Davy's manifesto and his career plan. He knew that he was a genius, destined for glory and immortality through imperishable discoveries, and he dreamed of becoming the Newton of chemistry – Dalton, who proposed a chemical atomic theory and formulated the laws regulating chemical combining proportions, subsequently emerged as the Kepler in this scenario. Genius was a preoccupation of Romantic poets and philosophers, but it was scarcely their private preserve.

The aspirations of genius fired Davy's ambitions for himself, his science, and his country. True glory was to be achieved through science. Politics and warfare might lead to temporary eminence, but advances in science led to the highest honours and distinctions, for these alone endured. Genius was, moreover, God-given, unlike merely temporal dignity. 'Persons of very exalted talents and virtues,' Davy remarked, 'may be said to derive their patent of nobility directly from God; and their titles are not registered in perishable court calendars, but written in the great histories of Nature or of Man.' In his last work, *Consolations in Travel; or, The Last Days of a Philosopher*, Davy put into the mouth of that work's hero, the all but autobiographical Unknown, a description of man ennobled and civilized through science, taming the earth and subduing it to his needs and comforts, 'perpetuating thought in imperishable words, rendering immortal the exertions of genius and presenting them as common property to all awakening minds, – becoming as it were the true image of divine intelligence of civilisation.'[13] In 'The Sons of Genius,' written in or around 1795, the scientist of genius was portrayed as one above mere terrestrial cares; thirty-five years later, Davy had come to see the material benefits deriving from the applications of science as important concerns of even the purest natural philosopher.

But whether immortality sprang from the abstracted contemplation of nature, or from the triumphs of applied science, glory accrued to scientists of genius. The point may be illustrated by the contrast that Davy postulated between projectors and other alchemical charlatans on the one hand and '*true alchemical philosophers*' on the other. The latter, Davy argued, 'had often sublime and elevated views. The idea of glory was continually present to them. To ameliorate the condition of humanity, and to support the interests of religion, were constantly held out as their objects. ... [T]heir errors were the errors natural to an infant science; but their industry was unceasing, their *hopes glorious*, and their discoveries eminently useful.' The emergence in Davy of a marriage of the concepts of utility and glory enabled him to lecture on agricultural chemistry and to adopt an entrepreneurial ideology while at

13 H. Davy, *Consolations in Travel; or, The Last Days of a Philosopher*, 1st ed. (London, 1830); 5th ed. (London, 1851), 238. Davy, *Works*, 1, 212. *Consolations* (1851), 244.

the same time sharing Romantic concerns with genius, creativity, and the harmony of nature.[14]

It was this facet of Davy's receptive mind that made him so eagerly responsive first to Southey, and afterwards to Coleridge and Words-worth. Their admiration of him as a scientific prodigy could not but season his responsiveness. Southey left it to Davy to revise and publish his long poem 'Thalaba, the Destroyer.' Davy in turn cheered Coleridge on in the fight to purify language: 'You are to be the Thalaba of all the Daemons existing in the world of Language, the rooter out of all the weeds & unnatural plants that the hand of civilized man has sown in the idea of passion & of nature.'[15] Wordsworth and Coleridge sought Davy's aid in seeing their *Lyrical Ballads* through the press, and Wordsworth in the preface to that work addressed Davy about the respective claims and language of science and poetry.[16] Walter Scott was to write after Davy's death that he 'would have established himself in the first ranks of England's living poets, if the Genius of our country had not decreed that he should rather be the first in the first rank of its philosophers and scientific benefactors.' Only Southey's epitaph for Davy was perhaps ambivalent, stating that 'he had all the elements of a poet; he only wanted the art.'[17]

Art or skill aside, Davy was convinced that great powers were necessarily accompanied by intense feelings; he planned, as we have seen, to write a poem entitled 'The Lover of Nature'; he adopted the stance, albeit in semi-fiction, that wildness was part of the true poetical temperament; and he agreed with his fiancée that mountain scenery exalted the imagination. His 'Sons of Genius' were above all material cares precisely because of their love of nature, and they dutifully delighted not only in the pastoral but also in nature's grand scenes, the great, the sublime, and the terrible. In 'The Sybil's Temple,' inspired by a visit to Tivoli on his first continental tour, Davy wrote of a sublime sympathy with natural forms and sounds, in which the mind 'forgets/Its present being.'[18]

All the ingredients are present for the construction of a sociologist's extinct dream, the ideal type of the Romantic poet. But one may come to suspect that much of Davy's Romantic inspiration lay in his enthusiastic desire to emulate his friends the Lake Poets, and that his delight in

14 *Works*, 1, 146–7. Morris Berman, *Social Change and Scientific Organization: The Royal Institution, 1799–1844* (London and Ithaca, NY, 1978).

15 H. Davy to S.T. Coleridge, 26 Nov. 1800: Pierpont Morgan Library MS MA 1857 No. 11.

16 R. Sharrock, 'The Chemist and the Poet: Sir Humphry Davy and the Preface to the *Lyrical Ballads*,' *Notes and Records of the Royal Society of London*, 17 (1964), 57.

17 S.T. Coleridge, *Poetical Works*, ed. E.H. Coleridge (London, 1973), 595. Davy, *Fragmentary Remains*, 33.

18 Davy, *Works*, 1, 62, 60; *Consolations* (1851), 18; *Works*, 1, 24–5, 186.

nature was more that of the scientist and fly-fisherman than that of the poet. 'Oh, most magnificent and noble Nature!' he exclaimed in a notebook,

> Have I not worshipped thee with such a love
> As never mortal man before displayed?
> Adored thee in thy majesty of visible creation,
> And searched into thy hidden and mysterious ways
> As Poet, as Philosopher, as Sage?[19]

The natural philosopher's love of nature for its law-abiding harmonies was truly Davy's own. Poetic imagination was there too, but needing more deliberate cultivation. He succeeded, not long after 1795, in achieving a poetic experience at once romantic and Spinozistic. 'To-day, for the first time in my life,' he recorded, 'I have had a distinct sympathy with nature. I was lying on the top of a rock to leeward; the wind was high, and everything in motion ...; everything was alive, and myself part of the series of visible impressions' – visible impressions smack more of Hartley and Locke than of Wordsworth, and a later addition to this notebook entry completes the transition from Romantic poet to scientist. 'Deeply and intimately connected,' Davy concluded, 'are all our ideas of motion and life, and this, probably, from very early association. How different is the idea of life in a physiologist and a poet!'[20]

The difference became for Davy not merely one of kind, but also one of value. By the time that he was lecturing on geology at the Royal Institution, he had clearly subordinated poetic to scientific pleasures. 'The image of a mountain country, which is the very theatre of the science,' he told his audience, 'is, in almost all cases, highly impressive and delightful; but a new and nobler species of enjoyment arises in the mind when the arrangement in it, its uses and its subserviency to life, are considered.' Increasingly, he came to see poetry as but a vehicle for transitory pleasure, while science was enduring, beautiful, useful, and true. In 1812 Davy, lecturing on electrochemistry, asserted that all knowledge was acquired by the senses, and that 'nature has no archetype in the human imagination.'[21]

Here was a rejection of a philosophical position shared by many Romantics, cogently developed in England by Coleridge, in ways that

19 *Fragmentary Remains*, 14.
20 *Works*, 1, 66–7. Cf. T.H. Levere, 'S.T. Coleridge: A Poet's View of Science,' *Annals of Science*, 35 (1978), 33–44; T. McFarland, *Coleridge and the Pantheist Tradition* (Oxford, 1969); D.M. Knight, 'The Physical Sciences and the Romantic Movement,' *History of Science*, 9 (1970), 54–75; D.M. Knight, 'The Scientist as Sage,' *Studies in Romanticism*, 6 (1967), 65–88.
21 Lecture of 1811, based on lecture of 1805, *Works*, 8, 200. *Ibid.*, 347.

254

went well beyond Schelling's *Naturphilosophie*. Schelling had presented natural phenomena as the limited products of developing mind.[22] For Coleridge, there was a sense in which nature could be regarded as constituted by ideas of mind; laws of nature and ideas of reason thus exhibited a congruence based on their underlying unity. Given the intimate connection between Coleridge's conception of reason and imagination, it followed that nature did have its archetype in the human imagination. Davy, believing otherwise, was effectively disjoining himself from whole traditions of idealistic philosophy. He was as clear as could be about the need for that disjunction, while hazy about recent developments in Germany, where, he complained, 'the metaphysical dogmas of Kant which as far as I can learn are pseudo platonism are preferred before the doctrines of Locke and Hartley, excellence and knowledge being rather sought for in the infant than in the adult state of the mind.'[23]

Davy's mixture of ignorance of philosophical idealism and distaste for it, especially in its modern German guise, was orthodox among British scientists. John Herschel, whose *Preliminary Discourse on the Study of Natural Philosophy* (London, 1830) offered a popular statement of the reigning empiricism, castigated *Naturphilosophie* as false, delusive, and heretical. Davy was in the mainstream. His revulsion against philosophies outside British empiricism was accompanied by the recognition that he was to be a scientist, a natural and especially a chemical philosopher, and not a poet. Underneath a prospectus that he drew up for a volume of poems, he wrote definitively:

These were the visions of my youth
Which fled before the voice of truth.[24]

In 1801, leaving his youth in the West Country behind him, Davy, whose ideas had impressed Count Rumford, removed from Bristol to Rumford's Royal Institution, and from the society of poets, radicals, and democrats[25] to the society of established landowners. The latter were imbued with an entrepreneurial ideology of science new in England although already held by the improving landlords of Scotland and, albeit more theoretically, by the philosophers and virtuosi of the French and the prior English Enlightenment. Only now – with an

22 B. Gower, 'Speculation in Physics: The History and Practice of *Naturphilosophie*,' *Studies in History and Philosophy of Science*, 3 (1973), 301–56.
23 T.H. Levere, *Studies in Romanticism*, 16 (1977), 349–79; *Affinity and Matter: Elements of Chemical Philosophy 1800–1865* (Oxford, 1971), 33 (R.I. MS n.d., but *ca.* 1808). D.M. Knight, *The Transcendental Part of Chemistry* (Folkestone, 1978), chap. 4.
24 *Fragmentary Remains*, 13.
25 J. Colmer, *Coleridge, Critic of Society* (Oxford, 1959).

expanding population and scarcity of grain for bread and of oak bark for tanning leather for shoes, with an economy still in the throes of industrial revolution, and with the need to arm and organize society in the face of fears of French invasion and of revolution at home – only now did the ideology of science gain a new dynamic. The Royal Institution was in the vanguard of this process. Shrewd aims and, even more significantly, a substantial overlap between the membership of the Board of Agriculture and the early governance of the Royal Institution soon led the latter body into the more remunerative aspects of agricultural development.[26]

The Royal Institution in its first decade was, in short, precisely the foundation in which science emerged as a directing force in society; and it did so with the co-operation of great landowners and leading Fellows of the Royal Society, including its president, but in a far more equivocal relation to other commercial interests. Davy's appointment to the Royal Institution gave immediate and tremendous scope to his ambitions and abilities, neither of which he had ever sought to disguise.

He responded eagerly and shrewdly to the genteel audience and new social sphere to which his responsibilities now introduced him. Coleridge, himself a more fundamental critic of society, was disillusioned, even appalled, at what he saw as Davy's apostasy from youthful radical ideals. He feared that Davy's promise might be strangled by the serpent of ambition, and complained that Davy moulded himself more and more upon the age, so that the age might mould itself upon him.[27] But in a way that Coleridge totally failed to comprehend, Davy's ambition fired his enthusiasm for scientific research. Shortly after his promotion to lecturer in chemistry at the Royal Institution, Davy wrote to his old friend John King, working with Beddoes in Bristol: 'The voice of fame is murmuring in my ear – My mind has been excited by the unexpected plaudits of the multitude – I dream of greatness & utility – I dream of science restoring to Nature what Luxury, what civilization have stolen from her – pure hearts, the forms of angels, bosoms beautiful; & panting with joy and hope. ... So much for egotism – for weak, glorious, pitiful, sublime, conceited egotism.'[28] Coleridge could only hope that Davy's intellectual powers would protect his moral character. 'There does not exist,' he remarked hopefully, 'an instance of a *deep* metaphysician who was not led by his speculations to an austere system of morals.' He continued to fear for Davy's morals.[29]

Davy, for his part, saw his chance, and seized it. He had begun admiring Newton and the pure intellectual light of scientific discovery,

26 Berman, *Social Change*.
27 J. Colmer, *Coleridge. The Notebooks of Samuel Taylor Coleridge*, ed. K. Coburn, vols. 1–3 of 5 vols. (London, 1957–ぁ), II, entry 1855.
28 Bristol City Archives, MS 32688/31, 22 June 1801.
29 *Collected Letters of ... Coleridge*, 2, 768.

had gone on to work under Beddoes in an attempt to develop chemical and medical knowledge in the service of mankind, and had then been translated to London by Rumford, part-time philanthropist, entrepreneur, and adventurer extraordinary. Now, at the Royal Institution, he was called upon to give chemical lectures to the higher classes, to advise the Board of Agriculture on technical scientific matters, and to develop a research program in chemistry. This experience and these aims were not mutually contradictory. One needed only to appeal to Francis Bacon's notion of science yielding both fruit and light, material and intellectual benefits, in order to see how Davy's experience could serve his ambition. Davy's ideology proved compatible with that of the landowners. The time he spent on applied research, and the cost of such equipment as platinum crucibles or a voltaic pile of two thousand plates, suggest that experiments of light were important to the managers of the Royal Institution, just as Davy knew the need for experiments of fruit.[30]

Davy's greatest initial contributions were to chemical science in its intellectual rather than utilitarian aspects. He attacked Lavoisier's invention of caloric, the matter of heat, invoked to explain thermal phenomena in chemistry; he developed a theory of the relation of chemical to electrical action that was at least susceptible of an interpretation based on forces or powers; and he assailed Lavoisier's revolutionary table of the chemical elements. Seeking, as Coleridge had urged, for an understanding of power and arrangement in chemistry, he used the current electricity of the voltaic pile, discovered in 1800, as a source of polar power to investigate bodies.[31] The discoveries he made and his lectures about them delighted Coleridge, who sought and found in Davy's researches confirmation of philosophical views, and visible symbols of poetical truths. Chemistry in England and France was, in the early 1800s, based on essentially mechanical philosophy, to which Dalton's atomic theory gave succinct expression. Such a system made it hard to account for chemical qualities, or reactions, or relations between reactants and products. A contemporary alternative to atomic chemistry was a dynamical chemistry, based upon powers and their mutual modifications and relations, in conformity with the universal law of polarity. Coleridge, elaborating this alternative, saw the chemical elements of the laboratory as symbols of polar powers, whose dynamic reconciliation constituted chemical combination. The nature philosophers of Germany recognized the overriding importance of polarity in chemistry, philosophy, and all of physical and mental nature.[32]

Schelling and his followers were scarcely empiricist philistines. Even

---

30 *Pace* Berman, *Social Change*, esp. chap. 2; my indebtedness to Berman is none the less considerable and obvious.

31 Hartley, *Davy*, *passim*.

32 *The Friend*, ed. B. Rooke, 1, 94, 471. *Affinity and Matter*, chap. 4.

those among them most skilled in experiment were given to confusing theory with fact. Ritter was typical in this respect. Davy, however, although given to great theorizing, was condescending about Ritter's errors as a theorist, extracting empirical nuggets from accounts of Ritter's work, and discounting everything else. Coleridge shared Davy's unease at German failures adequately to distinguish the speculative from the empirical, and came for a while to see Davy as the only hope for dynamic and romantic chemistry.

Davy seemed, after all, to adhere to a dynamical theory of matter – at any rate, he discussed chemical reactions in terms of forces, and was interested in Boscovich's and Priestley's theories that matter *was* essentially force. He also knew and, at least for a while, admired Bishop Berkeley's writings: and Berkeley, as Coleridge saw it, 'needed only an entire instead of a partial emancipation from the fetters of the mechanic philosophy in order to have enunciated all that is true and important in modern Chemistry.' Davy was, in short, well prepared intellectually; with his undoubted genius in the laboratory, he was, or seemed to Coleridge, the ideal man in England to accomplish the much needed reform of chemistry. Not only was Davy using polar power – current electricity – to probe the relations of bodies, but, for reasons metaphysical and theological, he believed in the order, unity, and simplicity of the natural world. Lavoisier's table of elements, published in 1789, was neither rationally ordered nor simple. It was, moreover, French, and an enemy invention.[33] It is worth remembering that Davy's principal researches were executed during the Napoleonic wars; that French chemists were Davy's keenest rivals; and that, as Davy's visit to France in 1813 clearly showed, scientific debate was far from immune to the pressures of national prestige.[34]

Davy, imbued with eighteenth-century English philosophy, natural theology, and patriotic fervour, tinged ever so lightly with second-hand German metaphysics, and armed with electrical power and the conviction of his own genius, probed the weakest parts of Lavoisier's table. In his early lectures, following his experiments on the amalgamation of potassium and ammonia with mercury, he argued that nitrogen was not a simple body, but could be converted to oxygen and another, hitherto unknown substance, related to an inferred principle supposed to be common to all the metals. This argument fitted well with German philosophical and dynamic chemistry, and not at all with corpuscular chemistry; it was also, unhappily, based on faulty analyses.[35]

33 See note 16 above, and especially *Studies in Romanticism*, 16, 361. S.T. Coleridge, note on flyleaf of G. Berkeley, *Siris*, 2nd ed. (Dublin and London, 1744), in Beinecke Rare Book Library, Yale University.

34 G. de Beer, *The Sciences Were Never at War* (London, 1960), stresses the continuity of scientific exchanges during the wars.

35 Levere, *Affinity and Matter*, 46.

Not all Davy's attacks on Lavoisier's table were delusive. His discovery of the alkali metals in 1807 was dramatic, and his experimental demonstrations were beautiful in their logic and style. The chemical action of electricity was partially elucidated, and the caustic alkalis shown to be compound – all in a manner further supportive of dynamism, however casual and shifting Davy's commitment to dynamism may have been. Coleridge was positively exalted by the discovery of the alkali metals: Davy's 'March of Glory' had led him to 'discoveries more intellectual, more ennobling and impowering human Nature, than Newton's!' Berzelius called the paper 'one of the best ... which has ever enriched the theory of chemistry.' Even Brougham paid tribute through the *Edinburgh Review*.[36]

Davy was certainly fulfilling his ambition 'on Newtonian wings sublime to soar.' It is ironic that even his most striking discoveries brought tribulation. Alas, in discovering sodium and potassium, far from exposing greater simplicity in nature, he added to the number of chemical elements. His fame as a chemical philosopher rested largely upon the contradiction of his beliefs, beliefs made explicit in his lectures. 'It seems very probable,' he wrote, 'from the past [process] of discovery – ... That the number of elements will be diminished: and that arrangements of a very simple nature will explain these phenomena which are now referred to complicated and diversified agents.' When the parts of nature are seen in their proper relations, 'they appear as sounds of one voice, impulses of one eternal intelligence.'[37] Guided by this view of nature, he made discoveries that contradicted it, but that won him glory. And glory, as we have seen from the outset, was what he sought.

Davy was concerned, both within himself and in pleading his cause before society, to establish a proper sense of the nobility of the scientific enterprise. He was fond of quoting Bacon. In 1808 he told an audience that Bacon had said that 'The introduction of noble discoveries seems to hold by far the most excellent place among all human actions; and this was the judgment of antiquity which attributed *divine* honours to inventors, but conferred only *heroical* honours on those who deserved well of their country in civil affairs. And whoever rightly considers, will find this a judicious custom.' Davy believed that everything grand and dignified had arisen from the union of science with religion.[38] He assured

36 H. Davy, 'The Bakerian Lecture, on Some Chemical Agencies of Electricity,' Royal Society, *Phil. Trans.* 97 (1807), 1–56; 'The Bakerian Lecture, on Some New Phenomena of Chemical Changes Produced by Electricity, particularly the Decomposition of the Fixed Alkalies ... ,' *ibid.*, 98 (1808), 1–44. Both papers use Lavoisier's concept of an element while correcting Lavoisier's table of elements. *Collected Letters of ... Coleridge*, 3, 38, 41. Berzelius, *Traité de chimie*, trans. Jourdain & Esslinger, 8 vols. (Paris, 1829–33)1,164. Henry Brougham, *Edinburgh Review*, 11 (1808), 390–8, 394–401, 483–90.

37 R.I. MS 1, quoted in *Affinity and Matter*, 66–7.

38 *Fragmentary Remains*, 59, 164.

readers of his *Consolations in Travel* that 'there never has been a higher source of honour or distinction than that connected with advances in science.' To understand the operations of nature and their utility for man, 'to bring the lightning from the clouds and make it subservient to our experiments': in such activities lay glory, honour, even sublimity. Like Bacon, Davy felt that light was superior to fruit, that understanding was superior to application – but genius, he believed, consisted in the perpetuation of individual existence through ideas that in their applica-tion transformed society.[39] Thus light and fruit were interdependent, and both contributed to glory. In this scheme, Romantic and utilitarian ideals reinforced one another.

Davy wanted the immortality that was the due of scientific genius. He was not, however, immune from more immediate ambitions. 'It is not that honours are worth having,' he observed, 'but it is painful not to have them.' It was, after all, only just that civilized society should recognize the merits of those who had most contributed to its prosperity. 'In reality,' Davy explained, 'the origin, as well as the progress, and improvement of civil society is founded in mechanical and chemical inventions.' Even in his early years, he took a liberally but not exclusively utilitarian view of the sciences, which, he argued, 'ought to be considered as related to man only so far as they are capable of promoting his happiness.' Chemistry deserved well in such a scheme; it was not only conducive to intellectual delights, but it applied to the needs and operations of everyday life which, perfected by science, 'have become the sources of the most refined enjoyments and delicate pleasures of civilized society.' Science, in short, was more than speculation and theory; it was at the heart of progress and civilization.[40] Davy, as president of the Royal Society of London, was an effective spokesman for science, skilled in eliciting patronage from those in power.[41]

Davy's own useful contributions included his work in tanning and agricultural chemistry, and his attempts to reduce the corrosion of ships' bottoms.[42] These attempts were electrochemically sound, and did indeed reduce corrosion; but they foundered biochemically, increasing barnacle incrustation. The miner's safety lamp was Davy's greatest practical triumph. Among other tributes, he received a service of plate at a dinner in Newcastle in 1817. Davy's speech of acceptance expresses his satisfaction at the knowledge that his work had contributed to 'arts, ... manufactures, commerce, and national wealth.' 'To learn this from such practical authority,' he continued, 'is the highest gratification to a

39 *Consolations* (1851), 238, 258. *Works*, 1, 62.
40 *Works*, 1, 69; 2, 315; 8, 87.
41 G.L'E. Turner, *The Patronage of Science in the Nineteenth Century* (Leyden, 1976).
42 *Elements of Agricultural Chemistry* (London, 1813). Royal Society, *Phil. Trans.*, 114 (1824), 151–8.

person whose ardent desire has always been to apply science to purposes of utility.' He descanted upon the importance of science to the sources of wealth and power in the state, and concluded by stressing the circumstances that his invention of the safety lamp was the fruit of the pursuit of proper scientific method. In glory, in utility, in pleasure, and in rewards there should be no divorce between pure and applied science.[43]

Balance was crucial. Davy had a profound contempt for those who would debase science to mere application, and who failed to perceive the splendour of the discovery of a new law. The fabric of law that unified nature was what the chemical philosopher sought, and the dignity of science was independent of its applications.[44] But those applications, resting upon scientific discovery, were not to be despised. Light gave rise to fruit, and both contributed to pleasure and glory.

Certainly Davy's own pleasure was much enhanced by the renewed recognition that his discovery won for him. Sir Joseph Banks wrote cordially to him that, although his researches on the safety lamp were intrinsically less brilliant than those on the alkali metals, they would be of greater service to the Royal Society and to the public image of science. John Playfair, who had courted and lost Jane Apreece, generously wrote that 'it may fairly be said that there is hardly in the whole compass of art or science a single invention of which one would rather be the author ... This is exactly such a case as we should choose to place before Bacon, were he to revisit the earth, in order to give him ... an idea of the advancement which philosophy has made.'[45] In view of the rage for empiricist Baconianism, this was a compliment indeed. So too was the baronetcy that the safety lamp won for Davy. His career was punctuated by honours, which, combined with his humble origins, made him a perfect illustration of Samuel Smiles's *Self Help*. 'What I am,' said Davy, 'I have made myself. I say this without vanity, and in pure simplicity of heart.'[46] Elsewhere, he tells us what he is: poet, philosopher, sage, benefactor of mankind, and genius. Having considered him under the three last categories, it is time to return to the first two.

He had early determined to pursue a career in science rather than in poetry, making a clear distinction between the poetic and the scientific apprehension of nature, following a different path from the Romantics but yet admired by them. Real philosophers – pure scientists – had often through their researches conferred material benefits upon mankind, while offering delight and enrichment to the intellect. It was this double

43 *Works*, 1, 207–8.
44 *Fragmentary Remains*, 58.
45 Banks to Davy, 30 Oct. 1815, *Fragmentary Remains*, 208–9. *Works*, 1, 202.
46 S. Smiles, *Self Help*, 1st ed. (1859); reprint (London, 1908), p. 14.

function that marked the superiority of science to poetry. Poetry exalted the mind, but had no absolute utility. Scientific pursuits reached to the heavens in their 'sublime speculations,' although belonging in their application to the earth. In a complete reversal of the judgment of Coleridge, Davy compared great poets unfavourably with great natural philosophers. 'At that time, when Bacon created a new world of intellect, and Shakespeare a new world of imagination, it is not a question to me which has produced the greatest effect upon the progress of society – Shakespeare or Bacon, Milton or Newton.' Works of poetic imagination 'resemble monstrous flowers, brilliant and odorous, but affording no materials of re-production.'[47]

The message was clear. Scientific discovery was glorious, and the achievements of scientific imagination were for Davy higher than those of poetic imagination precisely because the former bore fruit while the latter were brilliant but materially barren. Davy may have provided Romantic poets with their prime English example of scientific genius and creativity, but except for a period of youthful mutual sympathetic admiration, Davy did not reciprocate their sentiments. Coleridge once described Shakespeare's writings as nature realized in poetry, and Davy's chemistry as poetry realized in nature. Davy would have denied that there was such a symmetry between poetry and science. He was no mere utilitarian; but his ambitious quest for glory has its utilitarian as well as Romantic aspect. His last book, *Consolations in Travel*, epitomizes the blend of dignity, utility, permanence, and consonance with the tenets of reason and religion that characterized his vision of science. And the utterances of the Unknown constitute Davy's own *apologia* for a life spent in science and society.

---

47 *Consolations* (1851), 257–9. *Works*, 1, 147, 212. Levere, *Annals of Science*, 35 (1978), 33–44.

XII

S. T. Coleridge: A Poet's View of Science

Summary

This paper is concerned with Coleridge's view of science as at once a branch of knowledge and a creative activity, mediating between man and nature, and thereby complementing poetry. Coleridge was well-informed about contemporary science. He stressed the symbolic status of scientific language, the role of scientific genius, and the need in science to rely upon reason rather than the unqualified senses. Kepler and, more recently, John Hunter and Humphry Davy provided his favorite instances of scientific genius, while chemistry—Davy's not Lavoisier's—was poetic. Science and poetry could both rely on reason, the power of language, and faithfulness to nature.

1. Introduction

The unity and variety of the thought of Samuel Taylor Coleridge (1772–1834) are by now commonplace, facilitating recognition of the sciences as significant in the formation and development of his thought.[1] Notebooks and other surviving manuscripts show that he was strikingly knowledgeable about the non-mathematical sciences of his day.[2] His approach to science was unusual in early nineteenth-century literary society. He was not content with the role of interested spectator, nor did he simply come to science as a poet seeking images.[3] Coleridge, as William Walsh wrote, was a critic with a poet inside him and a philosopher on his back.[4] He brought these three activities together, notably in the *Biographia literaria* of 1817, which was ' introductory to . . . the application of the rules deduced from philosophical principles to poetry and criticism '.[5] His sympathetic and thorough approach to science involved these three elements. Firstly, science provided a foundation for his philosophy.[6] Secondly, he came to regard science and poetry as complementary forms of creative activity.[7] Thirdly, he saw criticism's

---

[1] This is particularly well brought out in Owen Barfield's *What Coleridge thought* (1972, London).

[2] Craig W. Miller, ' Coleridge's concept of Nature ', *Journal of the history of ideas*, **25** (1964), 77–96. I discuss Coleridge's scheme of the sciences and his detailed knowledge of individual branches of science in a monograph on Coleridge and science, now in preparation.

[3] His approach here is very different from, for example, Tennyson's. See S. Gliserman, ' Early Victorian science writers on Tennyson's " In Memoriam ": a study in cultural exchange ', *Victorian studies*, **18** (1975), 277–308, 437–459.

[4] W. Walsh, *Coleridge. The work and the relevance* (1967, London), 51.

[5] S. T. Coleridge, *Biographia literaria* (ed. G. Watson: 1965, Everyman's Library, London and New York), 1.

[6] For example, Coleridge to J. H. Frere, 6 June 1826, in E. L. Griggs (ed.), *Collected letters of Samuel Taylor Coleridge* (6 vols., 1956–71; Oxford), vol. 6, 583.

[7] *The collected works of Samuel Taylor Coleridge, Bollingen series LXXV* (ed. K. Coburn): vol. 4, *The friend* (ed. B. Rooke: 1969, Princeton), vol. 1, 471.

ultimate end as the establishment of principles, in politics as in literature; and he believed that these principles were strongly influenced by the predominant philosophy of the age, that was in turn influenced by science.[8]   He made it his business to learn what he could of the sciences.   The unity of intellectual life was scarcely a new notion, but Coleridge's adoption of it was unique in detail and bewildering in form to most of his English contemporaries.   His view of science is closer to the dynamism of German Romantic philosophy and to the idealism of the Neoplatonists than to the materialism of late eighteenth- and early nineteenth-century British science, with its atoms and imponderable fluids.[9]

The ways that Coleridge incorporated science into his thought are reflected in the ways that he came to science.[10]   In 1796 Thomas Beddoes introduced him to chemistry, natural philosophy and physiology, and probably encouraged him to visit Germany in 1798.[11]   There he studied physiology and natural history under Blumenbach.[12]   When he returned in 1799 he met Humphry Davy, whose later galvanic researches were highly significant for Coleridge's view of dynamic science.[13]   Meanwhile he read Kant, and moved on to Schelling and *Naturphilosophie*.[14]   Readings in the philosophy of nature took him to the corresponding natural sciences.   When he came to Dr. Gillman's in 1816, he at first concentrated on physiology.[15]   In 1819 he studied chemistry systematically, and by 1820 moved on to the life sciences.[16]   These were also the years in which he sought to relate *Naturphilosophie* to chemistry, geology, physiology, cosmology and cosmogony.[17]   His interest in science thus dated from no later than 1796, while the bulk of his scientific reading was between 1815 and 1825.   In that decade, the focus though not the boundary of this paper, he tentatively and progressively incorporated his scientific knowledge into his own philosophy of nature.   The stimulus of Davy's work made chemistry seminal and prominent in that elaboration.

Coleridge's concern with science arose partly from personal sympathy with chemists and doctor,[18] but principally from his mutually illuminating interests

[8] *Biographia* (footnote 5), 217; *Collected letters* (footnote 6), vol. 4, 759–763.

[9] G. N. G. Orsini, *Coleridge and German idealism* (1969, Carbondale and Edwardsville, London and Amsterdam); F. Brinkley (ed.), *Coleridge on the seventeenth century* (1955, Durham, N.C.); A. Thackray, *Atoms and powers* (1970, Cambridge, Mass.); and W. Schrickx, ' Coleridge and the Cambridge Platonists ', *Review of English literature*, **7** (1966), 77–79.

[10] A general biography is J. D. Campbell, *Samuel Taylor Coleridge.   A narrative of the events of his life* (1894, London; reprinted 1970, Highgate).

[11] K. Coburn (ed.), *The notebooks of Samuel Taylor Coleridge* (5 vols., 1957–   , New York then Princeton), vol. 1, entry 249n.

[12] E. J. Morley, ' Coleridge in Germany (1799) ', in E. L. Griggs (ed.), *Wordsworth and Coleridge. Studies in honor of George McLean Harper* (1939, Princeton), 220–236.

[13] T. H. Levere, *Affinity and matter.   Elements of chemical philosophy 1800–1865* (1971, Oxford), chapter 2.

[14] Orsini (footnote 9).

[15] S. T. Coleridge, *Hints towards the formation of a more comprehensive theory of life* (1848, London) was begun in 1816.   The partial locus of this work is described in O. Temkin, ' Basic science, medicine, and the Romantic era ', *Bulletin of the history of medicine*, **37** (1963), 97–129; and in J. Toulmin-Goodfield, ' Some aspects of English physiology: 1780–1840 ', *Journal of the history of biology*, **2** (1969), 283–320.

[16] British Library Add. Mss. 47,525 and 47,526 (Coleridge notebooks 27 and 28).

[17] *Ibid.*; and Coleridge notebook 29, Berg collection, New York Public Library.

[18] R. Guest-Gornall, ' Samuel Taylor Coleridge and the doctors ', *Medical history*, **17** (1973), 327–342.

in the world of nature and in himself.   He sought parallels between development in nature and the powers of the human mind.[19]   German philosophers of nature, led by Fichte and Schelling, had started from Kant's doctrine of the self and had gone on to consider the relations between mind and nature.[20] Coleridge accordingly found support and encouragement in the enquiries of the *Naturphilosophen*.[21] Like them, he pursued the investigation of self deliberately to extend his consciousness.   His concepts of nature, self and consciousness contributed essentially to his view of science, and must therefore be considered here.

2. Self-consciousness and nature

I shall start with Coleridge and self-consciousness, moving thence to knowledge and to nature; from nature through language and symbol to science and to poetry; through science and poetry to harmony with the powers of nature and to an end of domination by the senses; and back again from poetry to the extension of consciousness.   The links in the argument reflect the complex unity of Coleridge's thought.

' [T]here is one knowledge ', he wrote, ' which it is everyman's interest and duty to acquire, namely SELF-KNOWLEDGE: or to what end was man alone, of all animals, endued by the Creator with the faculty of self-consciousness? '.[22] ' [C]onscious self-knowlege ' was simply Reason, the highest intellectual faculty, whose objects were ' God, the Soul eternal Truth '.[23]   Without such knowledge mankind was degraded: with it, mankind became the crown of creation.

Knowledge, however, including self-knowledge, was not only of essences, things known in and of themselves, but also of relations.   This was necessarily so, since Coleridge was passionately convinced that the world was not made up of disconnected fragments.   His world was not a chaos but a cosmos governed by laws.[24]   Laws were the highest kind of relation in the physical sciences: ' in whatever [physical] science the relation of the parts to each other and to the whole is predetermined by a truth originating in the *mind*, there we affirm the presence of a law . . . '.[25]   Nature's laws, originating in mind, were god given, and part of the unity of nature.   So too was the human mind.   The common source of rationality in man and nature made possible man's comprehension of nature.   Coleridge, in the *Biographia literaria*, followed Schelling in stressing ' the absolute identity of subject and object, which it calls nature, and which in its highest power is nothing but self-conscious will or intelligence '.[26] Mankind could thus come to self-knowledge only in relation to God and to

[19] D. Emmet, ' Coleridge on powers in mind and nature ', in J. Beer (ed.), *Coleridge's variety. Bicentenary studies* (1974, London), 166–182.

[20] B. Gower, ' Speculation in physics: the history and practice of *Naturphilosophie* ', *Stud. hist. phil. sci.*, **3** (1973), 301–356.

[21] For example, *Biographia* (footnote 5), 86.

[22] S. T. Coleridge, *Aids to reflection* (ed. Thomas Fenby: 1905, Edinburgh), xi (1st edition 1825). For an account of the significance of self-consciousness for Coleridge, see K. Coburn, *The self-conscious imagination, a study of the Coleridge notebooks* (Riddell memorial lectures, 44th series: 1974, London).

[23] *The friend* (footnote 7), vol. 1, 156.

[24] M. H. Abrams, ' Coleridge and the Romantic vision of the world ', in Beer (footnote 19), 101–133.

[25] *The friend* (footnote 7), vol. 1, 459.

[26] *Biographia* (footnote 5), 155.

nature. Knowledge of self was bound up with knowledge of the world of nature:

> 'Tis the sublime of man,
> Our noontide Majesty, to know ourselves
> Parts and proportions of one wondrous whole.[27]

Coleridge stressed the need to perceive and interpret relations, and sought in his educational schemes to inculcate the habit of looking for relations throughout nature.[28] He advocated the study of the sciences as admirably suited to revealing relations. Chemistry provided his favorite illustration of this theme, since it explored the hidden relations of elements: ' so water and flame, the diamond, the charcoal, and the mantling champagne, are convoked and fraternized by the theory of the chemist '.[29] Coleridge's dynamic philosophy also viewed the relations of chemical species as symbolizing the relations of polar powers underlying all natural phenomena. Electrolysis, for example, revealed the polar relations of hydrogen and oxygen, which symbolized the polarity of electrical power, itself a symbol of a stage in the construction of matter that Coleridge found in Schelling.[30] It is plausible to view his fascination with the natural sciences as partly motivated by the search for such relations, where substances could stand for underlying powers symbolizing the constitutive and generative processes of nature. Reason, conscious self-knowledge, was the instrument of this search and the unifying power in Coleridge's science, Imagination, the sometime equivalent of Reason, was equally a unifying power.[31] In the *Biographia*, Coleridge described the imagination as either primary or secondary. The former, as ' the prime agent of all human perception ', involved the relation between subject and object, knower and known, man and nature, man and himself; like Reason, it involved self-knowledge. The secondary imagination was identical in kind with the former, differing from it in degree and in its mode of operation. It ' struggles to idealize and to unify '.[32] Coleridge advanced these categories in discussing poetry. But he regarded science in the hands of genius as a unifying activity cognate with poetry; he saw Davy, his constant exemplar of scientific genius, as ' the Man who *born* a Poet first converted Poetry into Science and *realized* what few men possessed Genius enough to *fancy* '.[33] There was thus a symmetry between Coleridge's concepts of poetic and scientific activity. The poet could idealize nature in poetry, while the scientist could realize poetry in nature.[34]

---

[27] S. T. Coleridge, ' Religious musings ', lines 125–127, in *Coleridge. Poetical works* (1973 (from edition of 1912), London, New York, Toronto), 113–114.

[28] See, for example, S. T. Coleridge, British Library Add. Mss. 47, 521, f. 31; and *The friend* (footnote 7), vol. 1, 451, 458.

[29] *Ibid.*, 470. T. H. Levere, ' Coleridge and Romantic science ', in Knafla, Staum and Travers (eds.), *Science, technology, and culture in historical perspective* (1976, Calgary), 81–104 discusses these issues.

[30] *The friend* (footnote 7), vol. 1, 94n; Coleridge notebook 27 (footnote 16), f. 49. Schelling, 'Allgemeine Deduktion des dynamischen Prozesses ', in *Zeitschrift für spekulative Physik*, 1 (1800), pt. 2, 1–87; the copy of this journal annotated by Coleridge is in the British Library.

[31] S. T. Coleridge, Victoria College Library (Toronto, Canada), Ms. SMS 5: ' The Imagination is the synthetic Power '. Barfield (footnote 1) has chapters on Ideas and Laws, Reason and Imagination.

[32] *Biographia* (footnote 5), 167.

[33] *The friend* (footnote 7), vol. 1, 471, 530; *Collected letters* (footnote 6), vol. 5, 309.

[34] *The friend* (footnote 7), vol. 1, 471.

This was possible because Coleridge was convinced of an essential congruence between powers of mind and powers in nature.[35]   He argued that the creative scientist used reason to arrive at theories and above all at laws of nature. These laws embodied relations in nature, perceived through and constituted by ideas.   The status which Coleridge accorded to laws meant that he saw them as determining facts rather than summarizing them.   Now facts were the objective pole in Coleridge's polarity between subject and object, man and nature.   The scientist of genius seized on central phenomena as exponents of natural laws, and his genius lay precisely in his ability to identify a particular empirical fact as a central phenomenon in the light of an idea.[36]   John Hunter's selection of specimens for his Museum, Cuvier's arrangement of the animal kingdom, and Davy's selection of facts for his electrochemical researches were among Coleridge's illustrations of scientific genius at work.[37]

3. Observation and interpretation

The observation of selected facts is a part of science, as it is of poetry. Coleridge pondered the nature of observation and experience.   He read Kant's *Critique of pure reason*, and remarked: ' The perpetual and unmoving Cloud of Darkness that hands over the Work to my " mind's eye ", is the absence of any clear account of—Was ist Erfahrung?   What do you mean by a fact, an empiric reality . . . ?   I apply the categoric forms to a tree—well!   But first, what is this Tree?   How do I come by this Tree? '.[38]   Facts were the foundations of the sciences, and he tried to distinguish different sciences according to the way their facts were gathered.   Physics was made up of facts of observation, chemistry of facts of experiment.[39]

Such distinctions were part of the structure of his philosophy, but he was interested in the psychology of creativity quite as much as in epistemology and logic.   Coleridge was a poet who even in youth knew very well that his philosophical opinions were ' blended with, or deduced from ' his feelings, since

[35] Emmet (footnote 19).

[36] *The friend* (footnote 4), vol. 1, 464–471, 472–481, discuss Theory and Law respectively. Coleridge's ' *central phenomenon* ' (p. 475) perceived through an idea is analogous to Goethe's archetypal phenomenon (*Zur Morphologie* (1817, Stuttgart and Tübingen), vol. 1, 122); see H. B. Nisbet, *Goethe and the scientific tradition* (1972, London).   There are also similarities to Cuvier's method of identifying significant characteristics in *Le règne animal distribué d'après son organisation* . . . (1817, Paris), vol. 1, pp. 3 *et seq.*, 10–11.   Since Coleridge's discussion of scientific method gives an important place to Bacon, the relevance of his ' prerogative instances ' should be considered.   A modern account of Bacon's method is in P. Rossi, *Francis Bacon.   From magic to science* (1968, London).

[37] *The friend* (footnote 7), vol. 1, 474–475, 530.   The Royal College of Surgeons of England has published an admirable *Descriptive catalogue of the physiological series in the Hunterian Museum* (2 vols., 1970–71, Edinburgh and London).   There is a corresponding catalogue of the pathological series, of less immediate concern for Coleridge.   Coleridge's view of Hunter was sharpened by the Lawrence–Abernethy debate, discussed by Owsei Temkin (footnote 15).   Coleridge in *The friend* was alluding to Cuvier's *Le règne animal* (footnote 36).   Cuvier's *Lectures on comparative anatomy* (trans. W. Ross: 2 vols.; 1802, London) had an impressive section on methods of classification. Frank Bourdier's article on Cuvier in the *Dictionary of scientific biography*, vol. 3 (1971, New York), 521–528, is a useful introduction.   For Davy's electrochemistry, see Harold Hartley, *Humphry Davy* (1966, London); and T. H. Levere, *Affinity and matter* (1971, Oxford), ch. 2.

[38] Manuscript annotation by Coleridge at the end of his copy of I. Kant, *Critik der reinen Vernunft* (1799, Leipzig), now in the British Library, cat. no. C. 126 i. 9; transcribed Victoria College Library Ms. BT 22, f. 30.

[39] Coleridge to C. A. Tulk, 12 January 1818, in *Collected letters* (footnote 6), vol. 4, 807.

' I seldom feel without thinking, or think without feeling '.[40]   In a passage on Shakespeare that could apply equally well to poet or scientist, he wrote of ' that affectionate love of nature and natural objects, without which no man could have observed so steadily, or painted so truly and passionately, the very minutest beauties of the external world '.[41]   Genius required faithfulness to the world of nature, and sympathy with it.[42]

Coleridge certainly possessed such faithfulness and sympathy.   In an often quoted passage he used precise observation of nature to illustrate thought and, half-unconsciously, feeling:

> Most of my readers will have noticed a small water-insect on the surface of rivulets which throws a cinque-spotted shadow fringed with prismatic colours on the sunny bottom of the brook; and will have noticed how the little animal wins its way up against the stream, by alternate pulses of active and passive motion, now resisting the current, now yielding to it in order to gather strength and a momentary fulcrum for a further propulsion.   This is no unapt emblem of the mind's self-experience in the act of thinking.[43]

Coleridge's love of nature, and his thinking and feeling prompted by the observation of nature, were mainly devoted to the minutest beauties, to a single moss of flower rather than to the starry universe.   In keeping with this preferred perspective, his conversation poems, ' Frost at midnight ', ' This lime-tree bower my prison ', and the rest contain much of his finest writing. Kant's *Theorie des Himmels* in contrast failed to induce in him wonder at the majesty of the heavens; there was little sublimity, he thought, in an endlessly repeated image of ' a blind Mare going round and round in a Mill! '.[44]   Such an image was ultimately sterile, divorced from life and feeling.   When feeling and thought coalesced, they did so through the consciousness of a living unity in nature; when that failed, knowledge of nature appeared as distasteful, the perception of nature's unity was lost,[45] and poetic inspiration yielded to arid analysis.   ' I look at the Mountains (that visible God Almighty that looks in at all my windows) I look at the Mountains only for the Curves of their outlines; the Stars, as I behold them, form themselves into triangles—and my hands are scarred with scratches from a Cat, whose back I was rubbing in the Dark in order to see whether the sparks from it were refrangible by a prism.   The Poet is dead in me— ... '.[46]   The death of the poetic faculty and the transformation of living symbolic nature into lifeless abstraction were fundamentally the same:

> O Lady! we receive but what we give,
> And in our life alone does Nature live:
> Ours is her wedding garment, ours her shroud![47]

[40] Coleridge to J. Thelwall, 17 December 1796, in *ibid.*, vol. 1, 279.

[41] *The literary remains of Samuel Taylor Coleridge* (ed. H. N. Coleridge: 4 vols., 1836–39, London), vol. 1, 54.

[42] S. T. Coleridge, *Theory of life* (footnote 15), 86.

[43] *Biographia* (footnote 5), 72.   For another instance of Coleridge's precision in observation see Lucy Eleanor Watson, *Coleridge at Highgate* (1925, London, New York, Toronto), 57.

[44] Marginal note to I. Kant, *Vermischte Schriften* (3 vols., 1799, Halle), transcribed in Victoria College Library Ms. BT 21, ff. 24–25.   See I. Kant, *Cosmogony* (trans. W. Hastie, intro. G. J. Whitrow: 1970, New York and London).

[45] Coleridge to Thelwall, [14 Oct. 1797], in *Collected letters* (footnote 6), vol. 1, 349.

[46] Coleridge to Godwin, 25 March 1801, in *Collected letters*, vol. 2, 714.

[47] ' Dejection: an ode ', *Poetical works* (footnote 27), 365, lines 47–49.

In the same poem, ' Dejection ', Coleridge identifies the vivifying power and music of the soul with joy, which once was his:

> But now afflictions bow me down to earth:
> Nor care I that they rob me of my mirth;
>   But oh! each visitation
> Suspends what nature gave me at my birth,
>   My shaping spirit of Imagination.
> For not to think of what I needs must feel,
>   But to be still and patient all I can;
> And haply by abstruse research to steal
> From my own nature all the natural man—
> This was my sole resource, my only plan.[48]

He knew from experience the joy of the union of thought and feeling, and bemoaned its loss.   Such union, he believed, was essential to creative genius in science as it was in poetry.   Genius in both was commensurate with inter-communion with nature.   So it was that Kepler, owing sympathetic allegiance to nature, had achieved the greatest recorded glories of scientific genius. Newton was for Coleridge a lesser man, who merely albeit brilliantly developed Kepler's ideas.[49]   Coleridge was decidedly ambivalent in his view of Newton. He recognized the power of the Newtonian synthesis, and admired Newton's experimental genius in the *Opticks* while deploring his fragmentation of white light into seven independent components.   He was most distressed by the theological and philosophical implications that he saw in Newton's cosmology, seeing in him, as Leibniz had done, the enemy of religion.   Coleridge's Newton was the Newton of the Enlightenment and of the early nineteenth century, closer to Voltaire's sage than to the Newton of more recent historiography. The Pipes of Pan were far away, and Coleridge's preference was for inspired Kepler.[50]

As Kepler's example showed, faithfulness to nature demanded accuracy of observation.   It also demanded careful interpretation of observations. Coleridge pointed out that in using a microscope one had to contradict the evidence of one's senses in order to deduce the true size of the animalcule.[51] What was true of the use of optical instruments was equally true of the unaided senses, including sight.   The senses had to be subordinated to reason if they

---

[48] *Ibid.*, 366–367, lines 82–91.

[49] Coleridge, 8 October 1830, in *Table talk* (2 vols., 1835), vol. 1, 216–218. Coleridge's view of Kepler was, as D. M. Knight reminded me, an orthodox one in Germany, but not unique in England—see, for example, S. Vince, *A complete system of astronomy* (3 vols., 1814–23, London), vol. 1, 98–102; and Robert Small, *An account of the astronomical discoveries of Kepler* (1804, London).   These references are given in M. J. Petry's edition of *Hegel's philosophy of nature* (3 vols., 1970, London) vol. 1, 361.   The notes to this edition are invaluable as an introduction to early 19th-century science, especially in Germany.

[50] *Collected letters* (footnote 6), vol. 2, 708–710 (March 1801), 1046–1047 (January 1804); British Library Add. Mss. 47,519, ff. 53–54; British Library Ms. Egerton 2801, ff. 19–20.   See P. Rattansi, ' Newton's alchemical studies ', in A. G. Debus (ed.), *Science, medicine and society in the Renaissance* (1972, New York), vol. 2, 167–182; and J. E. McGuire and P. Rattansi, ' Newton and the pipes of Pan ', *Notes and records of the Royal Society of London*, 21 (1966), 108–143.

[51] Marginal note to F. W. J. Schelling, *Ideen zu einer Philosophie der Natur* (1803, Landshut), 302–303.

40

were not to lead to an evasion of reality. The tyranny of the senses was a constant target for his invective, and he held it responsible for many of the ills of the age. The subordination of reason to sense had led literally to a general superficiality and a carelessness of principle. He blamed the predominance of the sense of sight, and of fictions derived from it, for the vogue for imponderable fluids and atoms in chemistry, for materialism, atheism, and all the ills of a mechanic age. Principles leading to superficiality in science could be equally disastrous in other realms of thought and of consequent action. Hence, as Coleridge wrote to Lord Liverpool in 1817, ' The recent relapse therefore of the Chemists to the atomistic scheme, and the almost unanimous acceptance of Dalton's Theory in England, & Le Sage's in France, determine the intellectual character of the age with the force of an experimentum crucis '.[52] The natural philosopher's fidelity to nature thus opposed sensual materialism, just as the poet's idealizing and unifying imagination transcended the world of the senses. Here again poetry and science were complementary activities.[53]

4. Scientific language and poetic symbols

The practitioners of both poetry and science had language as a primary tool, and knew the technical utility of employing words with precision. Humphry Davy cheered Coleridge exuberantly on: ' You are to be the Thalaba of the Daemons existing in the world of Language, the rooter out of all the weeds & unnatural plants that the hand of civilized man has sown in the idea of passion & of nature '.[54] Coleridge was constant in this fight. ' I have neglected no occasion ', he wrote, ' of enforcing the maxim, that to expose a sophism and to detect the equivocal or double meaning of a word is, in the great majority of cases, one and the same thing '.[55] The craftsman cared for his tools.

But he held words to be far more than passive tools, regarding them as ' LIVING POWERS, by which the things of most importance to mankind are actuated, combined, and humanized '.[56] Words were vitally powerful because, as Prickett has pointed out, they were tools of self-knowledge, symbolic in their function.[57] Words were also symbolic keys to a knowledge of nature,

---

[52] *Aids to reflection* (footnote 22), 357; and Coleridge to Lord Liverpool, 28 July 1817, in *Collected letters* (footnote 6), vol. 4, 757–763. Le Sage explained gravitational and chemical forces as resulting from the action of corpuscular imponderable fluids, for example, in his *Essai de chymie méchanique* . . . (1758, Rouen). His concept of a gravific fluid was repugnant to Coleridge.

[53] Coleridge's comments on Plato, the supreme poet-philosopher (K. Coburn (ed.), *The philosophical lectures of Samuel Taylor Coleridge* (1949, London and New York), 158), are illuminating here. See, for example, his ' Opus maximum ', Victoria College Library, Ms. SMS 28, vol. 2, f. 210: ' . . . the frequency of musical and geometrical terms in the works of Plato and Platonists ' served to overcome the associations of fancy. ' In the same sense geometry itself was enjoined as the ⟨first⟩ purification of the mind, the first step towards its emancipation from the despotism of the senses '. The angled brackets indicate Coleridge's additions.

[54] H. Davy to Coleridge, 26 November 1800, Pierpont Morgan Library, Ms. MA 1857, no. 11. Thalaba was ' the Destroyer ' in Robert Southey's long poem ' Thalaba '.

[55] Coleridge, *Aids to reflection* (footnote 22), xiii. H. Spencer, *First principles* (1862, London), section 153, explained that Coleridge had told him that with the advance of language, words which were originally alike in their meanings acquire unlike meanings—a change expressed by the formidable word ' desynonymization '. S. Sheets-Pyenson gave me this information.

[56] *Aids to reflection* (footnote 3), xvii. The language here is reminiscent of much 18th century discussion of powers in a Newtonian tradition. A. Thackray (footnote 9) explores such traditions.

[57] Stephen Prickett, *Coleridge and Wordsworth. The poetry of growth* (1970, Cambridge), 197

which had its own powers and its own language, ' a subordinate Logos '.[58]
The beauties of nature were

> The lovely shapes and sounds intelligible
> Of that eternal language, which thy God
> Utters, who from eternity doth teach
> Himself in all, and all things in himself.[59]

Poet and scientist alike sought an effective mediation between the language
of nature and the language of man, the infusion of one with the other.   In
science, a central fact informed an idea, and thus achieved symbolic significance.
A phenomenon could be seen as exemplifying a law.   In Coleridge's dynamic
philosophy of nature, laws expressed the relations of powers, that could be
apprehended symbolically in things and their relations.   We have seen that
scientific genius consisted for Coleridge in the identification of central phenomena
and their perception as symbols.[60]   This was the intellectual process of science,
cognate with that of poetry.   Both functioned through the secondary imagination, while depending on the primary imagination, the creative agent of all
human perception.[61]   The intrinsic creativity of perception and the function
of symbols in language and perception alike furnished him with a major link
between poetic and scientific approaches to nature.

' In looking at objects of Nature while I am thinking, . . . I seem rather to
be seeking . . . a symbolic language for something within me that already
and forever exists, than observing anything new.   Even when that latter is
the case, yet still I have always an obscure feeling as if that new phenomenon
were the dim Awakening of a forgotten or hidden Truth of my inner Nature/It
is still interesting as a Word, a Symbol!   It is Λογος, the Creator! ⟨and the
Evolver!⟩ '.[62]   The senses encountered symbols,[63] phenomena that were real
in themselves and were also living parts of the unity they represented.[64]   They
were, in science, phenomena symbolizing powers and explained by laws.
Writing to C. A. Tulk, a Swedenborgian much interested in science, Coleridge
agreed that ' all true science is contained in the Lore of Symbols & Correspondences '.[65]

Coleridge wanted to grasp the forms of natural laws, the genetic relations
of powers, and, like the *Naturphilosophen*, the role of life as a power in the
development of universal organism.   The Cosmos was alive, and it was with
this perspective that he noted: ' The most pregnant historic Symbol on Earth

---

[58] *Literary remains* (footnote 4), vol. 2, 50.
[59] ' Frost at midnight ', *Poetical works* (footnote 27), 242, lines 59–62.
[60] See footnote 36 above.
[61] *Biographia* (footnote 5), 167.
[62] *Notebooks* (footnote 11), vol. 2, entry 2546.
[63]For all that meets the bodily sense I deem
   Symbolical, one mighty alphabet
   For infant minds . . .
Coleridge, ' The destiny of nations ', *Poetical works* (footnote 27), 132, lines 18–20.   See also
L. C. Knights, ' Ideas and symbol: some hints from Coleridge ', in K. Coburn (ed.), *Coleridge.
A collection of critical essays* (1967, Englewood Cliffs, N.J.), 112-122.
[64] S. T. Coleridge, *Lay sermons* (ed. R. J. White: 1972, London and Princeton, N.J.), 30.
[65] Coleridge to C. A. Tulk, 20 January 1820, in *Collected letters* (footnote 6), vol. 5, 19.   For
C. A. Tulk (not Alfred Tulk, translator of Oken) see the *Dictionary of national biography*.

is a Coral Bank on a Stratum of Coal . . . The Peat Moor and the Coral Bank, the Conjunctions copulative of animate and inanimate Nature!—Lime fertilizing Peat, and thus mutually effectuating each other's re-ascent into Life '.[66] Elsewhere, discussing modern chemistry, he presented the chemical elements of the laboratory, substances that could not yet be decomposed, as symbols of powers. Carbon in graphite and diamond, hydrogen and oxygen in water, thus played a dual role in his scheme, at once substantial and symbolic. Chemistry exhibited relations of composition underlying qualitative differences. The chemist's mind revealed underlying unity in nature where his senses found none. This reinforced Coleridge's sense of the correspondence between mind and nature,[67] and between poetry and science. The student of nature, whose science was comprised in the language of symbols, was ' a dramatic poet in his own line ':[68]

If in SHAKSPEARE we find nature idealized into poetry, through the creative power of a profound yet observant meditation, so through the meditative observation of a DAVY, A WOOLLASTON, or a HATCHETT;

By some connatural force,
Powerful at greatest distance to unite
With secret amity things of like kind,

we find poetry . . . substantiated and realized in nature: yea, nature itself dislosed to us . . . as at once the poet and the poem![69]

5. Nature and genius: Shakespeare, Newton and Davy

Coleridge saw this power to grasp nature and to mirror and idealize it in poetry as the essence of Shakespeare's genius. Shakespeare was, like nature, ' inexhaustible in diverse powers ', and ' equally inexhaustible in forms '. He was, said Coleridge, ' a nature humanized ',[70] and only as long as Shakespeare was the mirror to nature would Coleridge be willing to live.[71] With such an emphasis upon Shakespeare's integral harmony with nature, it comes as no surprise to find Coleridge frequently pairing his name with the names of natural philosophers, some of whom might otherwise seem in strange company. Shakespeare, Bernoulli and Bonnet were ' the good and wise '; England, true

[66] *Notebooks* (footnote 11), vol. 3, entry 4432. For background, see Gower (footnote 20); D. M. Knight, ' Chemistry, physiology, and materialism in the Romantic period ', *Durham University journal*, **64** (1972), 139–145; D. M. Knight, ' The physical sciences and the Romantic movement ', *History of science*, **9** (1970), 54–75; T. H. Levere (footnote 13); and W. D. Wetzels, 'Aspects of natural science in German Romanticism ', *Studies in Romanticism*, **10** (1971), 44–59.

[67] *The friend* (footnote 7), vol. 1, 470–471; and see footnote 12 above.

[68] *Lay sermons* (footnote 64), 79.

[69] *The friend* (footnote 7), vol. 1, 471. William Hyde Wollaston (1766–1828) was a natural philosopher whose style contrasted with Davy's and who sometimes appeared as Davy's rival. David Goodman has written a D.Phil. Thesis (1965, University of Oxford) on ' William Hyde Wollaston and his influence on early nineteenth-century science '; see also his article on Wollaston in the *Dictionary of scientific biography*, vol. 14 (1976, London), 486–494; and his ' Wollaston and the atomic theory of Dalton ', *Historical stud. phys. sci.*, **1** (1969), 37–59. Charles Hatchett (1795?–1847) was associated with Davy and with W. T. Brande, Davy's successor in chemistry at the Royal Institution. Coleridge particularly admired Hatchett's analyses of animal matter.

[70] *Literary remains* (footnote 41), 67–68, 83.

[71] *Letters, conversations and recollections of Samuel Taylor Coleridge* (ed. T. Allsop: 2 vols., 1836, London), vol. 1, 196.

England, would be Shakespeare, Milton, and Bacon, the British Plato; Shakespeare, Milton, and Boyle were ' the great living-dead men of our Isle '.[72] But what of Isaac Newton? Alas, with his material ether, his essentially passive atoms, his world of little things, he came far below Shakespeare, who outweighed him twenty times over.[73] Coleridge's measure of greatness in science was scarcely an orthodox one, depending as it did on harmony with active nature, not the abstract analysis of a passive world.[74] Symmetry between poetry and science obtained only when both operated through corresponding symbols, ideas of mind and nature.

For the living embodiment of scientific genius co-existing with poetic genius, Coleridge idealized Humphry Davy, whom he regarded erratically as the greatest man of the age, after Wordsworth.[75] He apostrophized Davy as the ' Father and Founder of Philosophic Alchemy ' who had first converted poetry into chemical science.[76] Chemistry illuminated by such genius was truly poetical, besides constituting a bulwark of Coleridge's educational plan. He explained, while in his mid-twenties, that he would not ' think of devoting less than 20 years to an Epic Poem. Ten to collect materials and warm my mind with universal science ' as a first step.[77] Philosophy embraced natural philosophy, and only a profound philosophical mind could hope to achieve poetic greatness.[78] Thus poetry could be seen as the crowning achievement of the study of man and of nature. Coleridge had formerly argued for an antithesis between science and poetry, the former being directed to truth, the latter to pleasure.[79] Here were echoes of his earlier communion and debates with Wordsworth.[80] But in 1826, after years of extensive theoretical scientific enquiry, Coleridge asserted: ' Poetry [is not the substitute but] the corolla & fragrance of the austere and many Sciences '.[81] The poet had to arrive at ' living and life-producing ideas, which shall contain their own evidence, the certainty that they are essentially one with the germinal causes in nature—his consciousness being the focus and mirror of both '.[82] The poetic process was one with the living power of nature, even being susceptible of description in precise physiological metaphors,[83] and by its own living power extending consciousness.[84] Thus poets and scientists of genius, exploring mind through

---

[72] *Notebooks* (footnote 11), vol. 2, entries 2584 (where a note suggests that Johann Bernoulli (1667–1748) is intended) and 2598; vol. 3, entry 3270. Bacon as the British Plato is discussed in *The friend* (footnote 7), vol. 1, 488.

[73] M. H. Abrams, ' Coleridge and the Romantic vision of the world ', in Beer (footnote 19), 117–119.

[74] H. W. Piper, *The active universe* (1962, London).

[75] *Philosophical lectures* (footnote 53), 25; Coleridge, marginal annotation to his copy of *John Barclay his Argenis* (trans. R. Le Grys and T. May: 1629, London), now in British Library, cat. no. C. 44, d. 34.

[76] Coleridge to Dr. Williamson, November 1823, in *Collected letters* (footnote 6), vol. 5, 309.

[77] Coleridge to Davy, 1 January 1800, in *Collected letters*, vol. 1, 557; Coleridge to J. Cottle, early April 1797], in *ibid.*, vol. 1, 320.

[78] *Literary remains* (footnote 41), vol. 2, 59.

[79] *Ibid.*, vol. 2, 7; *Notebooks* (footnote 11), vol. 3, entry 4111.

[80] R. Sharrock, ' The chemist and the poet: Sir Humphry Davy and the preface to the Lyrical Ballads ', *Notes and records of the Royal Society of London*, **17** (1964), 57.

[81] *Notebooks* (footnote 11), F⁰ notebook, f. 46.

[82] *Literary remains* (footnote 41), 224.

[83] For example, British Library Ms., Egerton 2800, f. 39.

[84] *Notebooks* (footnote 11), vol. 3, entry 3632.

44

nature and nature through mind, were full partners, collaborators in the vital enterprise of the extension of consciousness.

Acknowledgments

An earlier draft of this paper was presented to the British Society for the History of Science at a conference on Science and Literature, Sheffield, 15 May 1976. The research for this paper was carried out with the support of a Killam Senior Research Scholarship during sabbatical leave from the University of Toronto.

XIII

Coleridge, Chemistry, and the Philosophy of Nature

If any thing could have recalled the Physics & Physiology of the age to the Dynamic Theory of the eldest Philosophy, it must have been the late successful researches of the Chemists, which almost force on the very senses the facts of mutual penetration & intus-susception which have supplied a series of experimental proofs, that in all pure phænomena we behold only the copula, the balance or indifference of opposite energies. The recent relapse therefore of the Chemists to the atomistic scheme, and the almost unanimous acceptance of Dalton's Theory in England, & Le Sage's in France, determine the intellectual character of the age with the force of an experimentum crucis. . . . I persist in the belief . . . that a few brilliant discoveries have been dearly purchased at the loss of all communion with life and the spirit of Nature. (S. T. Coleridge to Lord Liverpool, 28 July 1817).[1]

C OLERIDGE loathed the passive mechanistic philosophies born of the eighteenth century, associating them with atheism, determinism, anarchy, and tyranny, and charging them with every contemporary offence against taste, character, religion, and politics. For him, the French Revolution, the

1. CL, IV, 760. The following abbreviations are used for references within text and in notes: CC—The Collected Works of Samuel Taylor Coleridge, gen. ed. Kathleen Coburn (London: Routledge & Kegan Paul; Princeton: Princeton U. Press, 1969–); CL—Collected Letters of Samuel Taylor Coleridge, ed. Earl Leslie Griggs, 6 vols. (Oxford: Oxford U. Press, 1956–71); CN—The Notebooks of Samuel Taylor Coleridge, ed. Kathleen Coburn, Vols. I–III of 5 (London: Routledge & Kegan Paul, 1957–); N—a Coleridge Notebook not yet published, cited by serial number; TL—S. T. Coleridge, Hints towards the Formation of a more Comprehensive Theory of Life, ed. Seth Watson (London, 1848, republished Westmead, Hants.: Gregg International Publishers, 1970). In the footnotes, Samuel Taylor Coleridge is referred to as C. Quotations from CL are made with permission of Oxford University Press, and from CN with permission of Princeton University Press.

Earlier versions of parts of this paper were first used in seminars in the Universities of Calgary and Montreal. The research for this paper was supported by a Killam Senior Research Scholarship. I am indebted to Kathleen Coburn for help and encouragement, and to George Whalley for valuable comments.

Terror, and Napoleon were all consequences of so-called Enlightenment. Coleridge's was not merely a conventional English response to events in France. It stemmed from a deeply considered, unified, and methodical philosophy which he recorded in books, letters, notes, and sketches.

Coleridge wanted others to learn his philosophy, and was fertile in propounding plans for education. "[O]ur plan will teach—first to distinguish & generalize the component parts of one subject of knowledge in order to understand that subject—which is Science—and then will consider that subject in its relation to ⟨the⟩ / ⟨happiness of man⟩ *Man*, which is philosophy."[2]

Coleridge's philosophy was neither selfish nor narrowly academic. He urged a philosophical reading of history for the discernment of principles, which he viewed as fundamental truths providing the motive force for thought and action. He observed in 1816 that religious, civil, social, and domestic revolutions had been accompanied by "the rise and fall of metaphysical systems." He argued for the social and persuasive power of abstract notions in troubled times, noted that metaphysics embodied and expounded principles, and asserted that every principle was actualized in an idea. Coleridge's doctrine of ideas would need a book for its exposition—he wrote one, which he did not publish.[3] In 1816, in his *Lay Sermon addressed to the higher Classes of Society*, he explained that every idea was living and productive, and, partaking of infinity, contained endless seminal power (*CC*, VI, 23–24). Science, "which consists wholly in ideas and principles," was power, as Bacon, the British Plato, had said (*Friend* [*CC*, IV], I, 488). It is little wonder then that Coleridge identified, as being among the causes of the French Revolution, misguided philosophy and the overrating of power from improvements in unsound science, including "a wonder-working chemistry" (*Lay Sermons, CC*, VI, 33–34). Coleridge did not criticize the French for their emphasis on science. His objection was to the philosophy of the senses which underlay and falsified their science. He contrasted science based on sensory empiricism with science based on a combination of ideas and faithfulness to nature. He viewed the adoption by a society of one or other kind of science as symptomatic of the intellectual character of that society, which could be reformed by a reformation of science.

Coleridge's understanding of the principles of science is thus fundamental to his philosophy in its widest reference. His philosophy of nature was especially significant because it opened the way to a verification of principles applicable to the life of man and the life of mind. The verification came from natural science, in many branches of which Coleridge was well informed. In his integration of a wealth of scientific information with a philosophy of na-

2. Pierpont Morgan Library: MS fragment bound into MS. MA 1916.

3. "On the Divine Ideas," in the Commonplace Book, Huntington Library MS. HM 8195, pp. 3–301 (odd-numbered pages, with scattered notes on the even-numbered pages).

ture, Coleridge was one of the most impressive although not the most accessible of spokesmen for the Romantic vision of the world.[4]

The vision did not find great favour among the Fellows of the Royal Society of London, and the transcendental language in which it was expressed was as foreign to them as it is to us. Coleridge's language, indebted to Germany and to seventeenth-century England, was alien to most British scientists.[5] Nevertheless, Coleridge's greatest inspiration to the study of science and his constant exemplar of scientific genius was his sometime friend and contemporary, Humphry Davy. Coleridge at one time considered Davy as second only to Wordsworth as the greatest man of the age.[6] The relations of Davy and Coleridge favoured the prominence of chemistry in Coleridge's comprehension and presentation of the sciences, and illuminate his views of science. These views, and his sources for them, are often equally unorthodox and impressive. They open many unexplored avenues in the history of early nineteenth-century science, some of which reveal lively contemporary debates. They suggest that science in Britain was less insulated from Germany than has been generally thought. And they decidedly add to rather than detract from Coleridge's intellectual stature.

I. Coleridge's Early Scientific Education

Beddoes, Germany, Davy

When Coleridge came down from Cambridge, he had little scientific knowledge, bold necessitarian views—"I go farther than Hartley and believe the corporeality of *thought*" (*CL*, I, 137, 11 Dec. 1794)—and radical political convictions. He had written a poem on the fall of the Bastille, had relinquished his hopes for but not his belief in an egalitarian pantisocratic community,[7] and argued against Pitt's policies. In 1795 he attended a public meeting to protest against the Pitt-Grenville "Gagging Bills," at which Thomas Beddoes was

---

4. M. H. Abrams, "Coleridge and the Romantic Vision of the World," in *Coleridge's Variety*, ed. J. Beer (London: Macmillan; Pittsburgh: U. of Pittsburgh Press, 1974), pp. 101–33.

5. National styles of science are explored in *The Emergence of Science in Western Europe*, ed. M. P. Crosland, (London: Macmillan, 1975).

6. For a variant characterization of Davy, see D. M. Knight, "The Scientist as Sage," *Studies in Romanticism*, 6 (1967), 65–88. K. Coburn discusses Davy and C in "Coleridge: A Bridge between Science and Poetry," in J. Beer, pp. 81–100. The early friendship between C and Davy is discussed in A. Treneer, *The Mercurial Chemist* (London: Methuen & Co., 1963).

7. James Dykes Campbell, *Samuel Taylor Coleridge* (1894; rept. Highgate: Lime Tree Bower Press, 1970), Ch. 2, discusses pantisocracy, which the *OED* defines as "A form of social organization in which all are equal in rank and social position; a Utopian community in which all are equal and all rule."

also present.[8] This may have been when Coleridge and Beddoes first met. They saw much of one another in Bristol from 1795, and Coleridge's interest in science significantly dates from the same year. Beddoes was the first individual who was seminal for Coleridge's scientific development, and he introduced him to Davy, whose influence persisted with Coleridge even after their estrangement.

Beddoes had come to Bristol in 1793, in part because his sympathy for the French Revolution had made his position in Oxford uncomfortable.[9] Once in Bristol, he set about establishing a Pneumatic Institution for investigating the use of airs in treating respiratory diseases. He was friendly with the members of the Lunar Society of Birmingham. He knew the Watts and Wedgwoods. The latter were especially generous in providing funds for the Pneumatic Institution, and later a pension for Coleridge. Erasmus Darwin advised Beddoes about establishing a practice in Bristol, and Beddoes married Richard Lovell Edgeworth's daughter Anna. Beddoes was intimately in touch, personally and scientifically, with the foremost group of late eighteenth-century British scientists.[10]

He was also a disciple of Locke, Horne Tooke, and Joseph Priestley.[11] The *British Critic* remarked that Beddoes manifested a sovereign contempt for all that was not of the age of reason,[12] while the *Gentleman's Magazine* asserted that "he was of that school, the doctrines of which have operated, with poisonous influence, on the great mass of society . . . his *philosophical* speculations had a direct tendency to Atheism. . . . In short, he was a disciple of Darwin."[13] And the work read most exhaustively by Beddoes at the turn of the century was Abraham Tucker's *Light of Nature*—he and Davy kept it almost continuously from the Bristol Library Society from 1798 to 1801. Tucker attempted "to try what may be done by the exercise of our reason either for the advancement of knowledge or guidance of our conduct," and acknowledged

8. J. Colmer, *Coleridge Critic of Society* (1959; rpt. Oxford: Clarendon Press, 1967), p. 47, n.

9. C. A. Weber, *Bristols Bedeutung für die Englische Romantik und die Deutsch-Englischen Beziehungen* (Halle: Niemeyer, 1935), p. 92.

10. J. E. Stock, *Memoirs of the Life of Thomas Beddoes* . . . (London: John Murray; Bristol: J. M. Gutch, 1811). T. H. Levere, "Dr. Thomas Beddoes and the Establishment of his Pneumatic Institution," *Notes and Records of the Royal Society of London*, 32 (1977), 41–49.

11. Review of Beddoes, *Observations on . . . Demonstrative Evidence* (1793) in *The Critical Review*, 81 (1794), 178. Priestley and Beddoes had similar political positions. Even in chemistry, and in spite of his sometime support of Lavoisier, Beddoes was attracted by Priestley's views. See, e.g., Beddoes, "Specimen of an arrangement of bodies according to their principles," in *Contributions to physical and medical knowledge, principally from the West of England*, ed. Beddoes (Bristol: Biggs & Cottle, 1799).

12. *British Critic*, 3 (1794), 561–64.

13. *Gentleman's Magazine*, 79 (1809), 120.

his debt to Locke. He also, like Hartley, moved from an empiricist philosophy to God.[14]

Tucker's work illuminated Beddoes' concerns in science, philology, and philosophy. In 1795 Coleridge already shared many of these concerns, and as a frequent visitor to Beddoes' establishment he came to share them still more widely. He appears to have had access to Beddoes' impressive library.[15] His notebooks for 1795 and 1796 show that he read in Erasmus Darwin's *Botanic Garden*, Joseph Priestley's *Opticks* (1772) and probably his *Disquisitions on Matter and Spirit*, Isaac Newton's *Opera* (ed. S. Horsley, 1779–85), works by Beddoes, and papers in the transactions of the Royal Society of London and the Manchester Literary and Philosophical Society (*CN*, I, 9–14, 32, 64, 93, 235, 258). Beddoes was introducing Coleridge to the best of English science, reinforcing his intellectual aspirations. In 1797 Coleridge proposed a plan of studies appropriate for a poet: "I should not think of devoting less than 20 years to an Epic Poem. Ten to collect materials and warm my mind with universal science. I would be a tolerable Mathematician, I would thoroughly know Mechanics, Hydrostatics, Optics, and Astronomy, Botany, Metallurgy, Fossilism, Chemistry, Geology, Anatomy, Medicine—then the *mind of man*—then the *minds of men*—in all Travels, Voyages and Histories" (*CL*, I, 320).

Here indeed was an encyclopedic program. It was appropriate that Beddoes introduced Coleridge not only to English but also to German sources. Beddoes knew German well and was one of the rare Englishmen of his time acquainted with Kant's philosophy. During the 1790's he accurately and clearly presented Kant to the English.[16] When Dr. Joseph Frank of Vienna met Beddoes in 1803, the conversation "turned upon foreign medical literature." Frank "soon found that Dr. Beddoes reads German as well as he does English and is intimately acquainted with all our best authors."[17] In 1793 Beddoes had observed that the doctrines of Kant were making their way at the University of Göttingen.[18] In 1796 Coleridge talked of going to Jena, "a

14. MS record of the Bristol Library Society. Tucker, alias Edward Search, *The Light of Nature Pursued*, 2 vols. in 5 parts (1768), I, xii, xviii, and II, ii, 155 ff. Tucker presents John Locke in a higher state of existence than ours as a guide to mental and cosmic progress. This provides the model for "the Genius" in Davy's *Consolations in Travel*. C also read Tucker (see *CL*, II, 949).

15. Stock (*Beddoes*, pp. 300–301) gives an indication of the richness of Beddoes' library. C could not then or for years afterwards afford to buy scientific journals (*CL*, III, 144), but he used Beddoes' library and that of the Bristol Library Society (see Whalley, "The Bristol Library Borrowings of Southey and Coleridge, 1793–8," *The Library, Transactions of the Bibliographical Society*, 5th series, 4 [1949], 114–31).

16. E.g., in *Demonstrative Evidence* (see n. 11 above), pp. 89–90; *Monthly Magazine* (1796), pp. 265–66. See again *CN*, I, 249, n., and Weber, p. 107.

17. Quoted in Stock, *Beddoes*, p. 301.

18. *Demonstrative Evidence*, pp. 89–90.

cheap German University where Schiller resides," and there studying chemistry, anatomy, Kant—and much more (CL, I, 209). It was perhaps through Beddoes that in 1798 he made his way to Göttingen. The following May he reported to his patron Josiah Wedgwood that he had learned German, and "I have attended the lectures on Physiology, Anatomy, & Natural History with regularity, & have endeavoured to understand these subjects" (CL, I, 518). Blumenbach, whom Kant cited approvingly, was Coleridge's instructor in physiology, and remained an important authority for him.[19] University studies were only a part of Coleridge's education. There was also a tour through the Harz mountains with, among others, George Bellas Greenough, subsequently founder and first president of the Geological Society.[20] Coleridge and Greenough may well have met the philosophical chemist and geologist Heinrich Steffens on this tour.[21] Steffens was later among Coleridge's principal sources in natural science and natural philosophy.[22]

Coleridge's studies in Germany were not primarily scientific. But when he returned to England in 1799, he had at least made a start on his preparations for writing the hypothetical epic poem, and had learned enough physiology to understand Beddoes' activities at the Pneumatic Institution. He was also well placed to appreciate the merits and to share the aspirations of Humphry Davy, employed by Beddoes as chemical superintendent since the fall of 1798. Coleridge had previously been intellectually convinced of the importance of science. Now his enthusiasm for the sciences, and especially for chemistry and its role in physiology, was increased by his admiration of Davy, whom he later described as "the Father and Founder of philosophic Alchemy, the Man who *born* a Poet first converted Poetry into Science and *realized* what few men possessed Genius enough to *fancy*" (CL, v, 309). Coleridge participated in Davy's experiments at the Pneumatic Institution, contributing to mental as well as chemical cures, dined in London with Godwin, and shortly afterwards wrote to his friend that chemistry had been their intellectual fare.

19. Kant has a paragraph on Blumenbach's contribution to epigenesis: see *The Critique of Judgement*, trans. J. C. Meredith (Oxford: Clarendon Press, 1952), part 2, pp. 85–86. C has many references to Blumenbach: e.g., in N 36, ff59–60, and in BM MS. Egerton 2800, f156. See also *CL*, I, 494, 590. A full list of these references, and their analysis, would require a separate paper. C annotated a copy of Blumenbach's *Über die natürlichen Verschiedenheiten im Menschengeschlechte*, trans. J. G. Gruber (Leipzig, 1798).

20. J. Morley, "Coleridge in Germany (1799)," in *Wordsworth and Coleridge. Studies in honor of George McLean Harper*, ed. E. L. Griggs (Princeton: Princeton U. Press, 1939), pp. 220–36.

21. Steffens was in the Harz in the same period as C and Greenough, and then at Freyberg with Greenough. A letter of 1818 from Steffens to Greenough (Cambridge University Library, Greenough MSS. Add. 7918 [7]) is so cordial as to suggest that he and Greenough had become friends.

22. See below, especially n. 41.

Godwin talks evermore of you with a lively affection.—'What a pity that such a Man should degrade his vast Talents to Chemistry'—cried he to me.—Why, quoth I, how! Godwin! can you thus talk of a science, of which neither you nor I understand an iota? &c &c—& I defended Chemistry as knowingly at least as Godwin attacked it—affirmed that it united the opposite advantages of immaterializing [the] mind without destroying the definiteness of [the] ideas—nay even while it gave clearness to them—And eke that being necessarily [per]formed with the passion of Hope, it was p[oetica]l—& we both agreed (for G. as we[ll as I] thinks himself a Poet) that *the Poet* is the Greatest possible character—&c &c. Modest Creatures! (*CL*, I, 557)

Coleridge tried and failed to persuade Davy and Wordsworth to join him in setting up a chemical laboratory in the Lake District, but persisted in the theoretical study of chemical philosophy. He contemplated translating Blumenbach's *Handbuch der Naturgeschichte* (Göttingen, 1799), sought Davy's metaphysical opinions together with his advice on the theoretical and practical study of chemistry, and looked forward to attacking chemistry "like a Shark" (*CL*, II, 672; I, 589–91, 605). In 1802 he was in London, taking detailed notes at Davy's chemical lectures at the Royal Institution, seizing on the poetry of chemistry and exhibiting, in the accuracy of sixty pages of notes, some real understanding of the science, and something more: "Oxygenated muriatic acid gas, from Oxyd of Manganese & common mur. acid of Commerce, of a yellow green color—oxydates mercury white—& is absorbed by white [white *canceled*] water speedily / of a pungent Taste, hateful smell, & even spasms the epiglottis if attempted to be inhaled— . . . If all aristocrats here, how easily Davy might poison them all—" (*CN*, I, 1098). Coleridge's delight in chemistry in 1802 was quite distinct from his philosophical pursuit of the subject in later years. Readings in *Naturphilosophie* and theosophy and Davy's Bakerian lectures on electrochemistry[23] contributed in the years from around 1816 to Coleridge's distinctive formulation of his philosophy of nature. Coleridge in 1802 was still closer to Priestley and Hartley than to Steffens and Kant.[24] Davy's chemistry, philosophically indebted to eighteenth-

23. H. Davy, "On some chemical agencies of electricity," *Phil. Trans.*, 97 (1807), 1–56; "On some new phenomena of chemical changes produced by electricity, particularly the decomposition of the fixed alkalies . . . ," *Phil. Trans.*, 98 (1808), 1–44. C wrote a large number of marginalia in his copy of *The Works of Jacob Behmen the Teutonic Theosopher* (4 vols., 1764–81: the "Law" edition): BM C. 126.k.1. For C's reading of Schelling and Steffens, see G. N. G. Orsini, *Coleridge and German Idealism* (Carbondale: Southern Illinois U. Press, 1969), and n. 41 below.

24. P. Deschamps, *La Formation de la Pensée de Coleridge (1772–1804)* (Paris: Didier, 1964).

century British natural philosophy, was correspondingly attractive to Coleridge.[25]

Davy owed much to Newton. He came to emphasize the forces and powers proposed in Newton's thirty-first Query to the Opticks and the simplicity criteria in the rules of philosophizing.[26] But, while working with Beddoes, he stressed the atomism of the thirty-first Query and of the third rule of philosophizing. He treated this atomism at first naively, with conventional corpuscular notions that he extended by analogy from matter to mind. Pursuing chemical issues into physiology and psychology, he announced that life "may be considered as a perpetual series of peculiar corpuscular changes; and the living body as the being in which the changes take place. . . . The laws of mind then probably, are not different from the laws of corpuscular motion." When Davy published this in a book edited by Beddoes, the reviewers naturally attacked him for his materialism.[27] He was cautious thenceforth in talking about atoms and about matter at all: "The common vague and unphilosophical acceptation of the word Matter ought to be altogether eradicated from Scientific Language."[28]

Davy continued, however, to wonder about the relations of chemistry, sensation, and life: he wrote in 1800 that his galvanic discoveries "seem to lead to the door of the temple of the mysterious god of Life."[29] There was a long controversy about the applicability of chemistry to physiology.[30] Davy's contribution was welcome to Beddoes and fascinating to Coleridge who was avid for chemical lore, but still far from incorporating it in a philosophical synthesis.

In 1804 Coleridge, in poor health and hoping for improvement from a change of climate, set out for Malta. Davy wrote him a generous letter on the eve of departure. "In whatever part of the world you are, you will often live with me, not as a *fleeting idea*, but as a *recollection possessed* of *creative energy,*—as an *imagination winged with fire*, inspiriting and rejoicing. You must

---

25. T. H. Levere, *Affinity and Matter* (Oxford: Clarendon Press, 1971), Ch. 2. A. Thackray, *Atoms and Powers* (Cambridge, Mass.: Harvard U. Press, 1970), describes eighteenth-century British natural philosophy.

26. Levere, *Affinity and Matter*, pp. 45–46. Newton stressed the simplicity and uniformity of nature, and advocated correspondingly simple explanations in science.

27. H. Davy, "An Essay on Heat, Light, and the Combinations of Light," in *Contributions*, ed. T. Beddoes, pp. 4–147. The passage quoted (p. 144) leads to a theory of perception. A typical review is in *The British Critic*, 14 (1799), 623–27.

28. Royal Institution (RI) Davy MS. 13h, p. 34.

29. Davy to C, 26 Nov. 1800: Pierpont Morgan Library MS. MA 1857, no. 11.

30. D. M. Knight, "Chemistry, Physiology, and Materialism in the Romantic Period," *Durham University Journal*, 64 (1972), 139–45.

not live much longer without giving to *all men* the proofs of Power, which those who know you feel in admiration."[31]

Proofs of power were forthcoming, but unevenly and painfully. Coleridge returned from Malta in 1806, struggling against his addiction to opium. Ten more years passed before he moved to Highgate and with Dr. Gillman's help began to regain control.[32] In the intervening years Coleridge gave his lectures on Shakespeare, published *The Friend* as a periodical, pursued his reading of Kant and Schelling, and maintained his interest in science.

Coleridge followed Davy's career with particular attention. He was en-thralled by the Bakerian lectures on electrochemistry. In November 1807 he wrote to Dorothy Wordsworth of Davy's "March of Glory, which he has run for the last six weeks—within which time by the aid and application of his own great discovery, of the identity of electricity and chemical attractions, he has placed all the elements and all their inanimate combinations in the power of man; having decomposed both the Alkalies, and three of the Earths, discovered as the base of the Alkalies a new metal . . . Davy supposes that there is only one power in the world of the senses; which in particles acts as chemical attractions, in specific masses as electricity, & on matter in general, as planetary Gravitation. . . . [W]hen this has been proved, it will then only remain to resolve this into some Law of vital Intellect—and all human Knowl-edge will be Science and Metaphysics the only Science" (*CL*, III, 38). Davy's discoveries were "more intellectual, more ennobling and impowering human nature, than Newton's!" (*CL*, III, 41). "Humphry Davy in his laboratory is probably doing more for the Science of Mind, than all the Metaphysicians have done from Aristotle to Hartley, inclusive." This last comment was writ-ten while reading the works of Jacob Boehme before 1812. In a subsequent reading, Coleridge observed that "Alas! Since I wrote the preceding note, H. Davy is become Sir Humphry Davy and an *Atomist*!"[33]

Davy's electrochemistry, when free from passive corpuscular theories, was valuable for Coleridge's developing philosophy of nature.[34] It indicated rela-tions if not a fundamental identity between the natural forces of electricity, galvanism, and chemical affinity. If chemical affinity was analogous to the polar powers of electricity, then chemical reactions could be understood as

---

31. Dove Cottage Library MS. 72; *variatim* in *Fragmentary Remains, Literary and Scien-tific, of Sir Humphry Davy*, ed. John Davy (London: John Churchill, 1848), pp. 94–95.

32. All biographical information for which no other source is given here is from Campbell's biography.

33. Marginal note to Boehme, *I*, 40, 43.

34. For an account of Davy's electrochemistry see Harold Hartley, *Humphry Davy* (London: Nelson, 1966); Levere, Ch. 2; D. M. Knight, *Atoms and Elements* (London: Hutchinson, 1967); C. A. Russell, "The Electrochemical Theory of Humphry Davy," *Annals of Science*, 15 (1959), 1–3, 15–25; 19 (1963), 255–71.

resulting from interactions of polar powers. Polarity thus became a chemical concept, and chemical properties were related to underlying powers. At the same time, if electricity was conceived as a polar power it became very difficult to maintain a belief in imponderable corpuscular fluids. Natural philosophy was made up of sciences based on powers. These were the principal features of Coleridge's interpretation of Davy's work, which was a rational enterprise going beyond superficial appearances to underlying causes.

Two Styles of Science

Davy's chemistry was quite different from Dalton's. It seemed to Coleridge to offer an explanation of chemical qualities derived from powers instead of inexplicably associated with corpuscles. The underlying continuity of powers also provided the possibility of a more unified and coherent explanation than a multitude of distinct and essentially passive corpuscles. Davy's and Dalton's chemistry exemplified two distinct styles of science.

Coleridge saw Dalton's chemistry as typifying the worst of English and French thought (*CL*, IV, 760). He saw that the French owed much to Newton, Locke, and Hume (*Lay Sermons, CC*, VI, 22). He regarded Condillac's logic, for example, as plagiarized from British materialistic psychology (*TL*, p. 61, n.), and thought that French philosophy should more truly be termed "Psilosophy"—"from the Greek, psilos slender, and Sophia Wisdom."[35] Coleridge also believed that the English had relinquished philosophy for psilosophy. So it seemed reasonable to identify English and French science as essentially one.

This "Anglo-French" science, in Coleridge's view, seemed symptomatic of "the sunk condition of the world . . . given up to Atheism and Materialism. . . . All Science had become mechanical,"[36] and ended by "Untenanting creation of its God."[37] Such science may be identified by a series of labels. It deals in analysis rather than synthesis, dissection rather than unification, abstraction rather than reality, plurality rather than unity, mechanism rather than organicism, and sensual empiricism rather than rational empiricism. It may perhaps be traced from Newton's third rule of philosophizing, his so-called principle of transdiction, which extrapolates from the experimentally observed to the unobserved and concludes that "the least particles of all bodies

35. *Biographia Literaria*, ed. John Shawcross, 2 vols. (Oxford: Oxford U. Press, 1907), I, 49. *CL*, IV, 922.

36. Quoted from T. Carlyle's description of Coleridge's discourse in *The Life of John Sterling* (London: Chapman & Hall; Boston: Phillips, Sampson & Co., 1851), pp. 46–54, in R. W. Armour and R. F. Howes, *Coleridge the Talker* (Ithaca, N.Y.: Cornell U. Press, 1940), p. 118.

37. "The Destiny of Nations," *Complete Poetical Works*, ed. E. H. Coleridge, 2 vols. (Oxford: Clarendon Press, 1912), I, 132, line 35.

[are] also extended, and hard and impenetrable, and movable, and endowed with their proper inertia."[38] This rule made the senses dominant and science mechanistic, and while Coleridge admired Newton's experiments in the *Opticks*, and admired the theory of gravitation insofar as he could understand it, he condemned Newton as "a mere materialist—*Mind* in his system is always passive—a lazy Looker-on on an external World. If the mind be not *passive* . . . there is ground for suspicion, that any system built on the passiveness of the mind must be false, as a system" (*CL*, II, 709).

Materialism in science, transdiction, and the dominion of the senses presented what Coleridge scornfully called a world of little things; and Locke, who had given it philosophical expression, was "a perfect Little-ist." For Locke's followers, knowledge of the world was derived on a supposedly empirical basis from a *tabula rasa*, and was therefore below the level of the idealists' reason. Locke's philosophy entailed the severance of science from theology and metaphysics and the compartmentalization of intellectual life. Dalton's essentially passive chemistry—chemical psilosophy—was a good example of Lockean science. Coleridge condemned all sciences without unifying ideas and he dismissed contemporary botany as "Little more than an enormous nomenclature; a huge catalogue, *bien arrangè* [sic]. . . . The terms system, method, science, are mere improprieties of courtesy, when applied to a mass enlarging by endless appositions, but without a nerve that oscillates, or a pulse that throbs, in sign of *growth* or inward sympathy" (*Friend, CC*, IV, 469). So much for mechanistic science and sciences of mere classification, and so much for Anglo-French science.

Coleridge considered that German science[39] and philosophy were in a much better state. In Germany—then politically divided but with some degree of intellectual identity—philosophy as opposed to psilosophy was still in repute, and the worst German work of speculative philosophy seemed superior to the best British empirical philosophy for half a century (*CL*, IV, 922, 793–94). German science was not subject to the tyranny of the eye—sensualism—and latterly Coleridge seemed hopeful that the "*dynamic* spirit" of the physical sciences was growing stronger even in England. This dynamic style of science can readily be defined in opposition to mechanistic science—it dealt with synthesis, unification, reality, unity, organicism, and rationality. It did not ignore observation, but used it to provide fuel for imaginative reason, that most creative faculty, and so emphasized the unity of intellectual life.

This style of science, in its late eighteenth- and early nineteenth-century

---

38. *Sir Isaac Newton's Mathematical Principles of Natural Philosophy and his System of the World*, trans. A. Motte, revised by F. Cajori, 2 vols. (Berkeley: U. of California Press, 1966), II, 399.

39. D. M. Knight, "German Science in the Romantic Period," *Emergence of Science*, pp. 161–78.

form, had its philosophical genesis in Kant's separation of noumena from phenomena. Kant had defined noumena as unknowable in principle, so post-Kantian philosophers sought to remove them from philosophy as superfluous. Fichte and Schelling thus sought to construct a thoroughgoing and self-consistent idealism. Their systems assumed the congruence and ultimate identity of laws of mind and laws of nature, and enabled them to deduce a priori the basic types of matter and the forms of the laws governing the action of matter.[40] Schelling in particular expressed these laws in terms of polar dynamism and continuity. In these respects they were in complete contrast with the laws governing the "world of little things." Schelling derived and stated dynamic laws of nature, and Steffens elaborated them. Coleridge read both authors with great care.[41] In their works he read that man is not apart from nature. He noted Schelling's attempts to reconcile philosophy with a form of theology. Later he came to perceive that *Naturphilosophie* led to pantheism, and so he had to reject it. But he remained sympathetic to the attempt at reconciliation.[42]

He was also happy to adopt the genetic form of the theories of *Naturphilosophie*, which viewed nature as the always evolving product of rational and living development. In addition, nature for Coleridge and the *Naturphilosophen* alike was unified—everything was related to everything else. Science

40. *Aids to Reflection*, ed. T. Fenby (Edinburgh: John Grant, 1905), p. 354. For an account of dynamic science see B. Gower, "Speculation in Physics: The History and Practice of *Naturphilosophie*," *Stud. Hist. Phil. Sci.*, 3 (1973), 301–56, with its presentation of Schelling's dynamical atomism. I am grateful to Dr. Gower for the clarification that the distinction here is not between dynamism and atomism as such, but between dynamical and mechanical, passive atomism. See also D. M. Knight, "The Physical Sciences and the Romantic Movement," *History of Science*, 9 (1970), 54–75, and W. D. Wetzels, "Aspects of Natural Science in German Romanticism," *Studies in Romanticism*, 10 (1971), 44–59.

41. C annotated the following works: Steffens, *Beyträge zur innern Naturgeschichte der Erde* . . . (Freyberg: im Verlag der Crazischen Buchhandlung,1801); *Grundzüge der Philosophischen Naturwissenschaft* . . . (Berlin: im Verlag der Realbuchhandlung, 1806); *Geognostisch-geologische Aufsätze* . . . (Hamburg: Hoffmann, 1810); *Anthropologie*, 2 vols. (Breslau: Max, 1824); *Caricaturen des Heiligsten*, 2 vols. (Leipzig: Brocthaus, 1819, 1821); *Die gegenwärtige Zeit*, 2 vols. (Berlin: Reimer, 1817); *Ueber die Idee der Universitäten* (Berlin: Realschulbuchhandlung, 1809); Schelling, *Einleitung zu seinem Entwurf eines Systems der Naturphilosophie* (Jena: Gabler, 1799); *System des transcendentalen Idealismus* (Tübingen: Cotta, 1800); *Zeitschrift für spekulativ Physik*, ed. Schelling, 2 vols. (Jena and Leipzig: Gabler, 1800–1); *Ideen zu einer Philosophie der Natur* . . . (Landshut: Krull, 1803;) *Philosophie und Religion* (Tübingen: Cotta, 1804); *Darlegung des wahren Verhältnisses der Naturphilosophie* (Tübingen: Cotta, 1806); *Jahrbücher der Medicin als Wissenschaft*, ed. A. Marcus and Schelling (Tübingen: Cotta, 1805–8); *Philosophische Schriften* (1809); *Denkmal der Schrift von den göttlichen Dingen &c. des Herrn F. H. Jacobi* (Tübingen: Cotta, 1812); *Ueber die Gottheiten von Samothrace* (Tübingen: Cotta, 1815). C's notebooks, especially N 27 and N 28, also bear witness to the critical thoroughness of his reading of these works.

42. T. McFarland, *Coleridge and the Pantheist Tradition* (Oxford: Clarendon Press, 1969).

was correspondingly comprehensive. Its reach is summed up in a sentence written by Steffens in a study of the history of the earth: "The first part of the problem leads us to a theory of the universe."[43] I shall call this the dynamic style of science, in contrast to the mechanistic kind.

Davy's chemistry was polar. His emphasis upon powers and scepticism about imponderable fluids was dynamic. His demonstration of the relations between chemical and electrical power supported the view that nature was a dynamic unity. And his decomposition of the alkalies was an attack on Lavoisier's table of elements. Davy's laboratory work, suitably edited, thus furnished Coleridge with an instance of dynamic science. Davy was moreover well prepared intellectually. He was interested in Boscovich's and Priestley's theories that matter was essentially force.[44] He also knew and, at least for a while, admired Bishop Berkeley's writings: and Berkeley, as Coleridge saw it, "needed only an entire instead of a partial emancipation from the fetters of the mechanic philosophy to have enunciated all that is true and important in modern Chemistry."[45] Because of this background, Davy was a likely reformer of chemistry, a being of hope for Coleridge. Not only had Davy used the polar powers of electricity to probe the relations of bodies, but for reasons metaphysical and theological he believed in the order, unity, and simplicity of the natural world. He thus appeared to Coleridge as the ideal embodiment of the philosophical chemist of genius, standing above mere talent and cleverness.[46] When Coleridge, disenchanted with Davy, discovered that Steffens had made predictions later fulfilled by Davy's experiments, Davy's genius was downgraded to cleverness. "The demonstration that Soda, Potash, Lime, Barytes, &c are metals of the incoherent Series, as given before 1800 by Steffens, were such that Davy's Exhibition of Sodeum [sic], Potassium, Calcium, Barium &c (in 1809) could scarcely increase our conviction."[47] Coleridge became "most indignant at the continued plagiarisms of Sir H. Davy from the Discoveries of Steffens and others . . ." (CL, v, 130). He believed that Davy had become an atomist: atomism as a theory was sterile, and atomists who pretended to discoveries must therefore be plagiarists—the nature of the debate, and Coleridge's leanings, are clear. Dynamic science, German science, was good science. "Anglo-French" mechanistic science was bad. By the time that Coleridge moved in with the Gillmans, this distinction was clear and firm in his mind.

43. Beyträge, pp. 93–94.

44. Cf. Levere, Affinity and Matter, Chs. 1 and 2.

45. Note on flyleaf of G. Berkeley, Siris, 2nd ed. (Dublin and London, 1744); Beinecke Rare Book Library, Yale University.

46. Coleridge on Shakespeare. The Text of the Lectures of 1811–1812, ed. R. A. Foakes (Charlottesville: U. Press of Virginia, 1971), p. 37.

47. Marginal note to Steffens, Beyträge, back flyleaf, referring to p. 138.

II. Coleridge's Philosophy of Nature, 1816–1826

Poetry Realized in Nature

Once in Highgate, Coleridge embarked on a sustained bout of productive work. In 1816 his *Statesman's Manual* appeared and he wrote at least the first draft of *Hints towards the Formation of a more comprehensive Theory of Life*. The year 1817 saw the *Biographia Literaria*, *Sibylline Leaves*, *Zapolya*, and the introduction to the *Encyclopaedia Metropolitana*. In 1818 he published a new version of *The Friend*, and gave three courses of lectures. Thereafter he published less frequently, but continued to develop his ideas vigorously. For perhaps ten or twelve years from 1816, Coleridge filled his notebooks with systematic entries covering almost every branch of science, pursued in accordance with his own plan of general and self-education, and based upon an impressive variety of sources. His enquiries were restricted by his irksome ignorance of mathematics.[48] Little else held him back. More than two hundred full notebook entries,[49] many of them virtually essays, demonstrate Coleridge's attempt to acquaint himself with scientific laws and the myriad details upon which they rest. He was thorough in amassing a large body of abstruse information, which he used to good effect in his *Theory of Life*. The philosophy of nature presented in that work is again apparent in manuscript volumes of the great encyclopedic work that he never completed for publication, the *Opus Maximum*.[50] In assessing the nature and purpose of Coleridge's scientific explorations, one must bear in mind their incorporation in his overall philosophical scheme, and must expect to discover traces of scientific lore in all his major intellectual productions. These traces sometimes achieve dominance in the argument, especially in *Aids to Reflection* (1825) and in *The Friend* (1818), with its extended passages on chemistry.

Chemistry for Coleridge was never a goal in itself, but was merely a step on the ladder of the sciences. But chemistry was at the mid-point of the ladder. Coleridge, a poet, a Christian, a man of wide-ranging intellect, and a friend of men of science, accorded chemistry neither logical nor ontological pre-eminence. But for both personal and pedagogic reasons it was his preferred science. His clearest and finest statement of the imaginative power and significance of chemistry is given in the following passage from the "Essays on the Principles of Method" in *The Friend*:

> ... the assumed indecomponible substances of the LABORATORY ... are the symbols of elementary powers, and the exponents of a law, which, as the root of all these powers, the chemical philosopher, whatever his the-

48. Marginal note in Boehme, front flyleaf.
49. *CN*, I–V. The bulk of the scientific notes will be published in IV.
50. 3 vols. of the work are in Victoria College, Toronto.

ory may be, is instinctively labouring to extract. This instinct, again, is itself but the form, in which the idea, the mental Correlative of the law, first announces its incipient germination in his own mind: and hence proceeds the striving after unity of principle through all the diversity of forms, with a feeling resembling that which accompanies our endeavors to recollect a forgotten name; when we seem at once to have and not to have it; which the memory feels but cannot find. Thus, as "the lunatic, the lover, and the poet," suggest each other to Shakspeare's Theseus, as soon as his thoughts present him the ONE FORM, of which they are but varieties; so water and flame, the diamond, the charcoal, and the mantling champagne, with its ebullient sparkles, are convoked and fraternized by the theory of the chemist. This is, in truth, the first charm of chemistry, and the secret of the almost universal interest excited by its discoveries. The serious complacency which is afforded by the sense of truth, utility, permanence, and progression, blends with and enobles the exhilarating surprise and the pleasurable sting of curiosity, which accompany the propounding and the solving of an Enigma. It is the sense of a principle of connection given by the mind, and sanctioned by the correspondency of nature. Hence the strong hold which in all ages chemistry has had on the imagination. If in SHAKSPEARE we find nature idealized into poetry, through the creative power of a profound yet observant meditation, so through the meditative observation of a DAVY, a WOOLLASTON, or a HATCHETT;

> By some connatural force,
> Powerful at greatest distance to unite
> With secret amity things of like kind,

we find poetry, as it were, substantiated and realized in nature: yea, nature itself disclosed to us, GEMINAM *istam naturam, quæ fit et facit, et creat et creatur,* as at once the poet and the poem! (*CC,* IV, 470–71)

Chemistry, and indeed Coleridge's whole scheme of the sciences and of the "Genesis and ascending Scale of physical Powers, abstractly contemplated," symbolized relations of law, exemplified creativity in nature, and served pedagogically to call forth in the student

the faculty of recognizing the same Idea or radical Thought in a number of Things and Terms which he had ⟨never⟩ previously considered as having any affinity or connection. . . . Who ever attended a first course of Chemical Lectures, or read for the first time a Compendium of modern Chemistry (Lavoisier, Parkinson, Thomson, or Brande) without experiencing, even as a *sensation,* a sudden *enlargement* & *emancipation* of his Intellect, when the conviction first flashed upon him that the Flame of the Gas Light, and the River-Water were the very same things (= elements) and different only as A *uniting* with B, and AB united? or AB balanc*ing* and AB balanc*ed*? (N 23, ff31–31ᵛ)

All nature was a single divinely created system. Laws of nature were ideas of reason and since for Coleridge man has his reason in God's reason, perception of laws of nature enabled one to experience an aspect of creative governance. The poetic use of symbolic language could also reveal aspects of the divine unity of nature, and so both the poet and the scientist—most often, in Coleridge's examples, the chemist—shared imaginatively and creatively in the apprehension of God's plan:[51] "Are we struck at beholding the cope of heaven imaged in a dew-drop? — The least of the animalcula to which that dew drop is an ocean presents an infinite problem, of which the omnipresent is the only solution. . . . even the philosophy of nature can remain philosophy only by rising above nature."[52] The intellectual pyramid that was Coleridge's goal, his never fully accomplished *Opus Maximum*, rested upon a foundation of scientific knowledge supporting philosophy, and culminated in theology. Experiment "dignified into experience" as an "organ of reason" (*TL*, p. 30) was fundamental to this system, and recourse to nature was always the test of theory, "for there a single just exception destroys at once ten thousand apparent confirmations" (*CN*, III, 4171).

This philosophy of nature was clearly not that of Wilhelm Ostwald's fictional *Naturphilosoph* who, when given the task of describing the camel, "needed only to go to his study, and there construct the nature of the camel from the depths of his spirit."[53] Coleridge needed nature as well as reason in building his system, and this intellectual reliance upon nature was complemented by a genius for detailed observation. This is manifest in his poems and notebooks, and witnesses to "that affectionate love of nature and natural objects without which no man could have observed so steadily, or painted so truly and passionately, the very minutest beauties of the external world."[54] Here is cause enough for the great bulk of scientific information in the notebooks of his productive middle age.

Natural Science and the Philosophy of Nature

After 1816 Coleridge began to work towards a philosophical arrangement of the sciences that would elaborate their formal similarities and differences,

51. K. Coburn, "Coleridge: A Bridge between Science and Poetry," in J. Beer, pp. 81–100. T. H. Levere, "S. T. Coleridge: A Poet's View of Science," *Annals of Science* (in press).

52. "Commonplace Book," Huntington Library MS. HM 8195, f9.

53. W. Ostwald, *Naturphilosophie*, 2nd ed. (Leipzig: Veit, 1902), p. 7.

54. *Coleridge's Shakespearean Criticism*, ed. T. M. Raysor, 2 vols. (Cambridge, Mass.: Harvard U. Press, 1930), I, 212. C. is here describing Shakespeare's qualities as a poet, but the passage could very properly be applied to its author.

and also indicate their unity.[55] The formal similarities and the unity both derived, in Coleridge's view, from the divinely initiated genetic development
of powers. He believed that since all things were part of a single system, created and maintained by God, individual things were significant because they
revealed symbolically the comprehensive laws governing them.[56] In order to
understand the system, one needed to grasp the genetic relations between its
components and between laws. One therefore needed to begin with the whole
of nature to understand the system before one could claim to understand any
one of its parts.[57] Coleridge accordingly needed and set about acquiring a
knowledge of all the sciences of his day in order to achieve a systematic intellectual synthesis of the world of nature.[58]

With such a cosmic scope, and with the all but impossible task of beginning
with the whole in order to comprehend its parts, Coleridge was in desperate
need of a method for reducing multeity to intellectual unity. His method was
based on his doctrine of ideas, and required one over-riding idea to provide
the basis for unification. His insistence upon correct method is nowhere more
fluent or convincing than in his "Essays on Method" in *The Friend*:

> But in experimental philosophy, it may be said how much do we not
> owe to accident? Doubtless: but let it not be forgotten, that if the discov-
> eries so made stop there; if they do not excite some master IDEA; if they
> do not lead to some LAW (in whatever dress of theory or hypothesis the
> fashions and prejudices of the time may disguise or disfigure it): the dis-
> coveries may remain for ages limited in their uses, insecure and unpro-
> ductive. How many centuries, we might have said millenia, have passed,
> since the first accidental discovery of the attraction and repulsion of light
> bodies by rubbed amber, &c. Compare the interval with the progress
> made within less than a century, after the discovery of the phænomena
> that led immediately to a THEORY of electricity. That here as in many
> other instances, the theory was supported by insecure hypotheses; that
> by one theorist two heterogeneous fluids are assumed, the vitreous and
> the resinous; by another, a plus and minus of the same fluid; that a third
> considers it a mere modification of light; while a fourth composes the
> electrical aura of oxygen, hydrogen, and caloric: this does but place the
> truth we have been evolving in a stronger and clearer light. For abstract

55. See especially BM Add. MSS. 47,525 and 47,526.

56. Stephen Prickett, *Coleridge and Wordsworth: The Poetry of Growth* (Cambridge:
Cambridge U. Press, 1970), Ch. 7, "Symbol and Growth." O. Barfield, *What Coleridge
Thought* (Middletown, Conn.: Wesleyan U. Press, 1971), passim—see index for sym-
bol(s).

57. Cf. J. H. Haeger, "The Scientific Speculations of Samuel Taylor Coleridge: Manuscript Transcriptions and a Commentary," Diss. U. of Washington 1970, p. 54.

58. C regularly perused the *Phil. Trans., Quarterly Journal of Science & Arts*, etc.

from all these suppositions, or rather imaginations, that which is common to, and involved in them all; and we shall have neither notional fluid or fluids, nor chemical compounds, nor elementary matter,—but the idea of *two—opposite—forces*, tending to rest by equilibrium. These are the sole factors of the calculus, alike in all the theories. These give the *law*, and in it the *method*, both of arranging the phænomena and of substantiating appearances into facts of science; with a success proportionate to the clearness or confusedness of the insight into the law.[59]

Laws are essential—"with the knowledge of LAW alone dwell Power and Prophecy, decisive Experiment, and, lastly, a scientific method"—and the law of polarity is the fundamental initiative law. "EVERY POWER IN NATURE AND IN SPIRIT *must evolve an opposite, as the sole means and condition of its manifestation:* AND ALL OPPOSITION IS A TENDENCY TO RE-UNION" (*Friend, CC*, IV, 470, 94).

Such universal laws tempt one through generality to speculation. Coleridge recognized that "It is of the highest importance in all departments of knowledge to keep the Speculative distinct from the Empirical. As long as they run parallel, they are of the greatest service to each other: they never meet but to cut and cross."[60] He had already acquired the philosophical competence to be a speculative thinker, having a fine grasp of logic and impressive erudition in the history of philosophy and in contemporary philosophy.[61] Now he set out to create for himself a solid foundation of empirical knowledge, culled from the most reliable sources regardless of their philosophical leanings—Lorenz Oken and William Thomas Brande were equally grist for Coleridge, even though "Anglo-Gallic" Brande dismissed the works of Oken and his fellows as so much Eastern allegory. No matter—Brande's *Manual of Chemistry*[62] was for Coleridge one of the best compendia of modern chemistry. Coleridge accordingly worked his way through it, extracting detailed information wherever it seemed either philosophically relevant or of intrinsic interest. Such discipline ensured an empirical foundation of fact for his system of the philosophy of nature.

It is of course a dynamical system, concerned with synthesis and organicism.

59. *CC*, IV, 478. See also *CN*, III, 4226. C's extended formal statement is given in *S. T. Coleridge's Treatise on Method as Published in the Encyclopaedia Metropolitana*, ed. A. D. Snyder (London: Constable, 1934).

60. Marginal note on H. C. Oersted, *Ansicht der chemischen Naturgesetze* (Berlin: Realschulbuchhandlung, 1812), p. 42, in K. Coburn, ed., *Inquiring Spirit* (London: Routledge & Kegan Paul, 1951), entry 192.

61. "Treatise on Logic," BM MSS. Egerton 2825, 2826, discussed in Orsini, pp. 246–62, and in A. Snyder, *Coleridge on Logic and Learning* (New Haven and London: Yale U. Press, 1929).

62. W. T. Brande, *A Manual of Chemistry* (London: J. Murray, 1819).

Coleridge is free with analogies based upon the growth of plants. Some commentators, notably M. H. Abrams,[63] have seen this as a key to Coleridge's understanding of nature. But in comprehending Coleridge's scheme, one must consider carefully what Coleridge meant by analogy. He wrote that "Analogy implies a difference in sort, and not merely in degree: and it is the sameness of the end, with the difference of the means, which constitutes analogy."[64] Analogy is not identity. To say that A is analogous to B is to assert that between A and B there are both similarities and differences.[65] So the statement that the universe is like a plant means that some aspect or aspects of the universe are like some aspect or aspects of a plant, while other aspects of the universe are unlike the plant. Coleridge also makes it clear that talking of the analogy with nature does not imply that all the universe is like some one element in that universe. So universal analogies do not suffice for an understanding of Coleridge's view of nature. One needs first to explore the form of his scheme, presented through a genetic scale of powers embodying distinctions as well as analogies, and then to see how these help him to interpret a wide range of scientific facts.

Coleridge's universe is one of productive unity, and in this respect is like Schelling's in his *Einleitung zu seinem Entwurf eines Systems der Naturphilosophie* (Jena and Leipzig, 1799), a copy of which Coleridge annotated. But whereas the universe of Schelling and of Steffens produces itself by an inner logical necessity, Coleridge's universe is produced according to divinely created laws following an initiating divine act—so both pantheism and atheism are avoided, and God's will governs all. The first divine act operated on chaos, just as Genesis states, because "in order to *comprehend* and *explain* the forms of things, imagine a state antecedent to form" (*TL*, p. 67, and *Church and State, CC,* x, 233).

Coleridge tried various schemes for resolutions from chaos. All these schemes obeyed the law of polarity. Powers evolved from prothesis to thesis and antithesis in polar opposition, yielding in their turn both an indifference or dynamic reconciliation and a new synthesis. The indifference arose as the mid-point or balance between opposites, while the synthesis was a composition of opposites. For example, church and state were opposites, for which the press was a mesothesis or indifference, while the Crown was their synthesis.

---

63. M. H. Abrams, *The Mirror and the Lamp* (Oxford: Oxford U. Press, 1953), pp. 68–69, 369 (n. 50).

64. *TL*, p. 64. See also pp. 32–33, 43–44; *CN*, III, 4225; *Friend* (*CC*, IV), 469–70.

65. See, e.g., M. B. Hesse, *Models and Analogies in Science* (Notre Dame, Ind.: U. of Notre Dame Press, 1966), p. 8, on positive and negative analogies.

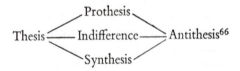

Chaos was the original prothesis, from which the first differential act produced light as thesis, and darkness or gravitation as antithesis. This polar pair was seminal and ubiquitous in Steffen's writings, most notably in his *Grundzüge der philosophischen Naturwissenschaft* (Berlin, 1806). Coleridge read this book critically and repeatedly.[67] Steffens was the author whose works Coleridge used most in constructing his system, and he made a sustained effort to correlate Steffens' developmental scheme with the Bible.

Coleridge clearly regarded Genesis as inspired philosophical cosmogony. He stated explicitly that he had nothing to do with elements but followed Moses (N 28, f53ᵛ). He noted eagerly that the latest philosophical science, whether geology, astronomy, or physics, seemed increasingly to vindicate the scientific authority of the Pentateuch (e.g., N 18, ff164–164ᵛ). But he asserted that he had built his scheme from science and philosophy, and only then perceived its congruence with the Mosaic account (*CL*, v, 18). Scientific evidence no less than revelation informed Coleridge of the emergence of light and darkness from the prothetic chaos, which was followed successively by the creation of water, the separation of water from the firmament, the separation of land from the waters, and the creation of living nature in a precise sequence culminating in man.[68]

Cosmogony, cosmology, astronomy and physics, geology, chemistry, botany, zoology, and the sciences of man were all comprehended within this scheme of cosmic evolution. The evolutionary or developmental plan was required by Coleridge's philosophy of nature and strengthened by his interpretation of the Bible and of modern science. The sequence was generated through a hierarchy of powers whose details varied but whose general form was established in a scheme of no later than 1815. In this scheme, represented by a circumscribed cross, the ends of the diameters and their intersection cor-

66. Derived from *CL*, IV, 807. Cf. C. W. Miller, "Coleridge's Concept of Nature," *J.H.I..* 25 (1964), 77–96. I discuss C's scheme of the sciences and his detailed knowledge of individual branches of science in a monograph on C and science, now in preparation.

67. Annotations in *Grundzüge*, especially pp. 26–40. *CL*, IV, 808–9.

68. N 18, ff163ᵛ–164ᵛ. The genetic aspect of C's dynamic philosophy epitomized in *CL*, IV, p. 807 pervades his writings. In this account of the creation, however, and elsewhere, the genetic aspect is soon subordinated to the polar aspect. Chaos is a prothesis, but C shifts from this form to stress a series of polar oppositions, light-darkness, water-firmament, land-waters. This transition is followed through in *CN*, III, 4226.

respond to five powers—powers at opposite ends of the same diameter are in polar opposition, the intersection of the diameters corresponds to the power that is the dynamic reconciliation or indifference of the two pairs of polar opposites, and the encompassing circle symbolises the overall unity of the powers represented. The same pentadic structure holds at every level in the hierarchy:

Ideal

NS = Line of *Being*: N = Fixive, S = mobile, motive.
EW = Surface of *Becoming*: E. Retractive, insulative,
W. dilative

M. Neutrant

Cosmical

N = Attraction, S. Repulsion. E = Morphic, W. Amorphic.
M = Gravitation.

Geological

N = Earth, S = Air, E = Fire, W = Vapor
M = Water. ※

Potential.

N = Magnetism, Negative Pole.
S.   Ditto, Positive Pole.
E.   Electricity, Positive Pole
W.   Ditto, Negative Pole
      M. Galvanism

Chemical

N = Carbon, S. Azote: E = Oxygen, W = Hydrogen.
M = Metal. ※ ※

Organics [*Organics* canceled]   *Vital*
N.S. Reproduction
E.W. Irritability
M. Sensibility

Organic
N.S. Glandular & Venous.
E.W. Arterial, Muscular
M. Nervous.

(*CN*, III, 4226)

The cosmogony did indeed follow Moses. It also relied selectively upon the cosmologies of Kant and Laplace, preserving their evolutionary arguments while rejecting their mechanism (*CL*, IV, 808; N 26, f24^v). He also invoked Jacob Boehme's theosophy.[69] Coleridge's cosmology followed Newton's laws, but explained them with the aid of concepts drawn from German philosophical writers from Steffens to Eschenmayer. Thus he saw the unity of gravitation and light manifested constitutively and constructively in the solar system, exemplifying the analogy of nature (*CN*, III, 4418). His geological account started from a watery chaos, the Biblical flood, and then proceeded through crystallisation and precipitation to produce both land formations and life (*TL*, pp. 70 ff.). Indeed, since Coleridge followed Schelling by defining life as the tendency to individuation, and since he saw this tendency even in geological formations and markedly in crystals, geology was related not only to all the previous sciences in his scheme, but also to the later sciences of chemistry and zoology.[70] The precipitation scheme of Werner, which could readily he assimilated to the story of Noah, at first had particular attractions for Coleridge:

> From the first moment of the differential impulse—(the primæval chemical epoch of the Wernerian school)—when Nature, by the tranquil deposition of crystals, prepared, as it were, the fulcrum of her after-efforts, from this, her first, and in part *irrevocable*, self-contraction, we find, in each ensuing production, more and more tendency to independent existence in the increasing multitude of strata, and in the relics of the lowest orders, first of vegetable and then of animal life. (*TL*, p. 70)

Subsequently Coleridge recognized that the life of nature rendered invalid all attempts to limit geology by chemistry. He attacked the chemical precipitation scheme as a waste of time, since it applied "to the plastic power of the Infinite a mete-wand borrowed from a chemist's Laboratory" (*CL*, IV, 804–5). But if geology could not be reduced to chemistry, far less could zoonomy

---

69. Marginalia in Boehme. See also A. C. Snyder, "Coleridge on Boehme," *PMLA*, 45 (1930), 616–18, and T. McFarland, pp. 325–32. C's marginalia are to be published, ed. G. Whalley in *CC*.

70. C defines life both as a tendency and a principle of individuation (*TL*, pp. 36, 42). This sentence summarises much of the argument of *TL*. Schelling's definition is in "Von der Weltseele," *Schellings Werke*, 3 vols. (Leipzig: Meiner, 1907), I, 663.

submit to such reduction. Between the sciences grounded in life and those not so grounded there was and could only be "a complete Saltus."[71]

Transitions between sciences were discontinuous, since powers operative at one step on the ladder of the sciences might correspond to powers at the next step, but could not merge with them. The intellectual ascent of the ladder, tracing out the genetic scheme of powers in nature, and identifying parallels and correspondences between distinct steps, was central to Coleridge's enterprise. The powers active in different sciences corresponded to different rungs on the ladder. The final stage of the construction of matter was through the ascent from the potential to the chemical realm, where the inward power of matter—chemical affinity—was first active. And organic life was on the next rung, beyond chemistry, which "must needs be at its extreme limit, when it has approached the threshold of a higher power" (*TL*, p. 32). Chemistry, situated between the life sciences and the sciences of inorganic nature and distinct from both, occupied as it were the very mid-point of Coleridge's ascent of the ladder of nature. It was central in his thought, and had been seminal in his discovery of the sciences. It thus provided him with many illustrations of philosophical, psychological, theological, and political arguments. Dynamical chemistry was based upon powers and their mutual modifications and relations, in conformity with the law of polarity. Coleridge gave his most concise statement of this universal law in explaining the natural opposition between civil and criminal law and religion, but he went on to illustrate it with a dynamic view of the constitution of water, which he saw as neither hydrogen nor oxygen, nor a mixture of both, but as the synthesis or indifference of the two.[72] Similarly, carbon and nitrogen were manifestations of power, corresponding to magnetic poles: they were *stuffs*, substances real in themselves, and also sensible symbols of polar powers, illustrating a law of nature (*Friend* [*CC*, IV], I, 470; *CL*, IV, 808–9).

Coleridge's four ideal elements (identical to those of Steffens) are: "pure Carbon, pure Azote, pure Oxygen, and pure Hydrogen, *ideally* indecomponible, and corresponding to these four elementary Bodies, practically [practically *canceled*] indecomponible ⟨into bodies,⟩ each supposing ⟨all⟩ the 4 ideal Elements, but as under the predominance of some one of them. Thus Carbon would ⟨be⟩ C.H.A.O. under the predominance of C" (*CN*, III, 4420, f19ᵛ). Thus the speculative or philosophical chemist saw that the simple substances of empirical chemistry must "*a priori* . . . be composite."[73]

Coleridge's view of the mode of composition of ideal elements is illuminated by his criticism of Steffens' view of the metals. Coleridge was neither

71. Notebook entitled "Marginalia Intentionalia," f20 (NYPL Berg Collection).

72. *Friend* [*CC*, IV], I, 94 and n. "Indifference" here means the dynamic product or combination of opposed but balancing powers.

73. See n. 60 above.

passive recipient nor uncritical enthusiast when reading the works of the *Naturphilosophen*. Steffens had seemed to propose that metals were compounded of the opposite forces represented by carbon and nitrogen respectively. Predominance of the former would result in a more coherent metal, and this predominance simply meant for Steffens more of the power of carbon in the metal's constitution. Such an additive and essentially passive notion of combination and constitution was unacceptable to Coleridge, who noted: "It is an error therefore and an inconsistency in Steffens to speak of the Metals as composed of Carbon and Nitrogen—unless where these are taken as the names of the Power predominant in each. And even so yet not as composed *of* them, but as constituted *by* them."[74] The tendency to re-union meant for Coleridge the mutual modification of powers in the process of dynamic synthesis.[75]

Chemistry in the hands of Davy, Ritter, and Oersted was truly a science of powers. Davy's electrochemical researches, involving use of the voltaic pile and a theory of the identity of chemical affinity and electrical power, were new, dramatic, and very agreeable to Coleridge's dynamism. Electrochemistry related chemistry to the potential level in the hierarchy of powers, just as organic chemistry related it to the vital.

Before looking at some of the details of Coleridge's chemistry, it is worth recalling the general structure of the hierarchy. Each step, each level was analogous to each of the other steps—hence Coleridge's universal application of the diagram of a circle with two diameters drawn at right angles. He regarded the analogy with nature as being comprehensive. But analogy is not identity, and the steps on the ladder were distinct although parallel.

The analogy held between the powers of matter-*in-potentia* and the ideal chemical elements, so that "the assumed indecomponible substances of the laboratory" were indeed symbols of powers. Coleridge described his cosmically significant diagram of a cross inscribed in a circle as a compass, admirably refraining from pointing out its other obvious symbolism. "But it must not be forgotten," he went on to say,

> that the Compass of Nature like the Mariner's Compass is not designated by the 4 great Points, N.S.E. and W. only, but by the intermediates—Of these we have [have *canceled*] know that we have discovered two, the

74. Steffens, *Beyträge*, pp. 262–63, and C's marginal notes.

75. Ibid. See also marginal notes at the rear of the volume, where he discusses the difference between modifying and substantiating powers, and the difference between the ideal directions and particular (chemical) forms. C's distinction between the imagination and the understanding, given its best-known expression in the *Biographia Literaria*, and his view of chemical synthesis, are mutually illuminated by his comment (Victoria College S MS. 5): "Difference between synthesis and juxta-position / illustrated by chemistry. I can put oil and water in juxtaposition, by adding an alcali I produce a synthesis or combination. . . . The Imagination is the synthetic Power."

position of which is probably between E. and South, or Oxygen, and
Azote—namely, Chlorine and Iodine.—It is possible that some known
Bodies may have been confounded under Hydrogen, or some supposed
decomponible—and others doubtless will be discovered. Oxygen itself
may not be the due East, or Hydrogen due West—. (CN, III, 4420)

Now if one viewed chemical substances in this dynamic way, it was clear
that transmutation of supposed elements could occur if the appropriate modification of power was super-induced. This was of great significance for Coleridge, who regarded the alchemists' dream of transmutation as "the theoretic
end of chemistry: there must be a common law, upon which all can become
each and each all."[76] The compass of nature, trinity in a pentad, multeity in
unity, was a profoundly revealing symbol of the powers in nature. It was also
heuristic. "Long before Sir H. Davy's attempts to establish the independent
existence of the Oxymuriatic as Chlorine, I had anticipated it a priori, tho'
whether as an East by North, or East by South, I could not determine, but I
conjectured the former. And such, I doubt not, it is."[77] This was written after
Steffens had replaced Davy as Coleridge's guide to the laws of chemistry.
Davy's initial work of aggression against Lavoisier's table of elements[78] had
suggested to him and to Coleridge that transmutation might be realized in
the laboratory. In his early lectures in London, Davy had argued that nitrogen
was not a simple body, but could be converted to oxygen and another hitherto unknown substance related to the principle common to all the metals.[79]
Such views fitted very nicely into Coleridge's later theoretical frameworks,
and could be described in terms of the modification of direction of magnetic
power—a stiff blow indeed at corpuscular chemistry. As Coleridge expressed
it around 1810:

⟨more probably, Azote is a tritoxyd of Ammonium—and Hydrogen the
protoxide—or in more philosophical Language, and according to the
dynamic View, Hydrogen is Ammonium in the state of + Magnetism
[Magnetism *canceled*] Electricity, and Azote the same in the state of +
Magnetism.⟩ . . . ⟨I doubt whether Oxygen exists as Oxygen in Azote
while it is Azote. I should suspect a priori Carbon in its highest state of
volatility and Atomism—and what if Carbon itself is capable of passing
into Oxygen by change of state, the magn. for the electr.?⟩ (CN, III, 4196)

76. March 18, 1832, *Table Talk*, ed. H. N. Coleridge, 2 vols. (London: John Murray,
1835), II, 27–28. C was much interested in alchemy and introchemistry. He read the
works of Paracelsus (see CN, I, 904, 1000) and was struck by Boehme's use of alchemical
lore, as shown by his marginalia (see n. 23 above).
77. Annotation on back flyleaf of Steffens, *Geognostisch-geologische Aufsätze*, referring
to p. 243.
78. D. M. Knight, *Atoms and Elements*, Chs. 2 and 3; see also n. 23 and n. 27 above.
79. RI: Davy MS. 3. Levere, *Affinity and Matter*, pp. 45–46.

Davy's view of the nature of nitrogen was unhappily based upon problematic analyses of ammonia amalgam. It was however consonant with phlogiston theory, and was widely held in the first decades of the nineteenth century.[80] It should be noted that Steffens regarded nitrogen as constituted by pure southerly power in the compass of nature, while Coleridge considered that ideal nitrogen as opposed to the stuff of real nitrogen was the symbol of the same power.[81] Evidence for transmutation provided from the "Anglo-Gallic' camp was particularly welcome. Transmutation had no place in Lavoisier's chemistry, and yet his followers sometimes seemed to support it. Berzelius, a superb experimentalist, reached conclusions about nitrogen that were similar to Davy's, through the application of laws of combining proportions to analyses of nitrogen compounds.[82]

Best of all was the evidence of William Thomas Brande, who lectured at the Royal Institution after Davy. Brande displayed such surpassing pedantry and scorn for German metaphysics that his unwitting support seemed conclusive proof of the dynamic philosophy that he had dismissed as the eastern allegory of Steffens.[83] He took much of his material from Thomas Thomson's popular textbook,[84] but at one point managed in transcribing a page to give a clumsy summary of a crucial paragraph; this made it appear to Coleridge that two very different organic compounds were in fact closely related by a simple transmutation of chlorine into oxygen. Now transmutation is of course impossible in the Daltonian chemistry to which Brande subscribed, but no surprise in dynamical chemistry, where matter is a manifestation of powers.[85] Coleridge may be excused for his satisfaction, mildly expressed in a notebook: "This, however, sufficiently favours my notion & gives a *sense* to my queries and suggestions, written before I had come to this passage" (N 27, f67). Brande provided Coleridge with several similar opportunities for satisfaction. When Brande ruled out any means for nitrogen to enter into the body of a plant, and then identified the presence of nitrogen in plant matter, Coleridge thought this was a "suspicious symptom of a reluctant approximation to the 'Eastern Allegory' or Dynamic Scheme" (N 28, ff7–7ᵛ).

Polar dynamical chemistry received a more thorough treatment in Coleridge's note-books than any other single branch of science. He often inter-

80. R. Siegfried, "The Phlogistic Conjectures of Humphry Davy," *Chymia*, 9 (1964), 117–24.

81. Steffens, *Gründzuge*, pp. 45 ff.; *Beyträge*, passim, and esp. pp. 262–63 with C's marginalia. *CN*, III, 4435, 4436. C's marginal note inside front cover of Boehme.

82. Berzelius to Davy, 30 June 1809, in *Jac. Berzelius Bref*, ed. Söderbaum, 6 vols. + 3 suppl. (Uppsala: Almqvist & Wiksells, 1912–32), II, 13.

83. Brande, *Manual*, p. 480.

84. *System of Chemistry*, 4 vols., probably 5th ed. (London: Baldwin, Cradock, & Joy, 1817).

85. Brande, *Manual*, p. 153.

preted geology and natural philosophy through chemical philosophy, and
even sought to explain Genesis in terms of transcendental chemistry. Chemistry was in the early nineteenth century perhaps the most accessible and the
richest of the sciences involving powers, and because of the unity of nature
and the unifying role of ideas, it shed light even on the vital realms. Chemistry was of the greatest importance to Coleridge and, for many years, Davy
appeared as chemistry's most brilliant exponent. Coleridge repeatedly stressed
the superiority of Shakespeare to Newton, yet he compared Davy to Shakespeare (*Friend* [*CC*, IV], I, 471). The true chemical philosopher, unlike the
mechanical psilosopher, revealed and created unity through his perception
of ideas of reason. Coleridge embraced Davy's work to produce his own
synthesis.

III Conclusion

Coleridge embraced Davy's work, but not his conception of science. Coleridge saw man's ideas as congruent with God's, and regarded laws of nature
as expressions of God's ideas. It followed that a law of nature once understood
was seen as necessarily true.[86] Davy's view was very different. "Nature," he
wrote, "has no archetype in the human imagination."[87] Here we seem to
have a clear opposition between the empirical scientist and the Romantic
spectator of science philosophizing in Platonic fashion. The two seem unlikely
to blend, and it is tempting to emphasize the dichotomy. The range of sources
consulted by Coleridge should, however, caution us against too simplistic a
distinction. Schelling is said to have castigated Ritter as an empiricist Philis-
tine; Ritter was latterly too careless of facts for Oersted's taste; Oersted knew
that the English thought him too much of a German metaphysician, and
Coleridge was offended by his mingling the speculative with the empirical.
Yet Ritter and Oersted provided at least empirical fodder for Davy who still
remained critical of German philosophy of nature. And Berzelius recoiled
before Davy's hypotheses.[88] The line dividing experiment from speculation
was important for every scientist, but there was clearly no unanimity in England or Germany about where the line should be drawn or how it should be
interpreted. Scientists did not fit into a clean dichotomy of respectable scien-

86. C's best discussion of Law is in *Friend* [*CC*, IV], I, 458 ff. For the "Divine Ideas,"
see Huntington MS. HM 8195. There is a useful account of "Ideas, Method, Laws" in
Barfield, Ch. 10.

87. *The Collected Works of Sir Humphry Davy, Bart.*, ed. J. Davy, 9 vols. (London:
Smith, Elder & Co., 1840), VIII, 347.

88. Oersted's correspondence with Ritter is in *Correspondance de H. C. Oersted*, ed. M.
C. Harding, 2 vols. (Copenhagen: H. Aschehoug, 1926). Oersted's comments on English
philosophical attitudes are in the same work, II, 404. Berzelius' comments on Davy's use
of hypotheses are in *Bref*, II, 35–39.

tists on one hand and Romantic ones on the other. This suggests that in constructing a history of scientific ideas, one might profitably examine a wide range of sources.

Davy's scientific education, for example, was indebted to Joseph Priestley and Isaac Newton—and also to a mathematician called Mako, who is obscure in all but his native Hungarian literature, to the Yugoslav Jesuit Boscovich, and to the *Naturphilosoph* Ritter.[89] Coleridge's eclecticism scarcely needs demonstration, but it is worth noting that it was aided by dealers who specialized in German books.[90] Beddoes clearly had no difficulty in obtaining German medical literature.[91] Thomas Thomson reviewed Oersted's essay on the identity of chemical and electrical forces without having read it, because he found French reviews more accessible than the book itself.[92] But Coleridge apparently had no problem in acquiring a copy, any more than in acquiring the works of Steffens, of Oken, or of continental animal magnetists.[93] British journals such as the *Philosophical Magazine* or the *Quarterly Journal of Science and Arts* published regular notices of foreign researches and of the proceedings of foreign scientific societies. Volta published his discovery of the pile in French in the *Philosophical Transactions of the Royal Society*,[94] and later on Taylor published his *Scientific Memoirs selected from the Transactions of Foreign Academies and Learned Societies and from Foreign Journals*. Davy went on a European tour during the Napoleonic wars, and Maria Edgeworth mingled with literary and scientific society in Paris shortly after the wars. British scientists were not insular in their interests, nor were they cut off from continental literature.[95] I do not mean to suggest that there was no real opposition between, say, Ritter and Davy. There was. Davy's severance of the forms of

89. Levere, *Affinity and Matter*, Ch. 2.

90. E.g., Thomas Boosey of Broad Street (see *CL*, IV, 664, 666, 730–31, 738). Crabb Robinson, Aders, and J. H. Green not only provided C with German books, but had direct connections with Europe that made it easy for them to provide him with books unavailable in London.

91. Stock, *Beddoes*, pp. 299 ff.

92. T. Thomson, "Sketch of the latest Improvements in the Physical Sciences," *Annals of Philosophy*, 5 (1815), 5, discusses Oersted, *Ansichten* (1812). He obtained M. de Serre's very free translation, *Recherches sur l'identité des forces chimiques et electriques* (Paris: J. C. Dentu, 1813) for review in *Ann. Phil.*, 13 (1819), 368, 456; 14 (1819), 47.

93. See n. 41 above for C's reading of Schelling and Steffens. C annotated: L. Oken, *Erste Ideen zur Theorie des Lichts* (1808); *Lehrbuch der Naturgeschichte*, 6 vols. (1813, 1816–26); *Lehrbuch der Naturphilosophie* (1809); J. H. Jung, *Theorie der Geister-kunde* [with] *Apologie de Theorie der Geisterkunde* (1808–9); C. A. F. Kluge, *Versuch einer Darstellung des animalischen Magnetismus* (1815); F. A. Mesmer, *Mesmerismus*, 2 vols. (1814–15). C used extensively *Archiv für thierischen Magnetismus*, ed. Eschenmayer, Kieser, and Nasse, 12 vols. (Leipzig and Halle, 1817–24).

94. A. Volta, *Phil. Trans.*, 90 (1800), 403.

95. G. de Beer, *The Sciences Were Never at War* (London: Nelson, 1960).

natural law from the human imagination would have been equally congenial to the Fellows of the Royal Society and unpalatable to the *Naturphilosophen*.

The official attitude of established British science to mere thinking was clear, from the attacks on Young's advocacy of a wave theory of light buttressed by no new experiment, to Herschel's presidential relief before the British Association for the Advancement of Science that the metaphysical heresies of German absolutists and ontologists were yielding to sound sense.[96] But even the fellows of the Royal Society had interests and institutional affiliations which, when followed in the light of Coleridge's concerns, lead into the fastnesses of *Naturphilosophie*.

Coleridge had many acquaintances among the fellows of the Royal Society, and followed developments at the Royal Institution. These two foundations furnished the membership of the Society for Animal Chemistry, which was active between 1812 and 1825.[97] H. Davy, Charles Hatchett, W. T. Brande, and E. Home were its most productive members. Coleridge assiduously read their publications in the *Philosophical Transactions* and elsewhere (N 27, 28, 29). Now Davy and Home were among the trustees of the Hunterian collection of the Royal College of Surgeons; Coleridge, a great admirer of Hunter, regarded the organization of this collection as a fine example of scientific method.[98] Not only did this furnish Coleridge with institutional and personal links between chemistry and physiology, but Coleridge's closest intellectual co-worker and disciple in later years, J. H. Green, was Hunterian Professor at the College. Green's lectures and books made extensive use of German physiology and philosophical zoology, and also of Coleridge's writings on these topics, with their admixture of chemistry.[99] Richard Owen, F.R.S., an enthusiast for Oken's ideas, was among Green's auditors,[100] and had obtained his post at the College through John Abernethy, F.R.S.[101] Abernethy and Coleridge had attended one another's lectures and supported one another's

96. J. F. W. Herschel, "Presidential Address," in *Report of the British Association for the Advancement of Science* (1845), p. xli.

97. E. Home, *Lectures on Comparative Anatomy*, 6 vols. (1814–28), V, 14.

98. Home, III, (1823), ix. *Friend* [CC, IV], I, 474.

99. Notes taken at J. H. Green's lectures, Royal College of Surgeons [RCS] of England: MS. 42 a.19, MS. 67.b.11. J. H. Green (*Vital Dynamics. The Hunterian Oration . . .* [1840], f. 56) refers to Carus, Oken, Meckel, Spix, Tiedemann, and others, and throughout his writings implicitly and explicitly acknowledges his indebtedness to C. Green was both C's co-worker and near–disciple, and became his literary executor.

100. RCS MS. 67.b.11 includes notes taken by Owen at Green's lectures. Owen wrote the article on Oken in *Encyc. Brit.*, 8th ed. (1858), XVI, 498–503.

101. For Owen's life and works, see *The Life of Richard Owen by his grandson the Rev. Richard Owen, M.A. . . . also an essay on Owen's position in anatomical science by the Right. Hon. T. H. Huxley, F.R.S.*, 2 vols. (1894).

ideas.[102] John Hunter and Coleridge between them linked the Royal Society with *Naturphilosophie*, through Green, Owen, and Abernethy. A scientific society has its own ethos. But just as one has to beware of assuming too much insularity in English science, so one should be receptive to the possibility of some eclecticism in any society—even the Royal Society.

Coleridge's grasp was certainly eclectic. He would learn where he could, and he regarded the science of the Royal Society as a mine of information needing only proper interpretation. He was also interested in the B.A.A.S., attending its meeting in Cambridge in 1833, just one year before his death.[103] But there was a side of Coleridge's interest in science that was but little advanced by the establishment familiar to English-speaking historians of science. In pursuing the relations between powers of mind and powers in nature he went to the medical profession.

Many of the sixty or more medical men[104] among Coleridge's acquaintance were interested in powers, whether through an interpretation of Hunter's theory of life or through Blumenbach's *nisus formativus*. Many of them again were concerned with the power of mind over body, with the problems of animal magnetism, and with psychosomatic diseases. The Royal College of Surgeons was a principal focus for their activities, and Coleridge, through Joseph Henry Green and others, availed himself of its resources (see, e.g., *CL*, v, 372). He owed much to the philosophical physicians of London and Bristol.

Coleridge's grateful recognition of the role of mind and powers in the natural philosophy of Schelling and of Steffens is well known. The little favour their works found in England led him to assert in frustration that Germany was "the only Country in which a man dare exercise his *reason* without being thought to have lost his Wits, & be out of *his Senses*" (*CL*, IV, 775; cf. 761). Rejection of "Eastern allegory" by Brande in despite of his own evidence brought from Coleridge repeated bursts of irritation against chemistry at the Royal Institution. "Sham, Flam, and Saintship, Humbug and holy-cant, rather than plead guilty of the horrid Heresy of Zoodynamism, and the *Life* of Nature" (N 28, f9ᵛ). The Royal Society was in no better case, and Coleridge hoped at one time that the London Philosophical Society (later given up as

102. K. Coburn, ed., *The Philosophical Lectures of Samuel Taylor Coleridge* (London: The Pilot Press, 1949), pp. 24–25. Owsei Temkin, "Basic Science, Medicine, and the Romantic Era," *Bulletin of the History of Medicine*, 37 (1963), 97–129, is helpful here. Abernethy, *An Enquiry into the Probability and Rationality of Mr. Hunter's Theory of Life* . . . (1814), pp. 48–52, draws extreme conclusions about chemistry and the "Anima Mundi" from Davy's Bakerian Lectures.

103. *Table Talk*, II, 200, n.

104. I have so far identified sixty-one physicians and surgeons and plan subsequently to publish a detailed elaboration of this paragraph. Pertinent information is given in R. Guest-Gornall, "Samuel Taylor Coleridge and the Doctors," *Medical History*, 17 (1973), 327–42.

the "London Psilosophical Society in Flower de Luce Court, or thereabouts")
might "be speedily raised into scientific Importance, . . . by pursuing the directly opposite course to that which the Royal Soc. has taken for the last 30
years"—an investigation that would destroy "the Anglo-Gallican Theory of
Chemistry" (*CL*, IV, 743–44, 788). Somehow or other Coleridge hoped to
bring together "the *Teutonics*, Germans & English"—and his nearest approach
to success in this enterprise came in philosophical intercourse with surgeons.

Coleridge used chemistry and philosophy to bear on life in a dynamically
constituted nature. He made especial use of German and English science, and
of scientists in several societies which often seem mutually exclusive. He was
critical, receptive, and methodical. And the philosophy of nature which he
evolved was very much his own.

XIV

Hegel and the Earth Sciences

Introduction

Hegel's lectures on the philosophy of nature were composed and delivered over a period of some twenty-five years, from the Jena period of 1805—1806, via the 1817 edition of his *Encyclopaedia*, through his Berlin period to the 1830 edition of the *Encyclopaedia*.[1] His first lectures on geology were delivered at a time when the Wernerian school was well established in Germany, but still more than a decade after Hutton's rival theory had first been promulgated.

The debate was at first one between schools generally termed Neptunist and Vulcanist, since water was the primary agency of geological change in Werner's scheme, while fire played a prominent role in Hutton's. Abraham Gottlob Werner (1749—1817) taught mineralogy at the mining Academy at Freiberg for forty years from 1775. He published relatively little, but was enormously influential through his teaching, which was based upon his knowledge of local formations. Werner's years as a teacher coincided with the development and fruition of the German Romantic movement, and also with the period in which the various earth sciences of mineralogy, lithology, stratigraphy, palaeontology, and the history of the earth coalesced into something ultimately recognizable as the science of geology.[2] Werner ceased teaching, and Hegel made the last additions to his lectures on geology, shortly before Charles Lyell published his uniformitarian manifesto[3], at once the last great work of the pre-modern age in geology, and the first great work of the newly emergent science.

The chronological coincidence favoured an interest among Romanticists for Werner's teaching[4]; his pupils at Freiberg included Franz

---

1 The four major chronological components in the composition of *Hegel's Philosophy of Nature* are indicated in M. J. Petry's edition, 3 vols. (London & New York, 1970), *1*, p. 123.
2 This thesis is presented in Roy Porter, *The Making of Geology. Earth Science in Britain 1660–1815* (Cambridge University Press, 1977).
3 C. Lyell, *Principles of Geology*, 3 vols. (London, 1830–33).
4 A. M. Ospovat, 'Romanticism and German Geology: five students of Abraham Gottlob Werner', *Eighteenth-Century Life*, 7 (2) (1982), 105–117.

Xaver von Baader, who was there from 1788 to 1792; Friedrich Leopold von Hardenberg — Novalis — who was there for a year and a half from December 1797[5]; Henrich Steffens, who came in 1799, and while in Freiberg wrote his *Beiträge zur inneren Naturgeschichte der Erde* (1801), an amalgam and development of Werner's teaching and Schelling's philosophy of nature; and Gotthilf Heinrich Schubert, who arrived in 1805.

Steffens (1773–1845) was the writer among this group who was most informed about the earth sciences, while also being thoroughly imbued with *Naturphilosophie*. Hegel, as one might except, accordingly both granted him credit in constructing his own system, and was critical of his metaphysical excesses. But whatever Hegel thought of Werner's students and commentators, he broadly based his own account of the rocks upon Werner's work.

Werner is today mainly remembered for his precipitation scheme[6], according to which the successive strata in the crust of the earth were precipitated from a universal ocean that many identified with Noah's flood. Here was a tool for unifying mineralogy with historical geology, for the sequence of deposition furnished both a history of the earth and a classification of its minerals. This theory functions at least as a heuristic device for the development of a scheme of mineralogical classification based upon Werner's detailed knowledge of the rocks in Saxony. It was possible to adopt the classification without being committed to its underlying theory, but Werner's physical and chemical theory of the deposition of strata did account for the origin and sequence of the rocks. Werner believed that the external forms and characteristics of minerals were correlated with their chemical composition.

Werner's system as it was first published in 1787[7] divided the formation of rocks into four periods. In the first or primitive period, rocks crystallized as chemical precipitates from a tranquil ocean. Granite was the first rock so formed, followed by gneiss, mica, porphyry, basalt, and other rocks; as the ocean increased in turbulence, the rocks formed were less crystalline. This whole period was azoic. Then came the *floetz*[8] period, which began with a shallow ocean, was stormy, and saw a vi-

5 R. Cardinal, 'Werner, Novalis and the Signature of Stones', in *Deutung und Bedeutung. Studies in German and Comparative Literature presented to Karl-Werner Maurer*, ed. B. Schludermann, V. G. Doerksen, R. J. Glendinning, and E. S. Firchow (Mouton, The Hague & Paris, 1973), pp. 118–133.
6 See e. g. A. Geikie, *The Founders of Geology*, 2 ed. (Dover, New York, 1962, reprint of 1905 Macmillan ed.).
7 *Classification der Gebirgsarten* (Dresden, 1787).
8 The use of this term goes back to the theories of Nicolaus Steno (1638–1686); see Pertry, ed. cit. (note 1 above; henceforth PN), 3, 221–222.

gorous development of life, followed by another universal flood. The *floetz*-formations deposited in this period include limestone, sandstone, chalk, and coal, formations whose depositions have carried on into recent times. Then came the volcanic and alluvial periods, whose rocks were the results of local conditions rather than of universal deposition from the oceans. In his revised system, formulated around 1796, Werner added a transition period with associated rocks between the *floetz* and primitive periods; transition rocks included slate, greywack, and some chalks formerly classified in the *floetz* series.

The system was most useful taxonomically, but it also addressed a number of issues that became central in geological debate, including "the relations between chemistry and mineralogy, the aqueous origin of most rocks, the unique status of granite as the most primitive rock, and the possibility of associating different stages in the development of life with different stages in the formation of the rocks of the earth's crust." [9]

Against this historically based taxonomy, James Hutton (1726–1797) offered an essentially ahistorical scheme [10] based upon a concept of endless process, in which the same forces obeying the same laws operated in a continuous cycle, forever eroding old rocks and producing new ones, and evincing "no trace of a beginning and no prospect of an end." Hutton's concern was with the relationship between changing landforms and unchanging processes; where Werner saw water as the active agent in geology, Hutton stressed the role of fire, which led to the production of granite and basalt.

Hegel viewed the Neptunist-Vulcanist controversy as missing the point, but he was concerned with questions of mineral classification, with landforms in relation to geological processes, to the sequence of rocks, to the question of the reality of historical change and its role in the development of the earth, and to the relationship between life and geology. Thus, while standing aside from the debate between Huttonians and Wernerians, Hegel adopted ideas and concepts from both parties.

By the time that Hegel was in Berlin, the focus of geology had shifted, thanks largely to the work of Georges Cuvier (1769–1832). Cuvier had worked on the rocks of the Paris basin [11], and on the fossils found in them [12], including those of large and clearly extinct animals. Now it was possible to claim that a fossil of a hitherto unknown species of shell-

---

9 T. H. Levere, *Poetry Realized in Nature. Samuel Taylor Coleridge and Early Nineteenth-Century Science* (Cambridge University Press, 1981), p. 160.
10 J. Hutton, *Theory of the Earth*, 2 vols. (Edinburgh, 1795).
11 *Essai sur la Géographie minéralogique des environs de Paris* (Paris, 1812).
12 *Recherches sur les Ossemens fossiles* (Paris, 1812).

fish, for example, might have a living exemplar somewhere on earth that had simply been overlooked by science; it was not, however, remotely reasonable to claim that mastodons or mammoths were alive and well, and had been overlooked by science.[13] Cuvier's work provided the most dramatic proof to date of extinction, and his interpretation of the fossil record in its correlation with the stratigraphic sequence of rocks persuaded him of the reality of a series of catastrophes that had led to widespread extinctions. Hutton's work, in contrast, appeared to present a uniform progression; geological debate moved from Neptunist-Vulcanist polarization to focus on the question of uniformitarianism versus catastrophism. Hegel, although aware of this facet of contemporary debate, was indifferent to it, being more concerned with the issues of the earlier controversy; the result was that here, as elsewhere, he knew more of recent science than he concentrated on in his lectures, and his reluctance to modify his lectures as science changed must have made them frustrating to philosophers learned in the latest developments in the sciences.

It should, however, be stressed that Hegel's knowledge of and interest in geology was extensive, and that the geological information in his *Philosophy of Nature* accurately represented the geological wisdom that he reported and drew upon.

Library and Sources [14]

Two hundred and thirty-five of the sixteen hundred and six titles in the auction catalogue of Hegel's library [15] deal with mathematics, science, and medicine; of these, the following twenty are on the earth sciences: [16]

1445. Brongniart, A., *Introduction à la minéralogie* (Paris, 1825).
1446. Brunner, J., *Handbuch der Gebirgskunde* (Leipzig, 1803).
1447. Cuvier, G. L., *Discours sur les révolutions de la surface du globe*, 5 ed. (Paris und Amsterdam, 1828).

---

13 M. J. S. Rudwick, *The Meaning of Fossils. Episodes in the History of Palaeontology*, 2 ed. (New York, 1976).

14 For a list of sources used by Hegel in compiling his geological lectures, see *Philosophy of Nature* ed. Petry, *1*, p. 136. There is also a discussion of sources in M. J. Petry, 'Editing Hegel's Encyclopaedia', in *Editing Polymaths: Erasmus to Russell. Papers given at the eighteenth annual Conference on Editorial Problems, University of Toronto, 5–6 November 1982*, ed. H. J. Jackson (Toronto, 1983), pp. 143–175 at pp. 166–167.

15 *Verzeichnis der von dem Professors Herrn Dr. Hegel ... hinterlassenen Bücher-Sammlung* (Berlin, C. F. Müller, 1832).

16 I am grateful to Prof. Michael Petry for this information.

1450. Ebel, J. G., *Über den Bau der Erde in dem Alpengebirge*, 2 vols. (Zürich, 1808).
1451–53. Emmerling, L. A. *Lehrbuch der Mineralogie*, 3 pts. (Giessen, 1793–1797).
1458. Gerhard, K. A., *Ueber die Umwandlung ... einer ... Steinart in die andere* (Berlin, 1788).
1373. Goethe, J. W., *Sammlung zur Kenntniss der Gebirge um Karlsbad* (Karlsbad, 1808).
1471–72. Lasius, G. S. O., *Beobachtungen ueber das Harzgebirge*, 2 pts. (Hannover, 1798).
1473. Lenz, J. G., *System der Mineralkörper* (Bamberg & Würzburg, 1800).
1477. Leonhard, K. C. von, *Handbuch der Oryktognosie* (Heidelberg, 1821).
1478–80. Leonhardt, K. C., *Charakteristik der Felsarten*, 3 pts. (Heidelberg, 1823–24).
1487. Mohs, Fr., *Die Charaktere der Klassenordnungen ... und Arten des Mineralsystems*, 2 ed. (Dresden, 1821).
1395. Neumann, F. E., *Ueber das Crystallsystem des Axinits*, in Poggendorffs *Annalen* vol. *80* pts. 1, 5 (Berlin, 1825).
1319. Neumann F. E., *De lege zonarum principio evolutionis systematum crystalliionorum* (Berlin, 1826).
1492. Raumer, K. G. von, *Versuch eines ABC-Buchs der Crystallkunde*, pt. 1 (Berlin, 1820).
1493. Raumer, K. G. von, *Nachträge zum ABC-Buch* (Berlin, 1821).
1101–2. Ritter, K., *Die Erdkunde im Verhältnis zur Natur und zur Geschichte des Menschen, oder Allgemeine, vergleichende Geographie, als sichere Grundlage des Studiums und Unterrichts in physikalischen und historischen Wissenschaften*, 2 pts. (Berlin, 1817–18).
1103. Ritter, K., *Erdkunde*, 2 ed., pt. 1 (Berlin, 1822).
1321. Rose, G., *De Sphenis atque titanitae systemate crystallino* (Berol., 1820).
1511. Werner, A. G., *Neue Theorie von der Entstehung der Gänge, mit Anwendung auf den Bergbau, besonders den freibergischen* (Freiberg, 1791).

Striking in this list is the predominance of German sources, French and British writings being significantly under-represented; striking also is the emphasis upon relatively local German mineralogy, although in the composition of his lectures on the philosophy of nature he drew, for example, upon *Hutton's Theory of the Earth*, and upon A. von Humboldt's *Personal Narrative of Travels to the Equinoctical Regions of the New Continent*.[17] He was to offer philosophical justification for the centrality of German geology, but was concerned with global developments.

Organic Physics

In Hegel's system, geology follows physics, and constitutes the first stage of "organics" or "organic physics"[18] in the development of nature. The geological process is immediately preceded by the chemical process, culminating in the process of separation, and bringing chemistry to the

---

17 *Travels ...*, trans. H. M. Williams, 6 vols. (London, 1818–26).
18 PN, 3, 9–44, sections 337–342.

threshold of life.[19] Chemistry and geology thus offer an interface between the physical and the organic sciences.

In introducing organic physics, Hegel wrote that "the real nature of
the body's totality constitutes the infinite process in which individuality
determines itself as the particularity or finitude which it also negates..."
(PN 3 p. 9). The self-determination of individuality has parallels with
Schelling's and Steffens's[20] identification of life with the principle of
individuation, the power whereby a totality was presupposed by its
parts. The process resulted in a productive tension that led to an ascent
of the hierarchy from mechanism to organism. "It is in this way that the
Idea has reached the initial immediacy of *life*." Hegel identified three
forms of life, the universal represented by the geological organism, the
particular, represented in vegetation, and the individual, represented
by the animal organism. The hierarchical sequence is at once logical, and
corresponding to the increase of complexity as one ascends; just as
geology depends upon the processes of chemistry, so zoology in its turn
depends upon those of geology.

Life in the geological organism was very much at the threshold, and in
the first stage. Indeed, it was not so much life as "the corpse of the living process. It is the organism as the totality of the inanimate existence
of mechanical and physical nature" (PN 3 p. 9). Clearly, the appropria-
teness of defining this or that level in the hierarchy as living depends
upon the perspective one adopts, because Hegel has already stated that
nature is *"implicitly* a living whole" (PN 1 p. 216), which undergoes
triadic progression and ascent.

More closely considered, the movement through its series of stages consists of the
Idea *positing* itself as what it is *implicitly*, i. e. the Idea passes *into itself* by proceeding out of its immediacy and externality, which is *death*. It does this primarily in
order to take on *living* being, but also in order to transcend this determinateness, in
which it is merely life, and to bring itself forth into the existence of spirit, which
constitutes the truth and ultimate purpose of nature, and the true actuality of the
Idea. PN 1 p. 216).

Now the overall ascent of the hierarchy of nature may be an ascent of
life, driven at once by logic and teleology, operating dialectically, and
ultimately spiritual. Hegel, however, was constantly working back and

---

19 PN 2 sect. 334. Ibid. sect. 335 p. 219 expresses the threshold status of chemistry:
"In general, the chemical process is in fact *life*" (passage dating from 1817); and
yet Hegel subsequently added the statement that "The beginning and end of the
process are not identical, and it is this which constitutes the finitude of the chemical process, and separates and distinguishes it from life."

20 F. W. J. von Schelling, *Von der Weltseele, eine Hypothese der höheren Physik zur
Erklärung des allgemeinen Organismus* (Hamburg, 1809). H. Steffens, *Grundzüge der philosophischen Naturwissenschaft* (Berlin, 1806), pp. 70 ff.

forth between levels, hierarchies, and spheres, and his discussion of life accordingly sometimes had a narrower and more exclusive reference. Living bodies, for example, were always on the point of succumbing to the chemical process (PN 3 p. 10); Hegel's implicit definition of life here seems little different from that of Xavier Bichat [21], who defined life somewhat tautologically as the sum of the functions by which death was resisted. But Hegel also reverted to his wider view of nature as a living whole, and of life as the "resolution . . . of oppositions in general" (PL 3 p. 11).

With that wider context re-established, he then addressed the question of why geological nature represents the lowest level, the "ground and basis of life."

Within each sphere, the triadic progression moved from what was universal and implicit to what was singular, in and for itself (PN 1 p. 97). The geological organism corresponded to the universal, lacking "an individual which would be implicitly active within itself" (PN 3 p. 12). The earth lacked self-consciousness and individuality, even though it "is a whole, and is the system of life. But as a crystal, it resembles a skeleton, which may be regarded as being dead, for its members still seem to have a formally separate subsistence, and its process falls outside it" (ibid.).

The metaphor of the earth as a crystal was one that Hegel explored and developed variously, mining it for its parallels with both mechanism and organism. Crystals grew, they possessed organization, and yet they were clearly inorganic; they exhibited a correspondence between composition and outer form, between inner and outer form, that if grasped would render rationally intelligible Werner's empirical classification of minerals.[22] And yet crystals were products, not agents: "The activity which has passed over into its product is shape, and is determined as crystal" (PN 2 p. 112). Hegel wrote of "the crystal of the Earth, which is the universal independence" (ibid. p. 113), and asserted that "the archetypal crystal is the diamond of the Earth . . . the firstborn son of light and gravity" (ibid. p. 123). Light and gravity were generative powers in the triadic process, so presented by the theosophist Jacob Boehme [23] in his elaboration of the story of creation, and by the *Natur-*

---

21 X. Bichat, *Recherches physiologiques sur la vie et la mort*, 4 ed. (Paris, 1822).

22 See above, and Werner, *Short Classification and Description of the Various Rocks*, trans. intro. & ed. A. Ospovat, with facsimile of original (1786) text (New York, 1971); Werner, *On the External Characters of Minerals*, trans. A. Carozzi (Urbana, Ill., 1972).

23 A. Koyré, *La Philosophie de Jacob Boehme* (Paris, 1929). A. Debus, *The Chemical Philosophy: Paracelsian Science and Medicine in the Sixteenth and Seventeenth*

philosoph Steffens.[24] Crystallinity was both the culmination of the inorganic process, and foreshadowed the organization of life. It provided
a conceptual entry into a consideration of the geological process, and of
the structural composition and life of the earth.

Geological Nature (The terrestrial organism)

In one sense, the earth was a chemical product: "the universal elements enter into the particular corporealities of the Earth, and are partly
causes and partly effects of the process" (PN 3 p. 15). In so far as the earth
was a product, it had a skeletal, dead aspect, like crystals. Its production
lay in the past. The process of that production arose from earth's connections and position within the solar system, and once produced the
earth simply "endures ... the process of the earth is simply an inner
necessity. *Considered* within the limits of the Earth's individuality, this
process is to be *seen* as a past event ..." (PN 3 pp. 16—17).

The use of italics was not casual, but drew attention to the perspective from which the problem was presently being considered. But there
is a distinction between history and nature, and between a temporal and
a logical productive sequence. The temporal sequence is what geologists,
students of the theory of the earth, have generally emphasised, although
for Hegel it was of much less importance than the logical sequence, philosophy being concerned with essence rather than accidence. Nevertheless, it is with traditional and empirical science that one has to begin,
for only the facts of the matter enable one to formulate qualitative differences, to arrive at an understanding of levels, hierarchies, and spheres, and to submit this understanding to dialectical interpretation. Hegel
accordingly, while constantly seeking qualitative differences and principles, was concerned to arrive at an understanding of the empirical
data and of the theories to which they have given rise. If one is alert to
the issue of levels — what set of problems Hegel addressed at any point,
and whether he was looking at the overall process, or at a limited range

---

Centuries, 2 vols. (New York, 1977) provides and account of the Hermetic and
Paracelsian traditions to which Boehme was heir. S. T. Coleridge in England, although far from sympathetic to Hegel's style, tackled similar issues in the philosophy of nature, drawing on many of the same sources and constructing a not
dissimilar scheme that illuminates the interaction of science, theosophy, trinitarian theology, and philosophy; his use of the light-gravitation diad is particularly
helpful here. See Levere, *Poetry Realized in Nature*.

24 *Grundzüge der philosophischen Naturwissenschaft* (Berlin, 1806).

within it [25] — then one removes the apparent contradictions [26] in his discussion of the earth here as product and there as process.

Looking at the history of the earth, viewed as a product, natural philosophers had developed geogonies — theories of the formation of the earth — and geognostic schemes. Geognosy [27] was essentially dynamic geology, dealing with the rocks, their probable origin, and their formation and arrangement. Hegel adopted the catastrophist scheme supported by Cuvier's work indicating massive extinctions. He speculated that these remote catastrophes might have had their origin in an extraterrestrial event or events which modified the angle of the earth's axis in relation to its orbit — a theory advocated in this century by Immanuel Velikovsky, but not generally accepted. Whatever the cause of the catastrophes, Hegel was fully convinced of their reality, agreeing with Cuvier that "Life ... has often been disturbed on this earth by terrible events." [28] Hegel pithily summarized the argument: "The surface of the Earth bears evidence of its having supported a vegetation and an animal world which are now extinct (a) at great depth, (b) in immense stratifications, and (c) in regions where these species of animals and plants do not thrive." (PN 3 p. 18).

Hegel briefly elaborated the palaeontological and stratigraphic evidence for the catastrophist's historical picture of the structure of the earth, referring in particular to Ebel's work *Über den Bau der Erde*.[29] Ebel's primary concern was with the structure of the Alps, whereas Hegel was concerned with a more general statement of the major categories of evidence, illustrating those categories by drawing on the factual information in Ebel, but also referring to other authors. He itemized the correlation of fossil trees with particular strata. Thus

petrified wood, even whole trees, and dendrolites etc., may be found in *floetz*-formations [30], and to an even greater extent in alluvial terrains. Immense forests, which have been flattened, lie buried below beds of deposit at depths of 40–100 feet, and sometimes even of 600–900 feet. ... on the banks of the Arno in Tuscany, fossilized oaks may be found, lying incidentally beneath palm-trees, and flung together with fossiled sea shells and huge bones (PN 3 pp. 18–19).

---

25 Petry, PN 1 p. 31: "Spheres consist of levels and hierarchies. They also contribute to the formation of more comprehensive spheres, within which they are levels ranged in hierarchies.

26 Cf. note by Michelet, PN 3 p. 18.

27 Werner, *A treatise on the external characters of fossils* (Leipzig, 1774, trans. T. Weaver, Dublin, 1805), p. 3; cited in Petry, PN 3 p. 218.

28 Cuvier, *Theory of the Earth*, trans. R. Jameson, 5 ed. (Edinburgh, 1827), p. 16, cited in Petry, PN 3 p. 220.

29 Auction catalogue (*Verzeichnis*) item no. 1450; see above.

30 I have preferred the use of the English spelling of the German term to the more anglicized "fletz".

Hegel was not restricting himself to the Alps. "These immense forests occur in all the alluvial terrains of Europe, the Americas and northern Asia." (ibid. p. 18)

Invertebrates had left the most numerous fossil remains in the animal kingdom, and again were widely distributed. "They are just as common throughout Asia, in Anatolia, Syria, Siberia, Bengal, and China etc., in Egypt, Senegal, and at the Cape of Good Hope, and in America. They are to be found at great depths in the strata immediately overlaying the primitive rocks, and to an equal extent at the greatest heights." (ibid.) Hegel, although basing himself mainly on Ebel, mentioned Voltaire's flippant explanation that oysters had been taken to the mountain tops and there eaten by travellers.[31] But what Hegel wanted to stress was the extensive distribution of these remains, and the correlation between palaeontology and stratigraphy. "Remains of this kind are not dispersed throughout the whole of the massif, but only in certain strata, where they occur in families in the strictest order, and are so well preserved, that they seem to have settled there peacefully." (ibid.) Most striking were the remains of giant extinct quadrupeds, which had fascinated scientists for more than a century.[32] Mammoths in Siberia,[33] von Humboldt's discoveries of giant animal remains in South America[34], Cuvier's series of finds among the fossil beds of the Paris basin — all these combined to make a strong case for extinction and cataclsym in the history of the earth, a case further srengthened by the state of the rocks themselves, "the frightful signs of tremendous laceration and demolition apparent in all primitive massifs, and granite ranges and rocks." (PN 3 p. 20).

This evidence for upheaval seemed to fascinate Hegel, at least in its detail, but the upheavals in themselves were ultimately of little importance to him: "All this is a matter of history, and has to be accepted as a fact; it is not the concern of philosophy." (PN 3 p. 21). The history of the

---

31 Voltaire, 'Dissertation . . . sur les changemens arrivés dans notre globe, et sur les pétrifactions qui'on prétend en être encore les témoinages', *Oeuvres complètes de Voltaire*, 2 ed. (Paris, 1828), 42, pp. 227–244; Petry, PN 3 p. 223.

32 Rudwick, *The Meaning of Fossils* (1976).

33 J. B. Breyne, "Observations, and a Description of some Mammoth's Bones dug up in Siberia, proving them to have belonged to Elephants", *Philosophical Transactions of the Royal Society of London* (1737; 1741), 124–128.

34 For detailed references, see Petry PN 3 p. 224. The South American fossils were particularly exciting for their novelty, size, and number. Charles Darwin during the voyage of H. M. S. Beagle concluded "that the whole area of the Pampas is one wide sepulchre of these extinct gigantic quadrupeds." (Darwin, *Journal of researches into the Natural History and Geology of the Countries Visited during the Voyage of H. M. S. Beagle Round the World, under the command of Captain Fitz Roy, R. N.* (London, 1891), p. 192.).

earth was literally and simply past. Geognosy described this by determining the order in which strata were laid down. Description was, however, very different from explanation, being "completely devoid of the necessity which characterizes comprehension" (ibid.). Hegel required of science very much what Coleridge did, and at very much the same time: "A ... real definition ... must ... be so far *causal*, that a full insight having been obtained of the law, we derive from it a progressive insight into the necessity and *generation* of the phenomena of which it is the law."[35] Hegel and Coleridge were here both in a line of descent from Aristotle through Kant.

Hegel dismissed as entirely inadequate both Werner's and Hutton's theories, appealing respectively to the agencies of water and of fire. They both offered merely a limited reduction of the geological process to what Hegel described as "aspects of organic fermentation[36] ... this explanation of events by mere succession has nothing whatever to contribute to philosophic consideration." (PN 3 p. 22)

We have seen that Werner more than Hutton had produced a scheme accounting for the composition and sequence of rocks in the earth's crust, but only in conventional physical and chemical terms. This approach, although entirely proper according to the canons of contemporary science, was in Hegel's view superficial for the philosopher, who sought to understand the "necessary relation" of the strata. "The universal law of this sequence ... may be understood without reference to its historical form, and this law is the essence of the sequence. It is only rationality which is of interest to the Notion." (ibid. p. 22) Nature was directed by an inner logic, teleological in its operation. The events of history could be understood in the light of that logical development, but nature was not history, and the philosopher, though he might start from the empirical phenomena, needed to avoid remaining mired in them.

Cuvier had produced one of the sets of facts from which scientist and philosopher alike might start. One of the most dramatic lessons of his observations had been the reality of extinction in the animal kingdom. But, especially with the geographical extension of palaeontological

---

35 S. T. Coleridge, *Hints towards the formation of a More Comprehensive Theory of Life*, ed. S. B. Watson (London, 1848), p. 25.

36 Fermentation was a widely used term from the alchemical period until the mid-nineteenth century, covering a great variety of chemical processes, mostly naturally occurring, e. g. in digestion, the smouldering of hay stacks, the growth of minerals in the earth and in the alchemist's laboratory, as well as in the operation of smelting; the word was also used "in various other vague application. *Obs-[olete]*." (Oxford English Dictionary) Hegel appears to have chosen a deliberately and excessively general word to indicate the inadequacy of the proposed explanations.

research, and the increasingly tight correlation between palaeontology and stratigraphy, Cuvier and his contemporaries were also demonstrating something potentially more problematic, the emergence of new life forms, and a sequence of apparent progression and ascent among those forms. Geology promised to shed light on the ascent of life.[37]

Hegel considered the problem of the origin and development of living beings,[38] rejecting the theory of epigenesis, according to which the germ is brought into existence by successive accretions, and tending to favour the rival theory of preformation[39], according to which all parts of the final organism exist preformed in the germ.

Preformation was compatible with the account in Genesis, according to which the first members of each species emerged "fully armed, like Minerva from the brow of Jupiter" (PN 3 p. 22). Moreover, these creations were distinct: "Man has not formed himself out of the animal, nor the animal out of the plant, for each is instantly the whole of what it is." Once again, the crystal's potential for growth was used as an illustrative metaphor.

Animal, vegetable, and human life had not merely a history but also a present distribution, as had the landforms themselves, with land concentrated in the northern hemisphere, and more continuous in the north, tapering towards the south. This, for Hegel, could not be mere accident, even though he did allow an unspecified rôle for accidence. "The activity of the Notion consists in grasping the necessary determinations of that which appears to sensuous consciousness as a contingency" (PN 3 p. 23). The differences between the continents were fundamental and essential. The new world was truly new, incompletely developed, weaker in its fauna although exuberant in its flora. The races of mankind were also geographically distributed, in ways supposedly rationally intelligible, and with characteristics associated with their geographical location. Africa, for example, was stunned by heat, corresponded to compact metal, and its humanity was "sunk in torpor"; Europe, in contrast, the third of three divisions of the old world, constituted the rational region of the earth, and formed an equilibrium of landforms whose centre was Germany (ibid. p. 24). Hegel was here elaborating and indulging in

---

37 P. J. Bowler, *Fossils and Progress: Palaeontology and the idea of progressive evolution in the 19th century* (New York, 1976).

38 Debates about this and related problems in the eighteenth century are examined in Jacques Roger, *Les sciences de la vie dans la pensée française du XVIIIe siècle* (Paris, 1963; 2 ed. 1972); P. J. Bowler, 'Evolutionism in the Enlightenment', *History of Science*, 12 (1974), 159–183.

39 P. J. Bowler, 'Preformation and pre-existence in the 17th century: A brief analysis', *Journal of the History of Biology*, 4 (1971), 221–244.

a kind of geographical anthropology[40] familiar in early nineteenth-century Europe. Blumenbach and Kant[41] had proposed the most widely know schemes for the classification of mankind, but it was Cuvier's scheme that most nearly corresponded to Hegel's, for Cuvier in 1817[42] identified three especially distinct races, the white or Caucasian, the yellow or Mongolian, and the negro or Ethiopian. Triplicities in geography, in geology, and in anthropology were essentially interconnected.[43]

The Earth's structural composition
(Geology and Oryctgonosy)

In dealing with the actual structure of the earth, Hegel was guided by Werner's mineralogy, which he subjected to his usual triadic analysis and dialectical development. Granite, for Hegel as for Werner, was the starting point, with the rocks of the calcareous series — chalk and the rest — standing in opposition. "Concrete graniticity ... exhibits the developed triad of moments within itself." The triad was manifested in silica or quartz, mica, and felspar. Granite was the core of volcanoes, the innermost substance, the primary rock. Through "siliceousness", it formed the first part of a triad, the other parts being "argillaceousness" and "calcareousness". Steffens had drawn attention to the opposition between the calcareous and siliceous series of rocks and formations, and had indeed made this opposition the key to his interpretation of the structure of the earth. Hegel acknowledged that this was one of Steffens's most valuable insights, but still felt moved to observe that "most

---

40 See also *Hegel's Philosophy of History*, trans. Sibree (Dover Publications, 1956) pp. 79–102.

41 J. F. Blumenbach, *De Generis Humani Varietate Nativa* (Göttingen, 1775; new ed. 1781); *Über die natürlichen Verschiedenheiten im Menschengeschlechte* (Leipzig, 1793). Kant, *Von den verschiedenen Racen der Menschen* (1775); *Anthropologie* (Königsberg, 1798).

42 Cuvier, *Le Règne animal distribué d'après son organisation*, 4 vols. (Paris, 1817), 1, p. 94.

43 Steffens was another who explored the relations between geology and anthropology, in a work that combined a wealth of empirical data with the extension and application of Schelling's philosophy. Hegel more than dismissed this work: "*Steffens'* "Anthropology" (2 vols. Breslau, 1822), mixes Geology with Anthropology to such an extent, that only about a tenth or twelfth of the whole is concerned with the latter. Since the whole of it is rustled up out of empirical material, abstractions and fantastic combinations, no attention being paid to the thought, Notion and method of science, such a work is of no interest, at least to philosophy." (*Hegel's Philosophy of Subjective Spirit*, ed. & trans. M. J. Petry, 3 vols. (Dordrecht & Boston: Reidel, 1978; 2 ed. 1979), 1, 103, 158.).

of his views are the crude and undisciplined utterances of a wild and hazy imagination however." [44]

Hegel drew on Ebel's work and on that of Johann Ludwig Heim [45] and of K. G. Raumer [46] to present an account of the sequence and relations of the rocks. He referred also to mineralogical lore, showing some familiarity not only with scientific technical names, but also with the distinctions maintained by miners, an indication of awareness of practice not commonly associated with Hegel. His concern, however, was not to summarize a systematic nomenclature, but rather to explain the elements of the relations of the rocks in a developmental sequence. Thus, for example, "the rock-structures closest to granite are modifications of it, for they are the further eductions of one of its aspects, in which the preponderance of the two aspects varies from place to place. Granite rocks are surrounded by beds of *gneiss, syenite, mica-schist* etc. which are clearly lighter transmutations of it." (PN *3* p. 27) Hegel stressed the importance of not allowing geology to degenerate into enumerative Baconian natural history, and opposed the practice in geology of taxonomical splitting. What mattered was "to grasp the lay-out of the general masses, and the Notion of the moments. ... It is most important to follow the nature of the transitions from one stratification to another." The basic process was the gradual reduction of "the basic determinations of granite", "the development ... from granite to the disappearance of its particular constituents." (PN *3* p. 28)

This approach was outside the battles between Vulcanists and Neptunists, and Hegel, while asserting the volcanic, and thus igneous origin of granite, was impatient with this classification as an explanation of the formation of granite. He worked instead through the moments of the Notion, presenting the transformation of granitic into *floetz* and alluvial rocks. "As graniticity becomes more of an indeterminate mixture, the

---

44 PN *3* pp. 24–26. Steffens's principal writings on geology are: "Ueber den Oxidations- und Desoxydations-Process der Erde", *Zeitschrift für spekulative Physik*, 1 (1800), 137–168; *Grundzüge der philosophischen Naturwissenschaft* (Berlin, 1806); *Beyträge zur innern Naturgeschichte der Erde* (Freyberg, 1801); *Geognostisch-geologische Aufsätze, als Vorbereitung zu einer innern Naturgeschichte der Erde* (Hamburg, 1810); *Vollständiges Handbuch der Oryktognosie*, 4 vols. (Halle, 1811, 1815, 1819, 1824). The opposition between the siliceous and the calcareous series is central to the argument of the *Beyträge* (1801) in particular. In spite of Hegel's strictures, Steffens did have a sound knowledge of mineralogy and geology.

45 *Geologische Beschreibung des Thüringer Waldgebürgs. Von der innern Einrichtung des Gebürgs nach seinen Gebürgslagern*, 3 vols. (Meiningen, 1796–1812).

46 *Geognostische Versuche* (Berlin, 1815). Hegel had two other works by von Raumer in his library; see above (cat. nos. 1492, 1493).

particular parts of the different formations emerge in greater abstraction; differences are therefore obliterated as in trap and greywack, which belongs to the transitional and *floetz* species." (PN 3 p. 29)

This was very well for an explanation in principle of the major rock formations. But what of the mineral veins that were of greatest interest to miners, and provided the direct motive and justification for Werner's lectures and for the Academy where he taught? The answer was provided, inevitably, by an appeal to the dialectical process. The transformations of granite and its associated formations, in which differences were obscured, had "affinity with a counter-sequence, in which there is a separation of various ores, and of the crystals which accompany them; iron separates out particularly early." (PN 3 p. 29.) Since this process accompanied the transformation of formations from granite downwards, they became more evident after the stage of the primitive rocks. There were, for example, no metals in primitive limestone, but only in secondary limestone; metals other than tin were almost completely absent in granite — a statement only partially correct, and at variance with Werner's[47] and his successors' account of the rocks of Saxony. Hegel's inaccuracy here was convenient for his theory, but he was, as always, careful to establish, although at second hand, a solid empirical base for his generalisations, providing extensive information about the association of metallic veins with particular rock formations, and drawing upon travel literature and geological texts alike.[48]

Metals were not associated with the final moment, the transition from floetz formation to alluvial terrain, which yielded the complete formlessness of clay and similar substances. In this moment, the primitive rock has been so far left behind that it has lost its mineral constitution, "and joins up with a vegetable being" — siliceous formations have been transformed into coal, "degenerate forms of *peat*, in which there is no distinction between mineral and vegetable". Similarly, calcareousness has passed into shell formations, "and it is difficult to say whether these are mineral or animal." There is azoic limestone, there are shells clearly animal in nature, there are fossils, and "there are also limestone formations which are not the residua, but merely the rudiments of the animal forms in which limestone formation terminates." Thus the limits of the calcareous and siliceous series link up with animal and vegetable na-

---

47 Werner, *Short Classification* . . ., trans. Ospovat (New York, 1971, from 1786 text) p. 52: "Granite contains metals, especially tin and iron."

48 E. g. J. B. Spix & K. F. P. Martius, *Reise in Brasilien*, pt. 1 (Munich, 1823), and F. W. H. von Trebra, *Erfahrungen vom Innern der Gebirge* (Leipzig, 1786). Petry's notes to PN 3 identify a wide range of sources.

ture respectively — a correlation which Steffens[49] had again identified, and developed in ways that Hegel found extravagant.

Hegel was particularly struck by proto-animal organic forms, in which "calcareousness expresses the transition to organic being." (PN 3 p. 33)

> It is nature in its organic-plasticity which engenders organic being in the element of immediate being ... The Notion ... immediately within the element of being ... has to work upon the material in which the moments of organic being are present in their totality. This is not a question of a universal life, in which the animation of nature is ubiquitous, it is a question of the essence of life. (PN 3 p. 33).

Hegel's caveat about the ubiquity of the life of nature was a direct rejection of Schelling's thesis in *Von der Weltseele*, and an attempt to comprehend the essence of life through its logical development, through the operation of the Notion. Geology has brought us to a further consideration of the nature of animation, and to an examination of the earth's life. The dialectical process has taken us so far in Hegel's system through the earth sciences that geology has manifestly become what it promised at the outset, the transitional science[50] between the physical sciences, and the study of vegetable and animal organism, of the life sciences as they are generally conceived.

The Earth's life

Hegel's discussion of the earth's life was thus in a sense a discussion of the point at which the geological process was superseded by the vegetable and animal process. Again, the metaphor of the crystal was called into service.

---

49 This identification was a principal argument of the *Beyträge* – but Steffens further correlates geological formations with vegetable and animal processes in the life of the earth, in turn correlating these processes with carbon and nitrogen (see Levere, *Poetry Realized in Nature*, chapters 4 & 6).

50 Coleridge was closer to Schelling than to Hegel, but it is instructive to explore parallels as well as differences between Coleridge's and Hegel's view of geology as a transitional science. Thus Coleridge wrote of the earth's formations that they were intermediate between crystallization and vegetable and animal life: "I regard them in a twofold point of view: 1st, as the residue and product of vegetable and animal life; 2d, as manifesting the tendencies of the Life of Nature to vegetation or animalization. And this process I believe – in one instance by the peat morasses of the northern, and in the other instance by the coral banks of the southern hemisphere – to be still connected with the present order of vegetable and animal Life, which constitute the fourth and last step in these wide and comprehensive divisions." (*Hints towards the formation of a more comprehensive theory of life*, ed. S. B. Watson (London, 1848), p. 48.) The developmental sequence is virtually identical in Hegel's and Coleridge's schemes, but the former eschews, as the latter does not, the universal life of nature.

This crystal of life, this inanimate organism of the Earth, which has its *Notion* in the sidereal connection outside it, but has its own peculiar process pre-supposed as its past, is the *immediate subject* of the meteorological process. As the *implicit* being of the totality of life, this inanimate organism is no longer fertilized by this process into individual formation, but into *animation*. The land, and to a greater extent the sea, are therefore the real possibility of life, and at every point they are perpetually breaking out into *punctiform* and *ephemeral* animation. The land breeds lichens and infusoria, the sea immeasurable multitudes of phosphorescent points of life. (PN 3 pp. 33–34.)

The crystal embodied organization and growth, and yet was not properly alive. So too the earth engendered growth. There was no universal life of nature, yet earth was capable through development of producing moments of organic being. Thus it was that the geological organism "excludes animation from itself, and surrenders it to other individuals. In other words, as the geological organism is only implicit animation, it is not identical with true living existence." (PN 3 p. 34) The distinction is of the utmost importance. Hegel's philosophy, like Schelling's, was inspired by trinitarian theology; Schelling's treatment of the life of nature led him, however, to pantheism[51] — Coleridge dismissed his *Naturphilosophie* as the Spinozismus of physics[52] — and so undermined the theological position that he sought to maintain. In order to avoid a similar frustration, Hegel had to be rigorous in his distinctions and his logic. The distinction of the life of nature from the potential for producing moments of organic being is a difficult one, but crucial for Hegel's enterprise.

Hegel discussed the earth as an organism, with springs of water as its lungs and secretory glands, volcanoes its liver or source of heat[53], and rivers its channels of excretion into the sea. (PN 3 p. 36) Our recognition of the overall intention of the imagery, to present the earth as organism, needs to be tempered by the constant recollection of Hegel's rejection of universal animation.

Hegel argued that the sea favours animality, while the land favours vegetation. He paid particular attention to fungi and lichens, which he described as universal vegetation clothing the earth, not arising from seed, and lacking individuality. (PN 3 p. 39) Cryptogamous vegetation had been of interest to eighteenth-century botanists and philosophers[54],

---

51 Thomas McFarland, *Coleridge and the Pantheist Tradition* (Oxford, 1969).
52 See e. g. Levere, *Poetry Realized in Nature* (1981), p. 245.
53 After the muscles, the secretory glands, especially the liver, are major sources of animal heat.
54 F. Delaporte, 'Des organismes problématiques', *Dix-huitième siècle*, 9 (1977), 49–59.

and remained of interest in the nineteenth-century[55], because of the challenge it posed to Linnean classification[56], and the fascination of unravelling its means of reproduction. Hegel was out of date in his view of these life-forms, which were in his day the subject of extensive study.[57] What was important for his argument, as always, was not so much empirical detail, although this would provide a reliable foundation for philosophizing, but rather the development of his scheme. Nascent animal forms in the sea, and nascent vegetation on the land, were what he addressed at the end of his discussion of the terrestrial organism, to provide bridge and introduction to the next stages in the scheme, the vegetable and animal organisms.

Life emerged in the geological process because it was already implicit, potential — "nothing emerges from the process but what is already there". The earth had inorganic being, but "the other moment of the universal life of the Earth is the actual organic living being ... Initially this is vegetable nature, which is the first stage of being-for-itself ... vegetable being begins where animation gathers itself into a point which maintains and produces itself ..." (PN 3 p. 43–44) At this point, geology and the earth sciences have been left behind, and one enters the realm of the vegetable organism.

---

55 E. g. C. F. B. de Mirbel, "Cryptogamous and agamous vegetation", *Quarterly Journal of Science, Literature, and the Arts*, 6 (1819), 20–31, 210–26; L. N. Vauquelin, "Experiments on Mushrooms", *Philosophical Magazine*, 43 (1814), 292–9.

56 The first issue of *Taxon* for 1976 has useful information about Linnaeus's classification. See also Henri Daudin, *Etudes d'histoire des sciences naturelles*, 1 vol. 1, *De Linné à Jussieu: méthodes de la classification et l'idée de série en botanique et en zoologie*, vol. 2, *Cuvier et Lamarck: les classes zoologiques et l'idée de série animale* (Paris, 1926); James L. Larson, *Reason and Experience: The Representation of Natural Order in the Work of Carl von Linné* (Berkeley, California, 1971).

57 Hegel based his views of lichens and fungi on works by Carl Asmund Rudolphi and von Humboldt. See Petry, PN 3 pp. 250–252 for an account of sources for mosses, lichens, and fungi.

Faraday, Electrochemistry, and Natural Philosophy

Michael Faraday was responsible for the addition of many new technical words to the vocabulary of science. He wanted them to express facts in electrical science without involving more theory than he could help.[1] Dr. Whitlock Nicholl, his personal physician, helped him to coin several new names, including electrolyte, electrode, and electrolization. Nicholl had also suggested a set of words identifying the positive and negative electrodes and the portions of the electrolyte migrating to them. Unfortunately Nicholl's awkward-sounding suggestions — eisode, exode, zeteisode, and zetexode — rested on the assumption of a single current of electricity passing through the electrolyte.[2]

Faraday considered that this was a very clumsy assumption since it implied that electricity was a fluid. Imponderable fluids were anathema to him, since they made it hard to conceive of nature as unified and simple.[3] If one postulated a different imponderable fluid to account for every different mode of activity in nature, then one could not explain the correlation and interconvertibility of forces. Faraday accordingly preferred in the early 1830's to think of electricity very generally in terms of progressive forces.[4] He wrote to William Whewell at Trinity College, Cambridge, for help in arriving at a theory-free set of terms. Whewell came up with anode, cathode, anion, and cation, words which "indicate *opposite* relations in *space*, and which yet *cannot* be interpreted as involving a theory".[5] Faraday was delighted and promptly adopted the new words.

There was however one new word invented by Whewell that Faraday would not willingly adopt. In 1840 Whewell proposed that a cultivator of science should be called a **scientist**.[6] Faraday never called himself a scientist. Nor did he consider himself as either a chemist or a physicist. He thought that it was senseless to divide chemistry from physics. "Such a difference," he stated, "is a mere play upon words, and shows ignorance rather than understanding".[7] Faraday considered himself as a natural philosopher, and devoted his life to the discovery and demonstration of the interconnection of natural forces.[8] His electrochemical researches were part of this enterprise, exploring the relations between the force of chemical affinity and the electricity of the voltaic battery.

Here he was extending and developing the electrochemical researches of Humphry Davy, his former mentor.[9] Davy had seen the various properties of matter as ultimately related; he had on occasion been outspokenly hostile to the notion of imponderable fluids, and correspondingly favorable to theories based on forces; his most brilliant researches had been in electrochemistry;[10] and he had demonstrated that there was some relation, if not identity, "between the primary attractive powers of the chemical elements and their electrical energies".[11] In 1826 Davy read before the Royal Society an essentially retrospective Bakerian Lecture "On the Relations of Electrical and Chemical Changes", in which he suggested that the electrical powers required to separate elements might give a measure of the intensity of their chemical union.[12]

With this suggestion and with Davy's example before him, one might expect that Faraday would have embarked on his own electrochemical researches in the 1820's. In his manual of *Chemical Manipulation* of 1827 he observed that "The powers of Electricity ... are so closely allied to those of Chemistry, and possess such vast influence in aiding or opposing them, that the experimenter in this science is continually resorting to them in his peculiar and ever varying examinations of matter".[13] But Faraday did not resort significantly to electrical powers in these years, although his *Diary* shows that he was considering them.[14]

From 1816 until 1830 he published a stream of apparently unconnected papers on chemical topics. He may have been cautious of trespassing on Davy's electrochemical preserve, or he may have been held back by the lack of success in a crucial experiment that would give direction and coherence to his researches.[15] In 1831, after a series of failures, he succeeded in such an experiment, and discovered electromagnetic induction.[16] Then between 1831 and 1834 came his superb sequence of electrochemical papers, the first major focus of his *Experimental Researches in Electricity*, in which induction was the unifying concept.

On 29 November 1831 Faraday wrote to his friend Phillips about this work: "The title will be, I think, 'Experimental Researches in Electricity: – I. On the Induction of Electric Currents, II. On the Evolution of Electricity from Magnetism; III. On a new Electrical Condition of Matter; ...' There is a bill of fare for you – and what is more, I hope it will not disappoint you".[17]

Faraday wound two insulated lengths of copper wire around a block of wood, attaching the ends of one to a galvanometer and of the other to a battery. A momentary current was induced in the secondary helix on making or breaking the primary circuit. Analogous effects were observed when a magnet was introduced into or removed from a wire helix connected to a galvanometer.[18] It is noteworthy that the first test Faraday applied after observing the deflection was to see whether the induced current would electrolyse metallic solutions.[19] Induction and electrolysis were from the outset associated in his mind.

An explanation of the association was provided by postulating the **electrotonic state**, in which strain was induced in the particles of matter in the secondary circuit and was maintained between the beginning and the end of the inducing currents. Faraday believed that electric impulses might arise from "the momentary propulsive force exerted by the particles during their arrangement". An electric current might thus be regarded as a succession of arrangements and rearrangements of molecular forces within the conductor. This led him to a conjectural explanation of electrolysis. Suppose that when a current was passed through electrolytes, they were thrown into the electrotonic state. The resulting strain might be sufficient to decompose the molecules into elementary particles that would then recombine in such a way as to relieve the strain. Maintaining the current would produce a succession of decompositions and recompositions with a net transfer "of the elementary particles of the opposite kind in opposite directions, but parallel to the current".[20]

The hypothesis of the electrotonic state and its alternate relief and restoration could explain electrolysis. Faraday nevertheless abandoned it in his second series of *Experimental Researches*, since his study of magneto-electric induction indicated that all the phenomena could better be accounted for by transferring the strain to lines of magnetic and electrical force.[21] Magnetic curves outside conductors could be rendered visible, and were accordingly closer to fact than to hypothesis. Faraday increasingly regarded them as physically real. They and the electrotonic state implied a relation between electrical action, chemical combination, and the spatial arrangements of particles and powers. They also implied the ultimate identity of electrical, chemical, and mechanical powers. Faraday constantly sought to reveal this identity.

On 11 June 1832 he found that blotting paper moistened with a solution of potassium iodide and starch provided a sensitive way of detecting the chemical action of an induced current.[22] This, together with his wider study of induction, took him a little further towards the demonstration of the unity of forces. His third series of researches showed that electricity was the same regardless of its source, differing only in quantity and intensity. He found that when static and voltaic electricity produced equal deflections on the galvanometer, they also liberated equal quantities of iodine from potassium iodide paper. Extensive quantitative experiments indicated that "for this case of electrochemical decomposition, and it is probable for all cases, that the chemical power, *like the magnetic force ... is in direct proportion to the absolute quantity of electricity* which passes".[23] His search for unity in nature had led him to his first law of electrolysis. He moved eagerly to a closer correlation of chemical, electrical, and mechanical power.

In December 1832 he asked in his *Diary*: "Can an electric current ... decompose a solid body ... If it can, does it give structure at the time".[24] He found, and announced in his fourth series of researches that solids were generally insulators, while liquids were generally conductors. Silver chloride, for example, was an insulator when solid, but when fused it became a conductor and could undergo electrolysis. He suspected that this was because particles in the solid state lacked the freedom to undergo the rearrangements necessary for electrolysis.[25] In his *Diary* on 15 February 1833 he asked, "Does not insulation by solid shew that decomposition by V. pile is due to slight power super added upon previous chemical attractive forces of particles when fluid? ... Does it not shew very important relation between the decomposability of such bodies and their conducting power, as if here the electricity were only a transfer of a series of alternations and vibrations and *not* a body transmitted directly".[26] He was developing the ideas adumbrated in his first and second series of researches. A state of strain was induced in the particles of the electrolyte along the lines of action of the electric current. Decomposition and recomposition relieved this strain, and, by constant repetition, resulted in electrolytic transfer, accompanying the passage of the current as a transfer of a series of alternations of electric power. Induction thus preceded conduction and electrolysis. This was at least a working hypothesis with Faraday in the spring of 1833. The next eighteen months would see its transformation into a theory incorporating laws of electrolysis.

Faraday's approach to the study of electrolysis was largely determined by his view that matter was experienced through the activity of its powers, such as attraction and repulsion. He even believed that it was probable that matter was constituted exclusively by these powers. He viewed electrical phenomena as products of the powers of matter, and was correspondingly sceptical about fluid theories of electricity.[27] If the electric current was not a flow of some imponderable fluid, but was, as he suggested, best conceived of as *"an axis of power having contrary forces, exactly equal in amount, in contrary directions"*,[28] then there was no need to limit this axis of power in electrolysis to the space between metallic poles. In his fifth series, read in June 1833, Faraday showed that contact with metallic poles was not necessary for electrolysis. The electric current could pass through the air from points to and from a moist pointed conductor, in which electrolysis would then take place.[29]

Grotthus's theory, based upon poles, was therefore wrong.[30] Davy's theory[31] had involved the decrease of electrolytic activity with increasing distance from the poles, and was thus doubly unacceptable to Faraday,[32] who rejected all the theories of his predecessors and sought a new, more precise, and better theory. He summarized his tentative theory of electrolysis in his fifth series:

> I conceive the effect to arise from forces which are *internal*, relative to the matter under decomposition -- and not *external*, as they might be considered, if directly dependent upon the poles. I suppose that the effects are due to a modification, by the electric current, of the chemical affinity of the particles through or by which that current is passing, giving them the power of acting more forcibly in one direction than in another, and consequently making them travel by a series of successive decompositions and recompositions in opposite directions and finally causing their expulsion or exclusion at the boundaries of the body under decomposition, *and that* in larger or smaller quantities, according as the current is more or less powerful.[33]

This account was predicated upon the assumption that the creation of power from nothing was impossible, so that chemical and electrical effects would stand in a determinate quantitative relation to one another. In this series Faraday cautiously suggested that *"for a constant quantity of electricity, whatever the decomposing conductor may be, ... the amount of electrochemical action is also a constant quantity...*".[34] He sought to demonstrate this with a new instrument that he invented and called a Volta-electrometer or Voltameter,[35] in which dilute sulphuric acid was electrolysed with platinum electrodes and the volume of the gases evolved was measured. Faraday found that the volume of gas began to diminish immediately after electrolysis. This confused the demonstration of constant action. He resolved the difficulty by appealing to the known powers of matter, identifying the cause of diminution with Döbereiner's observations on the catalytic action of spongy platina, and proposing his own mechanico-chemico-electrical explanation – a nice instance of the versatility of his view of the unity of forces and the dynamic nature of matter.[36]

With this out of the way, he returned in January 1834 to his main line of argument in his most important paper on electrochemistry, his seventh series of researches. He began by introducing his new electrochemical nomenclature, that has remained in use since then. Then, placing his voltameter in series with various electrolytes, of which fused stannous chloride was the most extensively used, he produced "an irresistible mass of evidence ... *that the chemical power of a current of electricity is in direct proportion to the absolute quantity of electricity which passes*".[37] The results were equally true for all electrolytes, so that these could be arranged into a single series, where the individual substances occupied definite positions, corresponding to the precise degree of their chemical affinities. The substances into which bodies divided in electrolysis were anions and cations; the numbers representing the proportions in which they were evolved in electrolysis were their *electrochemical equivalents* – and electrochemical equivalents "coincide, and are the same, with ordinary chemical equivalents". Faraday concluded that chemical affinity was a consequence of inter-particular electrical attractions.[38]

His quantitative results had established a relation between Dalton's laws of definite combining proportions and the electrochemical theory of affinity, and brought him to the verge of associating the particulate nature of matter with the novel concept of the particulate nature of electricity.[39] His theory had shown that the equivalent weights of bodies were "those quantities of them which contain equal quantities of electricity, or have naturally equal electric powers; it being the ELECTRICITY which *determines* the equivalent number *because* it determines the combining force. Or, if we adopt the atomic theory ..., then the atoms of bodies which are equivalent to each other in their ordinary chemical action, have equal quantities of electricity naturally associated with them". But Faraday held back from what might otherwise have come near to the deduction of the existence of the electron, for he was highly sceptical, indeed "jealous of the term *atom*".[40] His search for the unity of forces and his view of matter as knowable through its forces had led him to his laws of electrolysis, but made a corpuscular theory of electricity entirely unpalatable to him.

His seventh series had established the identity of the electricity that decomposed bodies with the electricity evolved by chemical decomposition. He considered that he had determined that the supply of electricity in the Voltaic pile was due to chemical powers.[41] But what was its origin?[42] Did it, as Volta had argued, come from the contact of dissimilar metals?[43] Or was it, as Fabbroni urged, chemical in origin?[44] Davy had attempted to show that both these views represented partial truths that had to be synthesized to provide an adequate explanation.[45] Controversy had continued since then, and Faraday now devoted himself, in the spring and summer of 1834, to its explicit resolution. His approach was again determined by his philosophy of nature, stressing the unity of forces and the powers of matter. He had rejected electrical fluids, and had shown that metallic poles were unnecessary for electrolysis. He no longer spoke of poles, but of electrodes, the surfaces bounding the electrolyte.[46] Electrolysis proceeded by an exertion of power by the individual particles; it followed that the current originated in an exertion of the chemical powers of the electrolyte, rather than in the contact of electrodes with the electrolyte. Faraday ignored the contact phenomenon of the e.m.f. on open circuit.

He demonstrated that metallic contact was not necessary for electrolysis by moistening a piece of turmeric paper with a solution of potassium iodide, placing it on a bent zinc plate and touching it with a platinum wire attached to a platinum plate. When the lower ends of both plates were dipped into a dilute acid solution, the iodide underwent electrolysis. Decomposition was polar, and dependent upon the direction of the current of electricity passing from the zinc through the acid to the platinum. When the plates were removed from the acid, electrolysis ceased. When the plates were connected together directly, electrolysis occurred in the opposite direction. This convinced Faraday that the current originated solely in the state of things in the vessel. The experiments also suggested to Faraday "a most extraordinary mutual relation of the chemical affinities of the fluid which *excites* the current, and the fluid which is *decomposed* by it".[47] This extraordinary relation obtained because "that power commonly called chemical affinity can be communicated to a distance through the metals and certain forms of carbon; ... the electric current is only another form of the forces of chemical affinity; ... its power is in proportion to the chemical affinities producing it; ... *the forces termed affinity and electricity are one and the same*".[48] As Faraday later put it, in a popular lecture on the forces ofnature, when metals were "burnt" in a voltaic battery, and heat thus given out through a platinum resistance wire, "this power is still chemical affinity ... If we call the power which is evolved at this point *heat*, or *electricity*, or any other name referring to its source, or the way in which it travels, we still shall find it to be chemical action." Within the voltaic battery, and in electrolysis, we see "chemical affinity producing electricity, and electricity again becoming chemical affinity".[49]

It is not surprising that Faraday saw no sense in dividing chemistry from physics. His whole train of electrochemical researches was directed by a view of natural philosophy that united those sciences, and brought to his experiments a sureness and a logic that made the years 1831 to 1834 a triumphal march in the history of electrochemistry. Faraday was not tackling problems piecemeal. He was constructing a unified electrochemical theory that rested on his conviction that forces acting on one another partook of a like nature. His approach assumed that all natural forces had "one common origin".[50] His view that matter was manifested by its forces provided another support for his approach, that remained valid whether Newtonian dynamism, a qualitative approximation to Boscovichean atomism, or Faraday's lines of force furnished the model.[51] The unity of force was his key to natural philosophy. It was a metaphysical assumption;[52] it directed a brilliant sequence of experimental researches; and it established foundations for electrochemical theory, and for electrochemical industry and technology.

REFERENCES

1. To Whewell, 24 April 1834, in *The Selected Correspondence of Michael Faraday*, ed. L. P. Williams. (2 vols., Cambridge,1971), vol. I, p. 264.

2. Ross, "Faraday Consults the Scholars: The Origins of the Terms of Electrochemistry", *Notes and Records of the Royal Society of London*, **16** (1961), 187-220.

3. T. H. Levere, "Faraday, Matter, and Natural Theology", *British Journal for the History of Science*, **4** (1968), 95-107.

4. M. Faraday, *Experimental Researches in Electricity* (3 vols., London, 1839, 1844, 1855), vol. I, para. 283, proposes this formulation.

5. *Correspondence*, vol. I, pp. 271-2.

6. W. Whewell, *Philosophy of the Inductive Sciences* (2 vols., London, 1840), vol. I, p. 113.

7. H. Hartley "Michael Faraday and the Theory of Electrolytic Conduction', *British Association for the Advancement of Science* (London, 1931), Section B. -- Chemistry: 1-21, cited p. 2. See also Hartley, "Michael Faraday as a Physical Chemist", *Transactions of the Faraday Society*, **49** (1953), 473-88.

8. This is developed in L. P. Williams' major biography, *Michael Faraday* (London and New York, 1965).

9. C. A. Russell, "The Electrochemical Theory of Sir Humphry Davy", *Annals of Science*, **15** (1959), 1-3, 15-25; **19** (1963), 255-71.

10. T. H. Levere, *Affinity and Matter* (Oxford, 1971), chapter 2.

11. *The Collected Works of Sir Humphry Davy, Bart. ...*, ed.J. Davy (9 vols., London, 1840), vol. VI, p. 109.

12. H. Davy, "The Bakerian Lecture. On the Relations of Electrical and Chemical Changes", *Phil. Trans.*, **116** (1826), 383-422.

13. M. Faraday, *Chemical Manipulation* (1827); new ed. (London,1830), p . 419.

14. *Faraday's Diary ...*, ed. T. Martin (7 vols. + index, London, 1932-36), vol. I, pp. 102, 191-2.

15. Cf. Hartley (1931), pp. 5-6 (ref. 7).

16. *Researches*, para. 4, (ref. 4), Williams, *Faraday*, chapter 4 (ref. 8).

17. *Correspondence*, vol. I, pp. 209-10 (ref. 1).

18. *Researches*, paras. 10, 38 (ref. 4).

19. *Ibid*, para. 22. Hartley, (1931), p. 6.

20. *Researches*, paras. 73, 76. *Correspondence*, vol. I, pp. 210-11.

21. *Researches*, para. 231.

22. Hartley (1931), pp. 6-7.

23. *Researches*, paras, 373, 377.

24. *Diary*, paras. 218-19, (ref. 14).

25. *Researches*, paras. 394, 412-13, 446.

26. *Diary*, paras. 286-87.

27. Williams, *Faraday*, chapters 2 & 6.

28. *Researches*, para. 517.

29. *Ibid*, para. 465.

30. F. T. von Grotthus, *Annales de Chimie et de Physique*, **58** (1806), 64,

31. H. Davy, "The Bakerian Lecture, on some Chemical Agencies of Electricity , *Phil. Trans.*, **97** (1807), 1-56, esp. 42.

32. *Researches*, para. 500.

33. *Ibid*, para. 524.

34. *Ibid*, para. 505.

35. *Ibid*, paras. 704 ff

36. *Ibid*, paras. 609, 656, 739.

37. *Ibid*, para, 821.

38. *Ibid*, paras. 824, 836, 839, 850.

39. *Ibid*, para. 852.

40. *Ibid*, para. 869.

41. *Ibid*, para. 877.

42. *Diary*, para. 1528.

43. A. Volta, *Phil. Trans.*, **90** (1800), 403.

44. Nicholson's *Journal of Natural Philosophy, Chemistry and the Arts*, **4** (1800), 120.

45. Levere, *Affinity and Matter*, chapter 2.

46. *Researches*, para. 662.

47. *Ibid*. paras. 880-887.

48. *Ibid*. para. 918, Levere, *op. cit.*, pp. 90-91.

49. M. Faraday, *On the Various Forces of Nature and Their Relations to Each Other*, ed. W. Crookes (London, ((1859,issued ? 1874)), pp. 160-61, 165.

50. *Researches*, para. 2562.

51. Williams, *Faraday*, chapters 2, 9. Levere, *Affinity and Matter*, chapter 3.

52. *Cf. Emporio Italiano*, no. 3, 1 May 1857, quoted in Levere, *op. cit.*, pp. 105-106.

XVI

FARADAY, MATTER, AND NATURAL THEOLOGY—REFLECTIONS ON AN UNPUBLISHED MANUSCRIPT*

THE publication of L. Pearce Williams's definitive biography of Faraday[1] has led to lively discussion of the influence of *Naturphilosophie* on Davy[2] and Faraday,[3] and of the role played by Boscovichean atomism in their scientific development. In a recent article[4] J. Brookes Spencer argued that Boscovich's force law, involving interaction between point atoms independent of surrounding particles, was only compatible with Faraday's view of gravity and not with his views on other forces.[5] This would of course contradict the notion of unity which is absolutely fundamental to Boscovich's *Theoria*.[6]

Davy's Philosophy of Nature

Before we deal with Faraday's attitudes to these problems, it will be useful to look briefly at Davy's ideas, for they profoundly affected Faraday's intellectual development. Davy's direct influence on Faraday is most clearly apparent in the latter's early lectures to the City Philosophical Society, where he cited Davy and Newton as equally revered authorities.[6a] The complexities and contradictions of Davy's mind are bound to make unambiguous interpretations of his ideas difficult.[7] Nevertheless, Davy and Faraday both become easier to understand when two related distinctions are borne in mind. These distinctions, although they seem obvious to-day, were frequently ignored in the nineteenth century,[8] and their subsequent neglect has tended to confuse historical classification. First, it was not necessary to accept the metaphysics of

* M. Faraday, "Matter", 19 Feb. 1844. The MS. is in the library of the Institution of Electrical Engineers, London. I am very grateful for permission to reproduce it here. I should also like to express my thanks to several people who have aided me in the preparation of this paper and particularly to Dr. Colin Russell and Mr. John Brooke.

[1] L. Pearce Williams, *Michael Faraday* (London, 1965).

[2] For mutually opposing viewpoints see R. Siegfried, *Isis*, lvii (1966), 325–335; D. M. Knight, *Ambix.*, xiv (1967), 181–182.

[3] E.g. T. S. Kuhn's review of Williams's *Faraday: B. J. Phil. Sc.*, xviii (1967), 148–154.

[4] *Arch. Hist. Exact Sc.*, iv (1967), 184 ff.

[5] Nineteenth-century commentators who could not dispense with the notion of imponderable fluids reached the same conclusion from different premises, e.g. R. Hare, *Phil. Mag.* [3], xxvi (1845), 602.

[6] R. J. Boscovich, *Theoria Philosophiae Naturalis* (Venice, 1763); trans. J. M. Child (Chicago, 1922).

6a The relevant MSS. are now at the Institution of Electrical Engineers.

[7] Indeed Davy has left so many contradictory statements in his MSS. that one can prove almost anything by selective quotation. This is because he considered both sides of every argument and not because his thought was completely chaotic.

[8] E.g. Oersted thought that Gowin Knight's work (see footnote 29) was Idealistic—but it definitely was not.

Naturphilosophie in order to think of chemical processes in terms of forces.[9] Secondly, Boscovich was not the only originator of force atoms.[10] Although Boscovich's atoms had no meaningful existence as individual entities (since their powers arose from their relations with other point atoms), they were essentially systems of forces around centres. In this, they had strong affinities with a variety of force atoms postulated by an exceedingly viable British tradition.[11] This tradition regarded the atomic centre, which could be either a geometrical point or a solid body, as being surrounded by a series of spheres of attraction and (in some cases) of repulsion. To postulate such atoms was to adopt a dynamical chemistry, which did not have to be Idealistic.

There can be no doubt that Davy's was a dynamical chemistry. In a sense, Coleridge was right in saying that his major discoveries were "made during the *suspension* of the mechanic Philosophy relatively to chemical Theory".[12] However, this need not imply that Davy subscribed to the concomitant Nature Philosophy. The hypothesis that he did so[13] is seductive, for it provides a convincing framework within which to interpret his ideas. In fact the positive evidence for it is slender. According to his brother John, writing after Humphry's death, he read Kant in 1786;[14] we know of his rejection of imponderable fluids, although he was not consistent in this;[15] he was friendly with Coleridge; and in a notebook of about 1800 he summed up a series of idealistic relations in the phrase "existence is unity".[16]

A few years later, however, Davy expressed a revulsion from these adolescent enthusiasms.

"[Ritter's] errors as a theorist seem to be derived merely from his indulgence in the peculiar literary taste of his country where the metaphysical dogmas of Kant which as far as I can learn are pseudo platonism are preferred before the doctrines of Locke and of Hartley, excellence and knowledge being rather sought for in the infant than in the adult state of the mind."[17]

[9] For an introduction to dynamical chemistry (including some Idealistic chemistry) see Knight, *op. cit.* (2), 179–197. Note that G. Eriksson, *Lychnos* (1965), 1–37, insists on the distinction between Kantian and Romantic dynamists. He makes it clear that in Swedish universities around the beginning of the nineteenth century, Kantian and Romantic dynamism were clearly differentiated from one another, and suggests that this differentiation may be significant for Berzelius's strong bias against Schelling. In general (Oersted was an exception), it was the atomists, with their blanket condemnation of dynamism, who confused the various forms of dynamical theories of matter.

[10] By "force atoms" I mean any atoms the properties of which are consequent upon inherent or constitutive forces.

[11] E.g. J. Rowning, G. Knight. See (28), (29).

[12] S. T. Coleridge to Lord Liverpool, 28 July 1817. *Letters*, ed. Griggs, 4 vols. (Oxford, 1956–59), iii, 760.

[13] L. P. Williams, *op. cit.* (1), 67–68.

[14] J. Davy, *Memoirs of . . . H. Davy*, 2 vols. (London, 1836), i, 36; but Davy could not read German, and there was then no English translation of Kant's dynamical work (10).

[15] Williams, *op. cit.* (1), 68. Note, however, that Davy's rejection of imponderable fluids was not always unequivocal; e.g. *Phil. Trans.*, cxvi (1826), 383–422; J. Davy, *op. cit.* (14), i, 314, 318. See (7) above.

[16] R.I. MS. iv, 15j.

[17] R.I. MS. iv, 1 (undated, but about 1808).

This passage strongly suggests that, for Davy, Kantian metaphysics was at best irrelevant to the pursuit of science. Moreover, it implies that he had never studied Kant.[18] Against this must be set the Neoplatonism of his *Consolations in Travel*.[19] But this work was written well after his active scientific career had ended. It may well be significant that no works of German metaphysics made their way into the Royal Institution's library while Davy worked there.[20]

While the nature of Davy's metaphysics remains a ripe ground for controversy, some broad trends in his theories do stand out clearly. Throughout his life he adhered to one kind of force atomism or another. In 1814[21] and again in 1829[22] he advocated Boscovichean point atomism; and an undated note[23] in the Royal Institution is reminiscent of Boscovich's library simile.[24] In one dialogue he even compared man to a point atom, and active powers to God's creative energy.[25] Another dialogue,[26] however, talks of *corpuscles* with form and inherent powers, and similar ideas are expressed at various stages of his career.[27] Examples could readily be multiplied. Such assumptions about the nature of matter correspond to hypotheses proposed by John Rowning[28] and Gowin Knight,[29] whose works were in the Royal Institution's library when Davy came from Clifton. Their general ideas were very much part of the background of Newtonian dynamism.

Besides adhering to this rather shifting force atomism, Davy displayed a constant substratum of religious feeling,[30] which was more than the conventional devotion of his time:

"It will not appear improbable that one law alone may govern and act

---

[18] Few Englishmen had studied Kant at the beginning of the nineteenth century. A fair picture is given by the *Edinburgh Review*:

" . . . we are content to be dully indifferent, and can hear of a system which has divided into patrons and opposers the whole thinking part of a large empire, without any public curiosity to become acquainted with its merits, or to know enough, even of its imperfections, to comfort ourselves with the certainty that our neglect of it has been deserved."

(Ed. Rev., i (1803), 254–255).

[19] *Consolations in Travel; or, The Last Days of a Philosopher* (London, 1830).

[20] Library catalogues were published for 1809, 1821, 1852. None of them lists any works by Ritter, Richter, Wenzel, Schelling or Kant; nor were Oersted's early works acquired.

[21] R.I. MS. iv, 12 (undated entry; next dated entry is of 9 Dec. 1814).

[22] *Collected Works*, ed. J. Davy, 9 vols. (London, 1839), ix, 388.

[23] R.I. MS. iv, 1.

[24] Boscovich, *op. cit.* (6), sect. 99. The 1763 ed. of the *Theoria* is not in the R.I.'s 1809 catalogue, but appears in that for 1821. There were several other sources in the R.I. which would have given him second-hand information about the theory.

[25] *Ibid.* (MS. iv, 9, consists of various unnumbered and undated dialogues.)

[26] *Ibid.* (MS. iv, 9, consists of various unnumbered and undated dialogues.)

[27] E.g. *Works*, vii, 11.

[28] *A Compendious System of Natural Philosophy* . . . , 2 vols. (London, 1744), ii, 5–6. (There were many other editions.)

[29] *An attempt to demonstrate, that all the phaenomena in nature may be explained by two simple principles, attraction and repulsion* (London, 1748). Although Knight used a dynamical approach, he would surely not have agreed with the tenets of *Naturphilosophie*. But Oersted, in his decidedly Idealistic *Ansichten der chemischen Naturgesetze* (Berlin, 1812), referred to it as being the nearest approach to the modern Philosophy of Nature.

[30] Cf. L. P. Williams, *Scientific American*, ccxvii (1967), 145.

upon matter,—an energy of mutation impressed by the will of the Deity, . . .

"The further we investigate the phenomena of nature, the more we discover simplicity and unity of design: an extensive field for sublime investigation is open to us."[31]

In Davy, natural theology and force atomism were mutually supporting, and Faraday inherited this combination.

Faraday and Force Atoms

Even before 1820 Faraday had indulged in speculations about point atoms.[32] Indeed, with Davy for his mentor, any other course would have been remarkable. In spite of this, however, he was able to write as late as 1834, "the more I think (in association with experiment) the less distinct does my idea of an atom or particle become".[33] Faraday always thought in association with experiment, and without it he remained "naturally sceptical on philosophical theories".[34]

As a result of this caution, Faraday's confidence in his theories germinated slowly. Williams has traced his scientific development with skill and clarity, so that it would be pointless to attempt to retrace the same path here. In the 1830's Faraday embarked upon his series of experimental researches in electricity, in the course of which he proved for himself the value of point atomism in directing his enquiries.[35] His papers on induction and conduction in particular were founded on the assumption of a dynamical theory of matter, a preconception of which his friends and contemporaries were largely unaware. They were therefore generally as mystified as they were admiring;[36] Tyndall, for example, wrote of Faraday's papers[36a] on induction:

"And then again occur, I confess, dark sayings, difficult to be understood . . .

"The meaning of Faraday in these memoirs on induction and conduction is, as I have said, by no means always clear: and the difficulty will be most felt by those who are best trained in ordinary theoretic conceptions."[37]

What, after all, were sober scientists expected to make of a viewpoint which assented to the question, "Do not all bodies act where they are not?"[32] Yet Faraday gave no explanation; when tackled directly, he claimed, "I have formed no decided notion."[38]

More research is needed on the problem of Faraday's reticence at

---

[31] Quoted by J. Davy, *op. cit.* (13), i, 76.

[32] *Common Place Book*, I.E.E. MS.

[33] Quoted by A. Hofmann, *Faraday Lecture* for 1875.

[34] Faraday to A. de la Rive, 12 Sept. 1821, expresses scepticism about Ampère's electrodynamic theory because of its lack of experimental support. Quoted by H. Bence Jones, *Life & Letters of Faraday*, 2 vols. (London, 1870), i, 354.

[35] For an account of this, see L. P. Williams, *Faraday*, chaps. iv–vii.

[36] *Ibid.*, 309–311.

[36a] *Phil. Trans.*, 1838.

[37] Bence Jones, *op. cit.* (34), ii, 85; quoted from J. Tyndall, *Faraday as a Discoverer* (London, 1868).

[38] *Phil. Mag.*, xvii (1840), 64.

this period. Nevertheless, it is tempting to agree with Williams that one reason for this reticence was the superficial correspondence between Faraday's approach and the dynamical chemistry of polar forces advocated by contemporary German metaphysicians. There can be no doubt that the latter notions were violently rejected by the majority of respected scientists in both France and England.[39] Thus Oersted's discovery of the magnetic effects of an electric current was at first coldly received in Paris. "We thought it was another German dream", wrote Dulong to Berzelius.[40]

An even greater obstacle to the acceptance of point atoms arose from their lack of properties. Atoms, if they are to serve any explanatory purpose, must have properties which are different from and fewer than those of the massive aggregates with which experience deals. Point atoms, being devoid of properties, were literally inconceivable, except as mathematical constructions. (This is strictly true only of Boscovich's atoms. Other force atoms did exist individually and independently by virtue of their powers.) English common sense[41] was unwilling to countenance the notion of these "unreal" entities. Daubeny complained, "I cannot . . . bring myself to assign any properties at all to mere space";[42] Donovan, while he was prepared to consider the theory, admitted that the student might find it impossible to "accept opinions revolting to his ordinary habits of thought";[43] and Davies Gilbert explosively opined that, "The most ingenious baseless fabrick that ever was reared, is in my opinion, that constructed by Boscovich."[44] It is scarcely surprising that Faraday hesitated in the face of so united an opposition.

It was only in the 1840's that he overcame his hesitation. Forced by the continuous pressure of laboratory work to rest from his experiments, he entered a fallow period, indulging in the unwonted luxury of speculation; thereby, he acquired the courage to announce his views.

"Speculations, dangerous temptations; generally avoid them; but a time to speculate as well as to refrain, all depends upon the temper of the mind. I was led to consider the nature of space in relation to electric conduction, and so of matter, i.e. whether *continuous* or consisting of *particles with intervening space* according to its supposed constitution. Consider this point, *remarking the assumptions* everywhere."[45]

Thus it was, in April 1844, that Faraday explained the genesis of his earlier paper, "A Speculation touching Electric Conduction and the

[39] Cuvier, *Rapport Historique . . .* (Paris, 1810), 9, and Berzelius, *Jahresbericht*, i (1822), 1–2, show typical hostility to *Naturphilosophie*.
[40] *Jac. Berzelius Bref* (Uppsala, 1916), iv, 17. Letter dated 2 Oct. 1820.
[41] Exemplified by the popularity of T. Reid's philosophy.
[42] *Introduction to the Atomic Theory* (2nd ed., Oxford, 1850), 47.
[43] *Chemistry* (4th ed., London, 1839), 40.
[44] Magdalen College, Oxford, MS. 400/46.
[45] Bence Jones, *op. cit.* (34), ii, 177-179.

Nature of Matter".[46] In this, he had first pointed out that if one accepted the usual atomic notions,[47] then the atoms could not be in contact, since cold or pressure would still lead to a decrease in volume. Thus in electrical conductors, the space between atoms would have to function as a conductor, while in insulators, the same space would necessarily behave as an insulator. To avoid this paradox (which Berzelius and many others attributed to ignorance of the nature of electricity), Faraday proposed to adopt what he thought were Boscovich's point atoms. These had the advantage of making the world a continuum, and dissolved the dichotomy presented by atoms and the void. He was left with a "Final brooding impression, that particles are only centers of force; that the force or forces constitute the matter." But "He is the wisest philosopher who holds his theory with some doubt . . ."[45]

Faraday must have been left in some doubt about the validity of his theory, for shortly after the published "Speculation" he wrote another memoir, this time apparently to himself, to clarify his ideas. It is this memoir which is reproduced in the following pages. Simplicity and unity are, as always, his ruling criteria. Here he identifies the former with the smallest number of assumptions, and interprets this as involving the fewest physical properties. Inevitably, therefore, he is led to conceive of matter as force.

The paper is of considerable interest both as a personal and as a scientific document. The argument is much more subjective than Faraday would publicly allow, so that the personal note is especially revealing. His scientific education derived largely from Humphry Davy,[48] and began in earnest during their continental tour together. If, as I have suggested, it is difficult to find any unequivocal evidence to show that Davy's theory of matter was influenced by *Naturphilosophie*, it is even harder to make the same claim for Faraday, who as a rule was not inclined to the study of speculative philosophy.[49] His *Journal*[50] and *Diary*[51] are empty of metaphysics,[49] and it is probable that he would have found the Gnostic undertones of *Naturphilosophie* incompatible with his strict Sandemanian evangelical Christianity. If he was not interested in the Idealistic Philo-

[46] *Phil. Mag.*, xxiv (1844), 136–144.

[47] I.e. Lavoisier's and Dalton's idea of hard incompressible atoms.

[48] Compare their use of analogy. Davy, R.I. MS. iv, 9 (and *Consolations*): "The imagination must be active and brilliant in seeking analogies yet intirely under the influence of the judgement in applying them". Cf. Faraday to Schoenbein, 13 Nov. 1845, in *The Letters of Faraday and Schoenbein*, ed. Kahlbaum and Derbyshire (Basle and London, 1899), 149: "You can hardly imagine how I am struggling to exert my poetical ideas just now for the discovery of analogies and remote figures respecting the earth, sun, and all sorts of things—for I think that is the true way (corrected by judgement) to work out a discovery."

[49] H. Helmholtz, *J. Chem. Soc.*, xxxix (1881), 277, went so far as to make the mistaken claim that Faraday's scientific method was "destined to purify science from the last remnant of metaphysics". Faraday did not identify religion with metaphysics!

[50] I.E.E. MS.

[51] *Diary*, ed. T. Martin, 7 vols. and index (London, 1932–6).

sophy of nature as a justification of his theory of matter, why then did he accept point atomism?

I think that the answer is quite simple. Faraday naturally valued force atomism for its explanatory power; but the main reason for his adherence to the hypothesis was that it fitted in with the world picture imposed by his religion.

The Influence of Faraday's Religion

The argument that follows in support of this assertion is, of necessity, suggestive rather than conclusive. Its statement is shielded by this reservation. Faraday was deeply religious[52]—perhaps even more so than Davy.[53] I have already suggested[30, 31] that, for Davy, the power of God was the final cause of the powers of matter, and that the connection between these powers was intimate.[54] God's activity in the universe was not restricted to an initial creation, but was rather a constant presence.[55] I shall not try to prove that religious convictions can be effective in shaping the content of a scientific theory; but such convictions can and do play a major role in the *selection* of theories.[56] The influence of Faraday's religious convictions on his life and thought—including scientific thought—cannot be ignored. Indeed, Stewart and Tait cited Newton and Faraday together as splendid examples of the compatibility of science with religion.[57] God created and sustained the universe; a single Architect implied a unified and purposeful plan. God worked through powers and through forces, and surely these agreed much better with a universe of force atoms than with one of billiard-ball atoms. Perhaps Faraday may even, like Priestley, have been attracted to point atomism because it made the world more truly continuous with the Divine activity. Such a religious association of the power of God with natural forces had been a commonplace interpretation to British "natural philosopher-theologians" from the time of Newton until the end of the eighteenth century.[58] Throughout

---

[52] L. P. Williams, *op. cit.* (1), 102–106.

[53] While on tour with Davy, Faraday wrote to Benjamin Abbott from Geneva (6 Sept. 1814; quoted by Bence Jones, *op. cit.* (34), i, 157): "Travelling . . . I find, is almost inconsistent with religion (I mean modern travelling), and I am yet so old-fashioned as to remember strongly (I hope perfectly) my youthful education . . ." Davy was not so troubled.

[54] Cf. (58) below.

[55] T. Exley, *Principles of Nat. Phil.* (London, 1829), xxvii, remarks that if matter exists solely by its powers, which are created by God, then the existence of matter is unremittingly maintained by the power of God.

[56] A good example is J. Priestley, *Disquisitions on Matter & Spirit*, 2 vols. (2nd ed., London, 1777), where his theology makes him adopt a form of Boscovichean atomism, e.g. i, 43.

[57] *The Unseen Universe* (1876), preface.

[58] For a good account of this see H. Metzger, *Attraction universelle et religion naturelle* . . . (Paris, 1937).
The most direct statement I have found, or indeed could wish to find on this topic, occurs in a letter which Sir William Rowan Hamilton wrote to Coleridge in 1832:
"Do I then at all express a possible view, or am I talking nonsense, when I say that I

[continued on page 102

Faraday's writings there are passages suggesting that his ideas were firmly in this tradition.[59] At any rate, he would surely have agreed with Davy that

"whenever we attempt metaphysical speculations we must begin with a foundation of faith. And, being sure from revelation, that God is omnipotent and omnipresent, it appears to me no improper use of our faculties, to trace *even in the natural universe*, the acts of his power and the results of his wisdom, and to draw parallels from the infinite to the finite mind."[60]

Gillispie, in *Genesis and Geology*, claims that Faraday was well able to separate science from religion, and this opinion seems to be of wide currency. The source for what I am convinced is an erroneous belief, expressing at best a partial truth, appears to be Faraday's statement that

"there is no philosophy in my religion. I am of a very small and despised sect of Christians, known, if known at all, as Sandemanians, and our hope is founded on the faith that is in Christ. But though the natural works of God can never by any possibility come in contradiction with the higher things that belong to our future existence, and must with everything concerning Him ever glorify Him, still I do not think it at all necessary to tie the study of natural science and religion together, and in my intercourse with fellow-creatures, that which is religious, and that which is philosophical, have ever been two distinct things."[61]

This statement of his views on the relation of religion to science is almost identical with that of Sir William Rowan Hamilton, as expressed

---

regard a certain atomistic theory as having a subjective truth, and as being a fit medium between our understanding and certain phenomena: *although objectively, and in the truth of things, the powers attributed to atoms belong not to them but to God?* The atomistic theory of which I speak is nearly that of Boscovich . . ." (R. P. Graves, *Life of Sir W. R. Hamilton*, 3 vols. (London and Dublin, 1882–9), i, 593; my italics).
Hamilton was both a Christian and an Idealist, and was inclined to Boscovichean atomism because of its religious associations, and also because Boscovich's views "seem capable of being incorporated with high metaphysical idealism" (*Life*, ii, 86, letter of 27 June 1834). It was in this same year, 1834, that Hamilton first became acquainted with Faraday, and discovered with delight that he and Faraday had almost identical views on the nature of matter. It does not appear unlikely that this coincidence of opinion may have extended to the theological implications of point atomism.

[59] E.g. *Experimental Researches in Electricity*, 3 vols. (London, 1839–55), sects. 2447, 2968 imply the acceptance of an economical theological teleology; *Lectures on the non-metallic elements*, ed. Scoffern (London, 1853), 2, tells us that chemistry is admirably suited to awaken within us "the sentiment of immortality". In R.I. MS. iv, 23 (lecture of 1847), he concludes a discussion of point atomism as follows: " . . . at last the molecule rises up, in accordance with the mighty purpose ordained for it and plays its part in the gift of *life itself*:—and therefore our philosophy, whilst it shews us these things should lead us to think of Him who hath wrought them:—for it is said by an authority far above even that which these works present that '*the invisible things of him from the creation of the world are clearly seen being understood by the things that are made even his eternal power and Godhead*'."

[60] *Consolations*, 279 (my italics).

[61] Bence Jones, *Life* (34), ii, 195.

in a letter of about 1835.[62] However, we have seen in an earlier footnote (58) that Hamilton did indeed conceive of a connection between natural theology and natural science. His concern for the distinction between religion and philosophy was merely to ensure that

"no reasonable complaint lies against religion for not presenting articles of faith under the form of Philosophical Theorems, though we may justly expect that the doctrines which it teaches should not be contradictory, nor capable of being proved to be absurd:—an *a priori* requisition of the mind with which it is my intellectual belief that Christianity complies."[62]

This necessary postulate of non-contradiction was the active agent of selection operated by religion upon science; it was, moreover, as we have seen (note 61), a postulate upon which Faraday was equally insistent, and whose negation would have struck him as being an utter impossibility. Had not Robert Sandeman, after whom Faraday's sect was named, held that Christianity was of an intellectual character, having its origins in the understanding?[63] It would seem to follow that, in the natural world, there must be an intellectually comprehensible unity and logical coherence. One could interpret the natural world in terms of the primary facts of God's existence and of His revelation to man. Faraday did occasionally employ natural theology, but his general theology of nature reversed the direction of Paley's argument from design in the physical world to the existence and nature of God. Paley's natural theology was, from the standpoint of evangelical (including Sandemanian) theology, valueless as a guide to divine characteristics, unless subjected to rectification by biblical revelation; it would have seemed presumptuous and even arrogant, when applied on its own. This evangelical attitude would have been even more strongly opposed to the far-reaching claims of *Naturphilosophie*, which argued, via its few metaphysical assumptions, from human to divine nature with *no* appeal to revelation. Faraday, in contrast, argued *primarily* from God to a limited but unimpeachable knowledge of the natural world. Within such a framework of religious ideas, the thorough-going divorce of science from religion makes absolutely no sense, nor did Faraday attempt it, for he realized that to distinguish science from religion was not to sever them, but only to indicate the latter's absolute and logical primacy, while limiting the former's sphere. Williams has pointed out that, in spite of Faraday's protestations, his deepest intuitions about the physical world arose from his faith in "the Divine origin of nature".[64, 64a]

[62] Graves, *Life of Hamilton* (58), ii, 397–398, Hamilton to E. O'Brien, winter 1835–6.

[63] J. Stoughton, *Worthies of Science* (Religious Tract Society, London), 273.

[64] Williams, *Faraday* (1), 4. The same point is made by R. E. D. Clark, *The Christian Graduate* (1967), 26–27.

[64a] After this article had been written, Dr. Colin Russell informed me of the article by R. E. D. Clark: "Michael Faraday on Science and Religion" (*Hibbert Journal*, 1967, 144–147). Clark's conclusions about Faraday's natural theology are very similar to mine.

104

Faraday was certainly too honest and methodical a natural philosopher to allow external factors, be they metaphysical or religious, to trespass overtly into his laboratory. On the interpretation proposed here, however, it is perhaps significant that, in his personal memoir on the nature of matter, God is thrice alluded to in support of the possibility of point atoms. "Is the lingering notion which remains in the minds of some, really a thought, that God could not just as easily by his word speak power into existence around centers, as he could first create nuclei and then clothe them with power?"

The scientific interest of the paper is less hypothetical. Here we have one more brick in the edifice of proof that Faraday did, at least at this date, seriously incline to a belief in point atoms. It is also interesting because of Faraday's ambiguous use of the word "force",[65] as in his discussion of the three atoms of silver. Sometimes he uses "force" to mean "power", with its wide and complex connotations, while at other times he means "force" as we understand it. He was aware of the difficulty, which for him was no ambiguity, but rather arose from a wider term which integrated with his theology. This appears clearly from a letter which he wrote to Clerk Maxwell in 1857:

"I dare say I have myself greatly to blame for the vague use of expressive words. I perceive that I do not use the word 'force' as you define it, 'the tendency of a body to pass from one place to another'. What I mean by the word is the *source* or *sources* of all possible actions of the particles or materials of the universe: these being often called the *powers* of nature when spoken of in respect of the different manners in which their effects are shewn."[66]

At periods distant from 1844, was Faraday's refusal to avow this hypothesis the result of caution and of his avoidance of controversy? Or did it stem from genuine uncertainty?

In 1847 he was still lecturing on force atoms.[67] But in January 1859 Sir Benjamin Collins Brodie wrote to him on the subject of atoms:

"I dare say you have forgotten, but I have not forgotten a conversation which I had with you long ago, in which I believe that you expressed yourself as agreeing with me in the opinion that of the ultimate structure of material bodies we neither have, nor can have any actual knowledge, and that neither the ordinary hypothesis of solid impenetrable molecules, nor Boscovich's hypothesis of mathematical points, is anything more than a contrivance for bringing these things down to the level of our limited comprehension."[68]

This letter, Faraday's note to Ward,[33] and numerous hesitations in print, all suggest that it was only in the 1840's that Faraday really considered point atomism as a *physical* theory. Before then, it served him

[65] Mr. Rom Harré first pointed this out to me.
[66] Cambridge U.L., Add. MS. 7655/II, 14. A similarly cautious and broad definition is proposed by Boscovich in his *Theoria*.
[67] R.I. MS. iv, 23.
[68] I.E.E. MS.

primarily as a guiding hypothesis, which postulated entities whose physical existence was merely plausible. Afterwards, he sensed that the theory as he formulated it was incapable of accounting for the force of universal gravitation.[68a] To avoid the incompatibility of this position with his views on the unity of nature, Faraday changed the emphasis of his ideas to lines of force, and consequently modified his theory of matter.

"MATTER

"As a natural philosopher and *purposely limiting* my object to the investigation of the phenomena presented by the *material* creation, I, in common with all having the same object, feel constrained to form some idea of matter. Whilst marshalling my thoughts into that order or condition which is least inconsistent with the phenomena, it seems to me very important that we assume as little as possible, since *all that we assume may be wrong*.

"God has been pleased to work in his material creation by laws, and these laws are made evident to us by the *constancy* of the characters of matter and the *constancy* of the effects which it produces. Matter, as far as we can observe it, is *invariable in itself*; and it acts by *forces* impressed upon it which, as far as we can judge, are also invariable; having undergone no change since man has been on the earth, and, as we have reason to believe, none from the first moment of their creation until now. Their integrity & the integrity of the laws which govern the material universe are bound up with each other.

"Then as to the nature of matter—take a piece of wood or iron or stone, I believe it to be matter as any other person would do, and I believe it to be manifested to our senses as a *particular* kind of matter *by its properties*; for we have no other way of knowing matter, either generally or specifically, than by the properties which it exhibits. But these properties belong to it by virtue of the *forces* which belong to it and in no other way; for, by the consent of all natural philosophers, the word force or forces is used to express that which gives to them their properties and powers. Thus, for instance, the *weight* or *gravitation* of a body depends upon a force which we call attraction; and this force is not something away or separate from the matter, nor the matter separate from the force; the force is an essential property or part of the matter &, to speak absurdly, the matter without the force would not be matter. Or, if we recognise matter by its *hardness*, what do we other than recognise by our sensations a force exerted by it? I press my finger against a piece of glass, and, because my finger is resisted by it I say it is *hard*; but how does this hardness or resistance arise? by a *force of repulsion* which existing in the particles of the glass & in the particles of my finger prevents their coming nearer to each other than a certain distance, fixed for the circumstances but varying if the circumstances vary. I say again that the glass is *hard* because its particles resist displacement; not that they are touching by any imaginary solid surfaces for we can easily place the particles nearer to, or farther apart from, each other by pressure, heat, &c; but because the forces of the particles hold them under the circumstances at a *given* distance & in a *given* position.

"Then let us pass at once to the ordinary notion of the particles or atoms

[68a] Cf. (4) above.

of matter, and see what it leads to. The ordinary notion is, that there is a something to be called matter which has certain forces (the forces of matter) impressed upon it; but that it exists independent of the forces, yet owes its properties to them, and that it & the forces may be conceived of apart from each other. Then let *a.a.a.* represent three atoms of silver, for instance, in a piece of solid silver. First of all they *gravitate* by virtue of a force in them, which extends to distances such as those of the sun & stars from us. Next they are held *fixedly apart* from each other, by forces which we call those of attraction & repulsion, and do not touch (except by their forces), for they never are so near but we can bring them nearer by a little more cold or a little more pressure. Next they *reflect light*, but as Brewster[69] has shewn the reflexion of light by a body begins before the ray of light has actually reached & touched the body, and this is also easily shewn in the case of any common reflector polished by ordinary means. Finally, its chemical properties are manifested long before the supposed real particles touch each other, both in electrolyzation & in the chemical action of gases; where, indeed, the supposed real particles of matter are considered as very far apart.

"All the properties, therefore, by which we are made aware of the presence of, & recognise, the matter are dependant on *forces* acting at some distance from the real nucleus; and of that, as a thing by itself, we cannot in any way be conscious. So then, for aught we can tell, the supposed material nuclei, instead of being so large as nearly to touch each other, may be of only half that size or diameter, or less still, or even mere points; for whether these nuclei be of the larger size, or of the next size, or of the still smaller third size, or little more than a mere point, if they have a constant amount of power for all the sizes, their effects and properties will be the same; i.e. they will *gravitate*, and *cohere*, and *reflect light*, & *act chemically*, exactly to the same amount in one case as in another: for the forces are assumed as definite & the properties are determined by them. If therefore we assume these nuclei of matter, it is clear we have no notion of their *size* as compared to the space they occupy in a mass of matter: we know this, that, according to the assumption & the facts, the sum of *their bulks* must be less than the *bulk of the matter* which they form as a mass; but whether it be nine tenths of this, or one half, or a fourth, or a tenth, or a hundredth, or a hundred thousandth, we have not the slightest means of judging.

"Well then;—as we cannot recognize this nucleus by any property or force it has, independant of those which are shewn by all the phenomena of nature to act at a distance from it, what reason is there to suppose that it exists at all? or how can we conceive of its existence away from these forces? Two of these assumed atoms never touch each other; they touch only by their forces; then suppose these forces away, what would happen? must not the silver vanish? There would be no more gravitation, no more reflexion of light, no more chemical action, and, if we could imagine it possible that the two particles were pushed together till they met really, & were then to think that they would (by a sort of impenetrable hardness) resist each other, this would be only to renew the idea of an atom *with its forces*; for we know of no resistance of this kind in nature except of particles acting at distances; and distances which we can make less or greater by heat, cold, & chemical influence.

"What real reason, then, is there for supposing that there is any such

---

[69] This would also agree with the Newtonian theory of light, as Brewster doubtless intended.

nucleus in a particle of matter? That an atom of matter is an unchangeable amount of power, I believe; and *as indestructible* as any of those atoms which Newton or others may have imagined consisting of nuclei; and that this power is grouped round & attached to a center I believe, just as others suppose it associated with a nucleus; but what the nucleus is wanted for, or how it is recognised, or what it is independant of the power around & about it, I cannot imagine: for, abstracted from the properties, no thought remains in my mind on which I can found the *idea of a nucleus*. Is the lingering notion which remains in the minds of some, really a thought, that God could not just as easily by his word speak power into existence around centers, as he could first create nuclei & then clothe them with power? Is there any thing more comprehensible to our minds in the complicated view of matter without power, and power without matter,[70] & matter & power mingled together, than there is in the simple view of power emanating from & around a center? which, after all, is only a part of the former view (namely power without matter) and therefore, amongst these incomprehensibles, the lesser assumption.

"I might go on until I should be lost in these considerations, which, after all, must rank only as assumptions whatever view we incline to adopt. But, returning to the first points expressed as the ground of natural philosophy, namely, that the Creator governs his material works by *definite laws* resulting from the forces impressed on matter, and, that matter is *that* of which we take cognizance by our external senses; then, I cannot imagine physical force without matter, or matter without force. Matter acts & is acted upon only by its forces, and the atoms of matter are to my imagination centers of force. [What force is I know not; the nature of our existence gives us only to recognize and to estimate it by its effects.]

M.F."[71]

---

[70] In a lecture of 1844 (R.I. MS. iv, 23), Faraday asks, "In radiation appear to have power separate from matter?" [*sic*].

[71] It is striking that this memorandum is more dynamical in character than the published "Speculation". Perhaps, as Dr. D. M. Knight has suggested (private communication), Faraday already saw his own logic pushing him beyond the Boscovichean position of the published paper, and towards his papers on ray vibrations and lines of force.

XVII

AFFINITY OR STRUCTURE:
AN EARLY PROBLEM IN ORGANIC CHEMISTRY

INTRODUCTION

IN the first third of the nineteenth century, inorganic substances alone seemed to obey more or less simple laws. Organic chemistry, however, resembled nothing so much as cookery by trial and error. In spite of all the determined spade-work of eighteenth-century, and even earlier, chemists who had come up against the organic realm, and who had confronted the problems of preformation and classification, organic chemistry as a coherent science dates only from around the 1830's.

Its provenance, its legitimacy, and its scope were all attacked, and the journals of the 1830's and 1840's are full of sound, fury and bewilderment. Although most chemists were certain that organic chemistry was a respectable part of science, they were much divided in their opinions on the nature of the beast.

The development of organic chemistry gave rise to a continuing debate that took place at two distinct levels. The first, and fundamental question was: Granted that there is such a thing as organic chemistry, loosely defined, what is the proper basis for exploring and describing the field? From which branch of chemistry should analogies be drawn to develop the whole of chemistry? Should organic or inorganic chemistry be regarded as easier to understand, as simpler, as a more suitable foundation from which to grope for knowledge among the murky thickets of the chemical forest?[1]

The conservative answer was provided by Berzelius. "In exploring the unknown, our only safe plan is to support ourselves upon the known".[2] Where chemistry was concerned, the known was the inorganic realm, in which the properties of compounds were explained in terms of the properties of their

---

[1] This problem has been the subject of a recent important study by Dr. J. H. Brooke. I have not read his Ph.D. thesis, *The Rôle of analogical argument in the development of organic chemistry*, University of Cambridge, 1969, but I owe a great deal to him for valuable discussion on many points.

[2] [*Taylor's*] *Scientific Memoirs*, **4**, 662, 1846.

constituent elements. After all, a mineral was what it was precisely because of its elemental constitution—this seemed self-evident to Berzelius.[3] Atoms owed their properties to their electrical natures, which might be positive or negative, to a specific degree for a given substance; hence any element could be unambiguously assigned a place on an electrochemical scale. This was the basis of Berzelius' system of chemical classification[4] in which chemical combination was explained in terms of the attractions of the opposite electricities associated with atoms.[5] All inorganic compounds were binary, composed of two parts in electrical opposition, in accord with Lavoisier's nomenclature, and also with the results of experiments on electrolysis. Thus, when Berzelius said that we should support ourselves upon the known, he meant that electrochemical dualism was to be the model for organic investigations. He laid down, as a methodological rule, that *"the application of that which is already or can hereafter be known concerning the laws of combination in inorganic nature, is the only guide to our researches concerning their mode of combination in organic nature"*.[6] He had, however, no intention of prejudging the results of organic researches.[7]

There were, by the 1840's, reasonable grounds for opposing Berzelius, resting on a denial of the truth of dualism even in the stronghold of inorganic chemistry. Electrochemical dualists believed that atomic properties, the powers, forces or natures associated with individual particles of matter, were the essential factors to be considered in the search for an explanation of chemical phenomena. Chemists who rejected dualism in favour of some kind of unitary theory gave a different answer. For others, including Laurent, molecular structure was in principle the fundamental concept, which easily led to conceived connexions between chemistry and crystallography. The overall debate may be broadly considered as taking place at two levels, one concerned with the direction in which chemical analogies should be applied, the other with the relative importance of atomic natures and positions. In some cases, crystallographic arguments complicate this analysis.

---

[3] *Rapport Annuel sur les Progrès de la Chimie*, **VII**, 167, 169, 1847.

[4] This is developed in Berzelius, *An Attempt to establish a pure scientific System of Mineralogy by the application of the Electro-chemical Theory and the Chemical Proportions*, trans. John Black, London, 1814.

[5] See his *Essai sur la théorie des proportions chimiques*, Paris, 1819.

[6] *[Taylor's] Scientific Memoirs*, **4**, 663, 1846.

[7] See J. J. Berzelius to R. Hare, 23 Sept. 1834, remarking that potassium sulphate could be split in different ways, e.g. $KO.SO^3$ or $K.SO^4$; the former had hitherto been generally accepted as being the correct representation, but as chemical theory developed, it became clear that both forms should receive equal consideration (*Jac. Berzelius Bref*, ed. H. G. Soderbaum, 6 vols. + 3 suppl., Uppsala, 1912–32, Part vii, pp. 141–2).

This paper will be concerned primarily with the second level of the debate, "affinity versus structure", with crystallographic incursions, within the established context of the first level. It will concentrate on the contributions to organic chemistry of J. B. Dumas and, especially, Auguste Laurent.

I. DUMAS[8]

In 1831 Dumas wrote an open letter to Ampère,[9] asserting that electrochemical dualism reigned equally in the organic and inorganic kingdoms. Three years later he stated flatly that: "All modern chemistry is based on the idea of duality among substances, which is in admirable agreement with electrical phenomena".[10]

In 1837, in his *Leçons sur la Philosophie Chimique*, Dumas discussed current theories of affinity. Electrochemical theories were the only ones he even considered, and there were three main contenders among them, proposed by Ampère,[11] Davy,[12] and Berzelius,[13] respectively.

Ampère, whose ideas have been described elsewhere,[14] regarded so-called elementary particles as compound, and of determinate primitive form. Their further combinations were regulated by considerations of structure, taking place only when the combining units could join to produce a regular form. Ampère seems to have derived parts of his theory from Haüy's crystallography, and to have used both chemical and crystallographic evidence therein. Such ideas had led him, in 1814, to an independent restatement of Avogadro's hypothesis. They also involved him in the identification of chemical with electrical forces. Detailed accounts, arriving at these conclusions, may be found in the recent literature.[15]

---

[8] S. C. Kapoor, "Dumas and organic classification", *Ambix*, **16**, 1–65, 1969, provides a valuable commentary on Dumas' methodology, and a summary of the influence of contemporary chemical theory on Dumas' work. See especially pp. 13–24 for a discussion of the influence of electrical theories.

[9] J. B. Dumas, *Annales de chimie*, **47**, 324–35, 1831.

[10] *Journal de Pharmacie*, **20**, 261 ff., 1834.

[11] L. Pearce Williams, *Michael Faraday*, London, 1965, pp. 148 ff.; *Contemporary Physics*, **4**, 113–23, 1962.

[12] C. A. Russell, *Annals of Science*, **15**, 1, 1959; **19**, 255, 1963.

[13] *Ibid.*, **19**, 117, 1963.

[14] See note 11 above, and note 15 below.

[15] Seymour H. Mauskopf, "The Atomic Structural Theories of Ampère and Gaudin: Molecular Speculation and Avogadro's Hypothesis", *Isis*, **60**, 61–74, 1969.

Dumas was initially captivated by these ideas,[16] but in 1837 he rejected them because he thought they failed to account for certain instances of chemical combination; for example, sulphur could combine with copper, which was electrically more positive, and with oxygen, which was more negative.[17] As it happens, Ampère's theory was very well able to take care of such difficulties.[18]

Davy's theory, although satisfactory chemically, relied on contact electrification, which Dumas looked on as discredited.

This left him with Berzelius' theory, which had so far withstood the attacks of both chemists and physicists.[19] However, although Dumas at this point regarded the electrical nature of atoms as the principal factor in determining chemical affinities, and hence reactions, he did allow a certain influence to arrangement also. He objected strongly to the prevalent notion of indivisible elemental chemical atoms, and was convinced, with Ampère,[20] that these were in fact integrant molecules. The different arrangements of their component atoms were responsible for the phenomena of elemental allotropy and of polymorphism in general. Thus differences in arrangement could lead to differences in chemical properties and, by implication, in chemical affinities.[21]

In spite of this, Dumas was still largely within the dualists' fold, and when he propounded his "theory or law" of substitutions, he at first did so without openly attacking dualism.[22] This did not prevent Berzelius from taking alarm at Dumas' ideas on substitution as contradicting his regulative principle with its methodological rule.[23] Dumas' subsequent extension of his work on substitution, well known to historians of chemistry, more than justified Berzelius' fears. From supporting dualism in 1837, Dumas progressed in a single year to a position where he doubted its value as a methodological tool, and ignored it in his new theory.[24]

---

[16] See his retrospective account, *Annales de Chimie et de Physique*, [Series 4], **15**, 70, 1868; Acad. des Science, MS. Dumas vii, perhaps around 1818–1820 (n.d.).

[17] *Leçons de la Philosophie Chimique*, Paris, 1837, 414–15.

[18] Académie des Sciences, MS. Ampère xiii, 250/8.

[19] Dumas, *Leçons*, pp. 409–19.

[20] Ampère, *Ann. Chim.*, **90**, 43–86, 1814; *Phil. Mag.*, **7**, 343–5, 1835, translated from *Ann. Chim.*, **58**, 434–44, 1835.

[21] Dumas, *Leçons*, p. 308.

[22] "The Theory of Substitutions expresses a simple relationship between the hydrogen evolved and the chlorine absorbed. . . . But . . . if you have me say that hydrogen is replaced by chlorine which plays the same part, then you attribute to me an opinion against which I strongly protest", *Comptes Rendus de l'Académie des Sciences*, **6**, 647, 1838.

[23] *Comptes Rendus*, **6**, 629, 1838. To postulate substitution was to call in question the guiding assumptions of dualism.

[24] *Ibid.*, **8**, 609, 1839.

Berzelius identified this change as nothing less than a complete revolution in the state of chemistry.[25] This, however, was an exaggeration. Dumas was unwilling to accept the complete denial of all previous ideas about chemical affinity, believing that the electrical nature of bodies still had some influence:

> . . . only it must be agreed, that it is at the moment when the combinations are made, at the moment when they are destroyed, that the role of electricity may be observed.
> But when the elementary molecules have taken their equilibrium, we no longer know how to define the influence that their electric properties may exercise, and no one has set forth views on this subject which agree with experience.[26]

Dumas was simply unable to disembarrass himself of the notion of chemical affinity as a principal determinant of chemical properties. Although his concessions to arrangement made impossible any precise ideas about the role and nature of chemical force, he was "far from denying that chemical and electrical forces may be the same".[27] In his more moderate moments, indeed, he went so far as to urge that a synthesis of aspects of electrochemical dualism with the theory of types[28] would provide the key to chemical phenomena.[29] It was, however, "above all from their situation" that particles derived their properties.[30]

Since situation was so important in his chemical theory, it will be useful to glance at some ideas on this topic which he proposed in 1840, and to which he briefly adhered. He suggested that, while atoms did have electrical properties, they were *not* arranged in static configurations, analogous to crystal structures; they were instead components of dynamical systems in equilibrium —something analogous to the pattern of planets in our solar system.[31] Dumas liked to think of himself as working within the Newtonian tradition.[32] The particles were held in equilibrium by "the diverse molecular forces whose resultant constitutes affinity", and even if electrical forces were part of this scheme, it was clear that there would no longer be room for the static dualistic schemes of Lavoisier and Berzelius.

---

[25] *Ann. Chim. Phys.*, **71**, 137 ff., 1839.

[26] *Phil. Mag.*, [3], **17**, 188, 1840.

[27] *Comptes Rendus*, **10**, 177, 178, 1840.

[28] For an account of Dumas' theory of types see J. R. Partington, *A History of Chemistry*, vol. iv, pp. 364–67.

[29] See note 27.

[30] *Op. cit.* (27), 171.

[31] *Ann. Chim. Phys.*, **73**, 73–103, 1840. "If, on the other hand, one pictures different chemical compounds as constituting so many planetary systems . . . one no longer sees the need for the universal application of dualism . . ." (p. 73).

[32] *Ann. Chim. Phys.*, [4], **15**, 94, 1868.

When one particle within such a system was replaced by another particle of a different kind, a new equilibrium would necessarily be established. The closeness of this equilibrium to the original would determine the degree of similarity of the reactions of the product to those of the reactant molecule.[33]

The picture was vague and qualitative, and Dumas clearly had no intention of using it either for purposes of prediction or for detailed explanation; perhaps its greatest utility was in demonstrating how complicated the system of molecular arrangement and molecular forces might be, and hence in removing these problems from immediate consideration. In 1868 Dumas stated explicitly that the theory of types had led to a recognition of the complexity of the problem of chemical affinity, and to a corresponding lessening of enthusiasm for and confidence in the search for a detailed theory of affinity within the chemists' fold.[34] His own concern with structural factors reflected the fragmentation of the concept of chemical affinity.

With this reminder of the role of structural factors, Auguste Laurent may be introduced.

II. Auguste Laurent

In 1836 Laurent entered the debate with his doctoral thesis,[35] presenting a new theory of organic combination, while criticizing the two main theories then current: dualism and the unitary theory.

Dualism assumed that certain groups which existed preformed before reaction were preserved thereafter. For example, potassium sulphate could be regarded as consisting of two groups, the negative and acidic group SO^3 and the positive basic oxide group KO. These groups existed preformed, and potassium sulphate arose when they combined.

To this theory, Laurent raised two distinct objections of his own, and another put forward by his contemporary Baudrimont. Baudrimont's objection was that chemical reaction involved the movement of atoms, altering their relative positions. How, then, could one infer anything about the relative positions of atoms in a compound from the reactions which the compound underwent?

---

[33] See note 31.
[34] *Ann. Chim. Phys.*, **15**, 89–90, 1868.
[35] Acad. des Sciences MS. Laurent, 1836. Part of this was published in *Ann. Chim. Phys.*, **61**, 125, 1836; the remainder is now available in the *Bulletin de la Société chimique de France*, Documentation 31, 1954, edited and introduced by J. Jacques. Dumas was one of Laurent's examiners.

Laurent's first argument was that the ideal chemical formula should express the totality of reactions undergone by a compound. But most chemical substances behave differently with different reagents and under different conditions, so that it was hard to select a satisfactory formula from the available alternatives. Although Laurent did not know it, the same difficulty troubled Berzelius.[36]

Laurent's second objection, distinctive of his approach to chemistry, was based on crystallographic arguments.[37] Many French crystallographers at this date still accepted Haüy's ideas, or others derived therefrom about crystal structure, postulating macroscopic crystals built up from molecular groups of related regular geometric form.[38] The basic building blocks were few in number—Haüy proposed three "primitive forms".[39] For example, suitable arrangements of cubic nuclei could yield dodecahedra, pyramids, etc. If one accepted this picture of crystal structure, then dualism, with its implicit concept of preformation, raised a serious difficulty. How could two separate molecules, with different crystalline forms, combine to give a third molecule whose crystalline form might well be incompatible, in terms of symmetry, with its constituents? The problem, earlier touched upon by Ampère, was one troubling to mineralogists in their search for a classification of mineral species, but generally ignored by chemists.[40] In America James Dwight Dana gave a clear statement of the problem in his *System of Mineralogy*, pointing out that compound molecules, similar in form to their crystals:

> cannot be formed by the *juxtaposition* of atoms. An atom of sulphur, the primary of which is the *rhombic octahedron*, united to an atom of lead, whose primary is the *regular octahedron*, could not in any way be made to receive the cubic form of galena; nor, were the molecules equal spheres, would it be a less difficult task—at least eight equal spheres would be required.[41]

In other words, Haüy's kind of crystallography could only work with preformation in chemistry when modified to admit compound units. Laurent

---

[36] See note 7.

[37] See *Acknowledgements*.

[38] J. C. Burke, *Origins of the science of crystals*, Berkeley and Los Angeles, 1966, p. 86.

[39] R. J. Haüy, *Traité de Minéralogie*, Paris, 1801, p. 31. This is discussed by D. C. Goodman, "Problems in crystallography in the early nineteenth century", *Ambix*, **16**, 152–66, 1969.

[40] There were exceptions to this generalization, both prior to and after Laurent, e.g. F. S. Beudant, *J. Soc. Arts*, **6**, 117, 1819, was concerned with the connexion between crystalline form and chemical composition, while Dumas, *Ann. Chim. Phys.*, [4], **15**, 93, 1868, was still worried about the relation of crystalline form to atomic arrangement.

[41] J. D. Dana, *System of Mineralogy*, 2nd ed., New York/London, 1844, p. 76.

came to adopt this conclusion, employing compound elemental "atoms".[42] Since he had worked under Dumas, who was interested in Ampère's ideas, a possible chain of influence is strongly suggested. This suggestion is strengthened by Laurent's reliance, in working out chemical formulae as a tool for classification, upon the hypothesis of Ampère–Avogadro.[43]

In 1836, however, Laurent seems not to have advocated compound atoms as a solution of the difficulty. Nor was he willing to accept the notion that in crystals the atoms were symmetrically disposed, without regard to their possible modes of combination; this would be sterile for chemistry, however much it simplified the problems of crystallographers. Strict dualism was untenable, for the reasons already given; but there was some evidence of the existence of regularly occurring groups within molecules—for example, Laurent thought that the constancy of colour through a series of salts, differing from the constancy of colour through another series of salts of the same metal, was due to the persistence of a particular group of atoms.

So far Laurent had merely criticized existing arguments; having cleared the ground, he was ready to propose his own theory, a compromise between dualism and the unitary theory. He stated his thesis compactly:

> When a molecule, containing atoms grouped according to a certain form, is confronted with another molecule, the atoms influenced by the presence of the new molecule adopt another arrangement, but without being withdrawn from their reciprocal influence; the same is true of the atoms of the new molecule.

It followed that, "in combining, the two molecules must thus lose their form, *but* the atoms of one of them do not pass into the other".

Laurent's detailed exposition of his thesis explains this passage. The model he offers for describing organic combination is a structural one, related to crystallography. He regards organic molecules as made up of a central radical, the structural kernel, surrounded by an external complex which can be modified in reaction without being destroyed. The kernel or nucleus of the molecule determines the group of compounds to which the molecule belongs, and it is resistant to modification. On the other hand, if it loses as much as as a single atom, it is destroyed, and the product molecules belong to different chemical classes. The external complex, the superstructure of the molecule, is, however, open to change, so that, for example, a hydrogen atom outside the nucleus may be replaced by a chlorine atom, without a change in chemical class or type.[44] This model gave a useful basis for a chemical classification.

---

[42] E.g. to explain allotropy; see below.

[43] Laurent, *Chemical Method*, translated by W. Odling, London, 1855, pp. 65–6, 68. Laurent's adherence to the hypothesis dates at least from the mid-1840's.

[44] This is all taken from Laurent's thesis; see note 35.

It also implied that the place of the individual atoms within a molecular structure was more important than the electrical nature of these atoms. Before going on, I shall briefly underline the major methodological features of the debate at this juncture. First, Laurent and Berzelius are both assuming, as a working rule, that there is some analogy between organic and inorganic chemistry; they differ with respect to the direction in which this analogy is to be applied, Berzelius starting out from the inorganic realm, Laurent from the organic. In both cases, the analogies are pursued as likely to be fruitful for chemistry. Thus far, the division is clean and clear.

The picture becomes somewhat complicated by Laurent's indebtedness to the French crystallographic tradition for his ideas on organic combination; this tradition was an inorganic one, though not in the line of Berzelius' dualism. Furthermore, Laurent himself constantly referred to inorganic substitution or isomorphous replacement as closely comparable with organic substitution.[45] Since the former had been known for more than a decade before Laurent developed his ideas,[46] it is reasonable to suppose that he drew his analogy from the prior theory; in which case, he *was* using analogies from inorganic chemistry, for guidance in organic chemistry. Berzelius was unhappy when he came to read Laurent's papers, simply because of the latter's neglect of the special analogies from electrochemical dualism.

Laurent was to insist repeatedly that organic substitution could be described in terms of the *isomorphism* of different substituents, such as that of chlorine with hydrogen, hydrogen with ammonium.[47] This emphasis led to his use, ever more confident, of structural models. He believed that structure determined reactivity, and was directly connected with crystalline form. Papers continued to flow from him on this connexion, and on the relation of form to constitution.[48] Systematic arrangement, recognizing these connexions, produced a simple classification of all substances, precisely similar to those of mineral chemistry—given Laurent's own classification of mineral substances![49]

Laurent and Berzelius started to correspond in 1843, both giving full and revealing statements of their positions. Laurent began[50] by seeking to persuade Berzelius that they really shared a great deal of common ground; both of

---

[45] E.g. *Comptes Rendus*, **20**, 357–66, 1845.
[46] Mitscherlich produced his first paper on isomorphism in 1819; *Abhl. Akad. Berlin*, 1818–19, 427; trans. in *Ann. Chim.*, **14**, 172, 1820.
[47] E.g. *Comptes Rendus*, **11**, 876, 1840; *ibid.*, **12**, 1193, 1841.
[48] E.g. *ibid.*, **15**, 350–2, 1842.
[49] *Ibid.*, **17**, 311–12, 1843.
[50] Berzelius, *Bref* (note 7), VII, pp. 181–5, letter of 12 May 1843.

them, for instance, were definite in their refusal to accept the idea of substitution in relation to Dumas' *mechanical* types, substitution products with similar chemical formulae but differing in chemical properties. Laurent went so far as to agree with Berzelius that substitution did lead to some change in properties, even when the type was preserved. In small molecules, an isomorphically–introduced substituent might produce a large mechanical imbalance, with a corresponding change in properties. Large molecules could absorb the mechanical disturbance much more readily, and hence isatin and chlorisatin, for example, scarcely differed in their chemical behaviour.

Berzelius, in return, admitted to some common ground, but insisted that he could not consider chlorine "as having adopted the nature of hydrogen, since chlorine always will remain chlorine", even though this retention of individual atomic electrical character might be masked by the phenomena which were classed under the heading of copulation or conjugation.[51]

It was probably then that Laurent read Berzelius' memoir on the allotropy of elemental substances, which referred to different states of the elements.[52] Laurent considered that these different "atomic" states, responsible for differences in chemical reactivity (different degrees of affinity, as Berzelius would have phrased it), were due to the molecular nature of elemental "atoms", so called; different arrangements of the constituent particles would result in different properties.[53] Berzelius, in contrast, based his methodology on the notion of atomic properties derived from experiments in inorganic chemistry. He therefore refused to believe that affinity could arise from structural factors derived from the obscure depths of speculations about organic compounds. He did not deny the potential usefulness of Laurent's approach, but insisted that, since it was diametrically opposed to his own, there would be no point in pursuing the correspondence. "It will be best", he concluded, "if we each follow our own route amicably, in the hope that science will draw profit from both".[54]

In the early 1840's, Laurent entered into another vigorous correspondence, more lasting and more fruitful than that with Berzelius. He exchanged long and frequent letters with Charles Gerhardt,[55] and soon, privately and publicly,

---

[51] *Ibid.*, pp. 188 ff., 20 October 1843.
[52] Published in translation in [*Taylor's*] *Scientific Memoirs*, **4**, 240–52, 1846, from *Jahres-Bericht* (1840), **20**, ii, 13, 1841.
[53] Berzelius, *Bref* (note 7), VII, p. 200, 5 January 1844.
[54] *Ibid.*, p. 208, 25 June 1844.
[55] The Laurent–Gerhardt correspondence is published in M. Tiffeneau (ed.), *Correspondance de Charles Gerhardt*, 2 vols., vol. i, Paris, 1918; E. Grimaux and C. Gerhardt junr., *Charles Gerhardt, sa vie, son oeuvre, sa correspondance*, Paris, 1900.

explained his attitude towards the structural models underlying his work. Laurent wrote in 1844 that:

> I do not claim to represent by my formulae the real arrangement of atoms. . . . Certainly, ideas on molecular arrangement have guided me in the system I expound; but one can, if one wishes, regard it as an abstraction, and see in my formulae only symbols, whose aspect recalls not only the nature and the composition of the bodies they represent, but also the series to which the body belongs, and the place it should occupy within the series.[56]

The formulae to which Laurent here refers are his "synoptic formulae", very different from the formulae of the dualists;

> I employ *synoptic formulae*, by the aid of which, I endeavour to manifest certain numerical relations presented by seriated bodies, and to give to analogous bodies analogous formulae. Thus, if I accorded to the sulphates this formula,
>
> $$SM^2 + O^4, [M = metal]$$
>
> and if I considered sulphatic ether as a sulphate, I should represent it also by
>
> $$SEt^2 + O^4,$$
>
> but if, on the contrary, I regarded it as a diamide, I should give to it the formula of the diamides. Be the formula that I employ what it may, for example that of the diamides, it might be considered as a hypothesis; for it is not demonstrated to the satisfaction of every one, that this ether really is a diamide.
>
> But on attentive examination it will be seen, that we have not to ascertain, whether in this ether there is such or such an atomic arrangement, but simply to determine, whether it has the properties of a salt or of a diamide. Here then, we are in the land of experiment.[57]

Laurent's formulae were *not* intended to indicate particular atomic arrangements—only the dualists presumed so far with their formulae. Laurent was content to construct formulae indicating analogies, and his structural ideas were merely used to suggest a theory of combination which would make sense of organic reactions, thereby facilitating chemical classification. He poked gentle fun at Gerhardt for his determination to avoid dealing with the arrangement of atoms in molecules, for such ideas, as Laurent clearly saw, were implicit in Gerhardt's work in a host of cases, and dominated him in spite

[56] Laurent, *Comptes Rendus*, **19**, 1098–9, 1844.
[57] *Chemical Method* (note 43), pp. 347–8.

of himself—all the more perniciously because Gerhardt thought he had banished them.[58]

Laurent and Gerhardt were agreed in rejecting the "rational" formulae of the dualists, and Laurent urged his friend to join him in constructing synoptic formulae "indicating relations of class and of properties. The others will look for formulae denoting arrangement, and we shall be able to attack them, at least until they find the *true formula*. But they are not there yet".[59] In the same year, 1845, he repeated his conviction that chemical substances owed their properties largely to their arrangement—which implied that formulae classifying bodies according to their properties would also classify them according to their internal arrangement. "We do not know what this grouping is. Shall we always be ignorant? Who knows?"[60] Laurent was convinced that the ideal goal of chemical research was a classification which would show how chemical properties were related to molecular arrangement.[61] His conviction that arrangement, although unknown, was influential over chemical properties, emerged repeatedly in his publications.[62] Arrangement was not the source of atomic properties, but rather the factor which modified these properties so as to determine the final properties of the molecular aggregate.

For example,[63] in 1846 he discussed the reactions between hydrogen and bromine, metals and hydrochloric acid, etc., arguing from one-volume formulae. "This volume, for simple bodies, represents one molecule or two atoms". (Note the reliance upon the Ampère-Avogadro hypothesis.) Thus oxygen, hydrogen, water (HH)O, phosphine (PH)(HH), etc., could be expressed as binary compounds. This, of course, did not imply the acceptance of electrochemical dualism; it was meaningless to ascribe a polar structure to the diatomic hydrogen molecule. Laurent suggested that the binary association of atoms perhaps allowed one to explain, to some extent, the affinity possessed by bodies in their nascent state. Let B,B′ be bromine atoms, and H,H′ hydrogen atoms. Mix BB′ with HH′, and the affinity of B for B′ will perhaps be enough, when joined to that of H for H′, to prevent combination; but if only atomic B and H are present, then there is no affinity to be overcome, and combination occurs readily.[64] Thus individual atomic properties were

---

[58] Laurent to Gerhardt, 4 July 1844, in Tiffeneau, *op. cit.* (55), I, p. 5.

[59] Laurent to Gerhardt, 19 April 1845, in *Charles Gerhardt* (note 55), p. 483.

[60] *Ibid.*, p. 487, Laurent to Gerhardt, 11 May 1845.

[61] *Ibid.*, p. 495, Laurent to Gerhardt, 29 May 1845.

[62] E.g. *Comptes Rendus*, **20**, 357–66, 850–5, 1845.

[63] *Ann. Chim.* [Series 3], **18**, 266–98, 1846.

[64] Cf. *Chemical Method*, pp. 69–70.

significant, but were subordinated to arrangement and to modes of combination. In 1849 Laurent stressed that the idea of different substances playing
the same role was "the most important part of my system, and the one which
the chemists will have the most difficulty in admitting".[65]

Laurent frequently used hypotheses—and this is just the point. He *used*
them, but tried to make his *classification* independent of them. "Such of them
as are to be met with [in my work]", he wrote towards the end of his life,
"are isolated, and may be left entirely on one side, without any detriment
to the progress of the work".[66] He defined the idea of causality in chemistry
as that of atoms and of their arrangement,[67] and added, in Galilean vein,
"I do not reject research after causes, although these may form perhaps but
a perpetual mirage, destined to impel us incessantly to an exploration of new
countries".[68] He did not expect answers to his questions about causes, but
he asked them, because the search for answers was fruitful—and a theory
was to be praised for its fruitfulness, or condemned for its sterility, not judged
as right or wrong.[69] Ultimate answers were going to remain hidden, and Laurent
was sure that his chemical classification was the important part of his contribution to chemical science.[70]

In 1854 Laurent's only extended account of his ideas received posthumous
publication, under the title of *Méthode de Chimie*. In the following year an
English version appeared, translated and introduced by William Odling, who
believed "the generalities of Laurent to be in our day as important as those
of Lavoisier were to his".[71] Laurent had introduced his book as an endeavour
to establish a method, "that is to say, a system of formulae, a classification
and a nomenclature, having the advantages of systems based upon facts, *and*
of those based upon hypotheses, but without their disadvantages".[72] The
hypotheses in the book (and there are many, dealing with molecular atoms,
substitution mechanisms and crystallographic hints) are mostly separable
from the classification.

---

[65] Institut de France, MS. 2379.
[66] *Chemical Method*, p. xv.
[67] *Ibid.*
[68] *Ibid.*, p. xvi.
[69] This is a constant theme throughout Laurent's work, from his doctoral thesis (where
he rejects symmetrical disposition of atoms with no preferred combinations because this
leads nowhere) to his *Chemical Method*, where he rejects a chemistry based merely upon
facts (p. xv) because this, too, leads nowhere.
[70] Cf. *Chemical Method*, p. 34.
[71] *Ibid.*, p. viii.
[72] *Ibid.*, p. xv.

Towards the end of the book, Laurent came out with an explicit statement of the relation between atomic properties and structural factors:

> I admit with all chemists, *that the properties of compound bodies depend upon the nature, the number, and the arrangement of atoms.* But I admit, moreover, *that order or arrangement has frequently a greater influence upon the properties of the body, than has the nature of the material of which it is composed.*[73]

After a detailed exposition of a series of reactions undergone by aniline and its derivatives, he concluded that mere consideration of affinities, independent of atomic arrangement, led to incorrect conclusions about chemical change. Laurent found this scarcely surprising: "What, moreover, do we know with regard to affinity?"[74]

Throughout this book,[75] as through the rest of his work, Laurent constantly stressed that arrangements of atoms, although unknown, were directly correlated with properties and reactions. The cardinal sin of dualism was that it attempted to ascribe a unique formulation and structure to each substance.[76]

Laurent had written to Gerhardt in 1845 that it was impossible to ascribe unique structural formulae to compounds, not because they did not have a determinate structure, but because: "It seems to me impossible, for the present, to represent a three-dimensional atomic arrangement by a linear formula".[77] Most chemists at that time, being unconcerned with crystallography, were unaccustomed even to thinking of structure in three dimensions—their preoccupation seems to have been more with the order in which atoms were joined, like links in a chain, not bricks in a house. Laurent, aware of these and other difficulties, used his synoptic formulae. Such formulae were amenable to arrangement in series; but it is clear that Laurent intended his formulae to relate to more than formal analogies of composition:

> by following out the system of volumes we obtain *the formulae which afford the greatest degree of simplicity; which best recall the analogies of bodies; which accord best with the boiling point and isomorphism; which allow the metamorphoses to be explained in the most simple manner, etc.; and, in a word, satisfy completely the requirements of chemists.*[78]

---

[73] *Ibid.*, pp. 321–22.

[74] *Ibid.*, p. 344.

[75] E.g. on p. 268 he sets down, as a principle to be proved, that: "*In the arrangement of atoms there is a predisposition, by which we are enabled to account for the chemical properties of certain compound bodies*".

[76] Or rather, different dualists were equally vigorous in advancing their own "unique" formulae; see discussion, *Chemical Method*, pp. 17–33.

[77] Laurent to Gerhardt, 25 March 1845, in *Charles Gerhardt* (note 55), p. 481.

[78] *Chemical Method*, p. 72.

In other words, although the only thing that he absolutely requires from his formulae, and the only thing which he will confidently infer from them, is analogy of composition, he still believes that these analogies are related to all other analogies between the various chemical and physical properties of bodies, and that chemists should bear in mind this overall unity of their subject in framing their laws and classifications. Analogies suggested by physical properties, especially those connected with crystallography, are, after the formal analogies of composition, those with which he makes the most play. Structural arguments are thus dominant.

This was his leading idea, and one whose heuristic value he clearly recognized. As he wrote to his friend and collaborator Gerhardt, ideas are essential to progress in science.

> Without a dominant idea, it is impossible to do anything. Do you ever get anything from your classification? No, nothing, absolutely nothing, because there is no idea there. A classification should offer a series of relations. And I am persuaded that, whatever the point of departure, one always arrives at interesting connexions. But still one must start out from an idea.[79]

Laurent's guiding idea, that crystallography[80] was somehow intimately connected with chemistry, and that crystallographic ideas would be fruitful for the whole of chemistry, was sound. His use of physical analogies to suggest chemical ones is noteworthy at a time when many chemists were oblivious of any significant connexion between chemistry and physics.

Conclusion

Dumas and Laurent have served as the principal actors in this narrative. They, with Gerhardt, were largely responsible for breaking the monopoly which dualistic ideas had held in chemistry.

At the beginning of the 1850's the theory of types and the radical theory were still at odds. The main difference between them at this stage was precisely the difference between Laurent and Berzelius: Arrangement versus Chemical

---

[79] Laurent to Gerhardt, 12 February 1845, in *Charles Gerhardt* (note 55), p. 474.

[80] Laurent's interest in crystallography went beyond his frequent references in publication (e.g. *Chemical Method*, pp. 129–56); he also compiled for students a *Précis de Cristallographie, suivi d'une méthode simple d'analyse au chalumeau*, Paris, 1847. Laurent's degree of commitment to structural arguments did in fact vary somewhat between 1836 and 1853. For example, his correspondence with Gerhardt in 1846–8 indicates a weakening of confidence in such arguments (*Correspondance*, note 55, I). These fluctuations do not affect the conclusions of this paper.

126

Nature. As the theory of types was repeatedly modified, and relative dualism was re-admitted to the chemical arena, a number of chemists[81] were able to reconcile the radical theory, based on a dualistic conception of affinity, with the theory of types, in which implicit structural concepts supplanted conventional ideas about affinity. In 1853 Liebig wrote to Gerhardt that "it is very strange that the two theories, formerly quite opposed, are now combined in one which explains all the phenomena in the two senses".[82] It should, however, be stressed that this seeming reconciliation was only effected by the substantial modification of both theories. The radical theory was able to survive only because the term "radical" ceased to indicate a stable and all but immutable organic analogue of the inorganic elements, and began to refer to something less stable; the "new" radical permitted substitutions to take place and its properties were capable of being modified by neighbouring substances in combination. Similarly, Berzelius' comparatively rigid electrochemical dualism, whether conventional or realistic, had yielded to the relative dualism of Gerhardt. The latter, being no longer absolute,[83] could serve reliably neither in a normative nor in a predictive role, but could be used only for *post hoc* explanations. Structural analogies suggested by the theory of types had meanwhile been recognized as representing less than the whole truth, and atomic properties began to re-assert themselves in the formulation of chemical theory, including valence theory.[84]

Acknowledgements

An earlier version of this paper was read to the History of Science Dinner Club, Toronto, in December 1969. I should like to thank an anonymous referee for a number of valuable comments, and especially for his stress upon the importance of crystallographic ideas for an understanding of Laurent's work.

[81] E.g. Bunsen, Frankland, Williamson, Hofmann. See T. H. Levere, *Affinity and Matter*, in press, ch. vi.

[82] Quoted by J. R. Partington, *A History of Chemistry*, London, 1964, vol. iv, p. 460.

[83] Gerhardt, *Précis de chimie organique*, 2 vols., Paris, 1844–5, vol. ii, pp. 495–6, admitted that the atoms of different elements did have, relatively to one another, differing electrical properties. Sometimes combination took place in a manner which could be correlated with the distance of two bodies from one another on the electrical scale; however, the opposite was sometimes true, and this, as Gerhardt noted, directly contradicted the ideas of the dualists as they were generally understood. It was essential, he argued, to realize that a classification of bodies based on their electrical properties could not be absolute, and could not, therefore, be used for the purpose of prediction.

[84] These assertions are developed and supported in Levere, *op. cit.* (81), chapters 5 and 6.

XVIII

Gay-Lussac and the Problem of Chemical Qualities

Abstract:

Two principal eighteenth-century modes of explaining chemical qualities, one through the chemical doctrine of principles, the other through essentially physical concepts, were variously taken up and modified by Lavoisier and Dalton. The theory of qualities that emerged following their work was essentially a chemical rather than a physical one, and it soon ran into difficulties. Berthollet's approach to chemistry sought a more physical account of chemical qualities than Lavoisier's, and Gay-Lussac, his disciple in the Society of Arcueil, attempted to resolve some of the problems raised by Lavoisier through the development of aspects of Berthollet's program. In doing so, he found himself working in increasing rivalry with Humphry Davy, who, starting with initially different assumptions and problems from Gay-Lussac, found himself in partial agreement with his rival over the problem of chemical qualities. It goes without saying that their running debate concentrated on their illuminating differences, rather than their equally illuminating agreements. This paper attempts to recognize both.

The problem of accounting for the chemical qualities of different kinds of matter is as old as chemistry. Two essentially distinct kinds of explanation were possible in principle and advocated in practice: one could either seek to subsume chemistry epistemologically under another science, or one could propose specifically chemical accounts of chemical qualities. Gay-Lussac inherited an explanatory framework that drew on both kinds of explanation. As one whose work developed partly within the society of Arcueil, even, as Michelle Sadoun-Goupil has written, Berthollet's spiritual son, Gay-Lussac worked with concepts deriving from eighteenth-century Newtonianism and from doctrines of chemical affinity and chemical principles.[1] He wanted to quantify chemistry where he could, in a complex operation that endeavoured to fuse two approaches often kept apart prior to Lavoisier's work, and even there only partially combined.

In this paper, I shall first discuss briefly two principal and familiar eighteenth-century modes of accounting for chemical qualities, and shall indicate how these were taken up by Lavoisier and Dalton. My purpose in going over such well known terrain is to define categories basic to the subsequent argument. The theory of qualities that emerged around the turn of the century was a chemical rather than a physical one; and it soon ran into difficulties, whose consideration may serve as a prelude to an account of Gay-Lussac's own attempts at resolving the problem. It will become clear as I proceed that Gay-Lussac's debates with Davy forced both of them to focus more intently on the problem of chemical qualities, and that, in following their debates, I am especially indebted to the researches of Maurice Crosland.[2]

Georg Ernst Stahl in the eighteenth century was well aware of English mechanistic attempts to explain chemical qualities. He considered that these attempts, whether deriving from Boyle's or Descartes's version of corpuscular philosophy, or from dynamic explanations in Newton's 31st query to the *Opticks*, were inadequate, for they only scratched the surface of things. What was needed was an explicitly chemical approach.[3]. A prominent feature of eighteenth-century chemistry in France and in Germany was the drive for the autonomy of chemistry from mechanism, and also from medicine, disciplines to which it had been subordinated in the preceding decades.[4] Two concepts were prominent in the assertion of this autonomy: affinity, and property-bearing elements or principles.

These two concepts between them gave chemistry a methodology and classification that were interdependent. Substances could be classified according to their properties, which were caused by their constitutent principles, and by their reactions, dependent upon their properties, and summarized in tables of affinities. The sterility of corpuscular chemistry, in which theory, practice and classification had no clear meeting ground, was now surmounted. When Lavoisier wrote his *Traité Elémentaire de Chimie*, he declined to treat the "science of affinities", which he described as holding "the same place with regard to the other branches of chemistry, as the higher or transcendental geometry does with respect to the simpler and elementary part". Moreover, he considered that all all that could be said "upon the number and nature of elements is ... confined to discussions entirely of a metaphysical nature". But although he refused to discuss the theory of these concepts in his treatise, he tabulated the combinations of bodies according to their affinities, approaching the problem of composition in an established eighteenth-century chemical tradition. He also made use of the old chemical concept of "principle", identifying and naming oxygen as the acidifying principle.[5] As Crosland has pointed out, Lavoisier's oxygen theory was "as much a theory of acidity as a theory of combustion", and it is also important to remark that oxygen was only a potentially acidifying principle for Lavoisier, its presence being a necessary but not a sufficient condition for the formation of an acid.[6]. That chemical qualities could be accounted for by the presence or particular chemical principles was an idea that, if true, might be valid for more than acidity. Berthollet had analyzed ammonia, and had shown that nitrogen or azote was its main constituent. The composition of the other alkalis was then unknown, but Lavoisier observed that "analogy leads us to suspect that azote is a constituent element of all of the alkalis" - by implication, it might be the principle of alkalinity.[7]

All this was strictly in the chemical tradition. But there was another aspect of Lavoisier's work that made chemistry once again more nearly a branch of physics, or at least of *physique*. The first part of his treatise deals with changes of state and discusses the relation of gases to solids in terms of interest to chemist and physicist alike. His collaboration with Laplace, his emphasis upon deductive geometrical reasoning in chemistry, and his extensive use of apparatus novel in chemistry but akin to the familiar apparatus for demonstration used by experimental Newtonians, all represented departures from established chemical paths.[8] These two aspects of Lavoisier's work, one traditionally chemical, the other novel and physical, could suggest that the development of chemistry might come to some extent through the application of physical methods to chemical problems, that nevertheless would remain strictly chemical. That is surely what one finds in the work of Berthollet and others in the Society of Arcueil — Gay-Lussac among them. One other development in chemical theory needs to be taken into account at this juncture: John Dalton's atomic theory. Dalton postulated a fundamental chemical heterogeneity of matter that, by ignoring forces, ran counter to mechanism, and his way of quantifying chemistry simply side-stepped problems of chemical affinity. What was new was not Dalton's atomism, but the simplicity and explicitness of his theory.[9] Thus there were fundamental differences in emphasis between the Society of Arcueil and Dalton. But the wide-spread existence of definite combining proportions was powerful support for a chemical atomic theory, and had corresponding implications for explanations of chemical qualities. The debate between Gay-Lussac, Davy, and Berzelius about the composition of ammonia amalgam revolved in part about the application of Dalton's laws, and, as we shall see, was important in the debate about alkalinity. There was, however, a more immediate and more general implication. Dalton had opened up what Lavoisier had regarded as the transcendental and metaphysical parts of chemistry. If chemical elements, differing in their qualities, were distinguished from one another by the different weights of their constituent atoms, and if compounds were formed by the regular arrangement of groups of atoms, then differences in chemical qualities might be caused either by differences in chemical composition, or by differences in the arrangement of constituent atoms, or by some combination of these two factors. And if arrangement was a factor, then a form of mechanism could survive in chemistry. Here, in spite of fundamental differences with the school of Arcueil, were possible grounds for a meeting of the two approaches. Both approaches were to feature in Gay-Lussac's controversies about chemical qualities. If one adopted a narrowly chemical theory, then differences in qualities had to be attributed to different constituent elements, whether these were regarded as atoms or principles.[10] There was, however, some evidence even before 1800 that this explanation was inadequate. Smithson Tennant's experiments on the diamond, for example, showed that a given weight of diamond would yield very nearly the same amount of carbon dioxide as Lavoisier had obtained by burning the same weight of charcoal in oxygen.[11] The difficulty was that the results were only very nearly the same. Exact equivalence would have made it possible to claim arrangement or mode of composition as the source of difference in chemical qualities. As it was, however, impure materials or imprecise analyses made it appear that several substances generally considered elementary after 1789 might in fact be compounds. Humphry Davy, as late as 1809, argued that diamond probably contained a minute amount of hydrogen, to which it owed its distinctive properties – a view that he was later to reject, with a consequent change in his account of chemical qualities. In 1809, however, he believed that not only was diamond compound, but that charcoal contained minute amounts of hydrogen, that sulphur in its common state contained both hydrogen and oxygen, that phosphorus was compound, and that, in general, "minute differences in chemical composition may produce great differences in external and physical characteristics".[12] Davy's results, or rather the analyses on which they were based, were disputed by Gay-Lussac and Thenard, who found no evidence for the compound nature of phosphorus and sulphur.

Davy's view at this date, however faulty its basis, was essentially a chemical one, in line with the doctrine of principles. The most fully developed theory in this tradition was Lavoisier's oxygen theory of acidity, which by then had received some criticism but was widely accepted. As late as 1814, when Gay-Lussac was developing a much more sophisticated account of chemical qualities in general and of acidity in particular, he stated that all bodies were neutral, or acidic, or alkaline; water was neutral, and since oxygen was acidic, it followed that hydrogen was alkaline. This statement occurs in Gay-Lussac's memoir on iodine,[13] and in order not to distort his argument, I shall discuss it later in some detail. Lavoisier's very tentatively adumbrated nitrogen theory of alkalinity attracted much less support, and the definition of alkalinity in relation to acidity made the latter the focus of debate. There were steadily more objections to the oxygen theory of acidity. Davy, as early as 1800, had remarked that nitric oxide contained proportionately more oxygen than nitrous oxide, but was nevertheless lacking in acidity.[14]. The problem of the relation between acidity and proportional oxygen content was one to which Gay-Lussac would give particular attention in 1814. Meanwhile, it was clear that there also appeared to be substances that were acidic but lacked oxygen. One has to remember both the role of oxygen as a potentially acidifying principle, and the logical point, made by Berthollet in his *Essai de Statique Chimique*, that the fact that oxygen conferred acidity on many substances didn't mean that no substance could be acidic without it .[15] Once more, Gay-Lussac in 1814 extended this observation: many bodies, he noted, shared acidity with oxygen, and it was better to define acids as bodies which neutralized alkalis – an empirical definition – than to pursue the search for a definition based on principles embodying chemical functions.[16] Davy's work on the alkalis, and his erroneous analyses of ammonia amalgam, led him to the view that oxygen "may be considered as existing in, and as forming, an element in all true alkalies".[17] Subsequent demonstrations that chlorine was not an oxy-compound were scarcely needed to ensure the demise of the oxygen theory of acidity.

That theory was, however, as Crosland has argued, a perfectly tenable one when Lavoisier proposed it. Phosphorus, sulphur, carbon, and nitrogen all formed oxy-acids, and it seemed reasonable to extend the argument by analogy, and to reach Lavoisier's conclusions. Argument from analogy would also be used in the application of the law of multiple proportions.[18] But analogy had its limitations, especially when used by one's opponents. Gay-Lussac and Thenard, criticizing Davy's work on ammonia amalgam, observed "that the most probable conclusions are those which best agree with the general analogy of chemistry". In 1814 Gay-Lussac again stressed the virtues of analogy, while cautioning the reader that one should not follow analogies too blindly. Davy, who was himself as willing as anyone to follow analogies, could not abide his rival's use of them. "The substitution of analogy for fact is the bane of chemical philosophy", he exclaimed. "The legitimate use of analogy is to connect facts together, and to guide to new experiments".[19]

If the oxygen theory of acidity was founded on inadequate analogies, then a new and stronger basis was needed for the theory of acidity in particular, and of chemical qualities in general. Following their initial electrochemical researches, Davy and Berzelius both for a while found a solution in the electrical characteristics of the component parts of bodies. Davy, for example, asserted in 1808 that there was a coincidence of certain chemical and electrical states of matter:

Thus acids are uniformly negative, allkalis positive, and inflammable substances highly positive; and as I have found, acid matter when negatively electrified, seems to lose all their peculiar properties and powers of combination. In these circumstances, the chemical qualities are shown to depend on the electrical powers, and it is not impossible that matter of the same kind, possessed of different electrical powers, may exhibit different chemical forms.[20]

The Académie des Sciences had awarded Davy a prize for his electrochemical researches. Napoleon, piqued as this, had a huge voltaic pile built and entrusted to Gay-Lussac and Thenard.[21] Their interpretation of the facts did not induce them to follow Davy and Berzelius in their view of chemical qualities. As Gay-Lussac observed in 1814, acidity and alkalinity were relative terms. The same body could function sometimes as an acid, sometimes as an alkali, and so one had to consider not only the electrical character of the substance in question, whether positive or negative, but also the character of the substance in relation to which it was being defined.[22] Acidity and alkalinity were correlative and inseparable properties. Such concern for the relation and interplay of forces was typical of the combination of physics and chemistry pursued at Arcueil, and marks Gay-Lussac once again as the heir of Berthollet. It was this approach that made Gay-Lussac ready to consider the interaction of different factors in producing a single result, and that at the same time impelled him towards quantification wherever possible. Gay-Lussac's law of combining volumes is one fruit of this endeavour. His studies of metallic oxides were similarly motivated by the desire to find regularities, preferably quantifiable ones, in chemical behaviour. He first found that those metallic oxides which best neutralized acids were in general able to precipitate others from solution. Further researches led him to conclude in 1808 that the capacity of metals for acids was inversely proportional to the quantity of oxygen that their oxides contained, when one considered corresponding degrees of oxidation. It followed that, for example, if copper needed to combine with twice as much oxygen as lead did in order to dissolve in an acid, then the saturation of a given quantity of acid required twice as much lead as copper.[23] These results served as prelude to an excursus note on acidity and alkality published in 1814 in his masterly paper on iodine.[24].Proportional composition, ratios, saturation, and neutralization were all important concepts in his discussion. Gay-Lussac began by dividing substances into neutral compounds, and acids and bases. In the former, the reciprocal properties of the components disappeared completely. Ethers, for example, could be considered as composed of two preformed parts, an acid and an alcohol, which perservered in the compound even though their properties or qualities were lost. In acids or bases, this loss of qualities was only partial, and the reciprocal properties of one of the components still showed. The notion of preformation was fundamental here, as it was in most nineteenth-century chemistry prior to the work of Laurent and Gerhardt in the development of organic chemistry. So too, it seemed, although in much diluted, even transmuted form, was the concept of principles, substances embodying chemical functions. We have already seen that the neutrality of water and the essential acidity of hydrogen implied for Gay-Lussac the alkalinity of hydrogen. But many oxides were alkaline, presumably because of their constituent metals. Here were grounds for one major modification of the concept of principles. Where oxides of the same substance ranged from basic to acidic, the acidic oxides were mostly those with the highest proportion of oxygen. This suggested to Gay-Lussac that oxygen lost or kept its character, according to the proportions in which it entered into combination.[25] The parallel with Berthollet's work on chemical statics is striking. Gay-Lussac then went on to consider acidic and neutral gaseous oxides, looking at carbon and nitrogen, and considering their formation in terms of volumes of reactants and products. The results of these considerations were complex; for example, it appeared that the combination of one volume of oxygen with one volume of members of "a certain class of bodies" would yield an acid, if and only if the condensation of elements was equal to half the total volume of the reactants.[26]

Not only was this kind of observation a continuation of the kind of quantification in which Gay-Lussac had already achieved success; it was also crucial for his understanding of chemical qualities. The proportion of oxygen in a compound generally affected its character as a neutral, acidic, or basic substance; but the degree of condensation of volume also seemed to be a highly significant factor. For example, two volumes of hydrogen plus one volume of oxygen yielded one volume of neutral water; one volume of nitrogen plus one volume of oxygen yielded two volumes of neutral nitric oxide; while one volume of carbon or sulphur plus one volume of oxygen yielded one volume of acidic gas. Generalising from these and other data, Gay-Lussac observed that when oxygen made up half or more of the total volume, acidity resulted.[27] There is no need to multiply examples in order to demonstrate the consistency of Gay-Lussac's investigation of chemical qualities with his law of combining gas volumes and with the research program developed from Arcueil. His distinction between the quantity of base neutralized by different acids and the energy of that neutralization was again in the same tradition. Without that distinction, he noted, "it would be ... remarkable to see the same quantity of base, whose electrical energy is constant, neutralize very different acids, whose energy varies". Clearly, combining energies were of only secondary importance, and it was necessary to follow Berthollet in considering other factors, such as solubility.[28]

We have already encountered Gay-Lussac's modified concept of principles. He still considered some acids as compounds of oxygen, the acidifying principle, with another element, for example nitrogen, sulphur, or phosphorus. But he admitted the existence of other acids. In hydracids, for example, those formed by the halogens, chlorine and its analogues served as acidifying principles, and Gay-

Lussac postulated an analogous arrangement of atoms within the molecules.[29] Combining all these pieces of evidence, Gay-Lussac was led to conclude "that the neutral, acidic or alkaline character of a compound does not depend solely on the character of its constituents, but is also dependent on their proportions and on their condensations in volume, or, in other words, on the arrangement of their molecules".[30]

1814 was also the year in which Davy's experiments on the combustion of diamond were published. Before these experiments, he had written that "it seems reasonable to expect, that a very refined or perfect chemistry will confirm the analogies of nature, and shew that bodies cannot be the same in composition or chemical nature, and yet totally different in all their chemical properties". After his experiments in Florence, he argued that the identity of composition with chemical nature now seemed "contrary to analogy, and I am more inclined to adopt the opinion or Mr. Tennant, that the difference depends upon crystallization". This was consistent with the view that he had developed in the previous year in his paper on iodine that acidity seemed "to depend upon peculiar combinations of matter, and not on any peculiar elementary principle".[31]

Thus in and around 1814 there was no great distance between Davy's and Gay-Lussac's views on acidity, although Gay-Lussac, more cognizant as he was of the variety of factors influencing chemical qualities, still allowed some role to the nature of constituent atoms. In 1816 Davy attacked this aspect of Gay-Lussac's synthesis, for it seemed to smack of the old chemistry of principles. This, Davy protested, unable to resist so splendid an opening, was

> an attempt to introduce into chemistry a doctrine of occult quantities, and to refer to some mysterious and inexplicable energy what must depend upon a particular corpuscular arrangement.... It is impossible to infer what will be the qualities of a compound from the qualities of its constituents.... When certain properties are found belonging to a compound, we have no right to attribute these properties to any of its elements to the exclusion of the rest, but they must be regarded as a result of combination.[32]

Had Davy read Gay-Lussac's paper more carefully, he might have found greater common ground than he was willing to admit in a French rival. But then he would have lost the chance to win a point in their long-standing game. Winning, for both of them, repeatedly took precedence over all else, and the rules by which they played countenanced strong tactics.[33]

There was one area in which Gay-Lussac's work showed consistent superiority to Davy's – his analyses were never hasty. Davy's tribute to Gay-Lussac very properly recognized his skill in the laboratory :he was, said Davy, "quick, lively, ingenious, and profound, with great activity of mind, and great facility of manipulation. I should place him at the head of the living chemists of France".[34]

When it came to arguments about the accuracy of experimental results, Gay-Lussac was usually right. One topic of protracted debate between Gay-Lussac and Davy bore directly on the problems of alkalinity, acidity, and of chemical qualities in general; this was the composition of ammonia amalgam, and the suppositious constitution of nitrogen. In 1808 Davy had decomposed ammonia, looking for oxygen in it, as analogy with caustic soda and caustic potash suggested. He found what he was looking for.[35] Gay-Lussac and Thenard went on to produce a compound from potassium and ammonia, and an amalgam of potassium, ammonia, and mercury. They initially interpreted the reactions of these compounds as indicating that potassium contained hydrogen, while maintaining with Berthollet that ammonia contained only hydrogen and elemental nitrogen.[36] Similar experiments were carried out by Davy, who kept reinforcing his initial opinion that ammonia was a compound containing oxygen and possibly also an unknown metal.[37] Berzelius and Pontin meanwhile had worked on the ammonia amalgam first produced by Seebeck, and they, following Davy's view on ammonia and on the alkalis in general, concluded that the amalgam of ammonia was a combination of mercury and the metal of ammonia.[38] Berzelius told Davy about this, and Davy prepared an amalgam by bringing moistened ammonium chloride into contact with negatively electrified mercury. When the amalgam was decomposed, Davy found that ammonia and hydrogen were liberated, in proportions that once again indicated to him that ammonium was a compound of a metallic base and oxygen; oxygen had been taken from water, so that hydrogen was inevitably liberated.[39] Gay-Lussac and Thenard found otherwise, arguing that ammonia amalgam was nothing but a compound of ammonia, mercury and hydrogen, into none of which did oxygen enter.[40] Berzelius wrote to Gay-Lussac, appealing to his latest analyses of these remarkably difficult amalgams, and urging that it was still possible to argue for the existence of oxygen in ammonia.[41] But Gay-Lussac was not convinced, and maintained his position. Davy had previously argued that, since ammonia, like the caustic alkalis, contained oxygen, one could claim that oxygen was a constituent of all the alkalis; this suggestion had been effectively designed to stand Lavoisier's oxygen theory of acidity on its head, and thus to refute any theory associating acidity with a single substance including hydrogen. Gay-Lussac in 1814 was having none of this, for he still believed, however much he hedged his bets, that oxygen was an acidifying principle. He denied Berzelius's and Davy's claims about ammonia, and, in an excursus note on ammonia following his note on acidity, asserted that one should consider nitrogen as akin to chlorine, oxygen, and iodine in some of its properties, and like them capable of combining with alkalifying substances to produce salifiable bases. Ammonia should therefore be considered a particular alkali in which nitrogen played the role of oxygen in other alkalis.[42]

It was this brief note on ammonia, far more than Gay-Lussac's longer note on acidity, that evoked Davy's wrath, and led him to complain of Gay-Lussac's discussion of acidifying and alkalizing principles as an attempt to introduce occult qualities into chemistry. And this note shows that, within the methodological and theoretical sophistication that Gay-Lussac deployed while developing and pursuing the new chemistry into the fastnesses of analysis, the chemistry of principles continued to play a powerful role in the debates over the problem of chemical qualities.

NOTES

1 M. Sadoun-Goupil, *Le Chimiste Claude-Louis Berthollet 1748-1822. Sa Vie -- son Oeuvre*, Paris, 1977, p. 71. M. P. Crosland, *The Society of Arcueil. A View of French Science at the Time of Napoleon I*, London, 1967. Crosland, *Gay-Lussac: Scientist and Bourgeois*, Cambridge, 1978.

2. Crosland, "Theories of Acidity in the Early Nineteenth Century", *Proceedings of the XIIIth International Congress on the History of Science*, Moscow, 1971, section 7, pp. 67-74. See also D. M. Knight, "Synthesis of Qualities in Nineteenth Century Chemistry", *ibid.*, section 7, pp. 74-80.

3. A. Thackray, *Atoms and Powers: An Essay on Newtonian Matter-Theory and the Development of Chemistry*, Cambridge, Mass., 1970, p. 172.

4. J.-C. Guédon, *The Still Life of a Transition: Chemistry in the Encyclopédie*, Ph. D. thesis, University of Wisconsin, 1974, discusses aspects of the drive for autonomy in 18th-century French chemistry. See also D. M. Knight, *The Transcendental Part of Chemistry*, Folkestone, 1978, esp. chap. 1; T. H. Levere, *Affinity and Matter: Elements of Chemical Philosophy 1800-1865*, Oxford, 1971, chap. 1; A. M. Duncan, *Annals of Science*, **18**, 1962, 189-194.

5. A. L. Lavoisier, *Traité Elémentaire de Chimie*, 2 vols., Paris, 1789 ; *Elements of Chemistry*, trans. R. Kerr, Edinburgh, 1790, pp. xxi, xxiv ; pt. 2 *passim*, e.g. pp. 232, 253.

6. M. P. Crosland, "Lavoisier's Theory of Acidity", *Isis*, **64**, 1973, 306-325, 306, 318.

7. Lavoisier, *Elements*, p. 156 .

8. H. Guerlac, "Chemistry as a Branch of Physics: Laplace's Collaboration with Lavoisier", *Historical Studies in the Physical Sciences*, 7, 1976, 193-276. Levere, chap. 3 of *Martinus van Marum Life and Work*, ed. E. Lefebvre & J. G. de Bruijn, vol. 4, G. L'E. Turner & T. H. Levere, *Van Marum's Scientific Instruments in Teyler's Museum*, Leyden, 1973.

9. Thackray, *John Dalton: Critical Assessments of his Life and Science*, Cambridge, Mass., 1972; *Atoms and Powers*, p. 278.

10. The debate was a persistent one. See, e.g., Levere,"Affinity or Structure: an Early Problem in Organic Chemistry", *Ambix*, **17**, 1970, 111-126.

11. Smithson Tennant, *Phil. Trans.*, **87**, 1797, 123.

12. *Phil. Trans.*, **99**, 39-104, 75.

13. Gay-Lussac, "Ueber Acidität und Alkalinität", Gilbert's *Annalen der Physik*, **18**, 1814, 341-363, 341; "Mémoire sur l'Iode" , *Annales de Chimie*, **91**, 1814, 5-160, Note B, 130 et. seq. "Sur l'Acidité et sur l'Alcalinité".

14. Crosland, *XIIIth Congress*, section 7, p. 68.

15. *Ibid.*, p. 67; C. L. Berthollet, *Essai de Statique Chimique*, 2 vols., Paris, 1803, vol. 2, p. 8

16. *Annalen*, **18**, 1814, 357.

17. *Phil. Trans.*, **98**, 1808, 41 .

18. Crosland, "Theories of Acidity . . . " (note 2). E.g. H.Davy, *Phil. Trans.*, **103**, 1813, 242-251.

19. Gay-Lussac & Thenard, *Annales de Chimie*, **75**, 1810, 294 .Gay-Lussac, *Annales de Chimie*, **91**, 1814, 128 . Davy, *Journal of Science and the Arts*, **1**, 1816, 288.

20. Davy, *Phil Trans.*, **98**, 1808, 333-370.

21. This is entertainingly sketched in P. Thenard, *Un Grand Français: le Chimiste Thenard 1777-1857*, Dijon, 1950, pp. 98-101.

22. *Ann. Chim.*, **91**, 146-147.

23. *Ann. Chim.*, **49**, 21-35 ; 67, 221-222.

24. *Ann. Chim.*, **91**, 1814, 5-160 (note 13 above).

25. *Ibid.*, 132.

26. *Ibid.*, 134.

27. *Ibid.*, 138.

28. *Ibid.*, 136-137.

29. *Ibid.*, 147.

30. *Ibid.*, 152.

31. *The Collected Works of Sir Humphry Davy, Bart.*, ed. J. Davy, 9 vols., London, 1839, vol. 5, pp. 436, 489, 456.

32. H. Davy, *Journal of Science and the Arts*, **1**, 1816, 283-288.

33. John Brooke's paper, "Gay-Lussac and Davy: The Acid Test", to be published in the Proceedings of the Davy Bicentenary Symposium, held at the Royal Institution, Dec. 1978, gives an exegesis both of the gamesmanship involved in this debate and of its logical structure.

34. Davy, *Works*, vol. **1**, p. 167.

35. *Phil. Trans.*, **98**, 1808, 1-44

36. *Ann. Chim.*, **65**, 1808, 325-326; **72**, 1809, 244-264.

37. *Phil. Trans.*, **98**, 1808, 333-370; **99**, 1809, 39-104.

38. Berzelius & Pontin, *Annalen der Physik*, **36**, 1810, 198.

40. Davy, *Works*, vol. **5**, p. 266.

41. *Jac. Berzelius Bref.*, ed. Soderbaum; 6 vols. + 3 suppl., Uppsala, 1912-1932, vol. 3, p. 114, 25 Sept. 1811.

42. *Ann. Chim.*, **91**, 1814, 159-160.

XIX

Arrangement and Structure: A Distinction and a Difference

At this celebration of the hundredth anniversary of two seminal papers by the founders of stereochemistry Jacobus Henricus van't Hoff[1] and Joseph Achille Le Bel,[2] I want to ask why views like those expressed in their papers were so long delayed, or, more fruitfully, why previous chemists, possessing most of the fragments which would be used to create the concepts of stereochemistry, came nowhere near the achievements of 1874. They did not try and fail, but instead they deliberately avoided concepts which might now seem akin to stereochemistry as one would avoid deserts, bogs, and other dangerous and misleading regions.

Let me state the problem more fully. Stereo-chemistry involves what van't Hoff in the title of the first publication of his paper called "the extension into space of the structural formulae at present used in chemistry". Note in passing something to which we shall have to return: most apparently structural formulae prior to the mid-1870s were not intended to express the spatial arrangement of atoms. This is implied in van't Hoff's title, and is con-firmed time and again by his predecessors.[3] Kekulé, who appears to have used structural formulae if any-one in the 1860s did so, was at pains to explain that this rational formulae were reaction formulae.[4] They were initially and primarily classificatory in function.[5] Kekulé's formulae, however, in common with almost everyone else's, except Benjamin Collins Brodie's in his calculus of chemical operations,[6] presented molecules as being made up of atoms, as for example in his representation of acetic acid.[7]

For all the perennial doubts through the nineteenth century about the existence of atoms,[8] almost all chemists recognized what J.B. Stallo in 1881 called "the merits of the atomic hypothesis as a graphic or expository device". He rightly went on to remark that "It is a fact beyond dispute that chemistry owes a great part of its practical advance to [the use of the atomic hypothesis], and that the structural formulae founded upon it have enabled the chemist, not merely to trace the connection and mutual dependence of the various stages in the metamorphosis of 'elements' and 'compounds' so called, but in many cases (such as that of the hydrocarbon series in organic chemistry) successfully to anticipate the results of experimental research".[9]

So stereochemistry involves the atomic theory and the concept of structure where this means the arrangement of atoms in space. It is well enough known that the concepts of atomism and of something like structure were implied simultaneously in chemical literature in 1808 in John Dalton's *A New System of Chemical Philosophy*. The last part of the volume presents the atomic theory, and ends by stating that "when three or more particles of elastic fluids are combined together into one, it is to be supposed that the particles of the same kind repel each other, and therefore take their stations accordingly".[10] The consequence was that he represented "An atom of sulphuric acid, 1 sulphur + 3 oxygen" as a central sulphur atom surrounded by three oxygen atoms symmetrically distributed at the corners of an equilateral triangle.[11]

Of course this is a very limited notion of structure, but others were advanced that were more sophisticated. Wollaston, for example, published a paper in 1808 in which he applied Dalton's law of multiple proportions to superacid and subacid salts. He found an unexplained gap in the potassium oxalates, and argued that an understanding of the interaction of elementary atoms would require not only arithmetical laws but also a geometrical conception of the relative arrangement of atoms in three dimensions.[12] Examples of such speculations could be multiplied.[13] Now if stereochemistry involves the ideas of atoms and their arrangement, and if these ideas were broadly familiar to chemists from 1808, then critical ingredients were at hand. Why were van't Hoff and Le Bel not anticipated long before 1874? The answer is not simple, and I shall merely suggest some of its components. Of course my strategy will be to argue that awareness of the ideas of atoms and their arrangement was a necessary but not a sufficient condition for the formulation of stereochemical theories, and to try to probe the area of insufficiency. If one assumes that atomism offered at least a useful hypothesis to most of the community of chemists after 1808, then concentration on the concept of arrangement should best illuminate the area of insufficiency. Easy access to this area is provided by one of the nineteenth century's most brilliant chemists, Auguste Laurent, in the preface to his *Chemical Method* of 1854.[14] Laurent there identified two stumbling blocks in the way of establishing a chemical system — facts, and their causes. If one restricted oneself to facts, then no true system would be possible, and one could achieve only a descriptive natural history of chemical species organized according to a natural classification.[15] Although Laurent did not say so at this point, he clearly believed that natural classifications were sterile, and he advocated an artificial system.[16] Mere facts were inadequate for chemical science. What of the other stumbling block? Laurent wrote:

> By setting out from the idea of causality, or of atoms and their arrangement, we must determine in any particular body, which of its atoms are combined simply, which of them are combined intimately, whether they are copulated or conjugated...
> But intermediate between facts and their causes, we have generalities and laws. Would it not be possible, by relying upon them, to establish a method, that is to say, a system of formulae, a classification and a nomenclature, having the advantage of systems based upon facts, and of those based upon hypotheses, but without their inconveniences?
> This is what I have attempted to do in this work, by endeavouring to render it as much as possible independent of all hypotheses. Such of them as are to be met with are isolated, and may be left entirely on one side, without any detriment to the progress of the work.

... I do not ... reject the research after causes, although these may form perhaps but a perpetual mirage, destined to impel us incessantly to an exploration of new countries.[17]

Laurent's identification of causality with "atoms and their arrangement" was unfortunate for arrangement, implying that it was probably undiscoverable. It could serve a heuristic function, but the search for the actual arrangement of atoms in molecules was likely to be long if not eternally frustrated. What Laurent has to say about arrangement is therefore not very different from what Auguste Comte has to say about causation in general – it serves its purpose during the adolescence of a science, but has no place in the final positive edifice of laws.[18] Comte was Laurent's contemporary. I have no grounds for claiming any influence of one on the other, and many of Laurent's speculations went beyond Comte's positivism, but the extent of their common ground is striking.[19] They both recognized that the inner arrangement of molecules was unknown, and, in the present state of chemistry, unknowable, so that whatever classification one adopted could serve only as a convention and a guide.[20]

Laurent and Comte admittedly differed in their choice of classification. Comte felt that electrochemical dualism offered the most appropriate guide to the classification of chemical substances and to the prediction of their reactions,[21] while Laurent rejected the doctrines of Berzelius and instead proposed his own nucleus theory.[22] In neither case, however, was method supplanted by ontology. Gerhardt could have been speaking for both of them when he wrote:

> we have a deep conviction that all the metamorphoses of a single substance are controlled by general laws, which we can scarcely envisage today, but which the united efforts of chemists will certainly succeed in discovering. ...We have been taken to task with a sort of disdain for performing chemical algebra; we are glad to accept this description, because we believe that the true progress of science does not consist of limitless multiplications of facts and experiments, but in establishing analogies, and generalizing them by formulae, thus finding the laws which are the only guides to the certain prediction of phenomena.[23]

The concept of arrangement was useful – it provided Laurent with the seminal idea behind his nucleus theory,[24] brought chemistry and crystallography closer together,[25] and underlined the unity of organic and inorganic substitutions.[26] Thus he proposed, for example a representation of lead sulphate inferred from crystallographic evidence,[27] in which lead oxide and sulphuric acid maintained their independent existence within an overall regular structure.[28]

But in spite of such attempts, arrangement was for Laurent primarily a heuristic concept which provided general ideas. As he stated in 1845, it was impossible to represent a three-dimensional atomic arrangement by a linear formula.[29] One should therefore leave to others the search for formulae indicating arrangement, attacking them as long as they failed to find true formulae. Instead, assuming that substances with similar but individually unknown arrangements should have similar properties, one could create a system of synoptic formulae, expressing analogies. As for arrangement, Laurent concluded, "Shall we always be ignorant of [it]? Who knows?"[30]

A knowledge of the detailed arrangement of atoms in molecules was thus at least temporarily ruled out by positivist attitudes towards science among precisely those chemists whose thought might otherwise have been inclined to consider arrangement. The same attitudes, reinforced by polemical bias, ruled out an aspect of atomism, that, incorporated in the theory of valency, was to be essential for the development of stereochemistry. I am referring to the concept of affinity.[31] Comte rejected it as metaphysical, and therefore unscientific.[32] Laurent[33] admitted that the nature of atoms, presumably including their affinities, influenced molecular properties, but stressed that arrangement was of greater importance than atomic natures. The wide-ranging successes of the theory of types, with its structural conceptual basis, distracted attention from the concept of chemical affinity,[34] which had provided the eighteenth century with its most successful classificatory tool and furnished the basis for Berzelius's electrochemical dualism. Since the theories of dualism and types were generally, if mistakenly, seen in opposition to one another, and since the theory of types was becoming dominant in mid-nineteenth-century organic chemistry, affinity ceased to be a prominent topic in that realm of chemical discourse. Dumas was one of the principal villains in the temporary demise of affinity,[35] and seems to have recognized and enjoyed his role. In the 1850s and 1860s several chemists, including Daubeny[36] and Wurtz,[37] emphasized this aspect of recent chemical history.

So far I have argued that those who adopted a unitary theory neglected affinity and were agnostic about arrangement. Their neglect of the former and agnosticism about the latter were not of course wholly polemical or philosophical. Crystallographic analogies had led to theories suggesting constitutional analogies, but as Beudant pointed out in 1843,[38] crystallographers had learned caution and were primarily concerned to establish a classification based upon the external characteristics of bodies, and not upon internal ones. Then too, as competent mineralogists like Dana were well aware,[39] it was all very well to say that in principle chemical and crystallographic classifications should agree, while in practice it was hard to see how they did so. At the very least, the doctrines of preformation in chemistry and in crystallography alike would need modification. There were hopes, expressed by Laurent,[40] Gerhardt,[41] Baudrimont,[42] Kekulé,[43] and others, that crystallography would one day reveal the relative positions of atoms in compounds – but of course, as Baudrimont[44] and Kekulé[45] stressed, these would be positions in unreacting compounds. Reactions would change structures, and so information derived from reactions could not lead to direct knowledge of structures. Laurent accordingly used synoptic formulae, e.g. $C^8H^2Cl^4O + O^2$ for chloracetic acid,[46] Kekulé used reaction formulae[47] and so on, quite properly, since chemists were concerned with predicting chemical changes and classifying chemical species. Williamson's brilliant work on etherification showed both the success and the limitations of a dynamic approach, expressed by the twin equations:

$$\frac{\begin{matrix}H\\H\end{matrix}SO^4}{\begin{matrix}C^2H^5\\H\end{matrix}0} = \frac{\begin{matrix}H\\C^2H^5\end{matrix}SO^4}{\begin{matrix}H\\H\end{matrix}0} \quad \text{and} \quad \frac{\begin{matrix}C^2H^5\\H\end{matrix}SO^4}{\begin{matrix}C^2H^5\\H\end{matrix}O} = \frac{\begin{matrix}H\\H\end{matrix}SO^4}{\begin{matrix}C^2H^5\\C^2H^5\end{matrix}0} \qquad 48$$

Kinetic theory, with its associated chemical kinetics – Berthelot's *Mécanique Chimique* – may have seemed to point the same way. Thus, although substitution and the rest seemed to encourage the view that arrangement was the principal determinant of properties, awareness of chemical change made knowledge of arrangement seem unobtainable. Besides, phenomena other than substitution were not so easily handled. For example, compounds produced by burning diamond and charcoal respectively in oxygen were indistinguishable,[49] but the ease with which carbon dioxide was produced was very different in the two cases, and even if one claimed that charcoal and diamond were chemically the same species, they were physically distinct. Berzelius in 1840 characterized such variations as instances of allotropy,[50] and went on in 1845 to suggest that this was not rare, but was probably a general property of the elements. He suggested that allotropes of a given element were different states of that element, but made no reference to arrangement as underlying the differences.[51] Laurent quickly provided the missing structural speculations, writing to Berzelius that there was a great analogy between their respective views. "The atom, according to its definition, cannot be modified; different varieties of a simple body α, β, γ, can therefore only be dIfferent groups. That, if I have understood it aright, is the consequence of your hypothesis. As I see it, the chemists' ordinary atom would be a group of elements, and different groups of these elements would constitute the varieties a, b, g."[52] Berzelius provided no illustration, and thought such speculation highly premature: "It is impossible to account for the cause of the difference of simple bodies according to their allotropic state, even if we could determine the properties possessed by each state. Does the difference perhaps reside in a particular grouping of the atoms of simple bodies, in such a way, for example, that 2, 3 or several atoms would combine to form groups of atoms which would play the part of a single atom, as seems to be the case with sulphur? or is an electric polarity modified or fixed up to a certain point ...? Our present knowledge does not allow us to answer these questions."[53] It was not even clear that these different states should be classified as representing the same element. Brodie, for example, analyzed graphite oxide, applied Dulong and Petit's law, and found that the atomic weight of graphite was 33. He concluded that this form of carbon "should be characterized by a name marking it as a distinct element".[54] And yet there were some who regarded isomerism and allotropy as analogous phenomena, both explicable in terms of arrangement,[55] even while isomerism itself remained perplexing to many. William Odling in 1864 told the chemical section of the British Association for the Advancement of Science that "Isomerism is, in fact, the chemical problem of the day. ... It is curious to note the oscillations of opinion in respect to this subject. Twenty years ago the molecular constitution of bodies was perceived by a special instinct, simultaneously with, or even prior to, the establishment of their molecular weights. Then came an interval of scepticism, when the intimate constitution of bodies was maintained to be not only unknown, but unknowable. Now we have a period of temperate reaction, not recognizing the desired knowledge as unattainable, but only as difficult of attainment. And in this, as in many other instances, we find evidence of the healthier state of mind in which, now more perhaps than ever, the first principles of chemical philosophy are explored. Speculation, indeed, is not less rife and scarcely less esteemed than formerly, but is now seldom or never mistaken for ascertained truth..".[56]

Perhaps it will be appropriate to leave the mid-century proponents of theories emphasizing arrangement with the reflection that trends such as Odling discusses, reflecting the changing status of imagination in science, may for a while be more important for the progress of science than substantive discoveries. After Gerhardt came to Paris in 1838, Liebig continued to send him advice, warning him that the Academy was "the implacable adversary of theories".[57] Even Dumas had suffered from theorizing, and if Gerhardt wanted to indulge himself, Liebig admonished, "For the love of God, don't write about theories, except for German journals!"[58] Later, Kolbe's blast[59] against van't Hoff's stereochemical nonsense was to be countered by the latter's assertion that imagination in the 1870s was not playing "the role that it is capable of playing; even today Kepler would have been able to raise himself as high above his surroundings as in his own time".[60]

So much, for the time being, for arrangement and speculation. What of electrochemical dualism with its emphasis upon atomic natures? Briefly, as Dumas wrote in 1840,[61] it is a theory which seeks in principle to derive the fundamental properties of bodies from the nature of their elementary particles. Within it, arrangement is therefore secondary. Its emphasis upon atomic polarities and its corresponding binary classification suggest a series of polar linkages, so that if one thinks of arrangement one is likely to do so in terms of order, links in a chain, rather than arrangement, bricks in a three-dimensional edifice. Berzelius, architect and champion of electrochemical dualism, was willing to consider more nearly structural notions. On one occasion he even went so far as to propose that organic atoms had a certain mechanical structure, "which enables us to deprive some of them of certain elementary atoms without altering the whole very much". Thus milk sugar, $80 + 10C + 16H$, could be converted to mucic acid, $80 + 6C + 10H$, by the removal of four carbon atoms and six hydrogen atoms.[62] Such speculations may on occasion have proved useful to Berzelius, but when he came to consider specific problems in which structural notions might have been useful, he clearly regarded the mutual satisfaction of electrochemical affinities as the determining factor, to which notions involving arrangement could lend at best circumstantial support. For example, in 1839 Berzelius wrote to Pelouze[63] that he had asked the Academy in Stockholm: "What is the greatest number of oxygen atoms which can be combined in a single oxide with a single or compound radical?" Yet he made no mention of geometric distribution, and it seems likely that he was thinking merely in terms of combining proportions and the mutual satisfaction of electrochemical affinities. A more striking instance is provided by Mitscherlich's discovery of the principle of isomorphism in Berzelius's laboratory in 1819.[64] Berzelius initially hesitated to accept isomorphism, but checked Mitscherlich's results at first hand, and was convinced.[65] He wrote to the crystallographer Haüy, whose theory was contradicted by Mitscherlich's findings, and who therefore remained unconvinced,[66] that "A new field is opening here, we are becoming aware of a whole new class of substances that, while conserving absolute regularity of their form, can vary in their elements between certain limits, without this variation being determined by chemical affinity, and without it conforming to the law of chemical proportions; it derives from the simple circumstances that these different substances can form integrant parts of the same crystalline form".[67] Isomorphism clearly had much to contribute to chemical and crystallographic theory, and Berzelius did allow it to modify his mineralogical classification, but in a characteristic and significant way. In his *Attempt to establish a pure scientific system of mineralogy by the application of the Eletrochemical theory and the Chemical Proportions* (1814), he had arranged minerals according to the electrical character of their positive constituents. Once Mitscherlich had demonstrated isomorphous replacement among these constituents, Berzelius's classification became invalid, and in 1824 he proposed a new system — this time based on the electrical characteristics of the negative constituents.[68] Ideas involving structure might have something to tell chemists, might even occasionally point out errors — but although structure and relativity were intimately connected, Berzelius's classification was always based upon the nature of atoms, whose forces interacted to produce the secondary phenomena of arrangement. Theories which greatly depreciated either notions of arrangement or notions of atomic natures could not support stereochemical ideas, which needed both atoms and arrangement. So the theory of types and electrochemical dualism had either to merge or to give way altogether before the concept of stereochemistry could become possible, let alone credible for the community of chemists. The two theories were in fact modified and merged gradually, so that as early as 1853 Liebig was able to write to Gerhardt, 'It is very strange that the two theories, formerly quite opposed, are now combined in one which explains all the phenomena in the two senses".[69] Radicals had ceased to function for chemists as the all but immutable organic analogues of inorganic elements, and might now even allow substitution to occur. The theory of types, on the other hand, was modified so as to allow for the role of individual atomic natures in determining molecular properties.[70]

Merging, however, was not enough. The structural aspects of the theory of types had initially been derived from crystallographic analogies, based upon the concept of a fundamental nucleus.[71] Other and earlier crystallographic analogies had used the concept of close packing to derive structure. Neither approach sufficed for the development of stereochemistry, which emerged after the development of valence theory, and directional valence theory at that.[72] The theory of types was useful here, but it provided a classification that was artifical.[73] What was needed was a description that was realistic. That is why van't Hoff in 1874 wrote: "It appears more and more that the present constitutional formulae are incapable of explaining certain cases of isomerism; the reason for this is perhaps the fact that we need a more definite statement about the actual position of the atoms".[74] As his statement implies, formulae illustrating relations of valency were already widely assumed to convey some information about the relative disposition of atoms. The tetravalency of carbon had been variously established, by Odling, Kekulé, Kolbe, Frankland, and Couper.[75] Pictorial representations of compounds of tetravalent carbon raised important questions, for they appeared to represent the physical disposition of atoms.

[76]

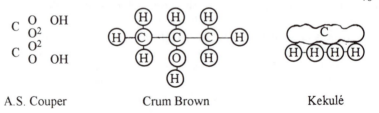

A.S. Couper   Crum Brown   Kekulé

Crum Brown[77] was among the first to pursue such questions critically. Kekulé came by the early 1860s to a position where he believed that "it must now indeed be held as a task of natural science to ascertain the constitution of matter, and therefore, if we can, the position of the atoms",[78] and although he refused to reach premature conclusions about stereochemistry, his views came to be seen as supportive of the stereochemical enterprise. The formal introduction of the notion of structure came, however, not from Kekulé, but fom Butlerov, who asserted in 1861: "Starting from the assumption that each chemical atom possesses only a definite and limited amount of chemical force (affinity) with which it takes part in forming a compound, I might call this chemical arrangement, or the type and manner of the mutual binding of the atoms in a compound substance, by the name of 'chemical structure' ".[79] The achievement of van't Hoff and of Le Bel was largely that of furnishing a conceptual tool which would enable chemical structure to be represented systematically and with precision. They refined the theory of structure and did indeed provide "a more definite statement about the actual position of the atoms". When Butlerov five years later defined structure as the arrangement of chemical bonds between atoms in a particle,[80] he was being both comprehensiveand retrospective.

LITERATURE CITED

1. van't Hoff, Jacobus Henricus, "Voorstel tot uitbreiding der tegenwoordig in de scheikunde gebruiktestructuur-formules in de ruimte, benevens een daarmee samehangende vermogen en chemische constitutie van organische verbindingen", J. Greven, Utrecht, 1874. Translated as "Sur les formules de structure dans l'espace", *Archives Neerlandaises des Sciences Exactes et Naturelles* (1874) *9*, 445-54.

2. Le Bel, Joseph Achille, "Sur les relations qui existent entre les formules atomiques des corps organiques, et le pouvoir rotatoire de leurs dissolutions", *Bulletin de la Société Chimique de France*, [2], (1874) *22*, 337-347.

3. E.g. Hofmann, A. W., "On the Combining Power of Atoms", *Chemical News* (1865) *12*, 166, 175, 187; Odling, W., *Outlines of Chemistry*, London, 1870, preface.

4. Kekulé, A., *Lehrbuch der organischen Chemie,* vol. 1, pp. 157-8, Erlangen, 1861.

5. Cf. Fisher, N. W., "Kekulé and organic classification, *Ambix* (1974) *21*, 29-52.

6. See Brock, W. H. (ed.) *The Atomic Debates. Brodie and the Rejection of the Atomic Theory,* Leicester University Press, 1967.

7. *Lehrbuch,* op. cit Kekulé introduced his formulae in vol. 1, p. 165n. See Russell, C. A., *The History of Valency,* p. 98, Leicester University Press,1971.

8. See Knight, D. M., *Atoms and Elements,* Hutchinson, London, 1967, passim.

9. Stallo, J. B., *The Concepts and Theories of Modern Physics,* p. 126, reprinted by the Belknap Press of Harvard University Press, Cambridge, Massachusetts, 1960.

10. Dalton, J., *A New System of Chemical Philosophy,* p. 216, Manchester, 1808.

11. Ibid. pp. 217, 219.

12. Wollaston, W., "On Super-acid and Sub-acid Salts", *Philosophical Transactions of the Royal Society of London* (1808) *98*, 96-102.

13. E.g. Davy, H., *Collected Works,* ed. Davy, J., vol. 5, pp. 435-6, London, 1839.

14. Laurent, Auguste, *Méthode de Chimie,* Paris,1854; trans. Odling, W., *Chemical Method,* London,1855.

15. *Chemical Method,* p . xv.

16. Cf. Fisher, N. W., "Organic classification before Kekulé", *Ambix* (1973) *20*, 108.

17. Laurent, op. cit, pp. xv-xvi.

18. Comte, A., *Cours de philosophie positive,* vol.1, pp. 4-5, Paris, 1830.

19. Brock, op. cit, pp. 145-152, has pertinent comments in his appendix on Comte, Williamson, and Brodie.

20. Comte, op. cit, vol. 3, pp. 104 et seq.. Levere, T.H., *Affinity and Matter. Elements of Chemical Philosophy* 1800-1865, p. 178, The Clarendon Press, Oxford, 1971.

21. Op. cit, vol. 3, p. 109.

22 . Laurent , A., doctoral thesis, 1836 , MS in the archives of the Academie des Sciences, Paris. Part of this was published in *Annales de Chimie et Physique* (1836) *61*, 125; the rest is published in *Bulletin de la Société Chimique de France (Documentation)* (1954) *31*, ed. J. Jacques.

23. Gerhardt and Chancel, *Compte rendu (mensuel) dest travaux chimiques* (1851) *7*, 65-84.

24. Laurent, op. cit

25. Laurent, *Compte rendu hebdomadaire des séances de l'Académie des Sciences* (1842) *15*, 350-352.

26. Ibid, (1840) *11*, 876.

27. This example is discussed by Kapoor, S. C., "The Origins of Laurent's Organic Classification", *Isis* (1969) *60*, 513, and Fisher, N. W., op. cit, 119.

28. Fisher has interpreted Laurent's description diagramatically: ibid. 119.

29. Grimaux, E., and Gerhardt, Ch. jun., *Charles Gerhardt, sa vie, son oeuvre, sa correspondence*, p. 481, Paris, 1900.

30. Ibid, pp. 483-7.

31. Levere, op. cit, passim.

32. Op. cit, vol.3 , p. 50.

33. *Chemical Method*, pp. 321-2.

34. Levere, op. cit, pp. 167-1.

35. Ibid.

36. Daubeny, C., *Report of the British Association for the Advancement of Science* (1856) 136 et seq.

37. Wurtz, Ad., *Dictionnaire de Chimie*, vol. 1, p. 77, Paris, 1869.

38. Beudant, F. S., "An Inquiry into the Connection between Crystalline Form and Chemical Composition", *Journal of Science and the Arts*. (1819) *6*, 117.

39. Dana, J. D., *System of Mineralogy*, p. 76, 2 ed. 1844 .

40. *Comte rendu...de l'Académie des Sciences* (1843) *17*, 311-12.

41. Gerhardt, C., *Introduction à l'étude de la chimie par le système unitaire*, p. 55 , Paris , 1848.

42. Quesneville's *Revue Scientifique et Industrielle* (1840) *1*, 35-8.

43. *Lehrbuch*, vol. 1, pp. 157-8, cited in translation by Russell, op. cit, pp. 143-4.

44. Op. cit, pp. 35-36.

45. Op. cit, pp. 157-158.

46. *Chemical Method* pp.65-6, 68 dicusses synoptic formulae, which are analogous for analogous bodies. The formula for chloracetic acid is from *Annales de chimie* (1836) 63, 377 (388).

47. Op. cit, p. 157.

48. *Alembic Club Reprint* no. 16, from Williamson's paper of 1850.

49. See, e.g., Davy, H., *Philosophical Transactions of the Royal Society of London* (1814) *104*, 557-70.

50. Jahres-Bericht (1840) *20*, ii, 13.

51. *Scientific Memoirs* (18) *4*, 240-252.

52. *Jac. Berzelius Bref*, ed., Soderbaum., vol. 7, p. 200, Uppsala, 1912-1932.

53. *Rapport Annuel sur les Progrès de la Chimie* (1845) *5*, 21-22.

54. Brodie, B. C., "On the Atomic Weight of Graphite ", *Philosophical Transactions of the Royal Society of London* (1859) *149*, 249-59.

55. Cf. Daubeny, C., *Introduction to the Atomic Theory*, pp. 182, 431, 2 ed., Oxford, 1850.

56. *Report of the British Association for the Advancement of Science* (1864) 24.

57. *Charles Gerhardt, sa vie...*, p. 38.

58. Ibid, pp. 42-3.

59. Kolbe, H,. *J. prakt. Chem.* [2] (1877) *15*, 473.

60. "De Verbeeldingskracht in de Wetenschap", trans. Benfey, O. T., *Journal of Chemical Education*,(1960), *37*, 467ff.

61. *Compte rendu...de l'Académie des Sciences*, (1840) *10*, 171, 176, 178.

62. *Annals of Philosophy* (1815) *5*, 274.

63. *Compte rendu...de l'Académie des Sciences*, (1839), *8*, 352-357.

64. Mittscherlich, E., *Abhandlungen der Königlichen Akademie der Wissenschaften zu Berlin* (1819) 427; trans. in *Ann. Chem. Phys.* (1820) *14*, 172.

65. *Jac. Berzelius Bref*, vol. 7, p. 124.

66. Ibid, vol. 7, 18 October 1821.

67. Ibid, vol. 7, p. 162.

68. *Annals of Philosophy*, N.S. (1826) *11*, 381, 422.

69. Quoted by Partington, J.R., 'A History of Chemistry', vol. 4, p. 460, MacMillan, London, 1964.

70. Levere, op. cit, pp . 185-193 .

71. See Laurent's thesis (22), and Mauskopf, H., Annals of Science (1969) 25, 229-242.

72. Russell, op. cit, pp. 159-167.

73. cf. Fisher, Ambix (1973) 20, 108.

74. Trans. Benfey, O.T., in 'Classics in the Theory of Chemical Combination', p. 151, Dover, New York, 1963.

75. See Russell, op. cit, pp. ll9ff.

76. See Benfey, op. cit, p. 148; Russell, op. cit, 98, 102; Larder, D., *Ambix* (1967) *14*, 112-32.

77. *Transactions of the Royal Socity of Edinburgh* (1864) *23*, 707.

78. Cited by Russell, op. cit, p. 144.

79. Ibid, p. 149.

80. "The Present Day Significance of the Theory of Chemical Structure", *Journal of the Russian Physico Chemical Society* (1879) *11*, 289-311; reprinted in G. V. Bykov, ed., *Centenary of the Theory of Chemical Structure*, pp. 111-29, Moscow, 1961.

INDEX